ADOLESCENTS AND WAR

ADOLESCENTS AND WAR

How Youth Deal with Political Violence

Edited By
Brian K. Barber

OXFORD
UNIVERSITY PRESS
2009

OXFORD
UNIVERSITY PRESS
2009

Oxford University Press, Inc., publishes works that further
Oxford University's objective of excellence
in research, scholarship, and education.

Oxford   New York
Auckland   Cape Town   Dar es Salaam   Hong Kong   Karachi
Kuala Lumpur   Madrid   Melbourne   Mexico City   Nairobi
New Delhi   Shanghai   Taipei   Toronto

With offices in
Argentina   Austria   Brazil   Chile   Czech Republic   France   Greece
Guatemala   Hungary   Italy   Japan   Poland   Portugal   Singapore
South Korea   Switzerland   Thailand   Turkey   Ukraine   Vietnam

Published by Oxford University Press, Inc.
198 Madison Avenue, New York, New York 10016
www.oup.com

Oxford is a registered trademark of Oxford University Press

Library of Congress Cataloging-in-Publication Data

Adolescents and war : how youth deal with political violence / edited by
Brian K. Barber.
        p.   cm.
    Includes bibliographical references and index.
    ISBN 978-0-19-534335-9
    1. Youth and war—Psychological aspects.   2. Youth and
violence—Psychological aspects.   3. Political violence—Psychological
aspects.   4. Violence—Psychological aspects.   5. War—Psychological
aspects.   I. Barber, Brian K., 1954-
    HQ799.2.W37A36 2009
    303.60835—dc22   2009002660

9 8 7 6 5 4 3 2 1

Printed in the United States of America
on acid-free paper

To Bonner Ritchie for planting the seed; to Bruce Chadwick for nurturing its growth; to Irv Sigel for the initial idea and opportunity for the book; to Jim Youniss for constant encouragement.

Most of all,

to the remarkable youth of a conflicted world.

Acknowledgments

Acknowledged first are the thousands of youths across the world who participated in the research reported in this volume. Next, I thank the various authors for their fine work, participation in the volume, and patience in seeing it to completion. Thanks also go to Paul D. Page of the Center for the Study of Youth and Political Violence at the University of Tennessee for his careful review and editorial work; to two anonymous reviewers; and to Jennifer Rappaport and Lori Handelman, editors at Oxford University Press. Gratefully acknowledged are the numerous institutions that have contributed valuable support to the work of mine that is presented in this volume and to the completion of the volume itself, including the U.S. Social Science Research Council, the Rockefeller Foundation Bellagio Italy Study Center, the Jerusalem Fund, the United States Institute of Peace, the BYU Jerusalem Center for Near Eastern Studies, the BYU Kennedy Center for International Studies, the BYU College of Family, Home, and Social Sciences, and the University of Tennessee Center for the Study of Youth and Political Violence, College of Education, Home and Social Sciences, and Child and Family Studies Department.

Contents

Contributors

BRIAN K. BARBER
Center for the Study of Youth and
    Political Violence
University of Tennessee
Knoxville

MIRELA BICIC
International Center on Responses to
    Catastrophes
University of Illinois at Chicago

NEIL BOOTHBY
Program on Forced Migration and
    Health
Columbia University
New York, NY

CLARE CASSIDY
School of Psychology
University of Saint Andrews
Scotland

ADANA CELIK
International Center on Responses to
    Catastrophes
University of Illinois at Chicago

JENNIFER CRAWFORD
Program on Forced Migration and
    Health
Columbia University
New York, NY

JOHN FULTON
Nationwide Children's Hospital
Ohio State University
Columbus

STERLING HILTON
Department of Educational Leadership
    and Foundations
Brigham Young University
Provo, UT

RANKA KATALINSKI
Electro-Technical Secondary School
Sarajevo, Bosnia and Herzegovina

ALMA KLEBIC
International Center on Responses to
    Catastrophes
University of Illinois at Chicago

KATHLEEN KOSTELNY
Erikson Institute for Advanced Study
   in Child Development
Chicago, IL

CHRISTOPHER M. LAYNE
National Center for Child Traumatic
   Stress
University of California at Los Angeles

DAHAI LIN
Wyeth Research
Cambridge, MA

AGOSTINHO MAMADE
Aga Khan Foundation
Maputo, Mozambique

ROBERT J. MCCOUCH
United Nations Secretariat
New York, NY

NICHOLA MCCULLOUGH
School of Nursing & Midwifery
Queen's University, Belfast
Northern Ireland

ORLA MULDOON
Department of Psychology
University of Limerick
Ireland

JOSEPH A. OLSEN
College of Family, Home, and Social
   Sciences
Brigham Young University
Provo, UT

ALMA PAŠALIĆ
Department of Psychiatry
University of Sarajevo Medical Center
Bosnia and Herzegovina

HAFIZA PAŠALIĆ
Teacher's Secondary School
Sarajevo, Bosnia and Herzegovina

RAIJA-LEENA PUNAMÄKI
Department of Psychology
University of Tampere
Finland

ROBERT S. PYNOOS
National Center for Child Traumatic
   Stress
University of California at Los Angeles

JULIE MIKLES SCHLUTERMAN
Department of Sociology
Arkansas Technical University
Russellville

MICHELLE SLONE
Department of Psychology
Tel Aviv University
Israel

JARED S. WARREN
Department of Psychology
Brigham Young University
Provo, UT

STEVAN WEINE
International Center on Responses to
   Catastrophe
University of Illinois at Chicago

MICHAEL WESSELLS
Program on Forced Migration and
   Health
Columbia University
New York, NY

ADOLESCENTS AND WAR

Chapter 1

Glimpsing the Complexity of Youth and Political Violence

Brian K. Barber

Countless thousands of youth confront the ravages of war and political violence. Although there is no way to calculate precisely just how many young people are affected by such conflict, the number is certainly many times higher than the estimated hundreds of thousands of child soldiers who have served as conscripted fighters and military personnel (see Chapter 5). Recently, focused and systematic efforts have been made to understand the experiences of this important group of youth who have heretofore remained politically and empirically in the shadows.

What do we actually know about adolescents who confront political conflict and its often intense violence? How do they understand, experience, respond to, and adapt to their exposure or involvement in political violence? This book addresses these basic questions to both lay a foundation for future, more refined research and assist those applied professionals charged with supporting and/or making decisions about conflict youth (e.g., from governmental, nongovernmental, clinical, education, and community development realms).

Regrettably, despite calls from as much as a decade ago for a more sophisticated and nuanced study of children and political violence (e.g., Cairns & Dawes, 1996), the knowledge base produced by (particularly quantitative and clinical) researchers remains limited. The primary drawback of the overall body of work is that it has approached the topic of adolescent functioning amid political conflict too simplistically (e.g., by primarily assessing violence exposure and stress-related, psychological impairment; see Chapter 2). There is actually a tremendous amount of intricacy associated with political conflict, a complexity that is manifest in all of the basic elements of the phenomenon—type and frequency of exposure to violence, motivation for involvement in the conflict, cognitive and emotional processing of the conflict and its violence, and response to it.

Thus, in addition to providing a review of existing knowledge, this volume discusses and illustrates much of this complexity. This opening chapter positions the contribution of the subsequent chapters in an elaborated discussion of much of that intricacy, centrally arguing that traditional approaches to the study of adolescents and political violence have understudied—and thereby underrepresented—youths' capacity to handle challenging circumstances. Those approaches have done so in large part by viewing adolescents through a narrow lens that has not adequately explored the totality of their conflict experiences, the sophistication with which they understand or attempt to understand conflict and its role in their identity, the array of broad cultural, political, and social forces that texture their experiences, and their dispositions toward and adaptation to those experiences.

Positioning the Book in Evolving Attention to Adolescents

This volume fits logically in a recently published, unplanned sequence of books on adolescents or youth that has advanced the theme of adolescent competent functioning in progressively more defined contexts. Several of these works emphasized the need to move away from the traditionally negative characterization of adolescents as unruly, unreliable, and reckless and to recognize and provide support for adolescent competence in meeting the transitional challenges confronting them (e.g., Eccles & Gootman, 2002; Villarruel, Perkins, Borden, & Keith, 2003). Some scholars have focused specifically on "civic engagement," in many parts of the world (e.g., Yates & Youniss, 1999) and in the United States specifically (e.g., Lerner, 2004). The focus was then tightened with the publication of a multiple-volume encyclopedia on youth activism in environmental, social, civic, and political issues that highlights the many ways youth can and have historically committed themselves to social change throughout the world (Sherrod, Flanagan, & Kassimir, 2005). More recently, Daiute, Beykont, Higson-Smith, and Nucci (2006) focused more specifically on youth experience with conflict situations, defined broadly to include conflict and violence in schools, against minorities, within nations, and transnationally.

The current book maintains this impetus to examine and document adolescent functioning, but with an even more defined focus—that is, their functioning in the context of political violence (see also Boothby, Strang, & Wessells, 2006a, for a compilation of social ecological approaches to children in war zones; Boyden & de Berry, 2004, for a treatment of children and youth of armed conflict and displacement; and Wessells, 2006, for a concentrated focus on child soldiers; among other relevant volumes). Although narrow, the restricted spotlight on political conflict is fruitful both because of the widespread global concern with war and political violence (and specifically young people's role in it) and because the phenomenon of political conflict is very complex. An initial appreciation of this complexity can be gained simply by recognizing the very large number of academic and professional pursuits that have important information to offer on the topic. These include (but are not limited to) anthropology, human rights, humanitarian assistance, international relations, political science, (multiple branches of) psychology, psychiatry, public health, public policy, refugee studies, and sociology.

Although adolescents have certainly been involved in political conflict historically, only recently has specific attention been focused on them. Some of this increased attention results simply from broader coverage afforded by technological advances of modern media. That is, the general world population has simply been made more regularly and thoroughly aware of the reality of adolescent involvement in political conflict through greater television coverage. However, the interest has also been inspired by iconic events (Kassimir, 2005) involving adolescents and violence (e.g., the Columbine High School shootings in the United States) and, more directly related to this volume, recent political conflicts in which adolescents were critically involved. In some of these, like the South African and Palestinian/Israeli conflicts, adolescents have been major front-line activists, often leading and sustaining the resistance. In others, like the several examples in other regions of Africa (e.g., Angola, Mozambique, Sierra Leone), adolescents and younger children have been coerced in large numbers to fight their elders' battles.

The complexity of political violence demands careful scrutiny and requires caution against making simplistic conclusions. With proper care, this area of research has the potential to produce informative and valuably nuanced views on the functioning of adolescents. Given the raw reality that the world is currently plagued with many ethnic or political conflicts (all the more sobering when recognizing that this level is not historically anomalous; Kleinman & Desjarlais, 1995), the study of this topic has the potential to encourage a needed merger of research and applied efforts that can be usefully implemented to care for the countless numbers of present and future young people who will witness and become involved in political conflict. The fact that these young people will be the world's next adults and leaders makes the task all the more compelling and essential.

In terms of content, a particular contribution of this book is that it conveys its overall message through a diverse assemblage of full and detailed scientific studies. Thus, individual chapters cover with precision and depth the varied relevant domains of scientific endeavor: theory (Chapter 3), reviews (Chapters 2 and 5), measurement (Chapters 4 and 7), and multiple methods of inquiry (Chapters 4 through 12). This strategy of compiling chapters of considerable depth was selected not only to provide the important and detailed data or arguments in the specific domains that inform the individual chapters but also to illustrate the multifaceted complexity of the topic as a whole and the rigors of its study.

A further contribution the book makes is the attention paid to youth perspectives on their conflict experiences. Youth have not typically been asked to comment on their own conflict experiences. As Muldoon and colleagues note (Chapter 6), the existing emphasis on adults' appraisal in determining the impact of stress and violence has not been extended to include children's perceptions of their experiences. This is unfortunate both because traditional concerns of researchers may not be of central concern to children, whose anxieties and troubles might be quite different than adults' (or what adults expect) (Boyden, 2003), and as Wessells and Kostelny note (Chapter 5), children (especially youth) form cognitive schemata relative to their involvement, identity, and attributions regarding their own behavior that critically define their experience with political conflict (see also Wessells, 2006). Several of the chapters herein make clear that adolescents are rich sources of detail as to the complexity of political violence by including first-person accounts of involvement with political violence from adolescents from Africa (Chapters 5 and 10), Bosnia (Chapters 11 and 12), Northern Ireland (Chapter 6), and Palestine (Chapter 12).

Adolescence and Youth

This book's title intentionally duplicates the ambiguous, frequent co-usage of the terms *adolescents* and *youth* to describe young people who are older than "children" and younger than "adults." In much of social science, the two terms are used interchangeably, not infrequently within the same sentence, largely because the terms have overlapping definitions and scope. In much of the youth development, civic engagement, and activism work already referred to, the discussion centers on adolescents to the extent that they are understood to differ from older youth by virtue of their educational status (i.e., in high school instead of in college or university).

In their recent volume on youth and conflict, Daiute and colleagues (2006) dealt with this ambiguity by substantially extending the downward reach of "youth" from the early twenties to include children as young as 8 years old. They did so in part to comport with international projects like the UN Convention on the Rights of the Child, which circumscribe age groupings similarly (see Boothby, Strang, & Wessells, 2006b, for a similar approach to defining children). Although that method aggravates any attempt to distinguish adolescents from youth, they reasoned importantly that the labeling of developmental stages of life (i.e., childhood, adolescence, young adulthood, etc.), largely a Western rationale, does not fit well in many of the world's societies where readiness for personal and social autonomy, maturity for work and family formation, and participation in civil service (volunteered or coerced) occurs with substantial variation across the age span. This issue of global salience will be addressed in detail shortly.

The ambiguity of age-labeling young individuals has an upward reach as well. Whereas at one time young people in their second decade of life could reliably be labeled adolescents (at least in Western cultures, where the concept of adolescence as a life stage predominates), it is now the case that adolescence's classic functions of exploration, identity seeking, and preparation for adulthood are thought to extend well into the twenties (the former domain of youth or young adulthood) because the transition to adulthood is considerably delayed due to significant social, demographic, and/or economic change (at least in many industrialized countries; Arnett, 2002). There are also political manipulations of this ambiguity. As Boyden (2003) notes, for example, at times during the South African conflict young activists were defined by the authorities as "youth" to establish their legal culpability, whereas the youth referred to themselves as "children" to avoid adult sanctions.

These definitional ambiguities make any attempt to demarcate adolescents from youth futile, and none is attempted here. However, although the vagueness is acknowledged here, as well as throughout the volume by way of the occasional, alternating usage of multiple labels as others have done (e.g., children, adolescents, youth, young people, etc.), this book is nonetheless concerned specifically with adolescents. By *adolescents*, we mean children in their teen years—an age grouping that is encompassed by virtually all definitions of adolescence.

Ironically, this interest in teenaged adolescents has not been motivated by compelling findings or theoretical notions that justify or call for a focus uniquely on teens. Instead, paradoxically, the interest has been motivated by the absence of such incentives. As to the lack of empirical findings that would illuminate the uniqueness of adolescence, we note in Chapter 2's review of available empirical studies that most studies have not concentrated on adolescents explicitly. Rather, consistent with the conceptual ambiguity already described, the large majority of studies have used very broad age ranges. These studies have often included (but typically have not tested for) differences between teens, younger children, and older youth. Moreover, of those studies that have investigated teens, most have not asked questions that would assess the developmental characteristics used classically to define adolescence as its own unique stage of development. Thus, there is little the empirical literature has to say explicitly about teenaged adolescents in zones of political conflict.

Why focus on adolescents, then? Four reasons have justified our attention: two are related to the specific study of political conflict, and two are associated more generally with the study of adolescence.

First, as noted, definitive estimates of the actual numbers of varying age groups of children that are exposed to or participate in political violence are virtually impossible to construct. Experts from nongovernmental organizations have concluded that a high number of them are actually adolescents (particularly those who are "child soldiers") and that they, distinct from other children, have been neglected by research and professional groups (Brett & Specht, 2004; Machel, 1996, 2001; Reynolds, 2004; Women's Commission for Refugee Women and Children, 2000).

Second, the large and elaborated bodies of literature from sociology and political science on social movements (e.g., Brinton, 1956; Epstein, 1991; Fendrich, 1993; Gurr, 1970; Jenkins, 1983; McAdam, 1989; McCarthy & Zald, 1977; Tilly, 1978), which often include attention to political movements, have not spoken adequately to adolescence as defined here. More typically in those literatures, university students or college-aged youth have been the subjects of interest. Relatively little study (particularly empirical work) or commentary about teenaged youth has been presented (see Braungardt, 1984, and Stagner, 1977, for exceptions), especially not on those involved in the sustained political conflict that often characterizes war.

Thus, as elaborated elsewhere (Barber & Olsen, 2006), relatively little is known from theoretical, empirical, or applied sources about the functioning of adolescents amid political conflict. This book focuses on them by inspecting the available work, providing authoritative commentary, and presenting new data.

The two other reasons for concentrating on adolescents were essentially corrective in nature. The first has to do with the lingering stereotypes of adolescent incompetence. Despite Western psychology's self-corrective reassessment of adolescence as a much more balanced and positive stage of life than earlier characterizations (e.g., Baumrind, 1991; Steinberg, 1990), and despite the formidable and vibrant work in recent years on positive youth development (e.g., among many, Eccles & Gootman, 2002; Larson, 2000; Larson et al., 2004; Lerner, 2004; Moore & Lippman, 2005; Villarruel et al., 2003; Youniss & Yates, 1997), there remains a suspicious characterization of adolescents and a predominant focus on the negative behaviors that some of them exhibit.

A telling illustration of this negative focus can be found in the most recent version of the *Handbook of Child Psychology* (Damon & Eisenberg, 1998). In that rich and prestigious set of volumes, an entire chapter (seventy-eight pages) is devoted to "children's" prosocial behavior, but in the single chapter devoted to adolescents, paragraphs totaling less than two pages discuss any positive aspects of adolescents' experience. That chapter's author (Grotevant, 1998), like many other scholars, laments the predominant focus in the scientific literature on mental and behavioral problems of adolescents (while they simultaneously cite the actual, opposing evidence that, by far, most adolescents function well; Dornbusch, 1989; Furstenberg, 2000; Youniss & Yates, 1997).

Grotevant (1998) attributes this concentration on the negative to biases inherent in the theoretical approaches to understanding adolescence and the interests of federal funding agencies. Evidence for this persistence of a broadly negative characterization of teenagers is available elsewhere when considering both the professional and lay literatures. For example, a perusal of in-print English-language books reveals that as many as 70% are problem-focused. Many are authored by academics or clinical professionals. Not surprisingly, the negative focus on adolescents has spilled over from the professional literatures into the trade book literature, the titles of which characteristically include such words as *turmoil, crazy, epidemic*, (parental) *survival*, and so on.

Although still nascent, the rapidly growing literature on youth and political violence consistently fails to find widespread dysfunction or reveals evidence of competent functioning that challenges this stereotype among many youth who are either exposed to or involved with political violence (see Cairns & Dawes, 1996, for an earlier review and similar conclusion). The relevant, available empirical work is reviewed in Chapter 2, and several of the other chapters comment on it or present new, supportive data. In a later section of this chapter, an attempt is made to situate the positive within a complex of multifaceted, psycho-social-civic functioning. Furthermore, in numerous chapters of this volume, attempts have been made to specify which adolescents in these environments have difficulty and which do not (see following elaboration). Thus, the volume's interest in teenaged adolescents has in part been motivated to provide yet more illustration of the misidentification of the potential or demonstrated competencies of most teens. Given the extremity of the circumstances that accompany war and political violence, such evidence might offer a meaningful validation of this capacity.

Finally, there is a second, broader reason to look anew at adolescent competence, particularly when studying them in the varied cultures and conditions that accompany political violence. Thus, it is not just the putative incompetence or troublesome nature of adolescents that needs to be challenged. The very theoretically fundamental presumptions of what adolescence is like deserve careful rethinking. Specifically, developmental psychologists—who have had a primary stake in defining adolescence as a stage in the life course—have recently added a long-overdue degree of caution in defining adolescence (see also Furstenberg, 2000, for a similar call from sociology for less parochialism in the U.S. study of adolescence). For example, in a volume impressive both in intent and content, Brown, Larson, and Saraswathi (2002) solicited elaborated commentaries on adolescence from a diverse group of (in some cases, native) experts from many parts of the world. A basic conclusion from that effort was that adolescence looks fundamentally different across the globe—at least different from the archetype that has been shaped heavily by U.S. and/or European scholars (see Brown & Larson, 2002; Larson, 2002; Nsamenang, 2002). Critically, beyond the earlier noted variability in chronologically demarcating adolescence as a period of the life course, these experts have concluded that very little of what classic developmental theory dictates about adolescents' experiences is evident in the non-Western world (which, as Kagitçibasi, 1996, aptly noted, amounts literally to the large majority of the world).

For some international political violence experts, the concern about the inadequacy of developmental theory is rooted even earlier than adolescence. As Boyden (2003) summarizes, cardinal principles of Western developmental psychology (e.g., focus on the early years, stage-wise development, attachment, etc.) have led to a universalized and individualized characterization of childhood that presumes vulnerability, incompetence, and constant need of protection. As will be elaborated, the concern extends critically to interventions, which, if based on such a portrayal of children, can actually undermine adaptation or coping.

Of course, this is not to say that there are no similarities among adolescents across the Western/non-Western chasm, but assertions about experiential commonality must be far less categorical, or they must be applicable to different realms of adolescents' experience. For example, Brown and colleagues (Brown et al., 2002; Larson, 2002) note that it would be appropriate to assert the less precise function of adolescence as preparation for adulthood (however varied adulthood might be across cultures), and within such a characterization there may also be common developmental, biological, cognitive, and psychological experiences or processes. There is also evidence from comparative empirical studies using both survey and interview data that adolescents from widely different cultures and nations perceive and respond to (parental) socialization quite similarly (e.g., Barber, Stolz, & Olsen, 2005; Rohner, 1986; Thomas, Weigert, & Winston, 1984; Vazsonyi, Hibbert, & Snider, 2003). However, there is no evidence to suggest that adolescents across the world are concerned with the largely self-oriented, classic preoccupations with emotional turmoil, psychic separation, or autonomy or with inordinate peer influence that have driven definitions of adolescence in the West (Barber, Schluterman, Denny, & McCouch, 2005; Brown & Larson, 2002; Larson, 2002).

If Brown and Larson's (2002) call for adults—professionals and nonprofessionals alike—to "divest themselves from Eurocentric, universalistic notions of adolescence" (p. 3) is a remedy for misunderstanding adolescent experience generally, then the prescription surely is all the more pertinent for understanding unique groups of adolescents—like those in zones of political conflict—whose experiences differ not only by culture but also by the extremity of their contexts and the rigorous demands of these contexts. So, again, we are interested in focusing on adolescents in our work on political violence because of the need for data that more accurately describe how adolescents actually function.

Approaching the Complexity of Adolescents and Political Violence

We asserted elsewhere that not enough is yet known about human functioning (of any age group) in the face of political violence to warrant solid conclusions or predictions as to how an individual or homogeneous groups of persons will process, participate in, or adapt to conditions of war (Barber et al., 2005). This reticence may seem surprising at first blush because of how violent and destructive war and political conflict clearly are. Indeed, some scholars have concluded the reverse: that demonstrable psychopathology in children is the nearly inevitable consequence of exposure to or participation in violence, particularly those types and levels of violence that often characterize political conflict (e.g., Shaw, 2003).

The conclusion that there is not evidence to support such automatic debilitation in the face of political violence comes from evaluating the scientific evidence (or lack of it). First, as could be said about many areas of important research, there has simply not been enough research to warrant firm conclusions about effects. For the overview presented next (Chapter 2), we were able to identify ninety-five empirical studies that explicitly (quantitatively) assessed the association between political conflict and some element of adolescent psychological, social, or civic functioning. Although it is very encouraging to see this many studies, the number is not large considering the prevalence of war and conflict; the diversity of purposes, intensity, and outcomes; the critical variations in historical, cultural, ethnic, religious, and political underpinnings; and the hundreds of thousands of adolescents that have been involved in them (who themselves differ broadly on a variety of personal, cultural, and economic factors that might inform the degree of their involvement, their reasons for involvement, and their response to it).

Apart from the overall lack of research, the caution about making definitive conclusions has much to do with the limitations of the basic design of the research body as a whole. As will be illustrated in Chapter 2, there is a single dominant trend in both the design of the research on children and youth and political violence and in the findings from that research. Regarding design, the primary focus has been to correlate political violence (most often exposure to it) with assessments of individual psychological difficulty (often measured as post-traumatic stress syndrome or other related negative psychological states or conditions). Not surprisingly, the main finding from that research has validated the driving hypothesis in regularly (i.e., in 80% of the studies) documenting correlations between violence exposure and stress or distress. Naturally, there are qualifications that must be placed on any such statistical finding, given the analytical methodologies used to produce it. Thus, for example, the finding should be clarified with "on average"—that is, it does not describe the experience of specific individuals but the average scores among a group. Also, although often significant, the strength of the correlation between violence exposure and negative functioning is not typically strong—thus, the finding holds for some members of the sample but not for others, or the increase in difficulty associated with exposure is high for some but not for others. However, these and other qualifications are certainly not unique to this one area of research or to the dominant trend within it; rather, they are salient to research in general. So the finding of a correlation between violence exposure and psychological difficulty should be taken at face value: it appears clearly to be the case that generally, individuals exposed to violence report heightened levels of stress or distress.

The essential intended contribution of this book has been to suggest, and in some cases to demonstrate, ways in which this finding can be more precisely understood and elaborated. In a later section of this chapter, focus will be placed on the limitations and consequences of the prototypical design of narrowly assessing violence exposure and concentrating on negative (predominantly psychological) functioning. First, however, it is useful to discuss the value of specifying, or qualifying, the main finding as it is.

Clarifying the Link to Difficulty

There are many questions that can be asked to refine the understanding of this basic research finding. In technical terms, these questions seek to identify the higher order relationships among the key variables, two of which are mediating and moderating effects. This book addresses both. The relevant question to describe mediating effects would be: "Why or how (i.e., by which pathways or mechanisms) does political violence place the individual experiencing it at risk for negative outcomes?" The corresponding question for moderating effects would be: "For whom (that is, which individuals or specific groupings of individuals) does the risk exist more or less strongly?"

Mediators and Mechanisms: Why and How Does Violence Injure?

Arguing that such detail is critical to preparing children of war for a postconflict future, Chapter 3 theoretically assesses the presumed though infrequently documented association between political violence and subsequent violence (i.e., aggressive and antisocial behavior) in those who have endured it. In so doing, the chapter illustrates nicely how complex the answers are to the question about why and how violence injures. Against the backdrop of what Punamäki judges as insufficient and nonsystematic research into this basic question, she draws out the potential cognitive, emotional, and psychophysiological mechanisms or pathways by way of which violence exposure might make its way to aggression in children.

Noting the "remarkable resiliency" of war's children, Punamäki suggests that to the extent that aggression surfaces in them, it is likely due to perceptions of threat and danger or biased and discrepant emotional processing of painful experiences. Her conclusions are consistent with those of others (Gibson, 1993; Liddell, Kvalsvig, Qotyana, & Shabalala, 1994) who have set the same task of understanding whether and why violence exposure begets violent behavior. Essentially, the answers to these simple questions are quite complex, requiring attention to a host of demographic, social, and intrapsychic conditions.

Based in part on her own extensive research, Punamäki also discusses social mechanisms. Her work and our own (Barber, 2001; Punamäki, Quota, & El Sarraj, 1997, 2001) converge in this regard by showing that one consequence of violence exposure among adolescents is a reduction in the quality of parenting—specifically, increases in an intrusive type of parenting referred to as psychological control, which has been shown in these and other studies to be associated with both internalized and externalized problems in youth, such as aggression (Barber, 2002; Barber et al., 2005).

Chapter 8 tests for the role of a number of psychosocial factors in understanding the effects of exposure to violence on Bosnian adolescents' postwar functioning. The degree to which these adolescents had developed a negative sense of the future fully explains (i.e., mediates) the effect of violence exposure on their later criminal behavior. That same negative sense of the future, together with feelings of depression and lowered perceived social competence, were also pathways (i.e., indirect effects) by which exposure to violence was associated with lower civic and political involvement postconflict.

Moderators: For Which Adolescents Is the Risk Highest?

Because it appears not to be the case that all children exposed to political violence substantially suffer psychologically or behaviorally, an advancement would be to identify more clearly which youth are at particular risk for negative responses to violence. Several of the chapters herein have taken seriously the need to detect precisely some of the individual and contextual factors that help distinguish levels of functioning in relation to experiences with political conflict.

Chapter 6 uses classic stress theory to investigate both individual and contextual factors in a careful analysis of the functioning of Northern Irish young people. Noting once again that many children of political violence function well, the analyses nicely illustrate the complexity of any study concerned with the effects of violence exposure. Critical to the authors' approach has been attention to children's own definitions and views of violent events. They demonstrate considerable variability in how stressful children rate specific events—depending in part on whether they have had prior experiences with that form of conflict and whether that particular form of conflict predominates at the moment. These appraisals are further complicated by diverse demographic moderators (social groupings, such as social class and ethnicity) in which youth appraise differently due in part to their greater exposure to conflict.

Building on stress theory and life events paradigms, Chapter 4 describes a programmatic effort to develop a research model and specifically an assessment instrument that accounts for subtle differences in the context, degree of exposure, and the subjective meanings ascribed to the political conflict that adolescents experience. The author's findings from a series of studies on Israeli and Palestinian adolescents are particularly useful in illustrating how the effects of political violence can be quite different within distinct populations of adolescents—even those who are experiencing the same conflict. Specifically, the author finds support for the dominant finding that for Israeli adolescents (Jewish and Arab alike), higher levels of exposure to political violence were associated with increasing psychological distress. In contrast, for Palestinian adolescents, distress was associated with low levels of exposure, whereas at high levels of exposure there was little or no evidence of psychological distress.

Slone contemplates that the explanation for this inverse pattern might be a youth's coping style. Thus, essentially, the active involvement of Palestinian adolescents—that is, resistance behaviors in the context of considerable and historic economic, political, and cultural constraint—transform into self-help and competence, whereas the different sociopolitical environment experienced by Israeli youth—that is, being victims of unpredictable violence in a context that does not provide for individual opportunity to contribute—does not offer the same logic or impetus for mastery or modulation of stress. This reasoning is consistent with Elbedour, Bensel, and Maruyama's (1993) findings that a belief that life is unjust and beyond their control was positively associated with emotional health of West Bank (Palestinian) youth, whereas for Israeli youth a sense that the world is incomprehensible was inversely related to emotional health.

Chapter 7 illustrates an important example of a key moderating variable—one that in this case can exert a "protective" or "buffering" effect on youth exposed to political violence. In a chapter otherwise impressive for its attention to theory, measurement, and data analysis (exemplifying thereby just how much rigor is called for in this kind of research), these authors highlight the role of social support in the lives of war-affected youth. They note the historic position of this construct in the study of stress and developmental psychopathology, but also its emerging significance in the research specifically on war-related contexts. Consistent with the theme of complexity, they maintain that the traditional methods of assessing social support have not adequately addressed the extensive array of potential sources, types, and functions of social support. Like Slone does in Chapter 4, Layne and colleagues conduct a systematic series of three studies, in their case on groups of Bosnian adolescents, to develop a new assessment instrument of sector-specific social support (i.e., nuclear family support, extended family support, peer support, and adult friend and mentor support). The effects of this version of social support on depressive reactions are themselves complicated (i.e., not simply linear). Empirical evidence for the importance of social relationships can also be found in our earlier work, whereby positive relationships with parents appeared to buffer Palestinian adolescents from negative effects (i.e., depression and antisocial behavior) of their involvement in political violence, but associations with deviant peers exacerbated those negative effects (Barber, 2001). Such findings for the protective role of family relations are also consistent with recent work on the effects of community violence (e.g., Kliewer et al., 2006).

Related to this issue of risk and protective factors, a body of research has identified certain cognitive and emotional features of youth exposed to political violence that help determine their response to their experiences. For example, Ramphele (1997) has noted the relevance of emotional, personality, and intellectual attributes of South African adolescents in understanding which youth suffer. Furthermore, work among Palestinian youth in Gaza has shown the importance of the rigidity of mental sets (Qouta, El Sarraj, & Punamäki, 2001), the variety of emotional coping styles (Näätänen, Kanninen, Qouta, & Punamäki, 2002), and the types of psychological defense styles (Punamäki, Kanninen, Qouta, & El Sarraj, 2002) youth possess.

In Chapter 12, attention is given to a different sort of cognitive functioning in response to repeated calls from researchers concerned with youth and political conflict to focus attention on the meaning that youth attach to their experiences. In comparing interview data from Gaza and Sarejevo adolescents, the construct of "identity-related meaning systems" is advanced to assist in interpreting the dramatic differences in the appraisals and reactions of these two groups to the substantial violence they were exposed to (see also Barber, 2008, for an elaboration using quantitative data as well). In that chapter, the extensive literatures on the role of meaning in human behavior (which generally describe posttrauma coping efforts) is reviewed, suggesting that the narratives from these groups of adolescents imply a different, "preconflict" type of meaning that potentially exists in a variety of sources or systems (e.g., historical, political, cultural, religious, etc.). Palestinian adolescents of the First Intifada sourced their commitment and sense of personal and social enhancement in the abundant detail that came from all of these meaning systems and, in particular, the explicit prescription this information gave for their active role in the popular struggle and its implications for their personal/collective identity development. Bosnian adolescents, on the other hand, mourned bitterly the absence of any such guiding information about the conflict they were confronted with—its historical origins, the logic of its timing, its moral or political purposes, or their role in it (a finding that is consistent with the substantial work on this population of youth; e.g., Chapter 11; Jones, 2002, 2004).

Expanding the Focus

The preceding section identified ways the understanding of adolescents and political violence could be refined, specifically by more precisely explicating the one dominant finding in the current literatures: the association between exposure to violence and impaired psychological functioning. This section is focused on another important strategy for understanding the task at hand: to modify the prototypical design for studying the phenomenon—namely, by expanding the scope of inquiry. Specifically, it is contended that a more accurate understanding of adolescent experience with political conflict—and critically, one that would maximize effectiveness for the key applied purposes of education, prevention, intervention, policy, and so on—is to broaden both how the conflict experience is assessed and how the functioning of adolescence is measured.

The Limits of Focusing on the Negative: Pathologizing Stress

Regarding the predominate focus on negative outcomes, it should first be said that the preoccupation with negative functioning in the face of conflict is understandable. As already noted, only very recently has research on adolescence in general shifted to include attention to competent functioning. Thus, it is not surprising that a circumscribed research literature, particularly one concerned with extreme and challenging contexts, would be heavily concerned with negative effects. As Daiute (2006) has noted, the harm that conflict causes encourages medical metaphors, such as recovery, resilience, and treatment. Moreover, it is also useful to note that the preoccupation with the negative is not a peculiar drawback of psychological sciences. As medieval historian Barbara Tuchman (1978) points out, a great hazard of recorded history itself is the disproportionate survival of the negative (e.g., evil, misery, contention, and harm; the "normal does not make news," p. xviii). Specifically regarding the research enterprise, of note is Grotevant's (1998) explanation that prevailing theories and funding priorities also explain the concentration on the negative. Both conditions, however, are probably informed by the same basic lack of allure of the positive.

Understanding why we gravitate to the negative does not, however, remove its substantial restrictions on understanding human experience. The consequences are particularly limiting when one traverses cultures to understand and help individuals who are faced with exceptionally demanding situations. One of the substantial challenges presented by concentrating on stress/distress as an outcome of violence involvement is avoiding the implication—or for some, the assertion—that those outcomes are themselves bad or unusual (and therefore seen as indicators of individual pathology that call automatically for remediation or therapy). Questioning this process often does not seem intuitive to those for whom the presence of stress symptoms is de facto evidence of maladaption or pathology. (For interesting evolutionary and cultural notions of the potential lasting negative effects of war trauma, see Belsky, 2008; Pick, 2003; and Sagi-Schwartz et al., 2003.) Anthropologists Kleinman and Desjarlais (1995) view this as particularly problematic for (U.S.) Americans, whose ideology includes the value that "there is nothing that needs to be endured. Even memories can be 'worked through,'" even though, as they add, America's poor, for example (just as the poor worldwide) actually must endure much (see Honwana, 2006, for recent similar criticisms). Moreover, they point out that both the definitions and diagnostic criteria that U.S. clinicians use for stress imply that normative functioning in response to difficulty would not include any continued complaint or discomfort.

Other anthropologists, political sociologists, psychologists, and psychiatrists have repeatedly raised similar points when considering political violence and its effects, including the tendency to exaggerate the prevalence of post-traumatic stress disorder (see very recent calls even in the PTSD and trauma literatures; e.g., Friedman, Resick, & Keane, 2007; Layne et al., 2008), the Western orientation to individual psychology and its proclivity to pathologize normative stress, and the concern that in doing so, well-intended professionals can sometimes actually do more harm than good (Barenbaum, Ruchkin, & Schwab-Stone, 2004; Becker, 1995; Boothby, Strang, & Wessells, 2006b; Boyden, 2003; Kleinman, Das, & Locke, 1997; Pupavac, 2004; Summerfield, 2000, 2003; Young, 1995; Yule, 2000). The apprehension is elaborated and extended further to include contentions by some that stress (particularly PTSD) has been both medicalized and commercialized, whereby individuals are separated from the overall social context of violence (and its normative suffering) and made into victims and patients. (See Ahmed & Boisvert, 2006, and Joseph & Linley, 2006, for similar concerns from positive psychology about the medicalization inherent in Western approaches to human functioning generally.)

As the argument goes, the victim status serves the purposes of the sensationalistic interest of the media, whose victim-preoccupied coverage distorts the nature and magnitude of disasters. Furthermore, it purportedly encourages the individual to buy into the characterization of victimhood, which in turn qualifies him or her for access to key resources and public assistance. The patient status, for its part, would serve the purposes of some well-intended but nevertheless commercially driven mental health professionals and organizations that compete for resources and client base (see Almedom, 2004, and Kleinman & Desjarlais, 1995, for elaborations of these arguments).

Drawing out this concern with the political economy of constructions of stress and distress is beyond the scope of this volume. It suffices to reinforce the simpler points that much of the world experiences persistent hardships that are unambiguously stressful, and specifically and regrettably, political conflict is a part of that hardship for much of the world's population (Honwana, 2006). The essential criticism here is not that stress or distress doesn't exist or shouldn't be measured but rather that the problem lies with relying on such difficulty as a valid indicator (and often the exclusive indicator) of well-being, particularly in the large majority of populations who do not suffer clinical levels of difficulty. Critics are quick to point out that political violence undoubtedly can have physiological, psychological, and social effects (even devastatingly so), but it is unhelpful to consider these as disease indicators, even among the minority of persons who experience the worst effects (Boyden, 2003; Kleinman & Desjarlais, 1995;

see Friedman et al., 2007, and Layne et al., 2008, for discussion of adopting a wellness orientation to the study of posttrauma adjustment).

The core of this widespread concern with current approaches to understanding conflict and its effects is that it gives inadequate attention to the role of culture in shaping not just the effects of conflict but its understanding and resolution. This neglect of the dynamics of cultural intricacy is related to such issues as the historical and symbolic role of conflict in a particular culture, the social meaning assigned to it (including attributions of supernatural, religious, and political causation; Summerfield, 2000), and the culturally specific rites or methods for assuaging negative consequences of conflict (Chapter 9; Honwana, 2006; Kostelny, 2006; Wessells & Monteiro, 2000).

This book devotes particular attention to this concern. Specifically, Michael Wessells and Kathleen Kostelny's analysis of youth soldiering leads them to conclude that an adequate understanding of even this subset of the war-involved youth population cannot be achieved through attention to individualized, clinical syndromes, such as stress (Chapter 5). Rather, the complexity of the experience of youth soldiers requires a holistic perspective, even when considering negative impacts—one that simultaneously considers the physical, emotional, cognitive, spiritual, social, and economic impacts of conflict. Critically, they maintain, the approach must be grounded culturally, arguing that the tendency of Western clinicians to focus narrowly on the impact of violence misses more prevailing concerns that youth themselves have, such as earning a living, fear of rejection by their home communities, or stigmatization (e.g., being unsuitable for marriage).

The elaboration of the interview narratives of Palestinian and Bosnian adolescents provided in Chapter 12 also illustrates the overriding role of culture in shaping experience with conflict. Despite long and consistent exposure to very harsh experiences, Palestinian adolescents rarely focused on the concomitant stress, and they virtually never complained of injury from it (psychological or otherwise). Rather, the conflict and its acute violence seemed to be givens, part of the package of being Palestinian in an ongoing struggle for relief and identity (Khalidi, 1997). No doubt Palestinian adolescents experienced stress at multiple levels (see Barber, in press, for an elaboration), but to center on it or, worse, pathologize it, would be to miss the essence of the conflict as they experienced it. To the contrary, the narratives of same-aged Bosnian adolescents—who also experienced years of violence—were riddled with the awfulness of the violence, precisely because, by their own account, it took them by surprise: they had no historical or cultural filter to render it normative or acceptable. Not surprisingly, therefore, studies assessing the effects of Bosnian youths' experiences with political conflict have been consistently and sharply negative (see Barber, 2008, for elaborations of these contrasting profiles).

In Chapter 10, Boothby, Crawford, and Mamade also reveal key cultural nuances in their work with former Mozambican male youth—the first longitudinal investigation to date of child soldiers. The reintegration of these child combatants (who, as Wessells and Kostelny also note in Chapter 5, witnessed and participated in extreme forms of violence) into their communities was facilitated by the interdependent blend of family/community acceptance and spiritual/religious practices. Traditional cleansing ceremonies were critical in repairing youths' key social relationships and realigning the boys' well-being with the spirit world, which in turn facilitated a sense of being "like everyone else," deepening their sense of acceptance. The authors note that this interplay of social and spiritual dynamics assisted both the youth (in dealing with guilt and shame over their misdeeds) and the community (by alleviating worries about how the youth would behave once back home). (See Honwana, 2006, for a discussion of similar issues relative to Mozambican and Angolan youth.) Notably, most of these former soldiers had become trusted and productive members of their communities.

Artificially Isolating the Individual

The dual concern of excessive attention to negative psychological states that it isolates the individual as the unit of analysis, an approach that is likewise incompatible with cultural realities. Although another classic way of understanding the human condition (i.e., classifying peoples or cultures as individualistic or collectivist in their orientation to self and society) is itself being faulted for oversimplification (e.g., Neff, 2003; Raeff, 2006; Spiro, 1993), it is nevertheless the case that many people do not focus intensively or primarily on personal well-being. Instead, many have natural preferences for collective integrity and security (Raeff, 2006; Summerfield, 2000). In fact, political conflict (its causes, locus, and consequences) is inherently social in nature, and its suffering is interpersonal (Honwana, 2006; Kleinman & Desjarlais, 1995), with adults and children collaborating to understand, cope, and envision futures (Boyden, 2003; Daiute, 2006; Reynolds, 2004) and work out cultural and national moral narratives (Rafman, 2004). Therefore, conflict is not logically or usefully understood via an unnatural individual lens. Such a separation from the social world in favor of an individual's internal processes is apparently new even to the West (Taylor, 1990), and it is rendered in the instance of political conflict, for example, via the psychologizing of social issues and war (Pupavac, 2004), personifying political violence (Kleinman and Desjarlais, 1995), and decontextualizing childhood (Boyden, 2003).

Given these realities of the social nature of political conflict and its effects, a meaningful expansion of research designs would be to assess the social aspects of adolescent experience with conflict. Several of this volume's chapters make preliminary attempts to do this. The earlier discussed concern of Layne and colleagues (Chapter 7) with better measuring social support structures in the lives of youth is a good example of acknowledging the sociality of conflict experiences. As just noted, reunification with family and community members and with religious ties was fundamental to the adaptation of Mozambican child soldiers (Chapter 10), and social competence and civic involvement were key variables for Palestinian youth (Chapter 9) (see also Almedom, 2004, for a theoretical model of the role of social support in mitigating war-induced psychological difficulty).

Glimpsing Competence

An additional important way to expand the investigation of adolescents and political violence is to broaden the focus to include attention to competent functioning during or after conflict. Instinctively, it might seem unreasonable to some to consider that the extreme experiences adolescents have with war could result in anything but degradation. In reality, however, there are several reasons to think otherwise.

It would not be sufficient here to rely too heavily on the evidence from the new focus on the positive in adolescence research (e.g., the "enormous potential that adolescents bring to society," Saraswathi & Larson, 2002, p. 344), because conflict situations are severe, and thus throughout them "positive" means actual behavioral and psychological adaptation to extremity and not just inherent potential to function well (presuming facilitative conditions and opportunity). Neither would it be adequate to rely too much on the evidence of competent functioning in the social movement literatures cited earlier (e.g., Fendrich, 1993; Flanagan & Syvertsen, 2005; McAdam, 1989; Whalen & Flacks, 1989) because in war, conflict is not only episodically severe but often durable and pervasive. Nevertheless, both types of information certainly recommend exploration of the possibilities of competent functioning. (See Straker, 1992, for a review of the history of psychoanalytic thought relative to the theorized benefits of involvement in violence.)

This thinking is reinforced by a growing body of research that is discerning competent functioning (or the absence of negative functioning) in extreme contexts. As reviewed in Chapter 12, these contexts range broadly—from social and parental health adversities, environmental stress, and severe personal grief or stress to trauma—with researchers characterizing the adaptation variably as "resilience," "hardiness," "fortitude," "strength," and "posttraumatic growth" (see Almedom, 2005, for a review of these literatures). Importantly, their arguments and evidence indicate not only the potential for humans to survive difficulties, but that most people often do. This judgment is consistent with the expanding literatures on positive psychology (e.g., Seligman, Steen, Park, & Peterson, 2005; Snyder & Lopez, 2002) and with trends in clinical and developmental psychology that are concluding that human adaptive functioning is apparently more normative than the classic "resiliency" construct (i.e., as an exceptional response to difficulty) has implied (e.g., Bonnano, 2004; Masten, 2002).

These notions are consonant with a similar trend in work specifically on political conflict. Barenbaum et al. (2004), for example, review studies conducted in Bosnia, Cambodia, and Nicaragua in which impairment was remarkably absent in the lives of most youth. (They also refer to contrary evidence in Holocaust studies that suggests the possibility that the negative consequences of violence exposure may take a very long time to surface; but see Sagi-Schwartz et al., 2003, for contradictory evidence.) The same conclusion has been made recently from an extensive UNICEF-sponsored project in Uganda about youth in general and youth child soldiers specifically (Annan, Blattman, & Horton, 2006; Annan, Blattman, Carlson, & Mazurana, 2008; Blattman & Annan, 2007). Further, Carmines (1991) noted the growing recognition that an adolescent's sense of personal competence is critical to understanding engagement in political violence.

In addition, some work shows that limited impairment is the compatible evidence of active, strategic, and competent functioning of children. Several researchers, for example, have noted the complexity with which children (some of whom have been in war environments) are able to make moral judgments (e.g., Daiute, 2006; Turiel, 2006; Turiel & Wainryb, 2000). Boyden (2003) notes how creatively children in Asia and South America have actively engaged in protecting themselves from risk, including feigning fictitious personalities; pretending to be deaf, mute, confused, or foolish; and heading households and earning income instead of using relief facilities. As will be noted in Chapter 2, available quantitative empirical studies that have assessed elements of youth competent functioning in response to political violence have often found evidence for it. Indicators of competence have included self-determination, tolerance and flexibility toward adversaries, cooperation toward building a future, coping, moral development, academic achievement, retained emphasis on educational aspirations or family values, creativity, employment, and so on. Moreover, recommendations for humanitarian agencies include interventions that focus on the ability of survivors to function effectively during transition to a postconflict society (Almedom, 2004; Bolton, Neugebauer, & Ndogono, 2002; Bolton & Tang, 2002).

To build on this growing body of work, several chapters in this volume have included a shift away from the largely deficit focus that carries the implication of youth as victims or damaged individuals (Boyden, 2003). In Chapter 5, Wessells and Kostelny recommend that a holistic focus on child soldiers—importantly, one that includes the judgments of youth themselves—reveals appraisals of competence and growth. Weine and colleagues (Chapter 11) write of the creative adaptive capacity of Bosnian refugee adolescents in coping with the multiple demands of being post-conflict refugees in a foreign urban environment (Chicago). Boothby and colleagues (Chapter 10) document long-term longitudinal evidence of productive, capable, and caring behavior of former Mozambican child soldiers that in some ways exceeds even that of their nonsoldier counterparts. In our own data, Palestinian adolescents' activism during the First Intifada was associated with several measures of psychosocial and civic competence assessed many years after the end of the struggle (Chapter 9; Barber & Olsen, 2006).

The Intricacy of Human Functioning

Clearly, shifting to a purely competence focus in research on adolescents and political violence would be unwise, both because of the consistent evidence of negative consequences to some youth and because such a focus would be equally as narrow and incomplete as the deficit model that it would counter. Indeed, one of the important lessons to be learned from the critiques of the dominant approach to this research is to avoid the compartmentalization of human functioning—generally and, perhaps even more important, to do so when studying populations undergoing extreme challenge. For in this realm we naturally tend to extend the extremity of people's experiences to their responses to them—that is, presuming that negative produces negative.

Yet how does one square the evidence of *both* disrupted and competent functioning in the same individual or groups of persons? There are numerous ways to interpret such evidence, all of which call for elaborations in how we approach research and understanding of youth (as well as younger and older individuals) experiencing political conflict. At least four juxtapositions seem relevant to the evidence being considered here.

A Flexibility Perspective   Strumpfer (2003) reminds that the "dispute between the pathogenic 'medical model' and the competence models of the wellness movement" (p. 69) is not new but is as old as ancient Greek philosophy and practice. Although Strumpfer's focus on workplace resilience and burnout is somewhat far from the fields of political conflict, his construal of the nature of resilience is instructive in understanding one way to view the concurrence of the negative and the positive. According to Strumpfer (2003), the root verb *resile* means to spring back or recoil to former size once compressed, stretched, or bent. Thus, quality of healthy functioning may be reduced by inordinate demands, but such reduction is temporary, after which the individual "resiles" to a level of normal functioning. Accordingly, the assessment of negative functioning—accurate as it may be—might be gauging just the first step in this resilience process. To stop there would be to prematurely conclude about the quality of functioning. (See Layne, Warren, Watson, & Shalev, 2007, and Layne et al., 2008, for compatible discussions of trauma recovery models that incorporate notions of stress resistance and restoration to homeostatic balance.)

Importantly, Strumpfer's (2003) approach to the flexibility in human response to difficulty is undergirded by the "sense of coherence" (Antonovsky, 1979) that humans possess (i.e., the degree to which one's environment is comprehensible, manageable, and meaningful). Any one of these features of coherence might be reduced temporarily by overload or excessive challenge, but once (or if) that condition is removed, the overall coherence of the environment is restored, enabling a restoration of effective functioning. This qualification of the role of coherence in adaptability appears to be critical in understanding youth experience with political violence. As is evident in comparisons of Bosnian and Palestinian experiences with political conflict (Chapter 12; Barber, 2008), some political conflicts are not at all coherent for those who endure them; for others, they are richly coherent. Relatedly, postwar environments, depending on how effectively they address or redress the conditions giving rise to conflict, can also vary substantially on the coherence they offer to those seeking place in them.

This flexibility perspective would suggest that research designs need to be substantially elaborated—extending beyond assessing either negative or positive functioning. Instead, both would need to be measured and, importantly so, over time—that is, pre-, during, and postconflict.

A Transformative Perspective   An augmentation of this flexibility perspective (also noted by Strumpfer, 2003) suggests that not only can humans return to levels of prechallenge functioning but we can adapt beyond them. For example, Tedeschi and colleagues (Calhoun & Tedeschi, 2006; Tedeschi & Calhoun, 1995) recognize the reports of survivors of various types of trauma in constructing what they refer to as "posttraumatic growth." This construct asserts that a potential result of exposure to trauma is positive change in cognitive, emotional, and perhaps behavioral functioning of a magnitude that surpasses mere coping. In their study of Bosnian youth refugees, Weine and colleagues (Chapter 11) echo this potential in commenting that although traumas may cause adverse or negative change, they may also stimulate adaptive responses leading to positive change. The extensive literatures on coping with stress (e.g., Lazarus & Folkman, 1984) could be situated under either of these perspectives, depending on whether coping is viewed as a tool to regain previous functioning (the flexibility perspective) or as evidence of adaptive, productive change (the transformative perspective).

Two further perspectives on the duality of negative and positive functioning also recommend alterations in the approach to the study of youth and political violence. Unlike the previous two, these do not hinge necessarily on an interaction between the positive and negative. One has to do with the determination of whether an element of functioning is either positive or negative. The other has to do with the compatibility of the two in describing the complexity of human experience.

An Ambiguity Perspective   Regarding adolescents generally, sociologist Furstenberg (2000) cautions against drawing a "sharp line between 'good' and 'bad' behaviors" (p. 900). Citing Becker (1973), he notes that behaviors have complex meanings that depend on both their social context and consequences. Furthermore, they suggest that social institutions and cultures (analogous perhaps in the present case to war and political violence) create competing demands or reinforce patterns problematic to successful (or optimal) development. Focusing on the study of "single domains of success or failure" (p. 905), it would seem, misses—or misconstrues—the ambiguous meaning of specific behaviors. Thus, what may be viewed as problem behavior in one context might well be understood (by the actors involved in the experience) as adaptive in another, depending on the realities and (multiple, often competing) demands of the immediate historical, political, or cultural context. Summerfield (2003) makes the same point when referring specifically to political violence: "how human beings experience an adverse event, and what they say and do about it, is primarily a function of the social meanings and understandings attached to it" (p. 459). The incidence of stress is a good example. Although elevated stress levels are problematic in many contexts and situations, they are both logical and expected in severely taxing environments. As noted, pathologizing them automatically is problematic. The more helpful approach would be to assess the extent to which they compromise broader functioning, requiring by definition the evaluation of multiple types of functioning before a judgment of well-being (or specifically, the costs to it of elevated stress) can be made.

Much of this task is subjective. This volume's emphasis on attending to the perspectives of youth concords with Furstenberg's (2000) recommendation that one way to reduce this type of "academic segregation" (p. 905; i.e., focusing either on success or failure) is to integrate qualitative research along with survey research—and thereby access the meaning and understanding that youth and their families make of the complexity of their circumstances.

A Balancing Perspective   In Chapter 7 and elsewhere (Layne et al., 2007, 2008), Layne and colleagues recommend the work of social support scholars (e.g., Kaniasty & Norris, 1993) that calls for the need to measure both negative and positive aspects of interpersonal relationships in contexts of disaster. The same approach would be sensible in studying the impact of exposure to or participation in political violence, given the inconsistent association in war refugee populations of growth indicators and symptom scores (from no correlation to moderately correlated; Powell, Rosner, Butollo, Tedeschi, & Calhoun, 2003). This perspective would acknowledge that lives are a complex of both positive and negative aspects of functioning (e.g., Ahmed & Boisvert, 2006; Joseph & Linley, 2006). Like the previous two perspectives, this view also requires the measurement of multiple forms of both positive and negative functioning, but analyses of these data would address questions of the relative balance of negative and positive functioning and weighting the relative salience of specific indicators of either type of functioning. Thus, for example, relevant questions are: How broadly across the multiple domains of one's life (e.g., social relationships, performance in key institutions, civic commitment, self-concept, etc.) is a youth functioning well or poorly? According to the prevailing cultures, in which of these domains is competent or problematic functioning more salient or critical to the overall assessment of well-being? (See Layne et al., 2007, for an extensive conceptualization from clinical psychology on the juxtaposition of negative and positive conditions in understanding recovery.)

Expanding the Assessment of Political Violence

One further element of the complexity of youth experience with political violence that this volume has approached is the understanding and assessment of the conflict itself. Two fundamentals of this complexity are addressed: (1) recognizing that the nature of political conflicts, and thus youth experience with them, vary substantially, and (2) assessing the broader social forces that typically precede, accompany, and endure the conflicts themselves.

Multiple Types of Violence and Conflict

In addition to the important variability in how violence is calibrated (e.g., its intensity, severity, and chronicity), which has been highlighted in some of this volume's chapters (Chapters 4, 6, and 10), violence and conflict vary substantially in both the underlying nature of the conflicts and, in turn, youths' reasons or motivations for being involved in it. Thus, the book has included attention to a variety of different political conflicts that in part illustrate the complexity of adolescent experience. Several chapters (Chapters 7, 8, 11, and 12) focus, for example, either exclusively or partially on the Bosnian experience because it is a good illustration of a conflict in which adolescents were unwitting, virtually defenseless victims of sustained and brutal political violence that moreover exploded on them without forewarning, explanation, or clarification.

In contrast, the Northern Ireland conflict is a very different phenomenon. Its long duration has included more sporadic violence in which adolescents were indeed victims but nevertheless have had to participate in a struggle that has been relatively well defined for all on ideological, religious, and political grounds. As Cairns and Darby (1998) noted, the Northern Ireland conflict differs importantly from many other conflicts also in that the combatants permanently inhabit the same territory, and therefore the everyday lives of opposing parties are tightly and inescapably interwoven. (This was and is partly true in the Bosnian case.) Such conditions can make conflict particularly intractable. Thus, unlike the South African conflict in which virtually all agreed that some change toward equality was necessary, or the Israeli-Palestinian conflict in which the conflicting parties essentially live apart from each other and the envisioned solutions are for sharing the overall land but not intermixing within it, in Northern Ireland there seems to be a zero-sum equation where compromise (being either part of the United Kingdom or part of Ireland) is automatically viewed as failure and essentially a sacrifice of identity by whichever group is making the concession (Cairns & Darby, 1998; Gallagher, 2004).

One of the key ways the Palestinian experience with political violence differs from many other conflicts has been the unparalleled levels of participation in the battles. There are numerous suggested demographic, historical, and strategic reasons as to why this might be the case (see Chapter 9 for a brief review of these), but for our purposes here, it is sufficient to highlight the point that understanding the impact of political violence on adolescents in some cases requires attention to the degree of their active involvement in it. As noted later in the volume (Chapters 9 and 12), their own activism was central to the conflict experience.

Different still is the experience of children and youth who are coerced into conflict. Indeed, even child soldiering is itself multifaceted, with some children being conscripted, some coerced, and some who volunteer (Brett & Specht, 2004; Wessells, 2006). Although concern for their often brutal victimization is obviously critical, as Wessells and Kostelny (Chapter 5) and Boothby and colleagues (Chapter 10) point out, even those youth who are forcibly recruited are not merely passive victims but rather can be actively involved in making sense of their situation and using cultural values to resist being fully exploited psychologically by their captors.

Conflict's Ecology: How Do Broader Forces Impact the Effects of Political Violence?

Political conflict most often occurs within a matrix of other strong forces—social, economic, ethnic, historical, or cultural. Some of these forces give particular meaning to the conflict (e.g., the history of relations between the conflicting parties) or inform how to navigate and cope with it (e.g., cultural beliefs, practices about conflict, suffering, peace, etc.). Other forces, such as economic disadvantage and other disparities related to ethnicity, are often actually part of the genesis, maintenance, perpetuation, or resolution of the conflict. These latter forces, among others, have their own negative impact on individual and social well-being quite apart from the impact of the concomitant conflict, and they can interact with it and ultimately affect individuals.

The reality of this multiplicity of impinging forces has important implications for assessing the impact of political violence on individuals and social groups. First, it is important to recognize that experience with political conflict is far more complex than simply exposure to violent events (i.e., to the trauma or victimization that has been the focus of most investigations). Rather, experience with political violence is a package of events and forces. In this regard, Weine and colleagues (Chapter 11) refer to the "trauma bundle" faced by Bosnian adolescents who survived ethnic cleansing and war and later become refugees in the urban United States. Consistent with the concerns already expressed about focusing narrowly on individual, negative psychological functioning in war-exposed populations, the authors argue against the tendency to prioritize the trauma of violence. For them, such an approach decontextualizes the conflict experiences and, as a consequence, misses not only the reality of multiple types of difficulty but likely also the geometry of their explanatory power.

Weine and colleagues detect in the narratives of refugee Bosnian youth that their trauma bundle, in addition to the experience with violence, consists of the socially and culturally marginalizing conditions of displacement, exile, and urbanization, factors that they suggest interact in affecting the lives of adolescents, their families, and their communities. By implication, therefore, to assess only violence exposure would be to insufficiently appreciate the extent of conflict and conflict-related experiences and only partially explain the effect of those experiences on well-being. Moreover, the complexity of multiple forces itself suggests that response might also be multifaceted; to the extent that the complex of forces is experienced in varying configurations by individual adolescents or groups of adolescents, it further complicates the generalization of effects across members of any sample being investigated. Thus, for these authors, the complex bundle makes it unreasonable to imagine or predetermine how individual adolescents fare in response to their bundle, but regardless, the response will be multifaceted—including adverse, adaptive, and positive changes.

This identification of other determining social forces that sometimes accompany political conflict resonates with Muldoon and colleagues' findings (Chapter 6) relative to social class and ethnicity. This specification of the different social positioning of youth and families is also consistent with Boyden's (2003) insight that social power resulting from status differences (i.e., gender, class, ethnicity, etc.) needs consideration to understand which youth will suffer more or less as a result of conflict. This recognition of the broader ecology of conflict also receives support from some earlier work of ours in which deteriorated neighborhood conditions more broadly predicted Palestinian adolescent difficulty (in part via disruptions in their social contexts) than did their specific experiences with political violence (Barber, 2001). Very similar findings were made in Bosnia by Jones and Kafetsios (2005), who discerned that socioeconomic conditions (e.g., neglected, isolated, and depressed community), worry about school performance, and friends and family could have as much effect on adolescents' well-being as their exposure to war-related events. Such attention to the broader ecology of which political violence is a part can also be found in several treatments of youth experience: in Northern Ireland (Cairns & Darby, 1998), the Middle East (Elbedour, Van Slyck, & Stern, 1998), and various parts of Africa (Higson-Smith et al., 2006; Honwana, 2006; Liddell, Kemp, & Moema, 1993; Nordstrom, 1997; Polgreen, 2006; Sommers, 2001).

Beyond informing critically on the experience of conflict, the relevance of the social ecology extends also to understanding the effects of conflict. Consistent with the theme raised earlier about suffering as a social experience, analyses of the social structural conditions postconflict are key to understanding its overall effects. Earlier in this chapter, the importance of attending to the social and civic functioning of conflict-exposed youth was noted. Highlighted here are the more macro forces that structure society, such as employment, education, and the degree to which postconflict youth have access, opportunity, and equity relative to them (see Chapter 8). Important also is the culturally specific fabric of social values and practices. Thus, as Barenbaum et al. (2004) have reviewed, the impact of war on children's mental health is a function not just of disruptions in critical social relationships (e.g., loss or estrangement of family members, as in Chapter 7) but also of the degree to which there has been destruction of social facilities and services and a breakdown of community values and practices. Further, Boyden (2003) notes that some of the most distressing aspects of conflict experience for children are the loss of educational and work opportunities, poverty, and social isolation, all of which can disrupt a sense of continuity in the lives of children and can bring humiliation to children and their families. Boothby and colleagues

(Chapter 10) came to the same conclusion when noting that former child soldiers reported that lost economic opportunity (which in turn aggravated achieving the life cycle tasks of choosing a wife and building a family) was more problematic for them than their actual war experiences were. Finally, as Boyden (2003) also observes, in many conflicts far more children suffer and die from the secondary effects of conflict, such as starvation, exposure, and untreated disease.

Conclusion

Would that this were a world without war. In that dream, no adolescent or youth (or child, or adult) would experience the tragedy and destruction of political conflict and violence. Current patterns of national, ethnic, and/or religious disharmony, however, make clear that the world's punctuated history of violence is not dissipating but, as many would argue, escalating in terms of scope and lethality. Regrettably, there is thus much opportunity and need to understand how exposure to and involvement in political conflict impact human experience.

This volume represents an effort to advance that understanding relative specifically to youth by synthesizing the growing sophistication of knowledge of human functioning in challenging conditions on the whole, the nature of adolescent experience generally, and the still very basic scholarly understanding of war-experienced adolescents specifically. As is the specific goal of this introductory chapter, the book as a whole illuminates and elaborates the substantial complexity of the topic. Specific recommendations for advancement in understanding this complexity are offered in Chapter 13. Most basically, the traditional approach of documenting the stress correlates of violence exposure needs to be refined to more precisely understand which youth (i.e., sex, age, social class, minority/majority status, psychological history, etc.) have been and will be significantly handicapped, and what the psychological and social mechanisms are that underlie this damage.

Beyond this, the volume encourages the recognition that the complexity of political conflict requires radically expanding both the assessment of conflict experience and the adaptation to it. As for the conflict experience, precision is needed as to the exposure youth have to violence (e.g., its intensity, frequency, familiarity, duration, proximity, attributed meaning, etc.) but also the degree of involvement in the conflict and its type (e.g., voluntary or coerced); youths' reasons/motivations/understanding of that involvement (e.g., duty, social unity, identity search, economic gain, escape from other hardship, personal and collective growth, etc.); the manifold historical, social, economic, and political forces and conditions that often predate and persist postconflict and can prevail over violence per se in their debilitating effects (e.g., poverty, substandard health services, ethnic discrimination, political inequality, forced migration, etc.); and the history, norms, beliefs, and philosophies of the cultures experiencing the conflict (e.g., the meaning, role, and purpose of violence and conflict in a given culture.)

As for adaptation to conflict experiences, much more comprehensive coverage of youth functioning is called for. This expansion should increase well past the predominant focus on negative psychological functioning to include broader assessments of psychological, social, and civic functioning. This expansion would not only represent a more accurate portrayal of the complex realities of day-to-day life for adolescents (and thus an enhanced ability to assess the relative weight of psychological stress or elements of adaptive functioning in defining overall well-being) but also encourage a more respectful and accurate orientation to adolescent capacity and potential competence (i.e., not relying overly on stereotypes of vulnerability, immaturity, and self-interest and self-absorption). Most fundamentally, the expansion needs to attend more sensitively to the cultural realities that define experience with war and violence (e.g., beliefs, values, and philosophies relative to individual and social suffering, death, growth, healing, reintegration, reconciliation, forgiveness, etc.).

References

Ahmed, M., & Boisvert, C. M. (2006). Using positive psychology with special mental health populations. *American Psychologist, 61,* 333–335.

Almedom, A. M. (2004). Factors that mitigate war-induced anxiety and mental distress. *Journal of Biosocial Science, 36,* 445–461.

Almedom, A. M. (2005). Resilience, hardiness, sense of coherence, and posttraumatic growth: All paths leading to the "light at the end of the tunnel"? *Journal of Loss and Trauma, 10,* 253–265.

Annan, J., Blattman, C., & Horton, R. (2006). The state of youth and youth protection in Northern Uganda: Findings from the Survey of War Affected youth (SWAY). A report for UNICEF Uganda. www.sway-uganda.org.

Annan, J., Blattman, C., Carlson, K., & Mazurana, D. (2008). The state of female youth in Northern Uganda: findings from the Survey of War Affected Youth (SWAY). A report for UNICEF Uganda. www.sway-uganda.org.

Antonovsky, A. (1979). *Health, stress, and coping.* San Francisco: Jossey-Bass.

Arnett, J. J. (2002). Adolescents in Western countries in the 21st century: Vast opportunities—for all? In B. B. Brown, R. W. Larson, & T. S. Saraswathi (Eds.), *The world's youth: Adolescence in eight regions of the globe* (pp. 307–343). Cambridge: Cambridge University Press.

Barber, B. K. (2001). Political violence, social integration, and youth functioning: Palestinian youth from the Intifada. *Journal of Community Psychology, 29,* 259–280.

Barber, B. K. (Ed.). (2002). *Intrusive parenting: How psychological control affects children and adolescents.* Washington, DC: American Psychological Association Press.

Barber, B. K. (2008). Contrasting portraits of war: Youths' varied experiences with political violence in Bosnia and Palestine. *International Journal of Behavioral Development, 32*(4), 294–305.

Barber, B. K. (in press). *One heart, so many stones: The story of Palestinian youth.* New York: Palgrave/Macmillan.

Barber B. K., & Olsen, J. A. (2006). Adolescents' willingness to engage in political conflict: Lessons from the Gaza Strip. In J. Victoroff (Ed.), *Tangled roots: Social and psychological factors in the genesis of terrorism* (vol. 11, pp. 203–226). NATO Security through science series, E: Human and societal dynamics. Amsterdam: IOS Press.

Barber, B. K., Schluterman, J. M., Denny, E. S., & McCouch, R. M. (2005). Adolescents and political violence. In M. Fitzduff & C. Stout (Eds.), *The psychology of resolving global conflicts: From war to peace* (vol. 2, pp. 171–190). Group and social factors. Westport, CT: Praeger.

Barber, B. K., Stolz, H. E., & Olsen, J. A. (2005). Parental support, psychological control, and behavioral control: Assessing relevance across time, method, and culture. *Monographs of the Society for Research in Child Development 70,* No. 4.

Barenbaum, J., Ruchkin, V., & Schwab-Stone, M. (2004). The psychosocial aspects of children exposed to war: Practice and policy initiatives. *Journal of Child Psychology and Psychiatry, 45,* 41–62.

Baumrind, D. (1991). The influence of parenting style on adolescent competence and substance use. *Journal of Early Adolescence, 11,* 56–95.

Becker, D. (1995). The deficiency of the concept of posttraumatic stress disorder when dealing with victims of human rights violations. In R. J. Kleber, C. R. Figley, & P. R. Gersons (Eds.), *Beyond trauma: Cultural and societal dynamics* (pp. 99–110). New York: Plenum Press.

Becker, H. S. (1973). *Outsiders, studies in the sociology of deviance.* New York: Free Press.

Belsky, J. 2008. War, trauma and children's development: Observations from a modern evolutionary perspective. *International Journal of Behavioral Development, 32*(4), 256–267.

Blattman, C., & Annan, J. (2007). The consequences of child soldiering. HICN Working Paper, 22.

Bolton, P., Neugebauer, R., & Ndogono, L. (2002). Prevalence of depression in rural Rwanda based on symptom and functional criteria. *Journal of Nervous and Mental Disorders, 190,* 631–637.

Bolton, P., & Tang, A. (2002). An alternative approach to cross-cultural function assessment. *Social Psychiatry and Psychiatric Epidemiology, 37,* 537–543.

Bonanno, G. A. (2004). Loss, trauma, and human resilience: Have we underestimated the human capacity to thrive after extremely aversive events? *American Psychologist, 59,* 20–28.

Boothby, N., Strang, A., & Wessells, M. (2006a). *A world turned upside down: Social ecological approaches to children in war zones.* Bloomfield, CT: Kumarian Press.

Boothby, N., Strang, A., & Wessells, M. (2006b). Introduction. In N. Boothby, A. Strang, & M. Wessells (Eds.). *A world turned upside down: Social ecological approaches to children in war zones.* Bloomfield, CT: Kumarian Press.

Boyden, J. (2003). Children under fire: Challenging assumptions about children's resilience. *Children, Youth and Environments, 13*(1). Retrieved July 2, 2006, from http://www.colorado.edu/journals/cye/13_1/index.htm.

Boyden, J., & de Berry, J. (Eds.) (2004). *Children and youth on the front line: Ethnography, armed conflict and displacement.* Oxford: Berghan Books.

Braungart, R. C. (1984). Historical generations and youth movements: A theoretical perspective. In L. Kriesberg (Series Ed.) & R. Ratcliff (Vol. Ed.), *Research in social movements, conflict and change* (vol. 6, pp. 95–141). Greenwich, CT: JAI Press.

Brett, R., & Specht, I. (2004). *Young soldiers: Why they choose to fight.* Boulder, CO: Lynne Rienner.

Brinton, C. (1956). *The anatomy of revolution.* New York: Vintage Books.

Brown, B. B., & Larson, R. W. (2002). The kaleidoscope of adolescence: Experiences of the world's youth at the beginning of the 21st century. In B. B. Brown, R. W. Larson, & T. S. Saraswathi (Eds.), *The world's youth: Adolescence in eight regions of the globe* (pp. 1–20). Cambridge: Cambridge University Press.

Brown, B. B., Larson, R. W., & Saraswathi, T. S. (Eds.). (2002). *The world's youth: Adolescence in eight regions of the globe.* Cambridge: Cambridge University Press.

Cairns, E., & Darby, J. (1998). The conflict in Northern Ireland: Causes, consequences, and controls. *American Psychologist, 53,* 754–760.

Cairns, E., & Dawes, A. (1996). Children: Ethnic and political violence—a commentary. *Child Development, 67,* 129–139.

Calhoun, L. G., & Tedeschi, R. G. (2006). *Handbook of posttraumatic growth: Research & practice.* Mahwah, NJ: Erlbaum.

Carmines, E. G. (1991). Psychological antecedents of adolescent political involvement: Personal competence and political behavior. *International Journal of Adolescence and Youth, 3,* 79–98.

Daiute, C. (2006). General introduction: The problem of society in youth conflict. In C. Daiute, Z. F. Beykont, C. Higson-Smith, & L. Nucci (Eds.), *International perspectives on youth conflict and development* (pp. 3–22). New York: Oxford University Press.

Daiute, C., Beykont, Z. F., Higson-Smith, C., & Nucci, L. (Eds.) (2006). *International perspectives on youth conflict and development.* New York: Oxford University Press.

Damon, W., & Eisenberg, N. (1998). *Handbook of child psychology,* vol. 5. Hoboken, NJ: John Wiley and Sons.

Dornbusch, S. M. (1989). The sociology of adolescence. *Annual Review of Sociology, 15,* 233–259.

Eccles, J. S., & Gootman, J. (2002). *Community programs to promote youth development.* Washington, DC: National Academies Press.

Elbedour, S., Bensel, R., & Maruyama, G. (1993). Children at risk: Psychological coping with war and conflict in the Middle East. *International Journal of Mental Health, 22*(3), 33–52.

Elbedour, S., Van Slyck, M., & Stern, M. (1998). Psychosocial adjustment in Middle Eastern adolescents: The relative impact of violent versus non-violent social disorganization. *Community Mental Health Journal, 34,* 191–205.

Epstein, B. (1991). *Political protest and cultural revolution: Non-violent direct action in the 1970s and 1980s.* Berkeley: University of California Press.

Fendrich, J. M. (1993). *Ideal citizens: The legacy of the civil rights movement.* Albany: State University of New York Press.

Flanagan, C., & Syvertsen, A. K. (2005). Youth as a social construct and social actor. In L. R. Sherrod, C. A. Flanagan, & R. Kassimir (Eds.), *Youth activism: An international encyclopedia. Vol. 1.* Westport, CT: Greenwood Press.

Friedman, M. J., Resick, P.A., & Keane, T. M. (2007). Key questions and an agenda for future research. In M. J. Friedman, T. M. Keane, & P. A. Resick (Eds.), *Handbook of PTSD: Science and practice* (pp. 540–561). New York: Guilford.

Furstenberg, F. F. (2000). The sociology of adolescence and youth in the 1990s: A critical commentary. *Journal of Marriage and Family, 62,* 896–910.

Gallagher, T. (2004). After the war comes peace? An examination of the impact of the Northern Ireland conflict on young people. *Journal of Social Issues, 60,* 629–642.

Gibson, K. (1993). The effects of exposure to political violence on children: Does violence beget violence? *South African Journal of Psychology, 23,* 167–173.

Grotevant, H. D. (1998). Adolescent development in family context. In W. Damon & N. Eisenberg (Eds.), *Handbook of child psychology*, vol. 5 (pp. 1097–1149). Hoboken, NJ: John Wiley and Sons.

Gurr, T. R. (1970). *Why men rebel.* Princeton, NJ: Princeton University Press.

Higson-Smith, C. (2006). Youth violence in South Africa: The impact of political transition. In C. Daiute, Z. F. Beykont, C. Higson-Smith, & L. Nucci (Eds.), *International perspectives on youth conflict and development* (pp. 177–192). New York: Oxford University Press.

Honwana, A. (2006). Child soldiers: community healing and rituals in Mozambique and Angola. In C. Daiute, Z. F. Beykont, C. Higson-Smith, & L. Nucci (Eds.), *International perspectives on youth conflict and development* (pp. 177–192). New York: Oxford University Press.

Jenkins, C. J. (1983). Resource mobilization theory and the study of social movements. *Annual Review of Sociology, 9,* 527–553.

Jones, L. (2002). Adolescent understandings of political violence and psychological well-being: A qualitative study from Bosnia Herzegovina. *Social Science & Medicine, 55,* 1351–1371.

Jones, L. (2004). *Then they started shooting.* Cambridge, MA: Harvard University Press.

Jones, L., & Kafetsios, K. (2005). Exposure to political violence and psychological well-being in Bosnian adolescents: A mixed method approach. *Clinical Child Psychology and Psychiatry, 10,* 157–176.

Joseph, S., & Linley, P. A. (2006). Positive psychology versus the medical model? *American Psychologist, 61,* 332–333.

Kagitçibasi, C. (1996). *Family and human development across cultures.* Mahwah, NJ: Erlbaum.

Kaniasty, K., & Norris, F. (1993). A test of the social support deterioration model in the context of natural disaster. *Journal of Personality and Social Psychology, 64*(3), 395–408.

Kassimir, R. (2005). Youth activism: International and transnational. In L. R. Sherrod, C. A Flanaga, & R. Kassimir (Eds.), *Youth activism: An international encyclopedia.* Westport, CT: Greenwood Press.

Khalidi, R. (1997). *Palestinian identity: The construction of modern national consciousness.* Chicago: University of Chicago Press.

Kleinman, A., & Desjarlais, R. (1995). Violence, culture, and the politics of trauma. In A. Kleinman (Ed.), *Writing at the margin: Discourse between anthropology and medicine* (pp. 173–191). Berkeley: University of California Press.

Kleinman, A., Das, V., & Lock, M. (1997). *Social suffering.* Berkeley: University of California Press.

Kliewer, W., Parrish, K. A., Taylor, K. W., Jackson, K., Walker, J. M., & Shivy, V. A. (2006). Socialization of coping with community violence: Influences of caregiver coaching, modeling, and family context. *Child Development, 77,* 605–623.

Kostelny, K. (2006). A culture-based, integrative approach: Helping war-affected children. In N. Boothby, A. Strang, & M. Wessells (Eds.). *A world turned upside down: Social ecological approaches to children in war zones.* Bloomfield, CT: Kumarian Press.

Larson, R. (2000). Toward a psychology of positive youth development. *American Psychologist, 55,* 170–183.

Larson, R. (2002). Globalization, societal change, and new technologies: What they mean for the future of adolescence. In R. Larson, B. Bradford Brown, & J. T. Mortimer (Eds.), *Adolescents' preparation for the future, perils and promises: A report of the study group on adolescence in the twenty-first century* (pp. 1–30). Ann Arbor, MI: Society for Research on Adolescence.

Larson, R., Jarrett, R., Hansen, D., Pearce, N., Sullivan, P., Walker, K., et al. (2004). Organized youth activities as contexts for youth development. In P. A. Linley & S. Joseph (Eds.), *Positive psychology in practice* (pp. 540–560). Hoboken, NJ: John Wiley and Sons.

Lazarus, R. S., & Folkman, S. (1984). *Stress appraisal and coping.* New York: Springer.

Layne, C. M., Beck, C. J., Rimmasch, H., Southwick, J. S., Moreno, M. A., & Hobfoll, S. E. (2008). Promoting "resilient" posttraumatic adjustment in childhood and beyond: Unpacking life events, adjustment trajectories, resources, and interventions. In D. Brom, R. Pat-Horenczyk, & J. Ford (Eds.), *Treating traumatized children: Risk, resilience, and recovery.* New York: Routledge.

Layne, C. M., Warren, J., Watson, P., & Shalev, A. (2007). Risk, vulnerability, resistance, and resilience: Towards an integrative model of posttraumatic adaptation. In M. J. Friedman, T. M. Kean, & P. A. Resick (Eds.), *PTSD: Science & practice—A comprehensive handbook* (pp. 497–520). New York: Guilford.

Lerner, R. T. (2004). *Liberty: Thriving and civic engagement among America's youth.* Thousand Oaks, CA: Sage Publications.

Liddell, C., Kemp, J., & Moema, M. (1993). The young lions: South African children and youth in political struggle. In L. A. Leavitt & N. A. Fox (Eds.), *The psychological effects of war and violence on children* (pp. 199–214). Hillsdale, NJ: Erlbaum.

Liddell, C., Kvalsvig, J., Qotyana, P., & Shabalala, A. (1994). Community violence and young South African children's involvement in aggression. *International Journal of Behavioral Development, 17,* 613–628.

Maçhel, G. (2001). The impact of war on children: A review of progress since the 1996 United Nations report on the impact of armed conflict on children. New York: Palgrave.

Maçhel, G. (1996). Impact of armed conflict on children. *Report of the expert of the Secretary-General submitted pursuant to General Assembly Resolution 48/157.* UN Document A/51/306 and Add.1. New York: United Nations.

Masten, A. (2001). Ordinary magic: Resilience processes in development. *American Psychologist, 56*(3), 227–238.

McAdam, D. (1989). The biographical consequences of activism. *American Sociological Review, 54,* 744–760.

McCarthy, J., & Zald, M. N. (1977). Resource mobilization and social movements. *American Journal of Sociology, 82,* 1212–1241.

Moore, K. A., & Lippman, L. (Eds.). (2005). *What do children need to flourish? Conceptualizing and measuring indicators of positive development.* New York: Springer.

Näätänen, P., Kanninen, K., Qouta, S., & Punamäki, R. (2002). Trauma-related emotional patterns and their association with post-traumatic and somatic symptoms. *Anxiety, Stress, & Coping, 15,* 75–94.

Neff, K. (2003). Understanding how universal goals of independence and interdependence are manifested within particular cultural contexts. *Human Development, 46,* 312–318.

Nordstrom, C. (1997). *A different kind of war.* Philadelphia: University of Pennsylvania Press.

Nsamenang, A. B. (2002). Adolescence in Sub-Saharan Africa: An image constructed from Africa's triple inheritance. In B. B. Brown, R. W. Larson, & T. S. Saraswathi (Eds.), *The world's youth: Adolescence in eight regions of the globe* (pp. 61–104). Cambridge: Cambridge University Press.

Pick, T. (2001). The myth of the trauma/the trauma of the myth: Myths as mediators of some long-term effects of war trauma. *Peace and Conflict Journal of Peace Psychology, 7,* 201–226.

Polgreen, L. (2006, July 30). War's chaos steals Congo's young by the millions. *New York Times,* p. 1.

Powell, S., Rosner, R., Butollo, W., Tedeschi, R. G., & Calhoun, L. G. (2003). Posttraumatic growth after war: A study with former refugees and displaced people in Sarajevo. *Journal of Clinical Psychology, 59,* 71–83.

Punamäki, R. L., Kanninen, K., Qouta, S., & El-Sarraj, E. (2002). The role of psychological defences in moderating between trauma and post-traumatic symptoms among Palestinian men. *International Journal of Psychology, 37,* 286–296.

Punamäki, R., Qouta, S., & El Sarraj, E. (1997). Models of traumatic experiences and children's psychological adjustment: The roles of perceived parenting and the children's own resources and activity. *Child Development, 68,* 718–728.

Punamäki, R. L., Qouta, S., & El-Sarraj, E. (2001). Resiliency factors predicting psychological adjustment after political violence among Palestinian children. *International Journal of Behavioral Development, 25*(3), 256–267.

Pupavac, V. (2004). Psychosocial interventions and the demoralization of humanitarianism. *Journal of Biosocial Science, 36,* 491–504.

Qouta, S., El-Sarraj, E., & Punamäki, R. L. (2001). Mental flexibility as resiliency factor among children exposed to political violence. *International Journal of Psychology, 36*(1), 1–7.

Raeff, C. (2006). *Always separated, always connected: Independence and interdependence in cultural contexts of development.* Mahwah, NJ: Erlbaum.

Rafman, S. (2004). Where the political and the psychological meet: Moral Disruption and children's understanding of war. *International Relations, 18,* 467–479.

Ramphele, M. A. (1997). Adolescents and violence: "Adults are cruel, they just beat, beat, beat!" *Social Science & Medicine, 45,* 1189–1197.

Reynolds, P. (2004). "Where wings take dream": On children in the work of war and the war of work. In J. Boyden & J. de Berry (Eds.), *Children and youth on the front line: Ethnography, armed conflict and displacement* (pp. 262–267). Oxford: Berghan Books.

Rohner, R. P. (1986). *The warmth dimension: Foundations of parental acceptance-rejection theory*. Thousand Oaks, CA: Sage.

Sagi-Schwartz, A., van Ijzendoorn, M. H., Grossmann, K. E., Joels, T., Grossmann, K., Scharf, M., et al. (2003). Attachment and traumatic stress in female holocaust child survivors and their daughters. *American Journal of Psychiatry, 160,* 1086–1092.

Saraswathi, T. S., & Larson, R. W. (2002). Adolescence in global perspective: An agenda for social policy. In B. B. Brown, R. W. Larson, & T. S. Saraswathi (Eds.), *The world's youth: Adolescence in eight regions of the globe* (pp. 344–362). Cambridge: Cambridge University Press.

Seligman, M. E. P., Steen, T. A., Park, N., & Peterson, C. (2005). Positive psychology progress: Empirical validation of interventions. *American Psychologist, 60,* 410–421.

Shaw, J.A. (2003). Children exposed to war/terroism. *Clinical Child and Family Psychology Review, 6,* 237–246.

Sherrod, L. R., Flanagan, C. A., & Kassimir, R. (Eds.). (2005). *Youth activism: An international encyclopedia*. Westport, CT: Greenwood Press.

Snyder, C. R., & Lopez, S. J. (Eds.). (2002). *Handbook of positive psychology*. New York: Oxford University Press.

Sommers, M. 2001. *Fear in Bongoland: Burundi refugees in urban Tanzania*. New York: Berghahn Books.

Spiro, M. E. (1993). Is the Western conception of self "peculiar" within the context of world cultures? *Ethos, 21,* 107–153.

Stagner, R. (1977). Egocentrism, ethnocentrism, and altrocentrism: Factors in individual and intergroup violence. *International Journal of Intercultural Relations, 1,* 9–29.

Steinberg, L. (1990). Autonomy, conflict, and harmony in the family relationship. In S. S. Feldman & G. R. Elliot (Eds.), *At the threshold: The developing adolescent* (pp. 255–276). Cambridge, MA: Harvard University Press.

Straker, G. (1992). *Faces in the revolution—the psychological effects of violence on township youth in South Africa*. Athens: Ohio University Press.

Strumpfer, D.J.W. (2003). Resilience and burnout: A stitch that could save nine. *South African Journal of Psychology, 33,* 69–79.

Summerfield, D. (2000). Conflict and health: War and mental health: A brief overview. *British Medical Journal, 321,* 232–235.

Summerfield, D. (2003). Mental health of refugees. *British Journal of Psychiatry, 183,* 459–460.

Taylor, C. (1990). Source of the self: The making of the modern identity. Cambridge, MA: Harvard.

Tedeschi, R. G., & Calhoun, L. G. (1995). *Trauma and transformation: Growing in the aftermath of suffering*. Thousand Oaks, CA: Sage.

Thomas, D. L., Weigert, A. J., & Winston, N. (1984). Adolescent identification with father and mother: A multi-national study. *Acta Paedologica, 1*(1), 47–68.

Tilly, C. (1978). *From mobilization to revolution*. Reading, MA: Addison-Wesley.

Tuchman, B. W. (1978). *A distant mirror: The calamitous 14th century*. New York: Ballantine Books.

Turiel, E. (2006). Social hierarchy, social conflicts, and moral development. In C. Daiute, Z. F. Beykont, C. Higson-Smith, & L. Nucci (Eds.), *International perspectives on youth conflict and development* (pp. 86–99). New York: Oxford University Press.

Turiel, E., & Wainryb, C. (2000). Social life in cultures: Judgments, conflicts, and subversion. *Child Development, 71,* 250–256.

Vazsonyi, A. T., Hibbert, J. R., & Snider, J. B. (2003). Exotic enterprise no more? Adolescent reports of family and parenting processes from youth in four countries. *Journal of Research on Adolescence, 13*(2), 129–160.

Villarruel, F. A., Perkins, D. F., Borden, L. M., & Keith, J. G. (2003). *Community youth development: Programs, policies, and practices.* Thousand Oaks, CA: Sage.

Wessells, M. (2006). *Child soldiers: From violence to protection.* Cambridge, MA: Harvard University Press.

Wessells, M., & Monteiro, C. (2000). Psychosocial intervention and post-war reconstruction in Angola: Interweaving western and traditional approaches. In D. J. Christie, R. V. Wagner, & D. DuNann (Eds.), *Peace, conflict and violence: Peace psychology for the 21st century* (pp. 350–362). New York: Prentice Hall.

Whalen, J., & Flacks, R. (1989). *Beyond the barricades: The sixties generation grows up.* Philadelphia, PA: Temple University Press.

Women's Commission for Refugee Women and Children. (2000, January). *Untapped potential: Adolescents affected by armed conflict: A review of programs and policies.* New York: Women's Commission for Refugee Women and Children.

Yates, M., & Youniss, J. (Eds.). (1999). *Roots of civic identity: International perspectives on community service and activism in youth.* New York: Cambridge University Press.

Young, A. (1995). *The harmony of illusions: Inventing post-traumatic stress disorder.* Princeton, NJ: Princeton University Press.

Youniss, J., & Yates, M. (1997). *Community service and social responsibility in youth.* Chicago: University of Chicago Press.

Yule, W. (2000). Emanuel Miller Lecture: From pogroms to "ethnic cleansing": Meeting the needs of war affected children. *Journal of Child Psychology and Psychiatry, 41*(6), 695–702.

Part I

GENERAL TREATMENTS OF YOUTH AND POLITICAL VIOLENCE

The four chapters included in Part I of this volume are broad treatments of the study of youth and political violence. These will be followed by Part II, which provides detailed specification of the effects of political violence on youth, and Part III, which expands the scope of inquiry of both the assessment of political violence and of youth functioning. The volume concludes with recommendations for future research (Chapter 13).

As for the general treatments provided in Part I, Brian Barber and Julie Schluterman (Chapter 2) first detail an overview of the quantitative empirical efforts to study political violence and its associations with youth functioning. They review ninety-five qualifying studies, concluding that the current state of research remains relatively simplistic in both scope and findings. In Chapter 3, Raija-Leena Punamäki gives a full theoretical treatment to the often invoked, yet inadequately validated or specified presumption that exposure to violence leads to violent or aggressive development in children. She outlines the variety of potential child, family, and social factors that inform if and when aggression in war-exposed children is likely to develop. In Chapter 4, Michele Slone summarizes her multifaceted program of research on youth in Israel and Palestine. She illustrates and implements in her systematic work many of the intricacies of conceptualization, measurement, sampling, and empirical analyses that are critical to this area of research. Finally, in Chapter 5, Michael Wessells and Kathleen Kostelny provide a thorough overview of the specific area of child soldiers, at once illustrating its own substantial complexity and recommending the need for holistic, integrative approaches to understand it.

Chapter 2

An Overview of the Empirical Literature on Adolescents and Political Violence

Brian K. Barber and
Julie Mikles Schluterman

The purpose of this book is to provide a thorough introduction to the study of adolescents in the context of political violence by critically reviewing prevailing approaches, offering new data from current approaches, and recommending how this particular field of study can be advanced. Fundamental to this goal is an evaluation of the empirical evidence as it now stands on how experiences with violence impact adolescents, both to understand what is known in this area and to view how research approaches can and should be refined to produce a more complete understanding. That has been the specific purpose of this chapter. As noted in Chapter 1, several reasons motivated the interest in adolescents (compared to younger children and older youth), including that adolescents make up large portions of the children involved in political violence; attention to them has been lacking; lingering stereotypes of adolescent troublesomeness still exist, despite evidence to the contrary; and recent work on adolescence internationally has advised that Western approaches to understanding them are largely unhelpful.

We are not concerned here with providing an empirical assessment of the strength of associations among the phenomena of interest (conflict experience and individual functioning), as would be done in a meta-analysis, for example. Rather, we provide an overview of the scope of the empirical, quantitative research. As will be seen, there is ample evidence that many youth who have experienced political violence are also likely to indicate higher levels of various forms of stress-related conditions or behaviors. This is an important and consistent finding, albeit not a particularly surprising one. Thus, although at some point it would be useful to provide a reliable estimate of the strength of that association, more important to the goal of improving the knowledge base at this stage is an assessment of how thoroughly the topic has been approached in empirical research.

Our primary concern in this chapter, accordingly, is organizing the information in an overview that will reveal the scope and comprehensiveness of the body of empirical work. Thus, for example, of concern are questions such as "How narrowly or broadly have researchers conceptualized experience with political violence?" "How specifically or comprehensively have researchers assessed the elements of youth functioning that might be impacted by this experience?" "How thoroughly has the common finding of a correlation between political violence exposure and negative psychological functioning been assessed (e.g., pathways of influence, buffers or moderators, variation by age or gender, etc.)?"

Although there is clearly not enough research on the functioning of this key population in the extreme context of political violence, there is a sizable and rapidly accumulating body of information to inspect. Not surprisingly, given the diverse groups of interested professionals, this corpus of information is quite diverse in scope and purpose. Therefore, it was necessary to make several screening decisions before settling on the final set of studies to include in this review.

We intentionally limited the coverage in this chapter to empirical work, leaving aside for now the scores of documents that are primarily historical, political, or anecdotal. Such material, of course, can be very valuable; nevertheless, in the requisite circumscription of scope of any single volume, we as social science researchers chose to focus on the available empirical evidence. We narrowed the selection further to include only quantitative empirical work. Because our essential purpose here is to evaluate the adequacy of the existing evidence for the impact of political violence on adolescents, we focus on studies that actually intended to calculate that impact. Naturally, very important and often critical information relative to understanding these questions comes from nonquantitative sources. In fact, elsewhere in this volume extensive attention is given, for example, to interview data, both as a way of fleshing out the variables that are typically assessed quantitatively and to suggest alternative, more salient issues as they are experienced, perceived, and reported by participants themselves (see Chapters 5, 10, 11, and 12).

Again, however, because some standardization is required to assess a body of information, we focus on those studies that attempted to actually assess the association between political conflict and adolescent functioning in a way that was intended to speak broadly for the populations under study. Our target was, therefore, work that (1) explicitly measured experience with political violence; (2) correlated such measures with one or more explicitly measured indexes of youth functioning (e.g., psychological, social, civic functioning, etc.); and (3) consisted of data from youth who were exclusively adolescents (e.g., in their teen years; see Chapter 1 for a discussion of the difficulties in defining adolescence) or from samples that included adolescents. Satisfying the first criterion was more difficult than anticipated, given the various ways researchers conceptualize and measure violence exposure or involvement. As much as possible, we kept to the strict standard that a study must have assessed (quantitatively) exposure or participation. This led to the exclusion of many studies. For example, there are many important works on migrating and refugee populations, but they do not necessarily include estimates of actual violence exposure or involvement.

Studies were located via multiple electronic searches using a combination of key words (e.g., adolescents, youth, political violence, political conflict, and war). Studies were also identified through inspection of the bibliographies of relevant articles or chapters. Naturally, no search is completely successful in identifying every relevant study, and we regret unintentionally excluding those that we did not locate. Some few studies are not included because we could not access the journal of publication. A clear limitation of the search criteria was the reliance solely on studies published in English. For better or worse, most of the empirical work of interest apparently has been published in English, as have been the debates and concerns surrounding the nature of adolescence and their specific experiences with political conflict that have motivated this book (see Chapter 1). A next step would be to consult findings published in other languages. With these limitations in mind, the set of studies reviewed herein should be fairly representative of the quantitative empirical evidence currently available.

The search procedures described produced a set of 243 citations (dating from 1972 to 2006). Fifty-one (21%) of these citations were either historical overviews or anecdotal reports and thus were not considered for review here. An additional ninety-seven studies (40%) were eliminated for a variety of reasons, most often because the study did not explicitly test (quantitatively) an empirical relationship between political violence and some form of adolescent behavior or characteristic. This left ninety-five studies to be reviewed for this chapter, four of which are part of this volume (see Chapters 6, 8, 9, and 10).

Overview of the Studies

Geographical Coverage

Table 2.1 is organized according to geographical region of study to give a view to the breadth of the scientific study of adolescents and political violence. Nine (10%) of the studies were conducted in Africa, with three of these in South Africa. Twelve (13%) of the studies were conducted in Asia, with all but one of these in Cambodia (or among Cambodian and/or Khmeri youth abroad). Nineteen (20%) of the studies were conducted in the Balkans (i.e., Bosnia, Croatia, Kosovo, Slovenia). Six (6%) of the studies were conducted in Europe, including five in Northern Ireland and one in Germany. Just over a third of the studies (forty-one studies [43%]) were conducted in the Middle East. Most were relatively equally divided between samples of Israelis (fifteen studies: twelve on Jewish adolescents, one on Arab-Israeli adolescents, and two with samples of both Jewish and Arab-Israelis) and Palestinians (nineteen studies, with samples from the West Bank, Gaza Strip, and/or East Jerusalem). Three studies were conducted with samples of both Israelis and Palestinians. Three additional studies were conducted in Lebanon, two in Kuwait, and one in Iraq. Finally, the review also includes one study conducted in South America and seven studies with samples from multiple countries.

Precision of Focus on Adolescents

It is clear from this set of studies that there has not been a precise focus on adolescents in the investigation of youth and political violence. In Chapter 1, the ambiguities

Table 2.1 Summary of Key Elements of Quantitative Studies on Adolescents and Political Violence

Article	Location	Size	Age Range	Negative Outcomes	Positive Outcomes
Africa					
Dawes et al., 1989	South Africa	65	2–17	PTSD, fears, emotional expression change, sleep & social difficulties	
Turton, Straker, & Moosa, 1991	South Africa	136	16–25	psychological distress	
Slone, Kaminer, & Durrheim, 2000	South Africa	540	mean 15.6	general distress; symptomatology indices; distress severity	
McIntyre & Ventura, 2003	Angola	231	13–16	PTSD; anxiety; depression; isolation; somatic complaints; social problems; problem thinking; delinquent behavior;	self-concept (lower)
Masinda & Muhesi, 2004	Congo	88	6–12, 13–20	traumatization	
Halcon et al., 2004	Somalia & Oromo refugees	338	18–25	physical, psychological, & social problems	
Geltman et al., 2005	Sudan refugees	304	Mean 17.6	*PTSD*	
Neuner et al., 2004	Uganda	3,179	15–55	*PTSD*	
Boothby, Crawford, & Mamade, Chapter 10 this volume	Mozambique	39	6–16; 22–32	recurrent thoughts/memories of traumatic events	cog strategies; acceptance; reintegration; household income; housing/food security; children's health/educ status
Asia					
Kinzie & Sack, 1991	Cambodia	46	14–20	PTSD; depressive symptoms	
Clarke, Sack, & Goff, 1993	Cambodia	69	mean 14.7 & 11.4	PTSD	
Sack et al., 1993	Cambodia	31	mean 14.7	PTSD; depression; financial assistance (few)*	college enroll (most); married (1/3)
Sack et al., 1994	Cambodia	209	13–25	PTSD, other psychpathologies	
Sack, Clarke, & Seeley, 1995	Cambodia	118	13–25	PTSD intergenerational; *depression intergenerational*	
Sack, Clarke, & Seeley, 1996	Cambodian refugees	170	mean 19.5	PTSD	

Reference	Sample/Country	N	Age	Outcomes	
Savin, Sack, Clarke, Meas, & Richart, 1996	Cambodian refugees	99	18–25	PTSD	*positive social functioning*
Mollica, Pole, Son, Murray, & Tor, 1997	Cambodia	182	12–13	emotional distress; *relation to physical health*	
Sack, Seeley, & Clarke, 1997	Cambodia	194	13–25	PTSD	
Kinzie & Sack, 2002	Cambodia	354	13–25	PTSD; depression; externalizing pathologies; drug & alcohol abuse; financial assistance (few)*	education or work (most)
Rousseau, Drapeau, & Rahimi, 2003	Cambodia (immigrants in Canada)	57	mean 13.6	emotional/behavioral problems; *racism(boys)*	*social adjustment; self-esteem*
Raddock, 1977	China	35	17–25	dissonance; fear; family contention	
Balkans					
Weine et al., 1995	Bosnian refugees	20	13–62	*PTSD, distress*	functioning (less)
Becker, McGlashan, Vojvoda, & Weine, 1999	Bosnia	10	13–19; 14–20	PTSD diminished	
Papageorgious et al., 2000	Bosnian refugees	95	8–13	depression, anxiety, intrusion, avoidance	
Zvizdic & Butollo, 2001	Bosnia	816	10–15	depressive reactions	
Jones & Kafetsios, 2002	Bosnia	337	13–15	anxiety/depression; *negative lifeline scores*	*schoolmarks*
Slodnjak, Kos, & Yule, 2002	Bosnia & Slovenia	460	14–15	PTSD; depression (low)*; sadness; worry; physical pains; *behavioral problems*	*school achievement*
Durakovic-Belko et al., 2003	Bosnia	393	15–19	PTSD; depression	
Jones & Kafetsios, 2005	Bosnia	40	13–15	anxiety, depression	
Hasanovic et al., 2005	Bosnia & Herzegovina	239	Mean 15.2	PTSD	
Hasanovic Sinanovic, Selimbasic, Pajevic, & Avdibegovic, 2006	Bosnia & Herzegovina	186	9–15	PTSD, depression	
McCouch, Chapter 8, this volume	Bosnia			depression; criminality: neg sense of future	polit; civic; labor particip; social initiative
Ajdukovic, 1998	Croatia	45	14–19	depression; posttraumatic stress reactions	

(Continued)

Table 2.1 (Continued)

Article	Location	Size	Age Range	Negative Outcomes	Positive Outcomes
Kuterovac, Dyregrov, & Stuvland, 1994	Croatia	134	10–15	intrusion, avoidance	
Kuterovac-Jagodic, 2003	Croatia	252	3rd–6th; 5th–8th	PTSD	
Begovac, Rudan, Begovac, Vidovic, & Majic, 2004	Croatia	322	13–19	sexual attitudes subscale of Self-Image; *Self-Image: emotional tone, social relations, psychopathology; mastering of the external world*	
Brajsa-Zganec, 2005	Croatia	583	12–15	depressive symptoms	
Kerestes, 2006	Croatia	349	mean 13.7	aggressive behavior	prosocial behavior
Jones, Rrustemi, Shanhini, & Uka, 2003	Kosovo	559	20 and under	stress disorders, nonorganic enuresis, learning disabilities, social & psychological difficulties	
Yurtbay et al., 2003	Kosovo	250	9–12, 15–19	trait anxiety; depressive symptoms	
Europe					
Maercker & Herrle, 2003	E. Germany	47	6–43	PTSD	personal growth
Lyons, 1974	N. Ireland	27	0–19	anxiety	
Blease, 1983	N. Ireland	115	10–16	psychological maladjustment	
Muldoon & Trew, 2000	N. Ireland	689	8–11		*global self-worth*; behavioral competence (low)
Muldoon & Wilson, 2001	N. Ireland	96	mean 15.2		self-esteem; ideological commitment
Muldoon, Cassidy, & McCullough, Chapter 6, this volume	N. Ireland	599	mean 10.3	distress (moderated by prior experience)	
Middle East					
Bat-Zion & Levy-Shiff, 1993	Israel (Jewish)	571	5th, 7th	distress; stressful appraisals	coping (active, emotion, trusting)
Punamäki, 1996	Israel (Jewish)	385	mean 12	anxiety; insecurity; depression; failure (as moderated by ideological commitment)	social support (less)
Bachar, Canetti, Bonne, Denour, & Shalev, 1997	Israel (Jewish)	871	mean 16.7	psychiatric symptoms (less)*	psychological well-being

Study	Location (Population)	N	Age	Outcomes
Hallis & Slone, 1999	Israel (Jewish)	88	12–13.5	global distress, somatization, depression, anxiety, paranoid ideation, social alienation
Slone & Hallis, 1999	Israel (Jewish)	397	12–13	psychological distress
Slone, Lobel, & Gilat, 1999	Israel (Jewish)	397	12–13	distress
Klingman, 2001	Israel (Jewish)	604	7th–11th	PTSD; stress; vulnerability; physical symptoms
Ronen et al., 2003	Israel (Jewish)	418	2nd, 6th, 10th	anxiety; behavior problems; war related symptoms
Laor et al., 2006	Israel (Jewish)	1,105	12–16	PTSD; dissociation; grief
Slone, Adiri, & Arian, 1998	Israel (Jewish/Arab)	259	13–14	*psychological distress*
Slone, 2003	Israel (Jewish/Arab)	625	15–19	psychological distress
Slone et al., 1998	Israel (Jewish)/ Palestine (Gaza)	209	12–13	psychological distress
Solomon & Lavi, 2005	Israel (Jewish)/ Palestine (Jewish settlements)	740	11.5–15	PTSD; attitudes towards peace negotiations; *future orientation*
Punamäki, 1982	Israel (Arab)/ Palestine (West Bank)	353	11	fears; aggression; favorable attitudes of war
Lavi & Solomon, 2005	Israel (Arab)/ Palestine (West Bank)	545	12–14	PTSD; pessimistic future orientation; attitudes toward peace negotiations; *psychological symptoms*
Punamäki, 1998	Israel (Arab)/ Palestine (Gaza)	412	6–15	poor psychological adjustment (as moderated/mediated by dreams)
Kostelny & Garbarino, 1994	Palestine (West Bank)	20,20	5–8, 12–15	personality & behavioral changes
Garbarino & Kostelny, 1996	Palestine (West Bank)	150	6–9, 12–15	behavioral problems
Punamäki & Puhakka, 1997	Palestine (West Bank)	185	10–13	coping (strength, hope)
Qouta et al., 1995a	Palestine (Gaza)	108,64	11–12, 12–13	neuroticism, low self-esteem; coping (multiple styles, some positive, some negative)

(Continued)

Table 2.1 *(Continued)*

Article	Location	Size	Age Range	Negative Outcomes	Positive Outcomes
Qouta et al., 1995b	Palestine (Gaza)	108	11–12	concentration, attention, & memory problems; neuroticism; risk taking	self-esteem (lower)
Punamäki et al., 1997a	Palestine (Gaza)	108	11–12	perception of parenting (strict, rejection, hostile)	
Punamäki, Qouta, & Sarraj, 1997b	Palestine (Gaza)	108	11–12	psychological adjustment problems	
Punamäki, Qouta, & Sarraj, 2001	Palestine (Gaza)	86	14	PTSD	
Qouta et al., 2001	Palestine (Gaza)	108	10–12,13–15	emotional disorders	
Qouta et al., 2003	Palestine (Gaza)	121	6–16	PTSD	
Thabet, Abed, & Vostanis, 2004	Palestine (Gaza)	403	9–15	PTSD: depression	
Punamäki, Komproe, Qouta, Elmasri, & deJong, 2005	Palestine (Gaza)	585	16–60	PTSD; anxiety; mood disorder, somatoform disorders	
Barber & Olsen, 2006	Palestine (Gaza)	917		*violent/disrespectful; pessimistic/ confused; loss*	personal growth; social integration; peace potential; fight again
Barber & Olsen, Chapter 9, this volume	Palestine (Gaza)	917		antisocial; (neg) mental health	social competence; civic/relig involvement; identity; orientation to others
Punamäki, 1989	Palestine (West Bank/Gaza)	135	8–14	psychological symptoms; anxiety; fear	
Punamäki & Suleiman, 1990	Palestine (West Bank/Gaza)	66	8–14	psychological symptoms; anxiety	coping (active, courageous)
Barber, 1999	Palestine (West Bank/Gaza/ Jerusalem)	6923	9th	antisocial behavior; depression; *aggression*	*family values; educational values; grades*
Barber, 2001	Palestine (West Bank/Gaza/ Jerusalem)	6000	9th	antisocial; depression; *deviant peers*	religion; *education*
Kaplan, et al., 2005	Palestine (Jewish settlements)	314	18–65	*PTSD; neurotic symptoms; acute stress*	
Punamäki, Muhammed, & Abdulrahman, 2004	Iraq	153	mean 12.26	PTSD; sleeping difficulties; aggressiveness; coping moderated by trauma nature	

Study	Region	N	Age	Outcome
Nader, Pynoos, Rairbanks, Al-Ajeel, & Al-Asfour, 1993	Kuwait	51	8–21	PTSD
Nader & Pynoos, 1993	Kuwait	54	7–17	PTSD
Farhood et al., 1993	Lebanon	540	adolescent	psychological symptoms; interpersonal relations problems; *somatization or depression*
Saigh, Mroueh, Zimmerman, & Fairbank, 1995	Lebanon	85	13	low self-efficacy
Macksoud & Aber, 1996	Lebanon	224	10–16	PTSD; adaptational outcomes
South America				
Hjern, 1991	Chilean refugees	55	2–15	sleep disturbances, dependency
Mixed Groups				
Punamäki, 1988	Palestine (West Bank) & Lebanon	139	8–14	coping (active, courageous; moderated by historical-political situation)
Locke et al., 1996	Immigrants from Central America	22	5–13	*PTSD*
Jagodic, 2000	Croatia, Israel, & Palestine	230	11–14	*war attitudes*
Rousseau & Drapeau, 2004	(immigrants in Canada from many countries)	1871	15–87	emotional distress
Montgomery & Foldspang, 2005	Middle East refugees in Denmark	311	3–15	anxiety
Kinzie, Cheng, Tsai & Riley, 2006	Refugees from many countries	131	<21	PTSD
Montgomery & Foldspang, 2006	Middle East refugees in Denmark	311	3–15	*PTSD*

Nonfindings are indicated by italicizing the variable for which no significant finding was discerned; opposite findings are indicated with an asterisked parenthetical, for example, "(less)*".

associated with defining adolescence (as well as children and youth), especially cross-culturally, were discussed, but it was concluded that virtually all renditions of it include the teen years. In the set of studies reviewed for this chapter, only fourteen (15%) of the ninety-five studies included samples with subjects who all were in their teen years. The others employed samples that included some or all of the teenage years but also contained younger children, older youth, or both. As examples, studies included age ranges as diverse as 0 to 19, 2 to 17, 8 to 18, 10 to 16, 17 to 25, 17 to 35, less than 17 years, and so on. For some studies, it was not possible to determine the age range, given that only a mean or median age of the studied sample was indicated. As will be noted, rarely were attempts made to test for difference across age groups in the studies that included broad age ranges.

Study Design

Overall, the research designs employed in this set of studies are relatively uniform and basic. Thus, for example, the large majority of the studies (N = 85, 89%) used a cross-sectional design—that is, assessing both exposure and outcomes at the same point in time. The ten (11%) studies that employed longitudinal designs varied in the time spans covered, but most involved a period of 1 or more years, with a few covering much longer time spans (e.g, Chapter 10; Maercker & Herrle, 2003). Most of the studies (N = 73, 77%) relied fully on survey research methods. The balance combined methods, such as survey/interview, survey/observational, interview/observational, and so on. Furthermore, most of the studies (N = 65, 68%) relied solely on child-reported data, with approximately one-quarter (N = 25, 26%) collecting data from multiple reporters, including parents and teachers. Sample sizes ranged from a low of 10 to a high of over 6,000, with a majority (N = 63; 66%) employing samples in the hundreds of youth.

As far as statistical analyses, just over half of the studies (N = 52, 55%) relied primarily on relatively basic statistical tests to assess the association between conflict experiences and youth functioning (e.g., proportions, correlations, analysis of variance). The other half of the set of studies used more sophisticated multivariate analytical techniques (e.g., multiple regression analysis, structural equation modeling, etc.).

Summary

In terms of a general overview of the set of ninety-five studies reviewed for this chapter, this literature appears to be relatively diffuse and basic. Thus, although studies cover youth experiences in many parts of the world (with a large minority of studies on the Middle East), there has not been a clear focus on adolescence as an age period, and despite large sample sizes, study design and analytical methodologies have been relatively narrow and limited. As a whole, the literature has not responded to calls for greater sophistication (e.g., Cairns & Dawes, 1996). The majority of the studies reviewed here (N = 64; 68%) were conducted and published since that review, but as an example, only seven of them (11%) employed longitudinal designs as recommended by Cairns and Dawes (1996).

Scope of Inquiry

One way to assess the overall nature of a body of scientific literature is to observe the scope of coverage—that is, to examine the specific variables researchers have chosen to include in their study designs. The selection of both the independent variables (in our case, experience with political violence) and the dependent variables (aspects of adolescent functioning) is typically guided by what either theory (invoked variably as a function of the researchers' academic disciplines; e.g., anthropology, psychology, psychiatry, sociology, etc.) or preferences (i.e., funding priorities, prevailing opinion or wisdom) dictate as to the critical components of the experience under investigation.

Assessing Exposure to Violence

The clear preference in this set of studies for assessing adolescent experience with political conflict has been understandably to measure the degree of exposure to the violence of war and conflict. Thus, all of the studies included some measure of exposure, with the clear majority (N = 75, 79%) assessing violence experienced directly by the youth (e.g., time spent in a security shelter, exposure to gunshot or use of other weapons, victim of an act of political violence, etc.). The balance of the studies (N = 20, 21%) assessed less direct exposure, such as living during a time of unrest, living in an area plagued by war, forced emigration due to political violence, and so on. Approximately half of the studies reviewed here (N = 46, 48%) relied solely on one or more measures of political violence exposure as independent variables. The balance (N = 49, 52%) also included other independent variables, such as caretaker post-traumatic stress disorder (PTSD), aspects of the community context, family relations, and so on. Only eight (8%) studies assessed adolescent participation (e.g., activism) in the conflict as a measure of conflict involvement.

Assessing Adolescent Functioning

Negative Functioning

Not surprisingly given the traditional focus in social science research discussed in Chapter 1 (i.e., Western, deficit, medical model), the most obvious pattern across these studies is the predominant focus on some form of negative functioning. Thus, ninety-one (96%) of the ninety-five studies included one or more measures of problematic functioning (the remaining studies focused exclusively on some form of competent functioning; see following discussion for an elaboration). This is evident in column 5 of Table 2.1, which lists the key dependent variables of the individual studies. Moreover, and again consonant with the traditional patterns of inquiry, eighty-six (95%) of the studies included one or more measures of negative *psychological* functioning. Twelve (14%) included some measure of problem *behavior*, only two of which measured behavioral difficulties exclusively. Of the eighty-six studies that included a measure of negative psychological functioning, the majority (N = 53, 62%) measured some form of stress or distress: just over a third measured PTSD explicitly (N = 37, 43%), with an additional 16 studies (19%) measuring either general stress or (psychological, emotional, or general) distress.

Other commonly studied negative psychological functioning variables were depression (N = 23, 27%) and anxiety (N = 13, 15%). Less frequently studied variables included confusion, disintegration, fear, neuroticism, problem thinking, psychological symptoms, (low) self-efficacy, (low) self-esteem, sleeping difficulties, somatization, violent dreams, and so on. The twelve studies that included a focus on behavioral problems measured these with a variety of constructs or scales, including aggression, antisocial behavior, behavior change, behavior disruption, behavioral problems, behavioral symptoms, delinquent behavior, externalizing behaviors, risk taking, social difficulties, and so on.

Competent Functioning

Just over one-quarter of the studies (N = 26, 27%) reviewed for this chapter included some form of competent psychological or social functioning. Fourteen (54%) of these twenty-six studies included a measure that could be considered to tap positive psychological functioning (e.g., cognitive development, moral maturity, personal growth, psychological well-being, self-esteem, etc.), including six that focused on a variety of types of coping; thirteen of the twenty-six studies (50%) assessed some form of competent functioning in society (e.g., academic success, college enrollment, educational values, employment [not relying on financial assistance], etc.); and one study assessed both psychological and behavioral competence and was thus counted in both groups. Other indices of competent functioning included behavioral competence, positive social functioning, satisfaction with friendships, social adjustment, and so on.

Summary

In terms of scope, the literature reviewed here has been quite consistent. The clear preference in decisions as to how to explore the experiences of youth with political conflict has been to assess the degree of their exposure to political violence and their psychological functioning, with a predominant focus on negative functioning.

Linking Political Violence and Adolescent Functioning

Another way to evaluate the content of a scientific literature is to inspect the significant findings made among the variables selected for study. Thus, whereas the previous section concentrated on the psychological and social functioning variables that researchers preferred to include to capture the experience of adolescents and political violence, this section evaluates the degree to which empirical associations between the selected violence and functioning variables have been discerned in these studies.

Negative Functioning

The consistent selection of negative functioning variables across studies that have assessed the impact of violence exposure—along with the theories invoked to support that linkage—makes clear that the expected impact of political violence has been a degradation of functioning of children exposed to the violence. Thus, we have evaluated the degree to which studies have (1) affirmed this expectation, (2) not found evidence for it, and (3) found that the effect was opposite to that expected.

Affirmative Findings

Of the ninety-one studies that focused on negative functioning, eighty (88%) found significant, positive associations between the selected form(s) of violence exposure and (in most cases) all of the measures of negative functioning that were included in the study design. These studies, then, affirmed the expected association between violence exposure and youth functioning. Some of the studies focused on a single, key index of negative functioning, whereas others included numerous indices in the same study.[1] Rather than compute some form of correlations between violence exposure and negative functioning as most studies did, some few studies compared frequencies of negative functioning in samples that did and did not experience political violence.

Nonfindings

In approximately a fifth of the ninety-one studies that assessed negative functioning (N = 17, 19%), no significant association with exposure was found for one or more of the indices of negative functioning that had been included in the study design.[2] In Table 2.1, these nonfindings are indicated by italicizing the variable in the negative functioning column for which no significant finding was discerned. The nonfindings included both negative psychological functioning variables (e.g., aggression, depression, emotional problems, psychological distress, etc.) and negative behavioral functioning variables (e.g., association with deviant peers, behavioral problems, externalizing problems, etc.), and were spread across the full geographic range of the set of reviewed studies (i.e., in, among others, Bosnia, Cambodia, Israel, Latin America [refugees in the United States], Northern Ireland, Palestine, and South Africa).

Opposite Findings

Finally, in five cases (4%) an "opposite finding" was made, where violence exposure was related to lower (as opposed to higher) levels of negative functioning. These findings are noted in Table 2.1 with an asterisked parenthetical (i.e., "(less)*"). In these studies of Cambodian, Balkan, and Israeli youth, violence exposure was associated with lower psychological difficulty (e.g., psychiatric symptoms, emotional problems) and fewer behavioral problems (e.g., risk behavior, externalizing problems, reliance on financial assistance).

Summary

In sum, the evidence relative to the association between political violence and negative functioning is relatively clear. In the large majority (88%) of studies, violence exposure was associated with higher levels of negative functioning. In approximately 20% of the cases, either no significant association was found between (one or more measures of) conflict and negative functioning, or the effect was reversed, that is, conflict was associated with lower levels of negative functioning.

Competent Functioning

Unlike for negative functioning, there has been no consistently articulated or hypothesized effect of political violence on competent functioning. That is, there has not been a well-developed rationale for expecting either a positive or negative effect on competent functioning. (Of course, a negative effect on competent functioning is implied by the expectation of the deleterious consequences of political violence that have both been clearly hypothesized and supported in the studies just presented.) Without a clearly articulated expectation for the nature of the effect (see, however, Chapters 1 and 12 for attention to the developing body of literature on post-traumatic growth), we have not characterized the findings of the (relatively few) studies that included indices of competent functioning as affirmative, absent, or contradictory as we have done for the studies assessing negative functioning.

Of the twenty-six studies that included an index of competent functioning, approximately half (N = 12, 46%) found a significant positive association between violence exposure and competent functioning—thus, the higher the reported violence exposure, the higher the reported self-esteem, coping, functioning in social institutions, and so on. (These findings are consistent with those already referenced where lower levels of negative functioning were associated with higher violence exposure; that is, the opposite finding). Half of these examined competent functioning as use of positive coping strategies. Supporting this positive statistical association are two additional studies that reported high frequencies of competent functioning (education, work status, and marital status) in groups also reporting high levels of political violence exposure.

Five (19%) of the twenty-six studies that assessed competent functioning found no significant associations between violence exposure and competent functioning (including academic performance, prosocial behavior, and positive social functioning). Four (15%) of the studies found a significant negative association between violence exposure and competent functioning (i.e., an opposite finding), such that the higher the violence exposure, the lower the competence (including reports of social support, self-esteem, self-concept, and a global assessment of functioning). The findings of these four studies are consistent with the findings of the bulk of the studies reviewed in the previous section that found exposure to political violence to be associated with negative functioning of youth.

Finally, three (12%) of the twenty-six studies reported mixed findings, with significant associations for one of the measured indexes of competence but not for another. In two of these studies, the significant finding was a positive association (i.e., the higher the violence exposure, the higher the competence—in these cases, self-esteem and religion). In the remaining study, the association was negative (i.e., the higher the violence exposure, the lower the competence, in this case, behavioral competence).

Summary

In summary, the picture relative to the association between political conflict and the competent functioning of youth is mixed and inconclusive. First, relatively few (twenty-six) studies have included competence indexes, and thus it would be premature to make firm conclusions, regardless of any pattern of the findings. Second, the findings are variable, with a few studies finding no relationship, some finding a negative relationship, and others finding both. To the degree that there is a tentative pattern within the set of findings, it would be the evidence for the positive association between conflict exposure and competence, with approximately half of the studies making this finding.

Specifying the Findings

To this point, the review has made clear that there has been one dominant trend in the quantitative, empirical work on youth and political violence—namely, identifying its degrading effects on youth functioning. This is evident both in the researchers' expectations for the effects (i.e., 96% of the studies included one or more measure of negative functioning, and most of them exclusively so) and in the empirical evidence itself (i.e., 88% of the studies that included a measure of negative functioning found it to be associated with conflict exposure). Although most of the reviewed studies have been relatively simple in design (see foregoing), some have attempted to specify that basic finding. Here, we review work that has included attempts to assess (1) mediators of the dominant finding (i.e., the pathways that violence exposure might take in predicting negative functioning); (2) moderators of the basic finding (i.e., conditions under which or groups for which the finding is stronger or weaker); and (3) the broader social ecology accompanying the conflict exposure (e.g., the other forces or statuses that impinge on the individuals experiencing conflict).

Refining the Dominant Trend: Evidence of Mediation

It is one matter to discern that violence exposure is predictive of negative functioning, it is another to understand why or how the risk is transmitted. The body of empirical studies is relatively silent on this issue, but there are a few that suggest possible mediators. Much of this work has been done by Punamäki, who in Chapter 3 elaborates substantially at a theoretical level about the potential pathways whereby exposure to violence might lead to violent behavior in exposed youth.

In her empirical work, Punamäki has made several findings that are of interest to this issue of mediation. In one study, for example, she determined that two consequences for children of trauma were a sense of persecution and the presence of unpleasant, repetitive dreams—both of which were in turn associated with lower levels of psychological functioning (Punamäki, 1998). An additional cognitive mediator in a different study was ideological commitment, which was enhanced by political hardships and associated with lower levels of psychosocial problems (Punamäki, 1996). The mediating role of ideology was, however, not found in a study of Jewish adolescents (Slone, Lobel, & Gilat, 1999).

There is also some preliminary evidence of social mediators in both Punamäki's work and our own. In studies of very different samples of Palestinian youth, it was evident that conflict exposure was associated with poorer quality parenting (e.g., punishment, rejection, strictness, lack of intimacy, parental psychological control), which in turn was associated with lower levels of psychological functioning (Barber, 2001; Punamäki, Qouta, & Sarraj, 1997a). In the Barber (2001) study, it was also reported that religious involvement on the part of Palestinian adolescents (e.g., religiosity, behavior, and salience of religion) mediated the effect of conflict involvement on antisocial behavior and depression (for females only).

McCouch (Chapter 8) demonstrated that Bosnian youths' self-reported "negative sense of the future" fully explained (mediated) the association between experience with political violence and postconflict criminality. Furthermore, although mediation was not evident, he demonstrated that experience with political violence—in addition to its direct effects—had indirect effects on postconflict functioning through this and other characteristics of youth. Thus, violence was associated indirectly with (lower) political and civic participation through youth depression and negative sense of the future. Exposure to political violence was also indirectly related to civic participation and criminality through youth social initiative.

Refining the Dominant Trend: Evidence of Moderation

Far more effort has been placed on identifying potential moderators of the impact of political conflict on youth than has been placed on tracing the paths (mediators) of effect. The evidence can be divided into several categories, some having to do with qualifying the violence (e.g., its severity), with individual characteristics of those experiencing the conflict (e.g., age, gender), and with the contexts of the violence (e.g., social, political, etc.).

Properties of Conflict

Several studies have found that the association between violence exposure and negative functioning is moderated by properties of the violence that was experienced. Thus, for example, Slone (1999) found among Jewish adolescents that their distress was high depending in part on their perception of threat and perceived impact of the political events they experienced. Among Palestinian and Arab/Israeli youth, Lavi and Solomon (2005) also found evidence for the moderating role of subjective appraisals of *threat*: at higher levels of subjective appraisal of threat, there was a positive correlation between objective intensity and symptom levels, but at lower levels, there was a negative correlation between objective exposure and symptoms. As for the severity of the conflict exposure, Punamäki and Puhakka (1997) found among Palestinian youth that coping styles were protective against psychosocial problems only during the Intifada, but not before it (presumably when conflict was lower or less intense). Relatedly, Macksound and Aber (1996) found that Lebanese children who experienced an accumulation of multiple war traumas exhibited more PTSD symptoms, as did Laor et al. (2006) among Israeli adolescents. When studying Bosnian adolescents, Jones and Kafetsios (2005) also noted that specific elements of war trauma were attributed different meaning (e.g., severity, with loss and injury to loved ones being among the worst) and that they therefore had different effects (both direct and moderated effects) (see Chapter 12 for an elaboration on the role of meaning).

Muldoon and colleagues (Chapter 6) demonstrated that young people in Northern Ireland rated specific types of political violence as less stressful if they had prior experience with conflict (although minority and lower income groups who had higher risk of actually experiencing conflict rated them as most stressful). Furthermore, their data indicated that children rate as more threatening forms of violence that predominate at the time (i.e., presumably because of the perceived likelihood that the event will actually occur).

Individual Characteristics: Parents

Three of the reviewed studies assessed the potential moderating effects of parental mental health. In South Africa, Dawes, Tredoux, and Feinstein (1989) found that youth whose mothers were diagnosed with PTSD were more likely to have multiple stress disorders. In studying Palestinians, Punamäki (1989) concluded that maternal mental health did not buffer children from the negative consequences for psychological well-being of exposure to political hardship (see following discussion for a review of studies that considered characteristics of youth, i.e., age and gender). In contrast, Qouta, Punamäki, and Sarraj (2003) found that the Palestinian youth most vulnerable to avoidance and intrusion symptomatology were those whose mothers showed high levels of PTSD (and who were also more highly educated).

Cognitive Functioning and Coping

In addition to the mediated findings already cited, Punamäki's (1998) study of Palestinian youth included evidence of the moderating effect of dreams, such that for youth who had certain types of dreams (e.g., vivid, active, bizarre, joyful), exposure to traumatic events was not associated with psychological symptoms. Qouta, El-Sarraj, and Punamäki (2001) found that for Palestinian children, traumatic experiences were associated with increased emotional disorders, but only among children with a rigid mental set. With Israeli adolescents, Hallis and Slone (1999) found evidence of moderation for both the amount of exposure and locus of control among the youth. Among Jewish youth with low political life event impact, those with external locus of control had higher symptom scores than those with internal locus of control. Among those with higher impact scores, those with internal locus of control showed higher depression than those with an external locus. In the same study, Hallis and Slone (1999) also found evidence of moderation for the impact of political life events and coping strategies. For those Jewish youth with low political life events, coping did not moderate the effect on symptom scores. However, for those with high scores on political life events, surprisingly, higher levels of coping were associated with higher symptom scores.

Political Orientations

Some of the reviewed studies tested for the potential buffering effect of political orientation for youth exposed to conflict. For example, some studies among Palestinian youth showed that political ideology or commitment can serve a buffering role for experience with violence (Kostelny & Garbarino, 1994; Punamäki, 1996; Qouta,

Punamäki, & Sarraj, 1995a). In a separate study, however, Qouta, Punamäki, and Sarraj (1995b) found no evidence that active participation in the conflict protected Gazan youth from developing emotional problems.

Social Context

The findings are mixed and complex in the few studies that tested for the moderating effects of social context on the impact of conflict exposure. Several studies have shown a buffering effect of family functioning and parenting among Angolan, Israeli, and Palestinian youth (Barber, 2001; Laor et al., 2006; McIntyre & Ventura, 2003; Punamäki, Qouta, & Sarraj, 1997a). Other studies have not found such moderation (Punamäki, 1989). Kerestes's (2006) study of Croatian adolescents demonstrates how methodology and variable selection can be factors in whether a significant moderating finding is made. In that case, good parenting did not buffer the effect of war exposure on aggression, but it did buffer the effect on (lower) prosocial behavior (when measured by teacher reports of youth prosocial behavior, but not when measured by parent reports).

As for other social contexts, Barber (2001) found that religious commitment buffered the effect of conflict involvement on Palestinian youth problem behaviors, and deviant peer association exacerbated that effect. McIntyre and Ventura (2003) found connection to tribal values to be protective for Angolan youth. Jones and Kafetsios's (2005) study of Bosnian adolescents reveals the complexity of understanding the joint role of multiple social contexts. For example, war exposure and displacement were associated with difficulty and lower well-being variably as would be expected, but this depended on the overall exposure level of the community. Thus, in a community where overall exposure to conflict was high (Goražde in Bosnia and Herzegovina), adolescents' exposure to conflict and displacement was associated with more symptoms and lower well-being. In contrast, in a community less exposed to war trauma (Foča in Bosnia and Herzegovina), displaced adolescents felt better than less-exposed local youth (as noted, this calculus was also influenced by the meaning youth attached to specific elements of war exposure).

Refining the Dominant Trend: Considering the Broader Ecology of Conflict

Although most of the reviewed studies concentrated on documenting exposure and its correlates, some investigated more broadly the social environment that either surrounded or accompanied the political violence. Clearly, conflict does not occur in a social vacuum, and thus, it is neither the sole nor necessarily the most consequential force or condition that individuals in some conflict zones might experience. For example, Kerestes (2006) found that the quality of parenting of Croatian adolescents predicted more unique variance in youth behavior than did their war experiences. In their study of the complexities of youth in Bosnia, Jones and Kafetsios (2005) concluded that in addition to the personal losses mentioned, negative aspects of the community (e.g., neglected, isolated) as well as worries about performance (e.g., in school) could have had as significant an effect on well-being as exposure to conflict. Similarly, Barber (2001) showed that among Palestinian refugee adolescents, neighborhood quality (e.g., the level of social disorganization) had wider impacts on the social networks and psychological and behavioral functioning than did experience with the conflict. Although not reviewed here, these findings are consistent with Elbedour, Van Slyck, and Stern (1998), whose broader version of social disorganization (extreme social upheaval) was found to be parallel in effects on mental health for Bedouin adolescents as was chronic social conflict for West Bank Palestinians or political violence for Gazan adolescents. Although it is difficult to tease out the unique effects of multiple stressors, Laor et al.'s (2006) study of Israeli youth assessed the reality and convergence of stressful life events not necessarily related to conflict (e.g., parents' divorce, birth of siblings, relocation, etc.) in understanding youth psychological functioning. The relevant social ecological impact can be viewed much more broadly as well, as in Halcon et al.'s (2004) study of Somali and Oromo refugees, among whom a lower likelihood of PTSD symptoms was associated with factors like fluency in English, leaving home a younger age, having emigrated with family members, and length of stay in the United States.

Not all studies found evidence for the relevance of the broader social ecology. For example, in a mixed sample of youth and adult Israelis, Kaplan, Mater, Kamin, Sadan, and Cohen (2005) found marital status, education, and employment background to not be associated with the incidence of stress or PTSD symptoms. Likewise, Locke, Southwick, McCloskey, and Fernandez-Esquer (1996) found no significant correlations of caretaker social support and PTSD symptoms among a sample of immigrants from Central America.

Developmental Differences

In general, the body of studies reviewed here has not been consistently concerned with identifying age- or stage-related differences in how young people experience political violence. As noted with specific regard to adolescents, very few studies explicitly sampled adolescents. Furthermore, of those studies that had breadth in the age range of their samples, less than 20% tested for age differences in either the prevalence of outcome measures or the strength of the effect between political violence and those outcomes. Some of those that did test for differences found no or minor differences by age in samples in Albania (Yurtbay, Alyanak, Abali, Kaynak, & Durukan, 2003), Croatia (Kuterovac-Jagodic, 2003), Israel (Kaplan et al., 2005), Lebanon (Macksoud & Aber, 1996), and Palestine (Lavi & Solomon, 2005 Qouta et al., 2003).

Although a few studies reported higher levels of certain difficulties among older (compared to younger) Israeli and Bosnian youth (Hasanovic, Sinanovic, & Pavlovic, 2005; Laor et al., 2006) and higher levels of difficulty among Bosnian adults than Bosnian adolescents (Weine et al., 1995), the majority of the studies that considered and detected evidence for age differences found levels of difficulty to be higher among younger youth in Croatia, Israel, and Palestine (Garbarino & Kostelny, 1996; Jagodic, 2000; Klingman, 2001; Kostelny & Garbarino, 1994; Kuterovac-Jogodic, 2003; Punamäki, 1989, 1999; Punamäki & Puhakka, 1997; Qouta et al., 2003).

One study among Israelis and Palestinians (Hoffman & Bizman, 1996) did explicitly test for cognitive-developmental differences in adolescents. They found support for all three of their hypotheses that adolescents, compared to elementary schoolchildren, (1) displayed a greater emphasis on the mutual agency of Israeli and Arab partners to the conflict, (2) attributed the conflict to more stable and less controllable factors, and (3) had expectations for the continuation of the conflict that were associated with the dimension of stability, whereas emotional responses were linked to the dimension of agency.

Gender

A similar minority proportion of the reviewed studies included assessments of potential gender differences in either the prevalence of difficulty among male and female youth or the effects of conflict exposure on their psychosocial functioning.

Differences in Levels of Difficulty

Two of the reviewed studies, both conducted among Palestinians, found higher rates of negative functioning (problem behavior and neuroticism, respectively) among males (Garbarino & Kostelny, 1996; Qouta et al., 1995b) compared to females. Overwhelmingly, however, studies that tested for gender differences found higher rates for females in Bosnia, Croatia, Israel, and Palestine. These included rates of fear (Punamäki, 1982, 1988, 1989), depression (Durakovic-Belko, Kulenovic, & Dapic, 2003; Zvizdic & Butollo, 2001), PTSD (Ajdukovic, 1998; Durakovic-Belko et al., 2003), and general or multiple psychological symptoms (Klingman, 2001; Laor et al., 2006). These findings are consistent with past work on gendered differences on expressed emotions and perceived stress (see Chapters 4 and 6) and with work focused specifically on trauma (Olff, Langeland, Draijer, & Gersons, 2007; Tolin & Foa, 2006). Three studies also found lower levels of coping among females compared to males (Klingman, 2001; Punamäki, 1988; Punamäki & Puhakka, 1997). Finally, Jagodic (2000) found Croatian females, compared to males, to be less ready to justify their nation's fight, feel responsibility, and demand loyalty in the state of war. (See Barber, 2008 for comparative, descriptive data in Palestine and Bosnia for exposure and functioning variables.)

Differences in Effects of Political Violence

Several studies conducted in the Balkans and in the Middle East concluded that there were either no or negligible differences in the effects of political violence on male compared to female youth (Kerestes, 2006; Kuterovac-Jagodic, 2003; Lavi & Solomon, 2005; Punamäki, 1982, 1989; Yurtbay et al., 2003). Four studies found stronger effects of conflict on female youth, including vulnerability to intrusion symptoms for Palestinian females (Qouta et al., 2003), anxiety and behavior problems among Israeli females (Ronen, Rahav, & Appel, 2003), and depression among Palestinian female youth (Barber, 1999, 2001). Two studies found stronger effects of conflict on Croatian male youth compared to Croatian female youth, including for depression (Brajsa-Zganec, 2005) and lower levels of expressed loyalty (Jagodic, 2000).

Conclusion

This chapter provided an overview of the state of empirical, quantitative research into the impact of political violence on adolescents. The primary goal was to inspect the focus and comprehensiveness of the body of work and not calculate a meta-analytic assessment of the strength of association between experience with conflict and individual functioning. Although such an empirical approach to the literature would be valuable, we deemed it more appropriate and useful to reveal how this important topic has been approached. Thus, our primary concern was organizing the information in a manner that would reveal the scope and comprehensiveness of the body of empirical work—that is, for example, how narrowly or broadly the two elements of interest (conflict experience and psychosocial functioning) have been conceptualized and measured, and how thoroughly the commonly found and not surprising basic finding of a positive association between violence exposure and stress has been explored (e.g., tests for mediation, moderation, age and gender differences, etc.), and how sophisticated research designs have been. This more topographical approach to the body of literature was viewed as most valuable in illustrating how research could and should proceed. In so doing, attention was given to English-language studies that explicitly assessed quantitatively the association between conflict experience and psychosocial functioning in samples that included teenaged adolescents. Other chapters in this volume have focused on less quantitative treatments of adolescents' experiences with political conflict (Chapters 10, 11, 12).

Despite the fact that nearly 100 qualifying studies were located and reviewed, it is apparent that the overall knowledge base produced by this set of studies is not yet very substantial; indeed, it appears that not much progress has been made in such quantitative empirical work since calls for more refined study were made as long as a decade ago (e.g., Cairns & Dawes, 1996; Ladd & Cairns, 1996). The body of research as a whole is rather thin and narrow, with most of the work still cross-sectional in design, constricted to limited assessments (and conceptualization) of both conflict experience (e.g., predominantly exposure to violence) and resultant functioning (e.g., primarily negative, psychological functioning), and inconsistently and inadequately concerned with variations associated with gender, age, and the condition of prevailing socioeconomic and political contexts.

This overview, coupled with the findings of the other chapters of this volume, has led to a series of recommendations for how research could continue on this topic to advance understanding of its complexities. Those recommendations are articulated in detail in the final chapter of this volume (Chapter 13). In brief, they include recommendations to more precisely focus on adolescents (in terms of both sampling and testing relevant domains of adolescent functioning); expanding the work identifying which youth are at most risk of suffering from political violence; seriously studying female youth experience with political violence; more thoroughly measuring the key elements of conflict exposure and involvement; acknowledging the economic and political forces that are often concomitant with conflict; elaborating the varieties of areas of youth social, psychological, and civic functioning that might be impacted by political violence (focusing particularly on identity-related issues); designing research that maximizes applied and policy relevance, and so on.

Notes

1. Because the multiple indexes are themselves typically highly intercorrelated (particularly for psychological functioning, e.g., anxiety, depression, PTSD), it is not surprising that the measure of violence exposure would be related similarly to all of them, particularly in the same sample of adolescents.
2. Because many studies employed multiple measures of negative functioning and some of these studies had differing effects depending on the specific measure, percentages of affirming and nonfindings do not add to 100.

References

Ajdukovic, M. (1998). Displaced adolescents in Croatia: Sources of stress and posttraumatic stress reaction. *Adolescence, 33*(129), 209–217.
Bachar, E., Canetti, L., Bonne, O., Denour, A. K., & Shalev, A. Y. (1997). Psychological well-being and ratings of psychiatric symptoms in bereaved Israeli adolescents: Differential effect of war- versus accident-related bereavement. *Journal of Nervous and Mental Disease, 185*(6), 402–406.
Barber, B. K. (2008). Contrasting portraits of war: Youths' varied experiences with political violence in Bosnia and Palestine. *International Journal of Behavioral Development, 32*(4), 294–305.
Barber, B. K. (1999). Political violence, family relations, and Palestinian youth functioning. *Journal of Adolescent Research, 14,* 206–230.
Barber, B. K. (2001). Political violence, social integration, and youth functioning: Palestinian youth from the Intifada. *Journal of Community Psychology, 29,* 259–280.
Barber, B. K., & Olsen, J. A. (2006). Adolescents' willingness to engage in political conflict: Lessons from the Gaza Strip. In J. Victoroff (Ed.), *Tangled roots: Social and psychological factors in the genesis of terrorism* (pp. 203–226). Amsterdam: IOS Press.
Bat-Zion, N., & Levy-Shiff, R. (1993). Children in war: Stress and coping reactions under the threat of scud missile attacks and the effect of proximity. In L. A. Leavitt & N. A. Fox (Eds.), *The psychological effects of war and violence on children* (pp. 143–161). Hillsdale, NJ: Erlbaum.
Becker, D., McGlashan, T., Vojvoda, D., & Weine, S. (1999). Case series: PTSD symptoms in adolescent survivors of ethnic cleansing. Results from a 1-year follow-up study. *Journal of the American Academy of Child and Adolescent Psychiatry, 38,* 775–781.
Begovac, I., Rudan, V., Begovac, B., Vidovic, V., & Majic, G. (2004). Self-image, war psychotrauma and refugee status in adolescents. *European Child and Adolescent Psychiatry, 13*(6), 381–388.
Blease, M. (1983). Maladjusted school children in a Belfast center. In J. P. Harbison (Ed.), *Children of the troubles* (pp. 21–32). Belfast: Stranmillis College.
Brajsa-Zganec, A. (2005). The long term effects of war experiences on children's depression in the Republic of Croatia. *Child Abuse and Neglect, 29*(1), 31–43.
Cairns, E., & Dawes, A. (1996). Children: Ethnic and political violence—a commentary. *Child Development, 67,* 129–138.
Calhoun, L. G., & Tedeschi, R. G. (2006). *Handbook of posttraumatic growth: Research & practice.* Mahwah, NJ: Erlbaum.
Clarke, G., Sack, W. H., & Goff, B. (1993). Three forms of stress in Cambodian adolescent refugees. *Journal of Abnormal Child Psychology, 21*(1), 65–77.
Dawes, A., Tredoux, C., & Feinstein, A. (1989). Political violence in South Africa: Some effects on children of the violent destruction of their community. *International Journal of Mental Health, 18*(2), 16–43.

Durakovic-Belko, E., Kulenovic, A., & Dapic, R. (2003). Determinants of posttraumatic adjustment in adolescents from Sarajevo who experienced war. *Journal of Clinical Psychology, 59*(1), 27–40.

Elbedour, S., Van Slyck, M., & Stern, M. (1998). Psychosocial adjustment in middle eastern adolescents: The relative impact of violent versus non-violent social disorganization. *Community Mental Health Journal, 34,* 191–205.

Farhood, L., Zurayk, H., Chaya, M., Saadeh, F., Meshefedjian, G., & Sidani, T. (1993). The impact of war on the physical and mental health of the family: The Lebanese experience. *Social Science Medicine, 36*(12), 1555–1567.

Garbarino, J., & Kostelny, K. (1996). The effects of political violence on Palestinian children's behavior problems: A risk accumulation model. *Child Development, 67,* 33–45.

Geltman, P. L., Grant-Knight, W., Mehta, S. D., Lloyd-Travaglini, C., Lustig, S., Landgraf, J. M., et al. (2005). The "lost boys of Sudan" functional and behavioral health of unaccompanied refugee minors resettled in the United States. *Archives of Pediatrics & Adolescent Medicine, 159*(6), 585–591.

Halcon, L. L., Robertson, C. L., Savik, K., Johnson, D. R., Spring, M. A., Butcher, J. N., et al. (2004). Trauma and coping in Somali and Oromo refugee youth. *Journal of Adolescent Health, 35,* 17–25.

Hallis, D., & Slone, M. (1999). Coping strategies and locus of control as mediating variables in the relation between exposure to political life events and psychological adjustment in Israeli Children. *International Journal of Stress Management, 6*(2), 105–123.

Hasanovic, M., Sinanovic, O., & Pavlovic, S. (2005). Acculturation and psychological problems of adolescents from Bosnia and Herzegovina during exile and repatriation. *Croatian Medical Journal, 46*(1), 105–115.

Hasanovic, M., Sinanovic, O., Selimbasic, Z., Pajevic, I., & Avdibegovic, E. (2006). Psychological disturbances of war-traumatized children from different foster and family settings in Bosnia and Herzegovina. *Croatian Medical Journal, 47*(1), 85–94.

Hjern, A. (1991). Persecution and behavior: A report of refugee children from Chile. *Child Abuse & Neglect, 15,* 239–248.

Hoffman, M. S., & Bizman, A. (1996). Attributions and responses to the Arab-Israeli conflict: A developmental analysis. *Child Development, 67,* 117–128.

Jagodic, G. K. (2000). Is war a good or a bad thing? The attitudes of Croatian, Israeli, and Palestinian children toward war. *International Journal of Psychology, 35*(6), 241–257.

Jones, L., & Kafetsios, K. (2002). Assessing adolescent mental health in war-affected societies: The significance of symptoms. *Child Abuse & Neglect, 26,* 1059–1080.

Jones, L., & Kafetsios, K. (2005). Exposure to political violence and psychological well-being in Bosnian adolescents: A mixed method approach. *Clinical Child Psychology and Psychiatry, 10*(2), 157–176.

Jones, L., Rrustemi, A., Shanhini, M., & Uka, A. (2003). Mental health services for war-affected children: Report of a survey in Kosovo. *British Journal of Psychiatry, 183*(6), 540–546.

Kaplan, Z., Matar, M. A., Kamin, R., Sadan, T., & Cohen, H. (2005). Stress-related responses after 3 years of exposure to terror in Israel: Are ideological-religious factors associated with resilience? *Journal of Clinical Psychiatry, 66,* 1146–1154.

Kerestes, G. (2006). Children's aggressive and prosocial behavior in relation to war exposure: Testing the role of perceived parenting and child's gender. *International Journal of Behavioral Development, 30,* 227–239.

Kinzie, J. D., Cheng, K., Tsai, J., & Riley, C. (2006). Traumatized refugee children—The case for individualized diagnosis and treatment. *Journal of Nervous and Mental Disease, 194*(7), 534–537.

Kinzie, J. D., & Sack, W. (1991). Severely traumatized Cambodian children: Research findings and clinical implications. In F. L. Ahearn Jr. & J. L. Athey (Eds.), *Refugee children: Theory, research, and services* (pp. 92–105). Baltimore, MD: Johns Hopkins University Press.

Kinzie, J. D., & Sack, W. (2002). The psychiatric disorders among Cambodian adolescents: The effects of severe trauma. In F.J.C. Azima & N. Grizenko (Eds.), *Immigrant and refugee children and their families: Clinical, research, and training issues* (pp. 95–112). Madison, CT: International Universities Press.

Klingman, A. (2001). Stress responses and adaptation of Israeli school-age children evacuated from homes during massive missile attacks. *Anxiety, Stress, and Coping, 14,* 149–172.

Kostelny, K., & Garbarino, J. (1994). Coping with the consequences of living in danger: The case of Palestinian children and youth. *International Journal of Behavioral Development, 17*(4), 595–611.

Kuterovac, G., Dyregrov, A., & Stuvland, R. (1994). Children in war: A silent majority under stress. *British Journal of Medical Psychology, 67*(4), 363–375.

Kuterovac-Jagodic, G. (2003). Posttraumatic stress symptoms in Croatian children exposed to war: A prospective study. *Journal of Clinical Psychology, 59,* 9–25.

Ladd, G. W., & Cairns, E. (1996). Children: Ethnic and political violence. *Child Development, 67,* 15–18.

Laor, N., Wolmer, L., Alon, M., Siev, J., Samuel, E., & Toren, P. (2006). Risk and protective factors mediating psychological symptoms and ideological commitment of adolescents facing continuous terrorism. *Journal of Nervous and Mental Disease, 194*(4), 279–286.

Lavi, T., & Solomon, Z. (2005). Palestinian youth of the Intifada: PTSD and future orientation. *Journal of the American Academy of Child and Adolescent Psychiatry, 44*(11), 1176–1183.

Locke, C. J., Southwick, K., McCloskey, L. A., & Fernandez-Esquer, M. E. (1996). The psychological and medical sequelae of war in Central American refugee mothers and children. *Archives of Pediatrics & Adolescent Medicine, 150*(8), 822–828.

Lyons, H. A. (1974). Terrorists' bombing and the psychological sequelae. *Journal of the Irish Medical Association, 67,* 15–19.

Macksoud, M. S., & Aber, J. L. (1996). The war experiences and psychosocial development of children in Lebanon. *Child Development, 67,* 70–88.

Maercker, A., & Herrle, J. (2003). Long-term effects of the Dresden bombing: Relationships to control beliefs, religious belief, and personal growth. *Journal of Traumatic Stress, 16*(6), 579–587.

Masinda, M. T., & Muhesi, M. (2004). Children and adolescents' exposure to traumatic war stressors in the Democratic Republic of Congo. *Journal of Child and Adolescent Mental Health, 16*(1), 25–30.

McIntyre, T. M., & Ventura, M. (2003). Children of war: Psychosocial sequelae of war trauma in Angolan adolescents. In S. Krippner & T. M. McIntyre (Eds.), *The psychological impact of war trauma on civilians: An international perspective* (pp. 39–53). Westport, CT: Praeger Publishers/Greenwood Publishing Group.

Mollica, R. F., Pole, C., Son, L., Murray, C. C., & Tor, S. (1997). Effects of war trauma on Cambodian refugee adolescents' functional health and mental health status. *Journal of the American Academy of Child and Adolescent Psychiatry, 36,* 1098–1106.

Montgomery, E., & Foldspang, A. (2005). Seeking asylum in Denmark: Refugee children's mental health and exposure to violence. *European Journal of Public Health, 15*(3), 233–237.

Montgomery, E., & Foldspang, A. (2006). Validity of PTSD in a sample of refugee children: Can a separate diagnostic entity be justified? *International Journal of Methods in Psychiatric Research, 15*(2), 64–74.

Muldoon, O. T., & Trew, K. (2000). Children's experience and adjustment to political conflict in Northern Ireland. *Peace and Conflict: Journal of Peace Psychology, 6,* 157–176.

Muldoon, O. T., & Wilson, K. (2001). Ideological commitment, experience of conflict and adjustment in northern Irish adolescents. *Medicine, Conflict, and Survival, 17*(2), 112–124.

Nader, K. & Pynoos, R. S. (1993). The children of Kuwait after the Gulf crisis. In L. A. Leavitt & N. A. Fox (Eds.), *The psychological effects of war and violence on children* (pp. 181–195). Hillsdale, NJ: Erlbaum.

Nader, K. O., Pynoos, R., S., Fairbanks, L. A., Al-Ajeel, M., & Al-Asfour, A. (1993). A preliminary study of PTSD and grief among the children of Kuwait following the Gulf crisis. *British Journal of Clinical Psychology, 32,* 407–416.

Neuner, F., Schauer, M., Karunakara, U., Klaschik, C., Robert, C., & Elbert, T. (2004). Psychological trauma and evidence for enhanced vulnerability for posttraumatic stress disorder through previous trauma among West Nile refugees. *Biomed Central Psychiatry, 25,* 4–34.

Olff, M., Langeland, W., Draijer, N., & Gersons, P. R. (2007). Gender differences in postraumatic stress disorder. *Psychological Bulletin, 133,* 183–204.

Papageorgious, V., Frangou-Garunovic, A., Iordanidou, R., Yule, W., Smith, P., & Vostanis, P. (2000). War trauma and psychopathology in Bosnian refugee children. *European Child & Adolescent Psychiatry, 9,* 84–90.

Punamäki, R. L. (1982). Childhood in the shadow of war a psychological study on attitudes and emotional life of Israeli and Palestinian children. *Current Research on Peace and Violence, 5,* 26–41.

Punamäki, R. L. (1988). Historical-political and individualistic determinants of coping modes and fears among Palestinian children. *International Journal of Psychology, 23*(6), 721–729.

Punamäki, R. L. (1989). Factors affecting the mental health of Palestinian children exposed to political violence. *International Journal of Mental Health, 18,* 63–79.

Punamäki, R. L. (1996). Can ideological commitment protect children's psychosocial well-being in situations of political violence? *Child Development, 67,* 55–69.

Punamäki, R. L. (1998). The role of dreams in protecting psychological well-being in traumatic conditions. *International Journal of Behavioral Development, 22*(3), 559–588.

Punamäki, R. L., Komproe, I., Qouta, S., Elmasri, M., & deJong, J. T. V. M (2005). The role of peritraumatic dissociation and gender in the association between trauma and mental health in a Palestinian community sample. *American Journal of Psychiatry, 162*(3), 545–551.

Punamäki, R. L., Muhammed, A. H., & Abdulrahman, H. A. (2004). Impact of traumatic events on coping strategies and their effectiveness among Kurdish children. *International Journal of Behavioral Development, 28*(1), 59–70.

Punamäki, R. L., & Puhakka, T. (1997). Determinants and effectiveness of children's coping with political violence. *International Journal of Behavioral Development, 21*(2), 349–370.

Punamäki, R. L., Qouta, S., & Sarraj, E. E. (1997a). Models of traumatic experiences and children's psychological adjustment: The roles of perceived parenting and the children's own resources and activity. *Child Development, 64,* 718–728.

Punamäki, R. L., Qouta, S., & Sarraj, E. E. (1997b). Relationships between traumatic events, children's gender, and political activity, and perceptions of parenting styles. *International Journal of Behavioral Development, 21*(1), 91–109.

Punamäki, R. L., Qouta, S., & El-Sarraj, E. (2001). Resiliency factors predicting psychological adjustment after political violence among Palestinian children. *International Journal of Behavioral Development, 25*(3), 256–267.

Punamäki, R. L., & Suleiman, R. (1990). Predictors and effectiveness of coping with political violence among Palestinian children. *British Journal of Social Psychology, 29,* 67–77.

Qouta, S., El-Sarraj, E., & Punamäki, R. L. (2001). Mental flexibility as resiliency factor among children exposed to political violence. *International Journal of Psychology, 36*(1), 1–7.

Qouta, S., Punamäki, R. L., & Sarraj, E. E. (1995a). The impact of the peace treaty on psychological well-being: A follow-up study of Palestinian children. *Child Abuse & Neglect, 19,* 1197–1208.

Qouta, S., Punamäki, R. L., & Sarraj, E. E. (1995b). The relations between traumatic experiences, activity, and cognitive and emotional responses among Palestinian children. *International Journal of Psychology, 30,* 289–304.

Qouta, S., Punamäki, R. L., & Sarraj, E. E. (2003). Prevalence and determinants of PTSD among Palestinian children exposed to military violence. *European Child and Adolescent Psychiatry, 12,* 265–272.

Raddock, D. M. (1977). *Political behavior of adolescents in China: The cultural revolution in Kwangchow.* Tucson: University of Arizona Press.

Ronen, T., Rahav, G., & Appel, N. (2003). Adolescent stress responses to a single acute stress and to continuous external stress: Terrorist attacks. *Journal of Loss and Trauma, 8,* 261–282.

Rousseau, C., & Drapeau, A. (2004). Premigration exposure to political violence among independent immigrants and its association with emotional distress. *Journal of Nervous and Mental Disease, 192*(12), 852–856.

Rousseau, C., Drapeau, A., & Rahimi, S. (2003). The complexity of trauma response: A 4-year follow-up of adolescent Cambodian refugees. *Child Abuse and Neglect, 27,* 1277–1290.

Sack, W. H., Clarke, G., Him, C., Dickason, D., Goff, B., Lanham, K., et al. (1993). A 6-year follow-up study of Cambodian refugee adolescents traumatized as children. *Journal of the American Academy of Child and Adolescent Psychiatry, 32*(2), 431–437.

Sack, W. H., Clarke, G. N., & Seeley, J. (1995). Posttraumatic stress disorder across two generations of Cambodian refugees. *Journal of American Academy of Child and Adolescent Psychiatry, 34*(9), 1160–1166.

Sack, W. H., Clarke, G. N., & Seeley, J. (1996). Multiple forms of stress in Cambodian adolescent refugees. *Child Development, 67,* 107–116.

Sack, W. H., McSharry, S., Clarke, G. N., Kinney, R., Seeley, J., & Lewinsohn, P. (1994). The Khmer Adolescent Project I: Epidemiologic findings in two generations of Cambodian refugees. *Journal of Nervous and Mental Disease, 182*(7), 387–395.

Sack, W. H., Seeley, J. R., & Clarke, G. N. (1997). Does PTSD transcend cultural barriers? A study from the Khmer adolescent refugee project. *Journal of the American Academy of Child and Adolescent Psychiatry, 36*(1), 49–54.

Saigh, P. A., Mroueh, M., Zimmerman, B. J., & Fairbank, J. A. (1995). Self-efficacy expectations among traumatized adolescents. *Behavior Research Therapy, 33*(6), 701–704.

Savin, D., Sack, W. H., Clarke, G. N., Meas, N., & Richart, I. (1996). The Khmer adolescent project: III. A study of trauma from Thailand's site II refugee camp. *Journal of the American Academy of Child and Adolescent Psychiatry, 35*(3), 384–391.

Slodnjak, V., Kos, A., & Yule, W. (2002). Depression and parasuicide in refugee and Slovenian adolescents. *Crisis: The Journal of Crisis Intervention and Suicide Prevention, 23*(3), 127–132.

Slone, M. (2003). The Nazareth riots Arab and Jewish Israeli adolescents pay a different psychological price for participation. *Journal of Conflict Resolution, 47*(6), 817–836.

Slone, M., Adiri, M., & Arian, A. (1998). Adverse political events and psychological adjustment: Two cross-cultural studies. *Journal of the American Academy of Child and Adolescent Psychiatry, 37,* 1059–1069.

Slone, M., & Hallis, D. (1999). The impact of political life events on children's psychological adjustment. *Anxiety, Stress, and Coping, 12,* 1–21.

Slone, M., Kaminer, D., & Durrheim, K. (2000). The contribution of political life events to psychological distress among South African adolescents. *Political Psychology, 21*(3), 465–487.

Slone, M., Lobel, T., & Gilat, I. (1999). Dimensions of the political environment affecting children's mental health: An Israeli study. *Journal of Conflict Resolution, 43*(1), 78–91.

Solomon, Z., & Lavi, T. (2005). Israeli youth in the second Intifada: PTSD and future orientation. *Journal of the American Academy of Child and Adolescent Psychiatry, 44*(11), 1167–1175.

Thabet, A. A. M., Abed, Y., & Vostanis, P. (2004). Comorbidity of PTSD and depression among refugee children during war conflict. *Journal of Child Psychology and Psychiatry, 45*(3), 533–542.

Tolin, D. F., & Foa, E. B. (2006). Sex differences in trauma and posttraumatic stress disorder: A quantitative review of 25 years of research. *Psychological Bulletin, 132,* 959–992.

Turton, R. W., Straker, G., & Moosa, F. (1991). Experiences of violence in the lives of township youths in "unrest" and "normal" conditions. *South African Journal of Psychology, 21*(2), 77–84.

Weine, S. M., Becker, D. F., McGlashan, T. H., Laub, D., Lazrove, S., Vojvoda, D., & Hyman, L. (1995). Psychiatric consequences of ethnic cleansing—Clinical assessments and trauma testimonies of newly resettled Bosnian refugees. *American Journal of Psychiatry, 152*(4), 536–542.

Yurtbay, T., Alyanak, B., Abali, O., Kaynak, N., & Durukan, M. (2003). The psychological effects of forced emigration on Muslim Albanian children. *Community Mental Health Journal, 39*(3), 203–212.

Zvizdic, S., & Butollo, W. (2001). War-related loss of one's father and persistent depressive reactions in early adolescents. *European Psychologist, 6*(3), 204–214.

Chapter 3

War, Military Violence, and Aggressive Development
Child, Family, and Social Preconditions

Raija-Leena Punamäki

The argument that violence breeds violence seems intuitively tempting to make. Thus, the expectation that children who experience abuse, cruelty, and injustice will themselves engage in aggression and antisocial behavior seems sensible. By the same logic, children who experience firsthand the hazards of war can be expected to develop aggressive behaviors as a result. This concern can be read, for example, in the common characterizations of the "lost generations" in Germany in the 1940s, in Cambodia in the 1970s, in Mozambique and Angola in the 1980s, and of aggressive youth in Palestine and Northern Ireland.

However, translating military aggression and a belligerent societal atmosphere into negative child and adolescent development is not as straightforward as it sounds. Various preconditions and complex sets of mediating processes are required for violent experiences to lead to aggressive behavior. This chapter discusses some of the mechanisms that underlie the link between exposure to war violence and the potential development of antisocial attitudes and aggressive behavior. These include cognitive, emotional, and psychophysiological processes, family relationships, political ideologies and social atmosphere. Awareness of their combined influences on human development helps us understand why and how environmental violence leads to aggression in some adolescents but not in others.

Violent Experiences and Aggression

Empirical evidence for linking violent experiences and aggressive behavior comes from the research on children exposed to community (Garbarino, 1995; Garbarino, Dubrow, Kostelny, & Pardo, 1992) and domestic violence (Fantuzzo, Boruch, Beriama, &

Atkins, 1997; Jaffe, Wolfe, & Wilson, 1990) and physical abuse (Kaplan, Pelcovitz, & Labruna, 1999). These studies show, for instance, that U.S. inner-city children who have witnessed shooting, killing, armed robberies, and violent detentions demonstrate more general aggression and externalizing disorders than children not exposed to such violence (Gorman-Smith & Tolan, 1998; Osofsky, Wevers, Hann, & Fick, 1993). According to the social learning models of aggression (e.g., Bandura, 1973), there is an increased risk for aggression because in crime-intensive environments children learn violent behavior by modeling and imitating others. The impoverished living conditions further deprive children of adequate and meaningful opportunities for learning social competence and prosocial ways of solving problems, regulating anger, and inhibiting harmful behavior (Berkowitz, 1993; Dodge & Price, 1994). Moreover, epidemiological data show that half of children exposed to domestic violence show severe emotional and behavioral problems, including externalizing symptoms (Jaffe et al., 1990).

A closer look at the violence-aggression link reveals that the correlations are dependent on the situation and personality. For instance, street violence leads to aggressive behavior only among children who show difficulties in emotion regulation and distortions in attention and interpretation of social situations (Schwartz & Proctor, 2000), lack parental sharing of their feelings and experiences, and suffer from insufficient community support (Kliewer, Lepore, Oskin, & Johnson, 1998). Also, empirical evidence does not support the argument of abused children growing up to be abusive parents, when various child- and family-related issues, such as temperament and parenting quality, are taken into account (Egelund & Sussman-Stillman, 1996; Haapasalo & Pokela, 1999; Kaufman & Zigler, 1987).

On the other hand, researchers agree that aggression as an inborn capability shows great individual variation and plays an evolutionary role in human survival (Loeber & Hay, 1997; Lore & Schultz, 1993). The evidence that an aggressive tendency is genetically transmitted is based, for instance, on twin studies showing a 50% concordance between monozygotic twins, compared to 17% concordance between dizygotic twins and siblings in externalizing disorders (Moffitt, 1993; Rushton, Fulker, Neale, Nias, & Eysenck, 1986). The heritability estimate of conduct disorder is 53% according to Gelhorn et al. (2005). The genetic transmissions are partly shown in temperamental differences between individuals. Characteristics such as high activity, irritability, novelty seeking, and low emotion regulation may, together with an unfavorable environment, lead to aggressive development (Plomin, 1995; Rothbart, Ahadi, & Hershey, 1994).

The social and biological aspects of aggression have traditionally been considered countervailing forces. Current models, however, emphasize the interaction and integration of biological, psychological, and social mechanisms in producing aggressive development. Caspi et al. (2002) showed, for instance, that childhood maltreatment leads to antisocial behavior when combined with genetic susceptibility. According to genetic models, there must be an environmental activator for the gene to manifest itself (Moffitt, 1993; Plomin, Nitz, & Rowe, 1990; Rutter, 2000). This integrative approach is salient among children living in conditions of war and military violence in that environmental influences, such as exposure to military violence and belligerent and hateful societal atmospheres, are necessary but not sufficient preconditions for the development of aggressive behavior. Similarly, psychological processes, physiological response, or child temperament may be necessary but not sufficient explanations for child and adolescent aggression in wartime. Also, exposure to war trauma may have stronger or weaker impacts depending on cultural, political, and personal characteristics.

To understand whether war violence leads to aggressive or prosocial behavior, we must study the combined effects of societal and child-related preconditions and mechanisms. Development occurs in a social (typically family) context, and therefore, relational vulnerabilities and protective factors are important preconditions for aggressive behavior. Figure 3.1 summarizes societal-, child-, and family-related preconditions and mechanisms that can contribute to adolescents' aggressive development in conditions of war and military violence. A belligerent society forms a risk for aggressive development through collective war propaganda and personal exposure to traumatic events. According to our understanding, children and adolescents in war and violence have to develop specific cognitive, emotional, and physiological responses to adapt and mentally survive in life-endangering environments and hateful atmospheres. However, if excessive and distorted, these originally adaptive mechanisms may constitute a risk for aggressive development. Life threats, traumatic experiences, and hateful war atmospheres burden family life and can interfere with the parental tasks of providing children protection and enhancing human virtues. This interference can result in a deteriorated familial relationship and, in turn, may be a risk factor for aggressive and antisocial behavior.

War Violence and Cognitive Processing

Cognitive processes of perceiving, interpreting, understanding, remembering, and responding to painful experiences are important for child and adolescent development both generally and in war conditions. However, research on the impacts of military trauma on cognitive processes is lacking, and thus we look elsewhere for information about specific cognitive mechanisms that either contribute to aggression or promote prosocial behavior. Research on social information processing in peaceful societies is fruitful in delineating specific paths through which violent experiences can constitute a risk for aggressive development (Crick & Dodge, 1994; Dodge & Price, 1994; Huesmann & Eron, 1989; Pakaslahti, 2000; Pakaslahti & Keltikangas-Järvinen, 1997). This research suggests that aggressive behavior would be more likely among children who perceive their environment as dangerous and other people as malevolent, use narrowed and distorted interpretations of their experiences, and apply inadequate problem-solving strategies.

Furthermore, research on peaceful societies shows that high arousal, anger, and intensive fear distort perceptions, which makes children with aggressive tendencies less able to use realistic environmental cues to guide their behavior (Dodge, Pettit, Bates, & Valente, 1995; Dodge & Tomlin, 1987). They consequently can dismiss gestures of reconciliation and cooperation and focus their attention on wrongdoings and injustices. They may also fail to recognize distress and fear in others and insist on interpreting others' behavior as threatening and dominating (Fisher & Blair, 1998). The interpretations of social situations of aggressive children are thus based more on their internal and personal schemas, causal models, and moods than on their peers' actual behavior and interactions with them (Dodge & Tomlin, 1987; Dodge et al., 1995). They typically blame others for their own bad mood and nervousness and attribute

Societal Preconditions			
War propaganda • Dehumanization of enemy • Enhancing hatred and revenge • Black and white & simplified information	Traumatic experiences • Loss and death • Witnessing humiliation • Witnessing violence	Human ideals and world view • Heroism & risk-taking • Endurance & persistency • Youth as a savior of the nation • Own superiority & disdain of others	National survival • Fear of death • Fear of annihilation

Developmental Preconditions:

Cognitive processes
• Intensified perception of threat & danger
• Generalized expectation of others' malevolence
• Narrow & biased problem solving strategies

Emotional processes
• Numbing of feelings
• Difficulty to recognize own and others' feelings
• Dominance of negative emotions
• Biased towards behavioral expression of feelings

Physiological changes
• Tolerance for violence
• Inhibition of aggression

Familial Risk Dynamics

Parent-child relationship
• Punitive parenting & disciplining
• Impossibility to protect children
• Fear disrupting early attachment

Child participation in fighting
• Early maturation & responsibility
• Reversal of roles
• Intrusive memories of violence

Figure 3.1. Societal, developmental, and familial preconditions and risks for aggressive child development in conditions of war and military violence.

their behavior to their own inner feelings (Saarni, 1999). They explain, for instance, that they ended up in violence toward others because they were in a bad mood and disappointed.

Life threats, personal losses, and destruction can constitute an overwhelming developmental burden to children and adolescents living in war conditions. They can tax their adaptive resources and considerably alter their perception and interpretations of themselves, others, and the world (Horowitz, 1999; Janoff-Bulman, 1985). Research shows that childhood trauma victims continue to be highly vigilant for new threats and dangers, expect malevolent intentions from others, and have a shortened and pessimistic view of the future (Terr, 1991). The altered schemata help children organize their coping responses in protective ways in acute life threat. However, if the schemata become automatic and rigid, they can form risks for aggressive behavior by biasing, distorting, and narrowing children's perceptions and attributions in safer conditions as well.

Children in war actually experience people deliberately harming them, and they have good reasons for mistrust and disappointment with human virtues. War propaganda, in turn, contributes to and escalates the negative and distorted perceptions by portraying the enemy as irredeemably bad, the environment as dangerous, and their own people as superior and honorable. It also creates an atmosphere of paranoia and generalized mistrust of others by fostering the belief that "nonpatriots, spies, and enemy collaborators" are pervasive and need to be exposed. Aggressive development is more likely if children's war-salient schemata continue to depict themselves as victims, others as persecutors, and the world as a dangerous place. Risk for aggressive behavior is also great if children generalize perceptions of humans as malevolent toward their own people and even family members. However, according to social information processing models, neither military violence and hostile atmosphere nor distorted and narrowed cognitive schemata alone are sufficient to predict aggression, but their interaction may do so.

Research on peaceful societies further shows that aggressive children provide inadequate and ineffective solutions to problems (Evans & Short, 1991; Keltikangas-Järvinen & Pakaslahti, 1999). For instance, they may avoid a problem when in fact they could control the outcome (i.e., failure or challenge in school work) or try persistently to change a situation when it is objectively beyond their control (i.e., adults' marital conflict). Analogously, war and military violence are likely to increase a risk for aggressive behavior through narrowed behavioral, emotional, and cognitive response repertoires and lack of alternative problem-solving and coping strategies.

Follow-up research shows that aggressive behavior decreases with age in peaceful societies. The peak of aggressive behavior appears to be in early adolescence (11 to 13 years of age), with behaviors such as fighting decreasing considerably between 14 and 16 years of age (Loeber & Hay, 1997; Tremblay, 2000). Sophisticated social information processing capacities are antecedents for decreased aggression (Dodge & Price, 1994). In early adolescence, thinking, reasoning, and interpreting become quicker, more comprehensive, automatic, and complex (Thornton, 2002). Children learn to perceive and interpret social interactions more accurately, understand complex causal relationships between their own and others' behavior, and are capable of comprehending conflicting and nuanced information. Subsequently, they increase their coping repertoire and refrain from immediate, impulsive, and aggressive responses (Eisenberg, 2000; Tremblay, 2000). War propaganda, on the contrary, relies on a simplified, fragmented, black-and-white worldview, which is discordant with nonaggressive, prosocial development. There may be a special risk for aggression, if the atmosphere of hatred and enmity interferes with normative development of complex cognitive processes and worldview and prevents development of rich and flexile problem solving strategies.

War Violence and Emotional Processing

Emotions are often adaptive responses to social, communicative, mental health, and survival functions (Cacioppo & Gardner, 1999; Frijda, 1987). In conditions of war and military violence, emotions seem to be especially salient. For instance, fear can serve as a warning of danger, and grief and sorrow can facilitate consolation and psychophysiological balance. Anger, in turn, is important in activating constructive coping strategies. The atmosphere of enmity and exposure to traumatic events can, however, compromise children's healthy emotional development, which in turn can form a risk for aggressive behavior. Two phenomena in particular are salient in delineating the possible paths through which war and military violence predict negative child development: (1) narrowed and behavior-dominated emotional expression, and (2) predominance and escalation of negative emotional response pattern.

In an atmosphere of war and military violence, some emotions are allowed and appreciated, whereas others are disregarded or punished. Boldness, aggression, and anger toward the enemy are encouraged; feelings of fear, helplessness, and compassion toward the enemy are condemned. The socially promoted, narrowed emotional repertoire also serves psychological needs by dulling the awareness of excessive physical and emotional pain. However, research has shown that both traumatized adults and children who numb their feelings often exhibit uncontrollable and impulsive behavior (Feeny, 2000; Moradi, Neshat-Doos, Taghavi, Yule, & Dalgleish, 1999; Näätänen, Kanninen, Qouta, & Punamäki, 2002). Impulsiveness involves a tendency to transform feelings and tensions directly into action, without cognitive evaluation or emotional processing, which may serve the immediate escape from danger. Research has shown increased risk for post-traumatic symptoms, for example, among Palestinian political prisoners whose emotional responses were characterized by action and behavioral readiness and included intensive anger, disappointment, and aggression. They also faced difficulties in recognizing, accepting, and understanding their own emotions and actions during interrogation and torture, which in turn evoked intensive feelings of shame and guilt (Näätänen et al., 2002).

In the same vein, it has been suggested that emotional expressions of children suffering from domestic and community violence are predominantly behavioral and lack appraising, evaluating, and interpretational processes (Perry, 1997). Researchers have shown that violent experiences in early and preverbal development are encoded as simple approaching or avoiding memory schemata, which in turn can explain why procedural and kinesthetic memory predominate in later aggressive behavior at the expense of more narrative and episodic memories (Crittenden, 1997, 1999; van der Kolk, 1996). When impulsive and aggressive tendencies decrease, for instance, in therapy, more emotionally colored, comprehensive, and multidimensional episodic memories emerge (Punamäki, 2000).

Humans tend to react more strongly and quickly to negative rather than positive stimuli, apparently because negative emotions are associated with danger and life threat, and quick reactions serve survival (Cacioppo & Gardner, 1999). There is also evidence that mood influences perceiving, interpreting, and remembering experiences. For instance, in sad moods, individuals more easily remember unpleasant events and tend to view others as similarly depressed (Power & Dalgleish, 1997, pp. 292–293); when angry, they view others as vicious and unpleasant (Keltner, Ellsworth, & Edwards, 1993). Research on peaceful societies shows that negative feelings are especially intense among children with aggressive tendencies, who also are highly sensitive to hostile signs and tend to overinterpret negative cues (Dodge & Newman, 1981).

Furthermore, seemingly arbitrary cues can activate their anger and make their "blood boil." Once activated, children with aggressive tendencies have difficulty calming down and soothing themselves, and their hostile feelings easily escalate to other situations (Osofsky et al., 1995; Perry, 1997). Aggressive behavior is more likely because negative mood continues to guide and organize interpretation and responses even in neutral and pleasant social encounters. On the contrary, balance and interaction between negative and positive moods are characteristic of people with high adaptive capacity, which allows them to both explore new issues and avoid dangerous ones (Cacioppo & Gardner, 1999).

In sum, adolescents living in conditions of war and military violence might be more at risk for developing aggressive behavior if their emotional responses are biased toward impulsive and behavioral activity at the expense of more comprehensive and reflective emotional processing. Furthermore, if the trauma-induced negative moods, suspicion, hostility, and anger are transferred into neutral domains of life (such as family and school relationships), the risk may be even greater. Aggressive arousals that are not easily moderated can lead to aggression in other situations, such as peer conflict and failure in school performance. By contrast, prosocial development is possible when "war children" learn to accurately recognize their own and others' feelings and are encouraged to express a diversity of emotions.

Violence and Psychophysiological Responses

Living in life-endangering conditions teaches children unique ways of mental survival and psychological balancing. The abnormally high arousal and constant vigilance for danger correspond with psychophysiological mechanisms, which partly explain the possible link between exposure to violence and aggressive behavior. They include, for example, habituation and threshold effects for increased tolerance for violence, and a lack of inhibitory processes and deficits in regulating and modulating aggressive impulses.

Habituation develops when violence-related arousal, activity, and strong emotional involvement seduce victims into seeking greater doses of excitement and dangers. Violence can numb senses and distort adequate fear responses. Originally the feelings of thrill can help victims maintain psychological and physiological balance, but gradually they may start to "feel at home" in highly stimulating and dangerous situations (Perry, 1997; Pynoos, Steinberg, Ornitz, & Goenjian, 1998). High arousal and vigilance can be adaptive in dangerous situations, but that state of mind is burdensome to children and adolescents if activated for extended periods. Analogously, research on the developmental effects of entertainment violence (TV, computer games) suggests that children who consume great amounts of virtual violence show an increased appetite for stronger doses of violence in both entertainment and real life. They can also become desensitized to real-life violence and be less sensitive to their own and others' pain and suffering (Kostelny & Garbarino, 2001; Murray, 1997).

The inhibition failure of aggressive activity is caused by neurophysiological alterations due to early and severe exposure to violence. They may contribute to development through disrupting normal biological maturation, such as attenuating fear-enhanced startle reflexes (Perry, 1997; Pynoos et al., 1998; Shalev et al., 2000). These alterations in turn disturb mechanisms that modulate anger and aggressive impulses.

It would be highly provocative to argue that living in life-endangering war conditions would alter such basic biological processes as aggression threshold and violence inhibition mechanisms. Most living creatures possess mechanisms for the control of aggression, which serves both social adaptation and biological survival. They involve recognition of submissive gestures of a fighting partner, which according to Blair activates violence inhibition mechanisms (VIM; Blair, 1995; Fisher & Blair, 1998). In child development, this recognition process is one of the crucial antecedents for prosocial learning and empathy development. Empathy development then guarantees that the inhibition of aggression is activated whenever another person displays distress. Further requirements of the development of the inhibition of aggression are the ability to reverse learning and stop ongoing activity (Patterson & Newman, 1993). However, the accelerating arousal of negative emotions may interfere with the modulating of an action and the reversal of learning (Saarni, 1999). Corresponding risk mechanisms were found in cognitive processing when adolescents generalize their threatened perceptions and malevolent expectations to safe conditions and escalate their negative emotions to neutral and pleasant experiences.

Family Dynamics

Family can provide children with the protection, consolation, and fortitude to endure dangerous and violent conditions. War and traumatic experiences, however, place hard burdens and specific demands on family relationships and parenting tasks. Table 3.1 illustrates that in war societies, children and parents have to cope with violence-salient developmental and parental tasks in addition to the normative challenges typical to peaceful societies. The table further shows how these tasks and challenges differ according to children's developmental stages.

Research in war conditions reveals three familial risk dynamics that may make children more vulnerable to aggressive development. First, traumatic experiences tend to compromise parental resources and enhance punitive and controlling parenting practices that can lead to hostile interactions between parents and children. Second, creating a secure early mother-child relationship is at risk in life-endangering conditions, which may then interfere with healthy development of emotion regulation, social competence, and trust in others. Third, belligerent societies tend to encourage children to assume adult roles in joining the military struggle, which may sacrifice their developmental needs and lead to negative outcomes.

Conflicting Family Interactions

The primary war-salient parental tasks in violent societies are to protect children from external dangers and alleviate negative consequences of traumatic experiences. However, functioning as a buffer against a dangerous environment can overwhelm parents. Research has shown, for example, that Palestinian parents in families exposed to high levels of military violence (e.g., detentions, home demolitions, killing) were harsher and more punitive when disciplining their children than were parents in less exposed families (Qouta, Punamäki, & El Sarraj, 1997). Parents who invoked harsher disciplinary

Table 3.1 Tasks and Challenges of Parents and Children in Peaceful and Violence Environments across Developmental Stages

	Child: Tasks and Challenges		Caregiver: Parenting Role and Tasks	
Developmental Stage	Peaceful Society	Violent Society	Peaceful Society	Violent Society
Infancy	• Creating safe base & exploring environment • Physiological regulation	• Safe base • Physiological regulation	• Sensitivity & responsiveness	• Protection of danger • Regulation of emotion
Toddler age	• Emotion regulation (anger) • Symbolic activity • Peer relationships • Right and wrong	• Emotion regulation (fear) • Reality testing • Peer thrusting • Survival strategies	• Emotional regulation (comprehensive) • Differentiate imagination & reality • Teaching limits	• Protection of danger • Emotional regulation (fear & anger) • Protecting from wrong-doings
Middle childhood	• Cognitive sophistication • School performance • Social acceptance • Moral development from concrete to abstract	• Cognitive complexity • National performance • Heroic conduct & social acceptance • Moral development; questions of life & death • Worry about family	• Indirect monitoring • Support & guiding • Open communication	• Protection of danger • Direct monitoring • Consoling & supporting • Negotiation of responsibilities
Adolescence	• Intimate relationships • Future plans • Worldview • Identity	• Intimate relationships • Shortened view of future • Ideological commitment • Collective sacrifice	• Granting psychological autonomy • Indirect involvement	• Enduring losses • Encouragement & support • Sharing of grief

strategies attributed it to their attempts to prevent children and adolescents from participating in life-endangering resistance activities. On the other hand, the same study indicated that exposure to traumatic events did not compromise positive forms of loving and caring parenting (Qouta et al., 1997), and positive parenting protected child adjustment via supporting children's cognitive and creative resources (Punamäki, Qouta, & El Sarraj, 1997). Very compatible findings were made in a large, representative sample of Palestinian adolescents by Barber (1999, 2001), who, after disaggregating the same parenting measured used in the Punamäki et al. (1997) study, determined that it was specifically parental intrusiveness (e.g., psychological control; Barber, Stolz, & Olsen, 2005) that was elevated in highly exposed families. Like the foregoing, he also found that positive relations with parents buffered the association between conflict expsosure/involvement and higher antisocial behavior.

Three studies have focused on the parental role in attenuating the impact of military violence as it relates specifically to aggressive behavior. Keresteš (2006) found that Croatian adolescents exposed to severe war trauma at preschool age showed higher levels of aggressive behavior than less exposed adolescents. Optimal parenting did not moderate this link between violence and aggression. Parenting did, in contrast, explain or buffer the effect of violence on aggressive behavior in two studies among Palestinian children and adolescents. In a large survey study of Palestinian families, Barber (1999) found that involvement in the Intifada (including exposure to and participation in political violence) was positively correlated with aggressive behavior of adolescents, but this effect was no longer significant in a multivariate model that included assessments of parenting. Aggressive behavior was, instead, predicted by lower parenting quality (see Barber, 2001). A study among Palestinian children showed that exposure to severe military violence involving losses, wounding, and witnessing killing was associated with increased aggressive and antisocial behavior (Qouta, Punamäki, Miller, & El Sarraj, 2007). In that study, supportive and nonpunitive parenting practices protected children from aggressiveness in severely victimizing conditions.

Patterson and colleagues (Patterson, 1982; Patterson & Dishion, 1988) provide a model of how punitive and harsh family interactions influence the development of children's aggression. The coercive cycles involve reciprocal negative interactions between children and parents that can be initiated by parents' inconsistent, harsh, and erratic efforts to set limits on their children's behavior: the children's aggressive reactions might be fueled by their disappointment in their parents' behavior, who in turn may invoke further punitive measures as a redress of their children's reactive behaviors. Subsequently, family members can end up in self-reinforcing cycles of aggression toward each other.

Research on veterans and prisoners of war suggest that paternal war experiences increase conflicting family interactions. Marital problems, lack of intimacy, and poor fathering have been documented among Middle Eastern (Solomon, Mikulincer, Fried, & Wosner, 1987), Australian (Westerink & Giarratano, 1999), and North American (Beckham, Lytel, & Feldman, 1996) war veterans. It might well be that psychological responses that are adequate in the battlefields, such as numbing of feelings, stoicism, and rational detachment, turn out to be counterproductive in civilian family life. Marital conflicts in war-traumatized families can contribute to children's aggressiveness.

There is general evidence of the correlations between family violence and children's externalizing symptoms and aggressive behavior (Cummings & Davies, 1994).

Finally, the UN report on women in war revealed that tortured political prisoners tended to act out their frustrations on their wives and children (Rehn & Johnson Sirleaf, 2002). We observed that Palestinian political prisoners often sought mental health consultation because they faced difficulties in intimate spousal and parental relationships. The men were haunted by vivid memories of humiliation and violence and felt unable to control the impulses to hurt somebody. These memories were a painful contradiction to the emotionally loaded expectations about returning to a satisfying family life they had cherished (Punamäki, 1986, 2000).

All told, it seems likely that interventions supporting warm and wise parenting and satisfactory marital relationships could protect against aggression and promote prosocial development in children in war conditions.

Parenting and Child Development in Danger

Early childhood experiences contribute to the formation of basic schemata about the security of the world, about adults' ability to provide protection against dangers, and about their own self-worth (Ainsworth, 1989; Bretherton, 1985; Crittenden, 1999). The maternal task is to create a safe place from which infants can explore the environment and train their sensorimotor coordination. Life threats communicated by maternal fear can interfere with the creation of a reciprocally warm mother-infant interaction and may result in the child developing an insecure attachment style. Such relational disruptions are often predictors of problematic development expressed through aggression or acting out (insecure-ambivalent children) or through withdrawal and depression (insecure-avoidant children) (Carlson, 1998; Crittenden, 1988). The insecure-ambivalent early mother-child relationship can thus be considered a possible link between war and military violence and the development of aggressive behavior.

Attachment experiences are important for the development of expression, recognition, and the regulation of emotions, including anger, frustration, and aggression. In early interactions with mothers, infants learn to integrate negative emotions as a part of communicative interactions (Grosmann, Grosmann, Winter, & Zimmermann, 2002). Infants typically protest with intensive anger when separated from mother, and a sensitive and responsive mother interprets the anger as a signal of insecurity and consoles and soothes the child. This mutual and rewarding interaction teaches the infant about the functionality of emotional expression and the predictability of others' behavior.

In contrast, if the mother interprets the infant's protest as aggression and disobedience, or chooses to ignore and reject his or her distress, the child's anger remains. Our observations of Palestinian mother-infant dyads suggest that a violent and dangerous environment increases the risk for maternal insensitivity and causes withdrawal and/or intrusive overprotection in mother-infant interaction. Expressions of fear and panic in mothers' eyes were particularly harmful for attachment development (Qouta, Kassab-Helmi, & Punamäki, 2003). Similar unfavorable characteristics of early mother-infant relationships have been documented among other stressed and traumatized families (Crittenden, 1988; Greenberg, 1999; Scheeringa & Zenah, 2001).

In the toddler years, children learn emotion regulation, including impulse control, causal analysis of others' behavior, and the soothing of oneself, first in interaction with parents and later within themselves. Follow-up research on peaceful societies has shown that emotional lability and general negative emotionality in toddler years, combined with compromised cognitive development, such as short attention span and restlessness, predicts aggressive disorders, antisocial behavior, and criminality in adolescence (Eisenberg, 2000). Hämäläinen and Pulkkinen (1996) showed that low emotion regulation and self-control in middle childhood predicted proactive aggression (without any provocation) in adolescence and criminality in adulthood. It is noteworthy that early childhood expression of aggression is not sufficient to predict later aggression, but compromised emotion regulation and distorted attributions of social interactions are the crucial moderators. Analogously, we may suggest that early and age-normative aggressive behavior among war-traumatized children would predict antisocial and aggressive development only when combined with failed emotion regulation and attributions that accept and idealize aggression.

The middle childhood period is characterized by intensive cognitive learning and importance of academic success (Thornton, 2002). Peer relations and popularity are highly important, to some extent at the expense of parental relationships (Parker & Asher, 1993). Children in war conditions, however, tend to worry about their parents' well-being and take on adult responsibilities before proper maturation. The reversal of roles has been documented, for instance, among refugee families in Europe when children adapt more easily into a new culture and more easily learn the new language. Thus, children help guide their parents in family crisis and critical communicative transmissions, rather than vice versa (Almqvist, 2000; Montgomery, 1998). The reversal of roles in a family can demand constant negotiations and sometimes involves conflicts between generations.

War and national struggle are salient for adolescents, who are intensively concerned with moral issues, justice, and their own and collective future. The illusion of invulnerability further contributes to their self-sacrificing attitudes and active participation in military and political struggles. War greatly challenges adolescents' moral and identity development: moral and ideological issues become a question of life and death. A successful resolution of moral dilemmas can lead to strengthened psychological integrity, high moral status, and healthy ideological commitment. An unsuccessful resolution, in turn, can lead to fragmented thinking, immature moral reasoning, and extreme views, which are often combined with aggressive tendencies (Van Ijzendoorn & Zwart-Woudstra, 1995).

According to Bell's (1968) systems theory, both parents and children have comfort zones and thresholds of tolerance for each other's behaviors. There are cultural, historical, and political variations in parents' upper and lower thresholds for children's aggressive behavior. Parents tune their expectations according to age-salient expression of aggression. For instance, biting is more readily accepted in infancy, and tantrums are considered normal in toddler years. Peer violence and bullying are common in school years, and parents and teachers can be somewhat tolerant or ignorant of this kind of indirect aggression (Salmivalli, Kaukiainen, & Lagerspetz, 1998). In adolescence, fighting, antisocial, and even criminal behaviors are normative to some extent

(Loeber & Hay, 1997; Tremblay, 2000). For their part, children respond in diverse and unique ways to parents' disciplining of aggressive conduct, soothing of aggressive impulses, and encouraging prosocial behavior (Rothbart et al., 1994). The reciprocal parent-child relationship is thus decisive in shaping children's and adolescents' expression of and their ability to control aggression.

More sophisticated research settings are imperative to more completely understand how family relations can prevent or exacerbate aggressive development in war violence. We do not know enough, for example, about whether and how socialization differs in dangerous and safer environments. Many conclusions from research have been based on cross-sectional studies in societies at war that lack country-level control designs. Furthermore, constant life threat may fundamentally shape priorities of social interaction, and thus, cross-cultural application of parenting and attachment measurements may be problematic.

Conclusion

Despite the fact that war is unhealthy and places tremendous burdens on child and adolescent development, there is evidence that "war's children" are remarkably resilient and can endure and in many cases even prosper developmentally despite the harsh conditions (Chapters 9, 10, and 12; Punamäki, Qouta, & El Sarraj, 2001; Straker, Moosa, Becker, & Nkwale, 1992). In essence, the human mind is not merely a mirror for external violence; rather, children and adolescents construct their experiences according to the meanings given to them and the various social and psychological preconditions that accompany violence.

In life-endangering conditions, children can learn to be sensitive to negative feedback and threatening cues. Risks for aggression occur if the war-salient cognitive processing interferes with a child's capacity to recognize safer and more neutral and peaceful messages. Furthermore, war and military violence bring about demands, challenges, and hazards to the parent-child relationship. In these situations, parents are challenged to protect children from external danger and provide security and compensatory experiences. If this does not occur, then the development of aggression in children appears more likely. Specifically, exposure to war and military violence creates risk for aggressive behavior if children experience their parents as punitive and nonloving and if the early mother-child interaction is frightening and insecure. If the developmental tasks of establishing a sense of security, trust, emotion regulation, and sophisticated cognitive and moral considerations are compromised, aggressiveness, particularly in adolescence, is more probable.

Aggression in adolescents is more likely if exposure to violence has a broad impact on an adolescent's cognitive, emotional, physiological, and social development. Violence can change the ways adolescents think, imagine, remember, and perceive. Aggressive behavior can evolve if adolescents continue to perceive others as threatening and if they are unable to recognize the suffering of others. Further, biased, discrepant, and narrowed emotional processing of painful experiences is a possible antecedent for aggressive behavior.

Implications for Interventions and Reconciliation

Research and interventions among "war's children and adolescents" will benefit from integrative approaches that combine individual, familial, and social antecedents of aggression. Because cognitive-emotional processes that form risks for aggression are closely related to both social experiences and neurophysiological maturation, psychological interventions among war-traumatized children should start early in development (Yule, 2002). Interventions are more likely to be effective if they are developmentally tailored and focused comprehensively on addressing deficiencies in cognitive, emotional, and psychophysiological processing of violent experiences.

Efforts in behalf of peace education, reconciliation, and trauma healing should also be tailored to comprehensively address the individual and societal risk factors and their underlying mechanisms. Peace education and reconciliation projects typically provide compensatory experiences and new kinds of encounters between former enemies (Sanson & Bretherton, 2001). In other words, they aim at enhancing cognitive processing that allows more realistic and comprehensive observations of other people and behavior that is based on real feedback from the environment rather than war-salient rigid and hostile schemata and negative memories. Interventions with war-traumatized children focus, inter alia, on teaching children to recognize accurately their own and others' emotional states and the physiological markers of fear and arousal. Such interventions enhance flexible and integrative interpretations and provide a repertoire of responses to traumatic experience (Smith et al., 1999; Yule, 2002), providing examples of the mechanisms that enhance prosocial development. That, in turn, is a precondition for both individual growth and political harmony.

References

Ainsworth, M. D. S. (1989). Attachments beyond infancy. *American Psychologist, 44,* 709–716.

Almqvist, K. (2000). Parent-child interaction and coping strategies in refugee children. In L. Van Willigen (Ed.), *Health hazards of organized violence in children, Coping and protective factors* (vol II., pp. 53–68). Utrecht: Pharos.

Bandura, A. (1973). *Aggression. A social learning analysis.* New Jersey: Prentice Hall.

Barber, B. K. (1999). Political violence, family relations, and Palestinian child functioning. *Journal of Adolescent Research, 14,* 206–230.

Barber, B. K. (2001). Political violence, social integration, and youth functioning: Palestinian youth from the Intifada. *Journal of Community Psychology, 29,* 259–280.

Barber, B. K., Stolz, H. E., & Olsen, J. A. (2005). Parental support, psychological control, and behavioral control: Assessing relevance across time, method, and culture. *Monographs of the Society for Research in Child Development, 70*(4).

Beckham, J. C., Lytel, B. L., & Feldman, M. E. (1996). Caregiver burden in partners of Vietnam veterans with posttraumatic stress disorder. *Journal of Consulting and Clinical Psychology, 64,* 1068–1071.

Bell, R.Q. (1968). A reinterpretation of the direction of effects in studies of socialization. *Psychological Review, 75,* 81–95.

Berkowitz, L. (1993). *Aggression: Its causes, consequences and control.* San Francisco: McGraw-Hill.

Blair, R. J. R. (1995). A cognitive developmental approach to morality: Investigating the psychopath. *Cognition, 50,* 7–15.

Bretherton, I. (1985). Attachment theory: Retrospect and prospect. In I. Bretherton & E. Waters (Eds.), *Growing points of attachment theory and research. Monographs of the Society for Research in Child Development, 50,* 30–35.

Cacioppo, J. T., & Gardner, W. L. (1999). Emotion. *Annual Review of Psychology, 50,* 191–214.

Carlson, E. (1998). A prospective longitudinal study of attachment disorganization/disorientation. *Child Development, 69,* 1107–1128.

Caspi, A., McClay, J., Moffitt, T. E., Mill, J., Martin, J., Craig, I. V., Taylor, A., & Poulton, R. (2002). Role of genotype in the cycle of violence in maltreated children. *Science, 297,* 851–854.

Crick, N. R., & Dodge, K. A. (1994). A review and reformulation of social information processing mechanisms in children's social adjustment. *Psychological Bulletin, 115,* 74–101.

Crittenden, P. M. (1988). Family and dyadic patterns of functioning in maltreating families. In K. Browne, C. Davies, & P. Stratton (Eds.), *Early prediction and prevention of child abuse* (pp. 161–189). New York: John Wiley & Sons.

Crittenden, P. M. (1997). Toward an integrative theory of trauma: A dynamic-maturational approach. In D.Cicchetti & S.Toth (Eds.), *Risk, trauma, and mental processes. The Rochester Symposium on Developmental Psychopathology, 10,* 24–84.

Crittenden, P. M. (1999). Danger and development: The organization of self-protective strategies. In E. Waters & J. A. Crowell (Eds.), *Atypical attachment in infancy and early childhood among children at developmental risk. Monographs of the Society for Research in Child Development, 64,* 145–171.

Cummings, E. M., & Davies, P. (1994). *Children and marital conflict.* New York: Guilford.

Dodge, K. A., & Newman, J. P. (1981). Biased decision-making processes in aggressive boys. *Journal of Abnormal Psychology, 90,* 375–379.

Dodge, K. A., Pettit, G. S., Bates, J. E., & Valente, E. (1995). Social information-processing patterns partially mediate the effect of early physical abuse on later conduct problems. *Journal of Abnormal Psychology, 104,* 632–643.

Dodge, K. A., & Price, J. M. (1994). On the relation between social information processing and socially competent behavior in early school-aged children. *Child Development, 65,* 1385–1397.

Dodge, K. A., & Tomlin, A. M. (1987). Utilization of self-schemas as a mechanism of interpretational bias in aggressive children. *Social Cognition, 5,* 280–300.

Egeland, B., & Susman-Stillman, A. (1996). Dissociation as a mediator of child abuse across generations. *Child Abuse & Neglect 20,* 1123–1132.

Eisenberg, N. (2000). Emotion, regulation, and moral development. *Annual Review of Psychology, 51,* 665–697.

Evans, S. W., & Short, E. J. (1991). A qualitative and serial analysis of social problem-solving in aggressive boys. *Journal of Abnormal Child Psychology, 19,* 331–340.

Fantuzzo, J., Boruch, R., Beriama, A., & Atkins, M. (1997). Domestic violence and children: Prevalence and risk in five major US cities. *Journal of American Child and Adolescence Psychiatry, 36,* 116–122.

Feeny, N. C. (2000). Exploring the roles of emotional numbing, depression, and dissociation in PTSD. *Journal of Traumatic Stress, 13,* 489–498.

Fisher, L., & Blair, R. J. R. (1998). Cognitive impairment and its relationship to psychopathic tendencies in children with emotional and behavioral difficulties. *Journal of Abnormal Child Psychology, 26,* 511–519.

Frijda, N. (1987). *The emotions.* New York: Cambridge University Press.

Garbarino, J. (1995). *Raising children in a socially toxic environment.* San Francisco: Jossey-Bass.

Garbarino, J., Dubrow, N., Kostelny, K., & Pardo, C. (1992). *Children in danger: Coping with the consequences of community violence.* San Francisco: Jossey-Bass.

Gelhorn, H. L., Stallings, M. C., Young, S. E., Corley, R. P., Rhee, S. H., & Hewitt, J. K. (2005). Genetic and environmental influences of conduct disorder: Symptom, domain and fullscale analyses. *Journal of Child Psychology and Psychiatry, 46,* 580–591.

Gorman-Smith, D., & Tolan, P. (1998). The role of exposure to community violence and developmental problems among inner-city youth. *Development and Psychopathology, 10,* 101–116.

Greenberg, M. T. (1999). Attachment and psychopathology in childhood. In J. Cassidy & P. R. Shaver (Eds.), *Handbook of attachment: Theory, research, and clinical applications* (pp. 469–496). New York: Guilford.

Grosmann, K. E., Grosmann, K., Winter, M., & Zimmermann, P. (2002) Attachment relationships and appraisal of partnership: From early experience of sensitive support to later relationship representation. In L. Pulkkinen & A. Gaspi (Eds.), *Paths to successful development. Personality and life course* (pp. 73–105). Cambridge: Cambridge University Press.

Haapasalo, J., & Pokela, E. (1999). Child-rearing and child abuse antecedents of criminality. *Aggression and Violent Behavior, 4,* 107–127.

Hämäläinen, M., & Pulkkinen, L. (1996). Problem behavior as a precursor of male criminality. *Development and Psychopathology, 8*(2), 443–455.

Horowitz, M. J. (1999). Introduction. In M. J. Horowitz (Ed.), *Essential papers on posttraumatic stress disorder* (pp. 1–17). New York: New York University Press.

Huesmann, L. R., & Eron, L. D. (1989). Individual differences and the trait of aggression. *European Journal of Personality, 3,* 95–106.

Jaffe, P.G., Wolfe, D., & Wilson, S. (1990). *Children of battered women.* Newbury Park, CA: Sage.

Janoff-Bulman, R. (1985). The aftermath of victimization: Rebuilding shattered assumptions. In C. R. Figley (Ed.), *Trauma and its wake: The study and treatment of post-traumatic stress disorder.* New York: Brunner Mazel.

Kaplan, S. J., Pelcovitz, D., & Labruna, V. (1999). Child and adolescent abuse and neglect research: A review of the past 10 years. Part I: Physical and emotional abuse and neglect. *Journal of the American Academy of Child & Adolescent Psychiatry, 38,* 1214–1222.

Kaufman, J., & Zigler, E. (1987). Do abused children become abusive parents? *American Journal of Orthopsychiatry, 57,* 186–192.

Keltikangas-Järvinen, L. & Pakaslahti, L. (1999). Development of social problem-solving strategies and changes in aggressive behavior: A 7-year follow-up from childhood to late adolescence. *Aggressive Behavior, 25,* 269–279.

Keltner, D., Ellsworth, P. C., & Edwards, K. (1993). Beyond simple pessimism: Effects of sadness and anger on social perceptions. *Journal of Personality and Social Psychology, 64,* 740–752.

Keresteš, G. (2006). Children's aggressive and prosocial behavior in relation to war exposure: Testing the role of perceived parenting and child's gender. *International Journal of Behavioral Development, 30,* 227–239.

Kliewer, W., Lepore, S. J., Oskin, D., & Johnson, P. D. (1998). The role of social and cognitive processes in children's adjustment to community violence. *Journal of Consulting and Clinical Psychology, 66,* 199–209.

Kostelny, K., & Garbarino, J. (2001). The war close to home: Children and violence in the United States. In D. J. Christie, R. V. Wagner, & D. D. Winter (Eds.), *Peace, conflict, and violence. Peace psychology for the 21st century* (pp. 110–119). New Jersey: Prentice Hall.

Loeber, R., & Hay, D. (1997). Key issues in the development of aggression and violence from childhood to early adulthood. *Annual Review of Psychology, 48,* 371–410.

Lore, R. K., & Schultz, K. (1993). Control of human aggression. A comparative perspective. *American Psychologist, 48,* 16–25.

Moffitt, T. E. (1993). Adolescence-limited and life-course-persistent antisocial behavior: A developmental taxonomy. *Psychological Review, 100,* 674–701.

Montgomery, E. (1998). Refugee children from the Middle East. *Scandinavian Journal of Social Medicine, 54*(Suppl.), 1–152.

Moradi, A. R., Neshat-Doos, H. T., Taghavi, R., Yule, W., & Dalgleish, T. (1999). Performance of children of adults with PTSD on the Stroop Color-Naming Task: A preliminary study. *Journal of Traumatic Stress, 12,* 663–671.

Murray, J. (1997). *Media violence and youth.* In J. Osofsky (Ed.), *Children in a violent society* (pp. 72–96). New York: Guilford.

Näätänen, P., Kanninen, K., Qouta, S., & Punamäki, R.L. (2002). Emotional patterns related to trauma and their association with PTS and somatic symptoms. *Anxiety, Stress and Coping, 15,* 75–92.

Osofsky, J. D., Wevers, S., Hann, D. M., & Fick, A. C. (1993). Chronic community violence: What is happening to our children? *Psychiatry, 56,* 36–45.

Pakaslahti, L. (2000). Children's and adolescents' aggressive behavior in context: The development and application of aggressive problem solving strategies. *Aggression and Violent Behavior, 5*(5), 467–490.

Pakaslahti, L., & Keltikangas-Järvinen, L. (1997). The relationship between moral approval of aggression, aggressive problem-solving strategies and aggressive behavior in 14-year-old adolescents. *Journal of Social Behavior and Personality, 12,* 905–924.

Parker, J. G., & Asher, S. R. (1993). Friendship and friendship quality in middle childhood: Links with peer group acceptance and feelings of loneliness and social dissatisfaction. *Developmental Psychology, 29,* 611–621.

Patterson, C. M., & Newman, J. P. (1993). Reflectivity and learning from aversive events: Toward a psychological mechanism for the syndromes of disinhibition. *Psychological Review, 100,* 716–736.

Patterson, G. R. (1982). *Coercive family process.* Eugene, OR: Castalia.

Patterson, G. R., & Dishion, T. J. (1988). Multilevel modes of family process: Traits, interactions and relationships. In R. Hinde & J. Stevenson-Hinde (Eds.), *Relationships and families: Mutual influences* (pp. 283–310). Oxford: Clarendon Press.

Perry, B. D. (1997). Incubated in terror. Neurodevelopmental factors in the "Cycle of Violence." In J.D. Osofsky (Ed.), *Children in a violent society* (pp.124–149). New York: John Wiley & Sons.

Plomin, R. (1995). Genetics and children's experiences in the family. *Journal of Child Psychology and Psychiatry and Allied Disciplines, 36,* 33–68.

Plomin, R., Nitz, K., & Rowe, D. C. (1990). Behavioral genetics and aggressive behavior in childhood. In M. Lewis & S. M. Miller (Eds.), *Handbook of developmental psychopathology* (pp. 119–133). New York: Plenum.

Power, M., & Dalgleish, T. (1997). *Cognition and emotion. From order to disorder.* Sussex: Psychology Press.

Punamäki, R. L. (1986). Stress among Palestinian women under military occupation: Women's appraisal of stressors, their coping modes, and their mental health. *International Journal of Psychology, 21,* 445–462.

Punamäki, R. L. (2000). Personal and family resources promoting resiliency among children suffering from military violence. In L. van Willigen (Ed.), *Health hazards of organized violence in children* (vol. II, pp. 86–116). Utrecht: Pharos.

Punamäki, R. L., Qouta, S., & El Sarraj, E. (1997). Models of traumatic experiences and children's psychological adjustment: The role of perceived parenting, children's resources and activity. *Child Development, 68,* 718–728.

Punamäki, R. L., Qouta, S., & El Sarraj, E. (2001). Resiliency factors predicting psychological adjustment after political violence among Palestinian children. *International Journal of Developmental Behaviour, 25,* 256–267.

Pynoos, R. S., Steinberg, A. M., Ornitz, E. M., & Goenjian, A. K. (1998). Issues in the developmental neurobiology of traumatic stress. In R. Yehuda, A. C. McFarlane, & B. A. Van der Kolk (Eds.), *Psychobiology of posttraumatic stress disorder* (pp. 176–193). *Annals of the New York Academy of Sciences, 821.* New York: New York Academy of Sciences.

Qouta, S., Kassab-Helmi, A., & Punamäki, R. L. (2003). *War and military violence and early child development: The role of mother-infant -interaction and intervention.* Research Proposal 23.06.2003. Bergen: Children and War Foundation.

Qouta, S., Punamäki, R. L., & El Sarraj, E. (1997). Experiences and coping strategies among political prisoners. *Peace and Conflict: Journal of Peace Psychology, 3,* 19–36.

Qouta, S., Punamäki, R. L., Miller, T., & El Sarraj, E. (in press). Does war beget child aggression? Military violence, gender, age and aggressive behavior in two Palestinian samples. *Aggressive Behavior.*

Rehn, E., & Johnson Sirleaf, E. (2002). The independent experts' assessment on the impact of armed conflict on women and women's role in peace-building. Retrieved from UNIFEM Web site: http://www.unifem.undp.org/resources/assessment/index.html.

Rothbart, M. K., Ahadi, S., & Hershey, K. L. (1994). Temperament and social behavior in children. *Merrill-Palmer Quarterly, 40,* 21–39.

Rushton, J. P., Fulker, D. W., Neale, M. C., Nias, D. K. B., & Eysenck, H. J. (1986). Altruism and aggression: The heritability of individual differences. *Journal of Personality and Social Psychology, 50,* 1192–1198.

Rutter, M. (2000). Resiliency reconsidered: Conceptual consideration, empirical findings and policy implications. In J. P. Shondoff & S. Meisels (Eds.) *Handbook of childhood intervention* (pp. 651–683). Cambridge: Cambridge University Press.

Saarni, C. (1999). *The development of emotional competence.* Guilford series on social and emotional development. New York: Guilford.

Salmivalli, C., Kaukiainen, A., & Lagerspetz, K. (1998).Aggression in the social relations of school-aged girls and boys. In P. Slee & K. Rigby (Eds.), *Children's peer relations.* London: Routledge.

Sanson, A., & Bretherton, D. (2001). Conflict resolution: Theoretical and practical issues. In D. J. Christie, R. V. Wagner, & D. D. Winter (Eds.), *Peace, conflict, and violence. Peace psychology for the 21st century* (pp. 193–209). New Jersey: Prentice Hall.

Scheeringa, M., & Zeanah, C. H. (2001). A relational perspective on PTSD in early childhood. *Journal of Traumatic Stress, 14,* 799–815.

Schwartz, D., & Proctor, L. J. (2000). Community violence exposure and children's social adjustment in the school peer group: The mediating roles of emotion regulation and social cognition. *Journal of Consulting and Clinical Psychology, 68,* 670–683.

Shalev, A. Y., Peri, T., Brandes, D., Freedman, S., Orr, S. P., & Pitman, R. K. (2000). Auditory startle response in trauma survivors with posttraumatic stress disorder: A prospective study. *American Journal of Psychiatry, 155,* 630–637.

Smith, P., Dyregrov, A., Yule, W., Gupta, L., Perrin, S., & Gjestad, R. (1999) *Children and disaster: Teaching recovery techniques.* Bergen, Norway: Foundation for Children and War.

Solomon, Z., Mikulincer, M., Fried, B., & Wosner, Y. (1987). Family characteristics and posttraumatic stress disorder: A follow-up of Israeli combat stress reaction casualties. *Family Process, 26,* 383–394.

Straker, G., Moosa, F., Becker, R., & Nkwale, M. (1992). *Faces in the revolution. The psychological effects of violence on township youth in South Africa.* Cape Town: David Philip.

Terr, L. (1991). Childhood traumas: An outline and overview. *American Journal of Psychiatry, 148,* 10–20.

Thornton, S. (2002). *Growing minds. An introduction to cognitive development.* New York: Palgrave.

Tremblay, R. E. (2000). The development of aggressive behaviour during childhood: What have we learned in the past century? *International Journal of Behavioral Development, 24,* 129–141.

van der Kolk, B. A. (1996). Trauma and memory. In B. A. van der Kolk, A. C. McFarlane, & L. Weisaeth (Eds.), *Traumatic stress: The effects of overwhelming experience on mind, body, and society* (pp. 279–302). New York: Guilford.

Van Ijzendoorn, M. H., & Zwart-Woudstra, H. A. (1995). Adolescents' attachment representations and moral reasoning. *Journal of Genetic Psychology, 156,* 359–374.

Westerink, J., & Giarratano, L. (1999). The impact of posttraumatic stress disorder on partners and children of Australian Vietnam veterans. *Australian and New Zealand Journal of Psychiatry, 33,* 841–847.

Yule, W. (2002). Alleviating the effects of war and displacement on children. *Traumatology, 8,* 25–43.

Chapter 4

Growing Up in Israel
Lessons on Understanding the Effects of Political Violence on Children

Michelle Slone

The potentially devastating effects of terrorism and political violence on children have become a focus of much concern in the current Middle East conflict. Beyond this specific conflict, the chronicity and complexity of this environment in the Middle East provides a setting from which broader issues related to children's ability to cope with political violence and terrorism may be studied. This chapter outlines a model for the study of the effects of political violence on children and presents a summary of data derived with the use of this paradigm. This model enabled the examination of the differing severity of exposure for children divided along different demographic categories, such as age, gender, residential location, and religious adherence. Furthermore, the scale allowed for the study of the consequences to children's mental health from exposure to differing levels of severity and for the detection of those factors that enhance resilience in coping with exposure to political violence. The paradigm prompted a wealth of data relating to risk factors for violence exposure, the emotional response of children, and buffering factors that can potentially be exploited for the enhancement of children's resilience in the face of uncontrollable violence.

Growing up in Israel is an intricate mix of negotiating the usual developmental tasks against the backdrop of a society torn apart by terrorism, politically motivated violence, and religious and ideological disputes. It should come as no surprise, then, that research findings indicate that Israeli children frequently manifest high levels of anxiety and other psychological and behavioral disturbances. These findings join the results of research from other areas of conflict that demonstrate the adverse consequences to children from living under circumstances of war, community violence, and the threats of physical harm. Notwithstanding the abundance of evidence to this effect, a glance at the daily processes of life in Israel raises a picture of children continuing to function on all societal levels. To a large extent, the familial, social, and academic structures continue to function with all the vagaries characteristic of any modern Western society. This apparent contradiction puts attention on the surprising resilience and adaptability that children frequently demonstrate, even under extremely adverse circumstances. This chapter discusses the consequences for youth of the long-standing Middle East conflict as an example case within which to understand the deleterious effects of political violence on children in general.

The chapter addresses two broad aims. The first is the development of a research model within which the exposure/outcome relation can be studied and the presentation of data on exposure and psychological outcome deriving from studies based on this model. This series of studies were conducted in Israel and framed by the conflicted Middle East environment. The second aim is the suggestion of extension of this basic research model to incorporate the study of resilience factors that may mediate the exposure/outcome relationship.

Growing Up in Israel

War is not novel to Israel. Since the establishment of the state, Israel has been involved in five wars, two wars of attrition, border skirmishes, missile attacks in the north, and two Palestinian uprisings. The past decade has been marked by various peace initiatives with neighboring Arab countries that brought the promise of new relations. However, despite the huge strides in concluding stable peace treaties with Egypt and Jordan, Israel has so far been unable to attain peace with the Palestinians or with Syria.

Israeli/Palestinian relations have been turbulent and contentious since the Six Day War in 1967, during which Israel acquired Gaza from Egypt and the West Bank from Jordan. This land was inhabited by about 700,000 Palestinians who came to live under Israeli rule and gradually developed a sense of hatred and frustration toward Israel, who they saw as depriving them of their land. In 1987, a Palestinian uprising occurred, the First Intifada, and it originated as a rebellion of the poor and the youth and spread into a clearly stated direction that called for an independent Palestinian state that would coexist alongside Israel. The Intifada laid the backdrop for the rise of fundamental Islamic organizations that advocated terror, armed force, and holy war (jihad) as the means to recover all of former Palestine (Smith, 1996).

Eventually, after months of secret negotiations in Norway, Israel and the Palestine Liberation Organization (PLO) announced in August 1993 that they had reached an agreement on mutual recognition and had outlined a plan for the end of Israeli occupation and an interim arrangement for Palestinian autonomy. Several agreements followed that implemented Israeli withdrawal and redeployment from various areas and transferred civil responsibility to the Palestinian authority. These agreements initiated a long, arduous, and controversial negotiating process. Many Israelis were concerned that the peace arrangements did not ensure Israel's security, and many Palestinians felt that the agreements were insufficient in advancing Palestinian aspirations. In addition, several problematic issues remained unsolved—namely, the final status of Jerusalem and the return of Palestinian refugees. One of the most immediate unresolved issues focused on the Israeli settlements that are or were dispersed throughout the West Bank and Gaza Strip. These settlements were established by Israel on conquered land based on the belief that this land is sacred and belongs to the larger Israel promised to the Jews as a homeland in the Bible. The existence of the religiously held settlements on land previously inhabited by Palestinians represents a center point of the religious and nationalistic roots of the conflict.

Attempts at orchestrating a Middle East peace settlement were dashed in October 2000 when a second Palestinian uprising erupted and became know as the Intifada el Aksa (or Second Intifada). The phrase derives from the events precipitating the outbreak of violence, namely, the visit of Ariel Sharon, then the Israeli opposition leader, to the Temple Mount, which also houses the el Aksa Mosque. The visit spurred a protest demonstration that was met with force by the Israeli military, resulting in significant casualties among the Palestinians. The unrest spread quickly and, over time, became forged into open Israeli-Palestinian conflict. The Second Intifada represents the most serious outbreak of hostilities in Israel since the Gulf War and has initiated a spiral of violence and desperation in the region.

Since the eruption of the Second Intifada, the Israeli-Palestinian conflict has reached unprecedented proportions of violence and mounting casualties on both sides. Present figures document 6,384 Israelis injured and 964 killed; Palestinian casualty figures report 2,806 killed.

For the Palestinian population, the forceful reacquisition of cities by the Israeli army, curfews, destruction of homes, and economic hardship have shattered the fabric of society and heralded untold suffering at every societal level. The conflict has resulted in massive destruction and a rising death toll on both sides. Violence pervades the area, disrupting daily living habits and undermining every dimension of personal safety.

For the Israeli population, all sense of security has been disturbed by the unrelenting spate of suicide bombings and terrorist attacks that have occurred with unprecedented frequency throughout the country. These attacks occur in buses, shopping malls, restaurants, and street corners and take the form of bombings, drive-by shootings, hit-and-run attacks, stabbings, and explosions. The unpredictability and ubiquitous nature of these terrorist events have laid a veil of fear and hopelessness over daily activities, stripping the civilian population of perceived control and security.

Exposure to this environment is by no means restricted to adults and has pervaded the very essence of childhood in Israel. The escalating statistic of Israeli children killed in the Intifada, frightening as it is, in no way serves as the only meter of their involvement in the violence. Many children have been wounded or have lost family members or friends. In addition, vast numbers have directly witnessed the most abhorrent scenes of violence; almost all have been exposed indirectly via the media to horrific scenes of explosions, charred remains of homes and public places, and the injured being evacuated to hospital.

This environment of terror, fear, and insecurity merges many elements that are noxious to children's healthy development. The current situation in the Middle East brings into focus many of the general issues related to the mental health outcomes of growing up under conditions of violence, conflict, and danger that have become so pertinent during the present era of global terrorism and political violence.

Research examining the consequences to children of growing up in conflict-laden environments has produced a mixed picture. Findings could be conceptualized as falling along a continuum, with evidence of marked disturbance at one pole and minimal effect and even precocious development at the opposite pole. Around the pole evidencing deleterious effects, a body of international studies indicates that exposure to war and political violence frequently leads to developmental impairment and psychiatric symptomatology, ranging from isolated symptoms, such as fear, anger, and insecurity, to profiles of disorder (Garmezy & Masten, 1990; Schwebel, 1992). Social crises, such as combat and political conflict, have been correlated with a sense of demoralization and depression (Steinmetz & Owens, 1992), and political violence has been associated with increased psychiatric symptomatology (Soliman, 1999). Studies emerging from countries besieged by war and conflict, such as the Middle East (Von-Hippel, 1997), Northern Ireland (Ferguson & Cairns, 1996), the Philippines (Protacio-Marcelino, 1989), and Latin America (Arroyo & Eth, 1984), have reported wide-ranging psychological disturbances among youth.

Around the opposite pole of the continuum is evidence, however scanty, that children growing up under politically violent and turbulent conditions actually manifest precocious emotional and cognitive development and abstract reasoning (Straker, 1993). Moral sensibility may be pronounced, and the capacity for moral reasoning may be unusually well developed (Coles, 1987; Straker, 1993).

Between these two poles, the bulk of research yields a mosaic of varying combinations of coping abilities and elevated distress indices. Children show a wide variety of individual differences in reactions to conditions of political conflict and often exhibit remarkable resilience in the face of adversity. Some studies report a degree of malfunction but low overall levels of stress (Erlich, Greenbaum, & Toubiana, 1994). Several resilience factors have been isolated that appear to reduce distress responses of children living under prolonged conflict. A study of Jewish Israeli preadolescents showed that high levels of ideological commitment serve as a protective factor (Punamäki, 1996), and good perceived parenting contributed to positive psychological adjustment among Palestinian children during the First Intifada (Punamäki, Qouta, & El Sarraj, 1997). In addition, in a large representative sample of Palestinian adolescents, social integration was found to protect against the potentially deleterious effects of Intifada conflict exposure (Barber, 2001). Research on children in Northern Ireland suggests the adverse emotional impact of exposure to traumatic political experiences, although there has been evidence of a surprising degree of resilience to stress (Joseph, Cairns, & McCollam, 1993). These studies reinforce the questioning of automatic dysfunction under conditions of chronic political violence exposure and exemplify the complex collage of varying interactions between conflict exposure and psychological outcome.

A Framework for Research on the Exposure–Outcome Relation

Research in this domain has captured the subjective meanings of growing up under conditions of political violence and yielded a rich harvest of valuable data on the wide-ranging consequences of these experiences to children. However, these fertile and important data have been hampered by a number of methodological difficulties that have curtailed the development of controlled, quantitative comparisons of the impact of sociopolitical events on children's mental health. Possibly because of the unpredictable and sporadic occurrence of political violence, research has tended to focus on acute traumatic events and their consequences for children, usually in terms of narrow symptomalogical indicators, such as anxiety, depressive symptoms (Cicchetti & Toth, 1992), or post-traumatic stress disorder (PTSD) (Eth & Pynoos, 1985). In view of this, researchers have begun to acknowledge the pressing need for the systematic study of the effects of chronic political violence and upheaval on children in a manner that allows for comparative and longitudinal exploration (Ladd & Cairns, 1996).

A general environment of political tension and violence usually cannot be captured as an isolated singular event or even as a series of unrelated events. Instead, the accumulation often leads to a sum that is greater than its parts. Furthermore, the focus on a singular dramatic or acute event presumes a universal traumatic experience for those exposed. However, the same event may be experienced in many different ways. For example, in a bus explosion, one child who has lost a friend in a previous explosion may witness the event from close proximity. Another child who has had no previous exposure may have seen the explosion from a great distance. A third child may have heard about the explosion and viewed the event on television, interspersed with viewing of other programs. Various experiences of the same event under these different circumstances may produce very different meanings assigned to the same event and, by implication, different outcomes for these three children.

Thus, the assessment of the consequences of exposure must take cognizance of both subtle variations of that exposure for the child and of multiple exposures. Such factors as differential previous experiences, subjective meanings, and different surrounding circumstances complicate the attempt to determine the outcomes of exposure to violent political events. These issues highlight the need for a standardized, quantitative measure of exposure to political violence, particularly in an environment in which it is endemic and chronic (Cairns & Dawes, 1996).

To address some of these issues, this chapter lays out a research model for the study of the effects of political violence. This model was developed by transporting a paradigm from another research domain, namely, that of general stress research (Slone, 1997). To measure the environmental factors of political violence and their impacts, the basis of the model was the adoption of the life events paradigm and its translation into applicability in the political sphere.

The life events paradigm studies consequences of adverse events by separating precipitant stressor from response by means of the quantification of social experiences (Monroe & Peterman, 1988). Comparable events across individuals are considered classifiable in a manner that reflects the external demands placed on them. Most life events research has relied on questionnaire or checklist methodology, with the occurrence of events conceptualized as the independent variable in the prediction of various psychological functioning indices (Cohen, 1988). This research has extended from the assessment of the influence of life events on psychological functioning among adults to a rapidly developing literature suggestive of a link between life events and the psychological adjustment of children and adolescents (Johnson & Bradlyn, 1988).

Within this framework, political events could be construed as representing a special category of life events located within a particular historical and cultural context and result in collective experience. There seems to be no reason to oppose this theoretical extension because political events do not form a category that is clearly divisible or differentiated from other personal or social life events. In addition, all are rooted in a particular context, and indeed, there may be some degree of overlap among them.

The adoption of the life events model as a template for the measurement of political events is a new conceptualization that opens avenues blocked in previous attempts to develop political scaling instruments. The legitimacy of the quantification of politically stressful events in cultural studies was recognized by Punamäki (1989) in her study of Palestinian children's fears and coping modes. However, the scale developed for her study was descriptive and not validated, thereby entailing limited generalizability.

Another index of political violence was constructed in South Africa, where the need for quantitative measures has long been recognized. This scale, the Township Life Event Scale (TLES) (Bluen & Odesnik, 1988), was regionally useful in quantifying political violence exposure endemic to living in the disadvantaged black townships of apartheid South Africa. However, the scale was targeted at adults and contained community-specific items that curtailed its generalization. Moreover, the scale has not been updated in pace with the historic changes occurring in South Africa.

An additional scale that has been developed is the Childhood War Trauma Questionnaire (CWTQ), which is designed to assess children's exposure to war trauma in Lebanon (Macksoud & Aber, 1996). Although the scale displays impressive psychometric properties, its format as a semistructured interview restricts large group administration and nonexpert objective scoring. Furthermore, it specifically measures war-related experiences and does not encompass chronic, minor, and non–war-related political trauma.

This armament of instruments has broken ground in facilitating a quantitative approach to the appraisal of children's exposure to political violence. Nonetheless, despite appreciation of the need for quantifiable scales, particularly in regions saturated by political violence, most existing instruments remain context-bound, locally relevant, and nontransferable across different arenas of conflict. Construction of a generally applicable instrument based on the life events model could address some of these methodological difficulties. Its development would overcome the integral need for a life events standard from which to compare differential group adjustment processes situated at the base of any quantitative cross-group study in the political domain.

Although the life events model holds potential for surmounting the pivotal problem of environmental unpredictability that hampers the political research field, its extension entails adoption of some of the conceptual and psychometric difficulties that inhere in the paradigm itself. First, the attempt to standardize and assign differing outcomes to the infinite array of adverse experiences and their appraisal will inevitably be reductionistic. Second, the separation of an event from the personal meaning attributed to it is a general methodological difficulty in all life events research (Cohen, 1988). It is questionable whether the event itself, the underlying meaning, or its appraisal elicits the trauma response. The methodology generally posits a linear relation between the number and meaning of experienced events and outcome, referred to as the additivity assumption (Holmes & Rahe, 1967). However, simple cause-and-effect interpretations of the life events–psychological functioning relation are frequently nonfeasible because curvilinear or recursive relations are possible. A particularly subtle consideration pertains to factors that may mediate between the life event and outcome chain. It has been proposed that appraisal processes that reflect the psychological significance of an event are crucial in determining its impact (Lazarus & Folkman, 1984). Thus, the processes that create adversity may derive not solely from the events themselves but from their appraisal and assessments of options for response. Third, the paradigm raises the problem of measuring events that have different meanings in different contexts. Can political events be described in a way that allows for cross-group comparisons? This difficulty poses a dilemma. On one hand, the lack of a cross-group standard restricts study to the descriptive comparison of adjustment indices of samples of children from different groups. On the other hand, the standard must be applicable both across groups and transculturally, such that it provides a common denominator of group-specific meanings and appraisals attributable to events.

General life events research accepts the compromise that complete freedom from specific meaning is untenable. However, to address this issue maximally in the construction of the Political Life Events (PLE) scale, an attempt was made to pare down the cultural specificity of events. For example, injury to a family member may have resulted from many causes, including combat, confrontation, and military accidents. This type of political life event was formulated neutrally as an item worded "Injury to a family member as a result of political or military violence."

Second, another mode by which personal meaning attribution can be addressed is by the assignation of different weightings to events. Generalized weighting on the basis of judges' personal and vicarious experiences is an acceptable scoring system for life events scales (Paykel, Prusoff, & Uhlenhuth, 1971) with adequate predictive value for psychological adjustment indices (Zuckerman, Oliver, Hollingsworth, & Austrin, 1986). Weightings based on event desirability can be determined either by judges or by subjects themselves because correlations between the two methods are high (Pilkonis, Imber, & Rubinsky, 1985). However, there is a potential confounding inherent in any reliance on subjective evaluation that could lead to "meaning after the effect" in which individuals attempt to explain their distress by evaluating life experiences negatively. Therefore, in scale development, item calibration should preferentially be achieved by independent judges similar to the target population on demographic variables that could influence judgments (Askenasy, Dohrenwend, & Dohrenwend, 1977).

The Measurement of Political Life Events

With these advantages and shortcomings of the life events model in mind, the PLE scale was constructed in a series of pretests. In the first phase, the range of politically violent event exposure was determined by means of in-depth interviews conducted with 150 Israeli children and adolescents representative of the demographic constituents of Israeli society. Samples of children differing along the variables of religion, degree of religious adherence, residential location, political ideology, and socioeconomic status were interviewed to determine the spectrum of violent political events to which they had been exposed. A pool of items was extracted from the themes of reported events and were factor analyzed to produce a list of items encompassing the possibilities for event exposure. An attempt was made to formulate items neutrally and derive common denominators that were transcendent of individual cases and cultural specificity. For example, children reported, "I saw a bomb blast on TV," "I read in the newspaper about children being shot." These specific cases, which cohered into one factor, were worded neutrally as an item, "Exposure to acts of political violence through the media, e.g., on television or in the newspapers." The final version of the PLE scale consists if twenty items representing stressful political events to which respondents are requested to report their exposure.

The second phase consisted of a pretest in which the item pool was administered to fifty adolescents aged 12 to 18 years, evenly divided by gender, who were requested to note their exposure to the described events and to comment on item inclusivity and clarity. On the basis of this pretest, five items were removed due to their duplication or vagueness, one new item was inserted, and the format was altered in line with subjects' comments. The final version of the scale comprised twenty items representing a series of politically stressful events to which children are requested to note their exposure (see Table 4.1).

To reflect increases in the severity of events, items on the PLE scale were calibrated in a separate pretest according to valuations of event severity by independent judges on the basis of their personal and vicarious experiences. In this test, forty Israeli youth were requested to evaluate items on a scale of 1 to 3, as mild, moderate, or severe according to their perception of the severity of the experience, irrespective of individual actual exposure to the events. Averages of these evaluations were calculated to produce item weightings. Thus, for research use, the scale is scored by weighting all items marked positive for exposure on each participant's profile according to the formula: mild items are multiplied by 1, items categorized as moderate are multiplied by 2, and items categorized as severe are multiplied by 3. A global measure, called the PLE score, is derived by summing weighted items across a research participant's entire questionnaire.

The PLE scale has been used in a series of different studies and has yielded good reliability (Cronbach's alpha coefficients ranging from 0.80 to 0.94). Validity studies assessing cross-nationality transferability for Jewish and Arab Israeli youth, for Palestinian youth (Slone, Adiri, & Arian, 1998), and for black and white South African adolescents (Slone, Kaminer, & Durrheim, 2000) have yielded excellent results and shown predictive validity for these communities. These results support the cross-nationality transferability of the PLE scale, enabling its utilization as a standard for comparison of cross-cultural adjustment mechanisms.

The PLE scale, allowing for the quantification of political violence exposure, would now enable the assessment of the exposure of a range of traumatic events associated with direct and indirect victimization, threat, insecurity, and loss of control within a chronically conflictual and violent political environment.

The Measurement of Psychological Outcomes

To measure mental health outcomes to exposure of political violence with the PLE scale, the present series of studies used the Brief Symptom Inventory (BSI) (Derogatis & Spencer, 1982). This instrument is a self-report scale to which respondents are asked to rate their experience of symptoms over the past 6 months on a distress scale. Items assess the presence and perceived depth of psychopathological symptoms, such as inferiority feelings, concentration difficulties, loneliness, fear of open spaces, appetite and sleep disturbances, uncontrollable temper outbursts, compulsive urges, and others. The scale yields two types of measures—the Global Severity Index (GSI), which is a

Table 4.1 Political Life Events (PLE) scale

1. A security drill at school	Yes	No
2. Time spent in a security shelter	Yes	No
3. A security check when entering a public place (for example, a shopping center)	Yes	No
4. Presence in a situation where there is a suspected dangerous weapon	Yes	No
5. Harm to property as a result of political violence	Yes	No
6. Exposure to gunshot or the use of other weapons	Yes	No
7. Absence of a family member for an extended period due to political or military involvement	Yes	No
8. Participation in a political demonstration	Yes	No
9. Witnessing a political demonstration	Yes	No
10. Knowing someone who was involved in a political demonstration	Yes	No
11. Exposure to acts of violence through the news on television or in newspapers	Yes	No
12. Victim of an act of political violence	Yes	No
13. Witnessing an act of political violence	Yes	No
14. Knowing someone who has been witness to an act of political violence	Yes	No
15. Death of a family member as a result of political or military violence	Yes	No
16. Death of a friend or acquaintance as a result of political or military violence	Yes	No
17. Injury to a family member as a result of political or military violence	Yes	No
18. Injury to a friend or acquaintance as a result of political or military violence	Yes	No
19. Confiscation of land of a family member	Yes	No
20. Confiscation of land of an acquaintance	Yes	No

single summary measure that serves as an indicator of depth of psychological distress, and a set of ten subscales that indicate the symptom pattern from which the distress evolves, specifically depression, anxiety, phobia, hostility, somatization, social alienation, paranoid ideation, obsessive-compulsive disorder, interpersonal sensitivity, and an additional subscale of miscellaneous symptoms.

The Measurement of the Effects of Exposure to Political Violence

With these two measures—the PLE scale and an outcome measure reflecting psychological distress and symptom load patterns—the stage is set for the study of the effects of political violence on youth. The basic paradigm is the detection of relations between the severity of exposure to political life events and indices of psychological distress and pathology, that is, the relations between these events and BSI indices.

A proviso in this formula is the need to control for the mental health consequences of exposure to other traumatizing social experiences to isolate the distress manifestations deriving purely from exposure to political violence. In all the studies reported here, respondents completed an age-appropriate personal life events inventory as a control for the contribution of stressful personal and social life events to the presence of psychopathology. The inclusion of both the political and personal life events questionnaires was necessary to ascertain the relative contribution of each to psychopathology. However, it raises the issue that political life events are both conceptually and methodologically intermeshed with general nonpolitical life events. The loss of a close family member in political violence, for example, would count as a stressful event on both scales. This means that there should be high levels of multicolinearity between the PLE and Social Life Events (SLE) scales, leading to difficulty in making a clear decision regarding whether general life events or political life events are related to symptomatology. This multicolinearity was taken into consideration statistically. Thus, in the present research framework, the model takes the form of partialing out from the mental health outcome measure the degree of distress associated with exposure to general social life events. This enables determination of the unique and specific association between exposure to political life events and psychopathology, over and above hazards and outcomes to mental health deriving from other, non–political-related personal and social life events. Thus, in specific terms, the basic model for the present research framework can be represented as political life events (PLE) (with life events [LE] partialed out) related to BSI.

This model was utilized in a series of studies that assessed the exposure to violent political events and the psychological outcomes of this exposure across different groups of Israeli children living under the conflict conditions in the Middle East. The findings of these studies gave rise to a global picture for levels of exposure to political violence, general distress of youth growing up in this environment, and the relation between exposure and distress.

Levels of Exposure to Political Violence

Over the past 8 years, the majority of Israeli children and adolescents tested reported that they had been exposed to a significant array of incidents of political violence (Slone & Gil-Ad, 2004; Slone & Hallis, 1999; Slone, Lobel, & Gilat, 1999). These included severe and traumatic events, such as the death or injury of family members or friends from terrorist attacks or army combat, loss of property, presence in the vicinity of an explosion or gun shots, participation in or witnessing of violent political demonstrations, and viewing the aftermath of a terrorist attack on television. This is an unnerving picture because it indicates that Israeli children are exposed to a background of extreme violence. This pertains to periods of both peace negotiations and overt conflict. Even during the relatively peaceful Israeli-Palestinian peace negotiations, children reported exposure to violence from intermittent terrorist attacks, rocket launches from Lebanon into northern Israel, and heated political and ideological clashes among segments of the Israeli population. The chronicity of violence stands out as one of the predominant features of the country.

However, beyond this baseline, there are significant demographic differences in severity of exposure. Regarding residential location, the pattern of exposure has changed since the beginning of the Intifada. Before, the highest levels of political life events exposure were reported by adolescents living in the north of the country, the second by youth in the settlements, and the lowest levels by adolescents in the large cities and urban areas (Slone, Lobel, & Gilat, 1999). Since the outbreak of the Intifada, the highest levels of political life events exposure have been reported by children from the settlements, thereafter by children form large cities and urban areas, and finally, by those living in the north of the country.

The high reported levels for adolescents from the settlements are probably related to two defining characteristics of this residential location. First, like most settlements, the areas investigated in these studies are located deep in the West Bank. Since the beginning of the Intifada, almost all settlements have been enclosed by barriers and fences, and most require passage through belligerent and violent areas on a daily basis, frequently resulting in contact with hostility, shootings, and ambushes. During the period of peace negotiations, prior to the Intifada, daily life was relatively routine. However, since the uprising, the danger has amplified to dramatic proportions, such that access to the settlements may even involve armed convoy travel. In addition, there have been several incursions into the residences in the settlements, leading to shootings, hostage taking, and killing.

Second, underlying the establishment of the settlements lies a coherent system of intertwined religious and political ideology. This ideology holds that the land in question is sacred and promised to the Jewish people, such that claims for the land and resistance to its surrender become inseparable from religious belief. Both conditions of unswerving religious belief fused with political activity and residential location amid hostility may predispose an increased exposure to violent political events.

The second highest levels of political life events are reported by adolescents living in large cities and urban areas. This reflects one of the defining features of the Second Intifada, which has been characterized by a spate of suicide and car bombings and drive-by shootings in densely inhabited public places. The Second Intifada has unhinged any order that could be assigned to the attacks. Once these attacks appeared to occur mainly in the early morning on buses, whereas now they have begun to occur outside night clubs and in restaurants late at night, at a hotel during a Passover dinner, at bar mitzvah halls, at train stations, and outside schools. Israeli children living in urban areas can make no order out of this situation, depriving them of the sense of control over their safety.

Finally, the lowest levels of political life events exposure are reported by children living in the north, possibly because the frequency of terrorist attacks has been lower in the far northern areas than elsewhere in the country. However, even here children report significant exposure to violence. The few terrorist attacks that have occurred in the north, the increased danger of living on the border, and involvement in security arrangements that protect the area compound the routine risks of living in a country characterized generally by high levels of tension and violence.

In addition to residential location differences in political violence exposure, measurements reflect gender and age differences (Slone & Hallis, 1999; Slone, Lobel, & Gilat, 1999). PLE scores accumulated over numerous studies show that older children and males report the highest levels of exposure to political violence. It could be speculated that older children are more autonomous, spending more time in public places outside of the home. In addition, boys and older adolescents may involve themselves more actively in political events, thereby increasing their exposure. Nonetheless, this evidence suggests that there are specific demographic variables that predispose toward the risk of exposure to violent political events.

These findings are furnished with some support from research in other arenas of political conflict. In war-torn countries such as Lebanon, older children are reported to have been exposed to a greater number of war traumas, probably due partially to the fact that they have been exposed to more years of war (Macksoud & Aber, 1996). Boys were also found to have been more exposed than girls, who tend to assume more domestic roles in the family unit. These researchers speculate that in Lebanese society, it may be easier to protect and control younger children and girls, thereby shielding them to some extent from the harsh realities of the conflict. The findings for Israeli children concur with this evidence of the influence of roles and societal positioning on children's exposure to political violence. It seems plausible that families and communities monitor, supervise, and protect children differentially according to gender and age, resulting in differential risk of exposure.

Levels of Psychological Distress

Results of this series of studies conducted over the past 8 years show a disturbingly sharp increase in psychological distress indices for Israeli children and adolescents (Slone & Gil-Ad, 2004; Slone & Hallis, 1999; Slone, Lobel, & Gilat, 1999). Prior to the Intifada, Israeli youth scores for general psychological distress on the BSI were significantly higher than the norms for children in the United States, approximating the norms for children living in South Africa during the riots preceding the disintegration of apartheid. However, since the beginning of the first Intifada, norms for Israeli children have shown a significantly steep escalation, both for general distress and for all the subscales. Figure 4.1 shows the General Severity of Distress Index (GSI) means for American adolescents (Derogatis & Melisaratos, 1983), for South African adolescents during the riots preceding the dismantling of apartheid (Slone, Kaminer, & Durrheim, 2000, 2002) and for Israeli adolescents prior to the Second Intifada (Slone, Adiri, & Arian, 1998; Slone & Hallis, 1999; Slone, Lobel, & Gilat, 1999) and since the beginning of the First Intifada (Slone & Gil-Ad, 2004). Scores reflect mean measures adjusted for standardization across studies (see Fig. 4.1).

This graph shows that prior to the Second Intifada, levels of psychological distress for Israeli adolescents approximated those of South African children during the period of violent riots that preempted the first free elections. The South African sample was

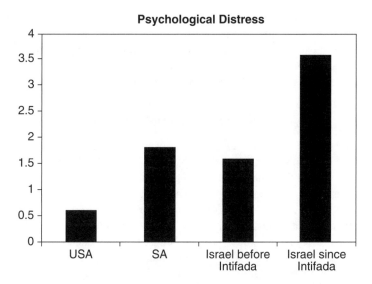

Figure 4.1. Psychological distress means across populations. SA = South Africa

representative, including black, white, colored, and Indian children, many of whom participated at the forefront of the riots. This is a striking result given the fact that the Israeli environment was supposedly relatively peaceful at the time. However, the graph shows an even further steep increase in distress levels since the beginning of the First Intifada, indicating very significant symptomatology among Israeli youth during the present historical juncture.

Accumulated findings for psychological distress also reflect a consistent pattern of gender differences in which levels are higher for girls than for boys. This is in alignment with studies showing greater emotionality and expression of distress among girls than boys (Ptacek, Smith, & Zanas, 1992; Vaux, 1985).

Relations Between Exposure to Political Violence and Psychological Outcome

The research framework that has been laid out here provides a model for the examination of the relation of exposure to political violence and psychological distress. This model translates into an examination of the relation between PLE and BSI, with the effects of other personal and social life events partialed out of the equation. With this model, a series of studies were undertaken to examine PLE to BSI relations across groups of adolescents differing along demographic variables, such as ethnicity, residential location, religion, and degree of adherence to religious belief. The guiding motivation prompting this set of studies was the attempt to determine whether the psychological outcome of exposure to equivalent levels of political violence (low, moderate, or high levels) is constant or differs across groups. The implications of the finding of constant outcomes across different groups would suggest that psychological outcome is essentially determined by severity of exposure to political violence. The implications of the alternative finding of cross-group differences in outcome for equivalent levels of exposure would suggest the existence of intervening variables emerging from the characteristics of the cross-group differences and would question the verity of automatic maladjustment under exposure conditions.

Cross-Cultural Differences in the Exposure–Outcome Relation

Cross-cultural differences in the effects of exposure to political violence were investigated in two studies. One researched responses of Jewish and Arab Israeli children residing in Israel, and the other investigated responses of Palestinian children residing in Gaza and a matched sample of Israeli children. The motivation underlying these studies was to provide an indication of adjustment reactions to political violence and their possible differential impact and culturally specific patterns.

In the Arab-Jewish Israeli study, the Arab children resided in and attended school in Jaffa, a city in Israel consisting of a mixed Arab and Jewish population. The Arabs residing in this area live an urban lifestyle, and the children were all from Muslim families who were traditional to secular in their religious orientation. The Jewish children were from a neighborhood in Tel Aviv approximating the low middle to middle-class socioeconomic status from which the Arab children were sampled.

Within Israel (as defined by the pre–June 1967 borders), Arabs and Jews are citizens who enjoy formal civic and legal equality. The Arabs, who were granted citizenship when Israel was established in 1948, constitute approximately 16% of the citizens (Rouhana & Fiske, 1995). However, constellations of religious, cultural, and political differences have given rise to complex difficulties, and the relation between Jewish and Arab citizens is permeated with cooperation in some areas and conflict in others (Kretzmer, 1990). Conflictual areas include land ownership rights, power sharing, and the distribution of resources, complicated further by the Israeli–Palestinian conflict. Arab citizens identify to some extent with Palestinians in the territories, although they have not shown a readiness to join in the uprisings or move to a Palestinian state if one is established. Although these conflictual areas have been almost completely devoid of physical violence, relations have often been strained (Smooha, 1992).

In terms of this unequal alliance, it would be expected that the political experiences and concomitant psychological adjustment of Arab and Jewish Israeli children would be different. They are separated along a religious, ethnic, cultural, residential, and national identity divide that could influence coping with political violence exposure. Thus, the underlying assumptions of this study suggested that Arab Israeli children would be exposed to more political life events than matched Jewish children. This was predicated on the postulation that the difficulties of being an Arab minority group living in Israel would be compounded by the Israeli–Palestinian conflict, possibly leading to more intimate involvement in and awareness of the intricacies of the political environment. In addition to the significance of the actual findings of differential exposure to political violence, support for this assumption would provide a criterion validity measure of the PLE scale. The central hypothesis predicted, in line with the basic assumption underlying general life events research, that there would be a linear relation between exposure to political life events and psychological distress.

Participants in the study were 118 Jewish and 140 Arab sixth- and seventh-grade children aged 13 and 14 years sampled from two demographically matched schools. Post hoc analyses of the demographic characteristics of the samples showed no significant differences between the groups on parental educational level or reported strength of self or familial religious commitment. All children responded to a battery of questionnaires in their native language: Jewish children in Hebrew and Arab children in the Arabic dialect used in the area. The battery was composed of the PLE scale, an age-appropriate life events scale (Coddington, 1990) and the BSI. Questionnaires were presented in randomly counterbalanced order to minimize response set. For both samples, the questionnaires were administered in the classroom in their instructional language by teachers who had received prior instruction.

The underlying assumption that Arab children would report greater exposure to political violence than Jewish children was confirmed, suggesting the criterion validity of the PLE scale. The central hypothesis posited that there will be a direct relation between level of exposure to political life events and psychological distress. Results showed that there was a significant linear relation between exposure to increasing levels of severity of political violence and higher levels of psychological distress. No significant interaction was found between nation and levels of political life events on the BSI, indicating that this direct relation held for the entire research population and for each nation.

These results showed that both Jewish and Arab children reported exposure to a significant array of events of political violence that were related directly to distress reactions. There were no significant differences between Jewish and Arab children for the amount and type of symptomalogical reactions, except for social alienation, which was higher among Arab than among Jewish children. This could be interpreted to mean that the variables in which these groups differ, such as culture and religion, do not intervene differentially in the response to political violence.

The second study in this series employed the same research design by examining the relation between exposure to political violence and psychological symptomatology outcomes. However, this cross-cultural study compared this relation for Palestinian children living in Gaza and for Israeli children. In light of the nature of the conflict and differential living conditions, the underlying assumption of the study stated that Palestinian children will report greater exposure to political violence than Israeli children. In addition to its quantitative value, this premise provides a further criterion validity test of the PLE scale. Again, in view of the general life events model, the central hypothesis of this study stated that after partialing out the effects of general personal life events, there would be a direct relation between severity of political violence exposure and distress. However, a cross-cultural comparison of the groups may yield differential patterns of adjustment mechanisms.

This study was conducted in 1995 during the height of peace initiatives between Israel and the Palestinians. The Palestinian children from Gaza have historically lived under foreign occupation that has stunted the establishment of autonomous societal and economic infrastructures as a nation, resulting in general socioeconomic disadvantage. At the time of the study, there were initiatives toward a peaceful settlement in the region that ultimately shattered into the Second Intifada. Thus, the Palestinians have always found themselves in a threatened position of insecurity about their national destiny, frequently divided among themselves regarding aspirations for its final form (Shikaki, 1996).

Participants in the study were 97 Israeli and 102 Palestinian sixth-grade children between the ages of 12 and 13 years. Access to Palestinian subjects was extremely complicated, thereby limiting controlled selection of this sample. Therefore, the Israeli sample was matched on the basis of the criteria of the Palestinian sample. The Palestinian children all resided in Gaza in a reportedly upper middle-class socioeconomic area with reference to local standards, representing a sector of the population with heterogeneous political orientations. They attended an academically competitive and relatively prestigious school. The Israeli children were selected from areas in Tel Aviv approximating as closely as possible the reported socioeconomic status and political heterogeneity of the Palestinian children. Considering residential conditions, parental educational level, and school characteristics, this was compatible with middle-class socioeconomic status for Israeli children. Post hoc findings revealed no significant differences between parental educational level for the two samples.

All children responded to the PLE scale, a life events scale (Coddington, 1990), and the BSI in their home language—Israeli children in Hebrew and Palestinian children in the dialect of Arabic used in the region.

Except for administrative logistics related to entry into Gaza, the procedure was equivalent to that of the first study. Questionnaires were administered in the classroom, in a randomly counterbalanced order—for the Israeli children by an experimenter and for the Palestinian children by a teacher who had received administration instructions.

The underlying assumption that Palestinian children would report greater exposure to political violence was confirmed. Although most of the Israeli children (74.2%) reported low to moderate exposure to political life events and only 3% reported very high exposure, most Palestinian children reported high to very high levels of exposure (71.5%), among whom 43.8% reported very high exposure. These findings extend the criterion validity of the PLE scale.

The basic central hypothesis that could logically be advanced for the relation between political violence and psychological distress is that there would be a direct relation between the two variables. However, in this study, the hypothesis of a direct relation was not confirmed. Results showed that in opposition to the hypothesis, the relation between the two variables, with the effects of personal life events partialed out of the equation, for the whole study population was not a linear relation; rather, an inverted U curve was produced. Figure 4.2 demonstrates the relationship between exposure to political violence (low, moderate, or high levels of exposure) to psychological distress as measured by the GSI index of the BSI.

To explore the effect of nationality within the overall picture, the means of psychological distress according to levels of exposure to political violence were examined for each nation separately. This examination produced an unusual finding: results showed that the inverted U–shaped curve for the entire research population was made up of two separate curves representing opposite relations for each nation. For the Israelis, there was a direct relation, indicating that increasing levels of exposure to political violence is associated with increasing psychological distress. However, for the Palestinians, an inverse relation emerged, indicating that at low levels of exposure to political violence,

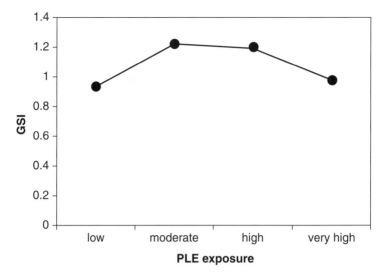

Figure 4.2. Global Severity Index (GSI) means according to Political Life Events (PLE) for Israeli and Palestinian population.

there are relatively high levels of distress. However, increases in severity of exposure, surprisingly, lead to decreases in psychological distress and ultimately very little (if any) expression of psychological distress. These relations are presented in Figure 4.3.

In general, these findings suggest that intervening strategies are used to regulate distress, and in this specific case, these are rooted in the cross-cultural variable. In terms of the cross-cultural difference, these findings raise two pivotal questions. (1) What underlies the counterintuitive decline in reported distress and symptomatology for Palestinian children at high levels of political life events exposure? (2) Why does this not occur among the two samples of Israeli children, including both Arab and Jewish Israelis?

The most likely explanation suggests that different coping strategies are used by the two groups of children. In light of the nature of the Middle East conflict, a possible mediating coping mechanism that explains the outcome for the Palestinian children may be the transformation of experience from passivity to activity. Active efforts to relieve a stressful situation are considered effective coping strategies in providing mastery and control over unpredictable or dangerous environments, frequently resulting in alleviation of perceived distress and enhanced mental health, whereas passive coping strategies are considered ineffective modes that do not ameliorate distress (Billings & Moos, 1981). The Palestinian experience of violence, personal threat, blocked national aspirations, and economic hardships could produce a pathogenic constellation with the potential to culminate in helplessness unless transformed in some way. The potential for adaptation and self-sufficiency lies in the transformation of helplessness into self-help and competence. The confluence of a particular sociocultural requisite situation and the ability to mobilize active participation would add the counterforce of control to an otherwise unpredictable situation.

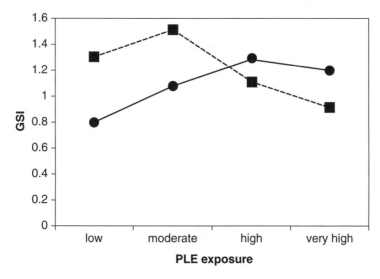

Figure 4.3. Global Severity Index (GSI) means according to Political Life Events (PLE) for Israeli and Palestinian children by nation.

For Palestinians, there may be an unique congruence between traditional cultural and collective modes of response and particular sociohistorical circumstances enabling the transition to active coping modes. The Palestinians perceive the conflict in terms of the need to create an autonomous state out of a situation that could be described as a national void, exacerbated by the experience of living as a conquered nation. To this end, Palestinian national aspirations require the channeling of activity to one clear target. In addition, underlying social frameworks enhance the potential for action-based strategies (Nixon, 1990). Densely populated residential areas and the traditional extended family produce high concentrations of people living in close proximity. In these areas, community structure and cultural and religious norms promote the formation of cohesive groups. When daily routines are disrupted by political events, such as closure of schools or curfews, children tend to gather together and rapidly form into united groups.

This explanation for the surprising finding of an inverse relation between political violence exposure and psychological distress outcomes for the Palestinian children aligns with previous research on their reactions to the conflict. Studies have indicated that traumatic experiences increased risk taking (Punamäki & Suleiman, 1990), and active participation in confrontation produced feelings of increased importance, pride, and self-esteem (Baker, 1990).

These premises raise the second question of the inability of Israeli children to modulate subjective distress. Both Jewish and Arab Israeli children find themselves in different sets of sociopolitical circumstances. The uncertainty of the political environment and the vulnerability of the country to internal and external attack have been reported to produce high levels of anxiety and distress reactions both among adults (Arian, 1996) and children (Klingman, Sagi, & Raviv, 1993). Although public opinion plays a crucial role in the sociopolitical theater, national policy is mediated via official channels, and initiatives are spearheaded at governmental level. In addition, cultural and religious norms encourage discussion and intellectual strategies to deal with social issues.

This generic sociopolitical structure could hamper attempts to attain mastery over the environment. For Israelis and Palestinians, there seems to be a juxtaposition in the locus of control (Rotter, 1975). For the Palestinian children, who have moved from a suppressed position of blocked national aspirations to hope for autonomous existence, the adoption of a personal sense of responsibility for resolving the conflict may have fostered an internal locus of control, which would result in an enhanced sense of empowerment. Circumstances are almost diametrically opposite for Israeli children, who are faced with relatively uncontrollable threats to personal security within the boundaries of the country. These definitions may produce an external locus of control, possibly resulting in feelings of vulnerability and lack of belief in one's own ability for restructuring the situation. Israeli children would be hard pressed to adopt instrumental problem-solving strategies that could impact significantly on the actual situation because attempts to master the environment must be focused through indirect channels.

The set of studies presented here cannot make assumptions regarding the specific dimensions of the cultural variable responsible for differences in psychological outcome, because this variable encompasses social, historical, religious, and political conditions that were not defined in the studies. Complementary qualitative research, such as focus or encounter groups, may be valuable in delineating more precisely the operative dynamics postulated to underlie the findings. Rigorously designed cross-cultural studies may prove fruitful in identifying societal mechanisms that impact adversely on children's mental health, although these are not always possible due to the nature of the appraisal of stress and the sociodemographic conditions of the context under investigation. However, such studies reinforce the thesis that individual and group differences may be attributed to the activation of mediating coping mechanisms that ameliorate distress under stressful circumstances. In this context, psychological coping may be perceived as the factor by which social stress is translated into individual psychological functioning and mental health (Lazarus & Folkman, 1984).

A Framework for Studying Resilience in the Face of Political Violence

The findings of cultural and individual differences in the response to conditions of political violence is consistent with the viewpoint that traumatic events and psychological responses frequently cannot be accommodated within the traditional linear model of cause and effect (Parkes, 1986). Instead, the relation between exposure and outcome is moderated by resilience or vulnerability factors.

The model outlined here that guided the present research offers a methodological conceptualization for the study of resilience factors in the face of exposure to political violence. This conceptualization raises a question concerning the traditional life events linear model and supports its modification to encompass an interactionist model based on a moderated or mediated connection between stressor and adjustment. The interactionist model entails extension of the exposure–psychological distress relation to include study of potential moderating variables according to the following formula:

$$\text{Exposure} \rightarrow \text{Resilience variable} \rightarrow \text{Outcome}$$

In terms of this formula, it would be expected that under conditions of exposure to political violence, individuals who have high levels of resilience would show better adjustment outcomes than those who have low levels of resilience and who would show more negative adjustment outcomes.

Implications

Beyond distress symptoms, much remains to be learned about children's responses to chronic political violence and its ramifications. The research underscores the need for a social ecological perspective that highlights broad contextual information in understanding the range of developmental adjustment difficulties that may result from exposure to political violence.

The significant challenges of the period of adolescence, defined by intrapsychic energy expended predominantly at establishing personal identity from among alternative identities (Erikson, 1963; Marcia, 1994), the quest for self-autonomy and social role consolidation formation, have been well established. However, these developmental difficulties are magnified when they occur within a conflicted social environment. Necessary developmental tasks of rebelliousness as a crucial process in identity consolidation (Marcia, 1994) are facilitated in a stable environment and may be compromised in a chaotic, insecure environment. Normative proactive agency on the environment for self-exploration, identity formation, and social role testing is more possible in stable social conditions.

The finding of a linear relation between political life events and emotional distress indices raises notable methodological, clinical, and political implications. Methodologically, it establishes that chronic exposure to political violence is measurable, releasing researchers from dependence on the unpredictable occurrence of acute traumatic events. The extension of the life events model to the political realm could open vistas of research previously untenable. The PLE scale described here represents an initial step toward expanding this research horizon.

The use of an exposure scale showed that children are affected not only by acute dramatic events but also by cumulative chronic forms of political violence. Reactions are not limited to singular symptoms, such as anxiety or PTSD, but manifest in a variety of symptom profiles. Future research should be directed toward depicting a more cohesive developmental picture by investigating pathogenic sociopolitical conditions on other age groups and for other adjustment outcomes. Additionally, extension of the research model should be directed toward encompassing more insidious types of political life events that characterize oppressed populations, undemocratic practices, restrictions on freedom of expression, and self-determination. Furthermore, self-reporting measures should ideally be corroborated by other measures, such as parent or teacher observations or descriptions of children's behavior. Most important, the adjunct value of qualitative research that captures subjective meanings and experiences cannot be underestimated.

The model laid out here focused on only one of many possible outcome measures of exposure to political violence. Aside from emotional distress and pathology, more subtle indicators of children's difficulties could be informative, such as increased substance abuse, school drop-out rates, academic and social difficulties, and changes in family functioning and needs. Moreover, in line with the thesis of increased resiliency and functioning under conditions of chronic violence, the model should be expanded to target positive outcomes, such as enhanced emotional growth, moral sensibility, hardiness, and maturity.

This series of studies is anchored on one specific conflict at a particular historical juncture, namely, the Israeli–Palestinian conflict. Although attention has been given to measuring the cross-cultural validity of the PLE scale, consideration also needs to be directed toward the ecological environment framing any specific conflict. Outcomes and resilience factors will be culturally influenced, and without a culturally sensitive reassessment of the nature of the political conflict and the relation between exposure and adjustment, generalizability of the model will be restricted.

The findings of the two central studies reported here contribute to the mosaic of evidence on the effects to children of growing up in conflictual and war-torn environments. Even within the narrow perimeters studied in this research, children demonstrate different mental health outcomes under conditions of political violence, with substantial evidence of wide-ranging individual differences. These findings cast a long shadow over the assumption of automatic malfunction outcome and highlight the need to focus on the subtle indicators in a culturally and contextually sensitive way in the quest to understand the complex implications for children who grow up under conditions of political violence and threat. Differential outcomes underscore the importance of formulating therapeutic interventions in an individually and culturally sensitive manner.

Notwithstanding the fluid and tumultuous nature of the sociopolitical environment and the considerable methodological difficulties of research in this domain, the impact of living under prolonged exposure to political violence on children's adjustment should not be overlooked. The multidimensional ramifications of growing up under conditions of protracted violence need to be assessed and reassessed, and adjustment mechanisms and therapeutic interventions must be monitored to disentangle short- and long-term implications for children's mental health.

References

Arian, A. (1996). *Israeli security opinion*. Tel Aviv, Israel: Jaffee Center for Strategic Studies.

Arroyo, W., & Eth, S. (1984). Children traumatized by Central American warfare. In S. Eth & R. Pynoos (Eds.), *Post traumatic stress disorder in children* (pp. 183–195). Washington, DC: American Psychiatric Press.

Ashkenasy, A., Dohrenwend, B. P., & Dohrenwend, B. S. (1977). Some effects of social class and ethnic group membership on judgments of the magnitude of stressful life events: A research note. *Journal of Health & Social Behavior, 18*, 432–439.

Baker, A. (1990). The psychological impact of the Intifada on Palestinian children in the occupied West Bank and Gaza: An exploratory study. *American Journal of Orthopsychiatry, 60*, 496–505.

Barber, B. K. (2001). Political violence, social integration, and youth functioning: Palestinian youth from the Intifada. *Journal of Community Psychology, 29*(3), 259–280.

Billings, A. C., & Moos, R. H. (1981). The role of coping responses and social resources in attenuating the stress of life events. *Journal of Behavioral Medicine, 4,* 139–157.

Bluen, S. D., & Odesnik, J. (1988). Township unrest: Development of the Township Life Events Scale. *South African Journal of Psychology, 18*(2), 50–57.

Cairns, E., & Dawes, A. (1996). Children: Ethnic and political violence—A commentary. *Child Development, 67*(1), 129–139.

Cicchetti, D. & Toth, S. (Eds.). (1992). *Child maltreatment, child development, and social policy.* Norwood, NJ: Ablex.

Coddington, R. D. (1990). *Child psychiatry: A primer for those that work closely with children.* St. Louis: Warren H. Green.

Cohen, L. (Ed.). (1988). *Life events and psychological functioning: Theoretical and methodological issues.* Newbury Park, CA: Sage.

Coles, R. (1987). *The political life of children.* Boston: Houghton Mifflin.

Derogatis, L. R., & Melisaratos, N. (1983). The Brief Symptom Inventory: An introductory report. *Psychological Medicine, 13,* 595–605.

Derogatis, L. R., & Spencer, P. M. (1982). *The Brief Symptom Inventory (BSI): Administration, scoring and procedures manual.* Baltimore, MD: Clinical Psychometric Research.

Erikson, E. H. (1963). *Childhood and society* (2nd ed.). New York: Norton.

Erlich, C., Greenbaum, C., & Toubiana, Y. H. (1994). Exposure to prolonged stress and sex differences in children's responses to the Gulf War. *Psychologia Israel Journal of Psychology, 4,* 123–133.

Eth, S., & Pynoos, R. (1985). Developmental perspective on psychic trauma in childhood. In C. Figley (Ed.), *Trauma and its wake* (vol. 1, pp. 36–52). New York: Brunner/Mazel.

Ferguson, N., & Cairns, E. (1996). Political violence and moral maturity in Northern Ireland. *Political Psychology, 17*(4), 713–725.

Garmezy, N., & Masten, A. S. (1990), The adaptation of children to a stressful world: Mastery of fear. In L. U. Arnold, (Ed.), *Childhood stress* (pp. 459–473). New York: John Wiley & Sons.

Holmes, T. H., & Rahe, R. H. (1967). The social readjustment rating scale. *Journal of Psychosomatic Research, 11,* 213–218.

Johnson, J. H., & Bradlyn, A. S. (1988). Life events and adjustment in childhood and adolescence. In L. H. Cohen (Ed.), *Life events and psychological functioning: Theoretical and methodological issues* (pp. 64–95). Beverly Hills, CA: Sage.

Joseph, S., Cairns, E., & McCollam, P. (1993). Political violence, coping and depressive symptomatology in Northern Irish children. *Personality and Individual Differences, 15,* 471–473.

Klingman, A., Sagi, A., & Raviv, A. (1993). Effects of war on Israeli children. In L. Leavitt & N. A. Fox (Eds.), *Psychological effects of war and violence on children* (pp. 75–92). New York: Erlbaum.

Kretzmer, D. (1990). *The legal status of the Arabs in Israel.* Boulder, CO: Westview Press.

Ladd, G. W., & Cairns, E. (1996). Children: Ethnic and political violence. *Child Development, 67,* 14–18.

Lazarus, R. S., & Folkman, S. (1984). *Stress, appraisal and coping.* New York: Springer Verlag.

Macksoud, M. S., & Aber, J. L. (1996). The war experiences and psychosocial development of children in Lebanon. *Child Development, 67,* 70–88.

Marcia, J. (1994). The empirical study of ego identity. In H. A. Bosma, L. G. Tobi, H. D. Grotevant, & D. J. de Levita (Eds.), *Identity and development: An interdisciplinary approach.* Thousand Oaks, CA: Sage.

Monroe, S. M., & Peterman, A. M. (1988). Life stress and psychopathology. In L. Cohen (Ed.), *Life events and psychological functioning: Theoretical and methodological issues* (pp. 31–63). Newbury Park, CA: Sage.

Nixon, A. (1990). *The status of the Palestinian children during the uprising in the occupied territories.* East Jerusalem: Radda Barnen.

Parkes, K. R. (1986). Coping in stressful episodes. The role of individual differences, environmental factors, and situational characteristics. *Journal of Personality and Social Psychology, 51,* 1277–1292.

Paykel, E. S., Prusoff, B. A., & Uhlenhuth, E. H. (1971). Scaling of life events. *Archives of General Psychiatry, 25,* 340–347.

Pilkonis, P., Imber, S., & Rubinsky, P. (1985). Dimensions of life stress in psychiatric patients. *Journal of Human Stress, 11,* 5–10.

Protacio-Marcelino, E. (1989). Children of political detainees in the Philippines: Sources of stress and coping patterns. *International Journal of Mental Health, 18,* 71–86.

Ptacek, J. T., Smith, R. E., & Zanas, J. (1992). Gender, appraisal and coping: A longitudinal analysis. *Journal of Personality, 60*(4), 747–770.

Punamäki, R. (1989). Factors affecting the mental health of Palestinian children exposed to political violence. *International Journal of Mental Health, 18*(2), 63–79.

Punamäki, R. (1996). Can ideological commitment protect children's psychosocial well-being in situations of political violence? *Child Development, 67,* 55–69.

Punamäki, R., Qouta, S., & El Sarraj, E. (1997). Models of traumatic experiences and children's psychological adjustment. The roles of perceived parenting and the children's own resources and activity. *Child Development, 68,* 708–728.

Punämaki, R., & Suleiman, R. (1990). Predictors and effectiveness of coping with political violence among Palestinian children. *British Journal of Social Psychology, 29*(10), 67–77.

Rotter, J. B. (1975). Some problems and misconceptions related to the construct of internal versus external control of reinforcement. *Journal of Consulting & Clinical Psychology, 48,* 56–57.

Rouhana, N. N., & Fiske, S. T. (1995). Perception of power, threat, and conflict intensity in asymetric intergroup conflict. *Journal of Conflict Resolution, 39*(1), 49–81.

Schwebel, M. (1992). Making a dangerous world more tolerable for children: Implications of research on reactions to nuclear war, threat, war and disaster. In G. Albee, L. Bond, & T. Monsey (Eds.). *Improving children's lives: Global perspectives on prevention.* Newbury Park, CA: Sage.

Shikaki, K. (1996). The peace process, national reconstruction and the transition to democracy in Palestine. *Journal of Palestine Studies, 25,* 5–20.

Slone, M. (1997). *Construction of a political life events scale.* Unpublished manuscript, Tel Aviv University, Israel.

Slone, M., Adiri, M., & Arian, A. (1998). Adverse political events and psychological adjustment: Two cross-cultural studies. *American Academy of Child & Adolescent Psychiatry, 37,* 1058–1069.

Slone, M., & Gil-Ad, S. (2004). *Individual differences in coping with political violence.* Unpublished manuscript, Tel Aviv University, Israel.

Slone, M., & Hallis, D. (1999). The impact of political life events on children's psychological adjustment. *Anxiety, Stress & Coping, 12,* 1–21.

Slone, M., Kaminer, D., & Durrheim, K. (2000). The contribution of political life events to psychological distress among South African adolescents. *Political Psychology, 21*(3), 465–487.

Slone, M., Kaminer, D., & Durrheim, K. (2002). Appraisal of sociopolitical change among South African youth: The relation to psychological maladjustment. *Journal of Applied Social Psychology, 32*(2), 318–341.

Slone, M., Lobel, T., & Gilat, Y. (1999). Dimensions of the political environment affecting children's mental health. *Conflict Resolution, 43*(1), 78–91.

Smith, C. D. (1996). *Palestine and the Arab-Israeli Conflict.* New York: St. Martin's.

Smooha, S. (1992). *Arabs and Jews in mutual intolerance* (vol. 2). San Francisco: Westview Press.

Soliman, H. (1999). Post-traumatic stress disorder: Treatment outcomes for a Kuwaiti child. *International Social Work, 42*(2), 163–175.

Steinmetz, S., & Owens, T. (1992, August 20–24). *"Real-time" war: Adolescents' physical and emotional responses to the Persian gulf war.* Paper presented at the annual meeting of the American Sociological Association, Pittsburgh, PA.

Straker, G. (1993, August). *The moral development among black township youth in South Africa.* Paper presented at the Third International Symposium on the Contribution of Psychology to Peace, Ashland, VA.

Vaux, A. (1985). Variations in social support associated with gender, ethnicity and age. *Journal of Social Issues, 41,* 89–110.

Von-Hippel, C. (1997). The effects of political violence on childhood aggression in Israel. *Dissertation Abstracts International,* 57(12-B), 7746.

Zuckerman, L. A., Oliver, J. M., Hollingsworth, H. H., & Austrin, H. R. (1986). A comparison of life events scoring methods as predictors of psychological symptomatology. *Journal of Human Stress, 12*(2), 64–70.

Chapter 5

Youth Soldiering
An Integrated Framework for Understanding Psychosocial Impact

Michael Wessells and
Kathleen Kostelny

A pervasive characteristic of contemporary political violence is that youth, mostly between the ages of 14 and 18 years, are prominent actors in these hostilities (Cairns, 1996; Wessells, 1998, 2006). Owing in no small part to the widespread availability of lightweight weapons, such as the AK-47 assault rifle, many of these teenagers serve as soldiers in government-sponsored armed forces or in armed opposition groups (Brett & McCallin, 1996; Cohn & Goodwin-Gill, 1994). Consistent with the United Nations Convention on the Rights of the Child (CRC) and other legal instruments, a child soldier may be defined as "any person under 18 years of age who is a member of or attached to the armed forces or an armed group, whether or not there is an armed conflict" (Coalition to Stop the Use of Child Soldiers [CSC], 2002, p. 11). As set forth in the Paris Principles (UNICEF, 2007), such a child need not have taken part in hostilities.

No hard data exist on the prevalence of child soldiering. Current estimates suggest there are approximately 250,000 to 300,000 child soldiers (Machel, 2001), including children as young as 6 or 7 years (Boothby & Knudsen, 2000; CSC, 2004; Wessells, 1997, 2006). Singer (2005) has estimated that children have served as fighters in over two-thirds of recent conflicts. Further, seventy-two different parties to armed conflict have recently used children as soldiers (CSC, 2002). In northern Afghanistan, for example, in the recent war by the United States and the Northern Alliance against the Taliban, nearly all boys between 14 and 18 years in villages along the line of fighting served with their local commander, many of whom continue to carry a gun (Wessells & Kostelny, 2002). In Sri Lanka, teenage girls have served regularly as combatants and suicide bombers for the Liberation Tigers of Tamil Eelam (LTTE), wearing cyanide capsules around their necks to use for suicide if captured by government forces (Keairns, 2002). In countries such as Angola, El Salvador, Ethiopia, Sierra Leone, and Uganda, among others, girls reportedly account for 30% to 40% of child soldiers (Mazurana, McKay, Carlson, & Kasper, 2002).

In Colombia, both government forces and armed opposition groups such as the Revolutionary Armed Forces of Colombia have used large numbers of youth soldiers (CSC, 2002). A similar pattern of recruitment by both government forces and armed opposition groups is evident in African countries such as Angola, Sierra Leone, Sudan, and Uganda (CSC, 2002), though it is mostly the nonstate actors who recruit youth. In Sierra Leone, for example, most youth recruitment was by the opposition group Revolutionary United Front (RUF) and the Civil Defense Force (CDF) that armed to protect their villages against rebel attacks. In addition, youth recruitment is not limited to developing nations—the United States and the United Kingdom, among other countries, regularly recruit people under 18 years of age into government forces. This practice is legal under the Optional Protocol to the CRC so long as youth under 18 years do not participate in combat. Youth soldiering, then, is a global phenomenon.

A profound issue that warrants urgent attention is how soldiering affects youth, who are among the most precious resources of any society. Media images have alternately portrayed youth soldiers as innocent victims or as hardened killers who constitute a "lost generation." Although careful analyses of the impact of child soldiering are needed, researchers face numerous complexities and obstacles. First, child soldiering is not a monolithic category because enormous differences exist in how children entered military activity, their roles and experiences while in the military, and the situations they faced following demobilization. Second, how young people are impacted depends on their experiences, ability to understand these experiences, and perceptions of their motives, choices, and identity. Two youth who have killed a person might be impacted very differently if one viewed the killing as necessary and justified, and the other felt forced to do it. Like adults, youth construct meanings around their life experiences. These meanings, which relate to culture, gender, class, and ethnicity, mediate the impact of life events and influence whether a particular experience creates risk or strengthens resilience. Unfortunately, these dimensions of child soldiering have not been analyzed thoroughly in the extant literature. Third, a tendency exists to impose Western psychological concepts, such as trauma and depression, that are fragmentary, individualized, and not grounded in local culture or in young people's lived experiences and their relations with family, peers, and community.

This chapter contributes to a more holistic understanding of the consequences of youth soldiering, recognizing the diversity within the category of "child soldiers" and using young people's testimonies to show how youth understand their experiences and choices. Having put the definitions of "youth" and "child soldiers" in critical perspective, this chapter analyzes various pathways for a young person's entry into soldiering, recognizing the linkage between how one enters and the impact of soldiering itself. Next, the chapter examines the varied roles and experiences of youth soldiers, connecting these with gender, the choices young people make while associated with an armed group, and their evolving sense of meaning and identity. Then the discussion probes the impact of youth soldiering within a holistic framework that links psychosocial wellbeing with health, cosmology, economics, and social roles and relations. The chapter concludes with reflections on the implications of this holistic conceptualization for social reintegration and peacebuilding. In writing, the authors draw on their own field experience and research, particularly in Afghanistan, Angola, Sierra Leone, and Uganda.

Definitional Issues

The term *youth* is a cultural construct that exhibits enormous variation and defies universalized definitions. In Western psychology, *youth* typically refers to someone between the ages of 13 and 18 years, the period of adolescence in which a key life task is to define one's identity (e.g., Erikson, 1968). In South Africa, however, *youth* refers to someone up to the age of 35 years. In Sierra Leone, people up to age 50 years may be considered youths. Furthermore, in many parts of Sub-Saharan Africa, particularly in rural areas where traditions run strong, people are considered adults once they have completed a cultural rite of passage or have married, typically in the age range of 13 to 15 years.

For these reasons, it is best to avoid reification of Western definitions of youth. One should also recognize that in every culture the authors have worked in, young people between the ages of 13 and 20 years are viewed as being in transition into the adult world, making key life choices, and defining their role and position in society. Typically, elders in these societies regard these young people as still being in need of mentoring and guidance. These aspects of social function are also characteristic of adolescents in Western societies. In these contexts, this chapter will refer to 13- to 20-year-olds as "youth," recognizing that locally they may be regarded more as young people or young adults.

The term *youth soldier* also needs to be problematized. This label can stigmatize people, invite attempts to rerecruit them, or increase risks that they will be attacked by people who remember what they had done. Keen ethical awareness is required in the use of such terms. In addition, *youth soldiers* sounds monolithic, when in fact, the phrase masks enormous differences in life experiences and roles. The term tends to be imposed in ways that young people themselves see as inappropriate or offensive. For example, a young girl who is abducted and forced to be a sex slave but who never engages in combat or adopts a military identity may see herself not as a youth soldier but as a person who has been captured and robbed of her civilian life and freedom. Being ashamed of her situation and fearing rejection on her return home, she might resist being labeled a youth soldier. In contrast, a 15-year-old boy who joined an armed group out of ideological fervor, serves as a commander, and experienced repeated firefights might relish being called a soldier. Recognizing this complexity, this chapter unpacks some of the diversity within the category of youth soldiers. This analysis begins with an examination of different modes of entry into military activity.

Entry into Military Activity

Broadly, youth enter into activity with armed groups or armed forces in three ways: forcible, voluntary, and compulsory recruitment (UNICEF, 2007). Forcible recruitment occurs when people are coerced through force or threat of force by illegal means, such as abduction at gunpoint. Voluntary recruitment occurs when people join without obvious force or state conscription. Compulsory recruitment is guided by national legislation and entails legal conscription into the government military. In reality, the lines between these categories are blurry. Life pressures and hardships can make it very difficult to distinguish between forced and voluntary recruitment (Brett & Specht, 2004; Wessells, 2006). A youth who joins an opposition group because he has no means of obtaining food or health care may appear to make a voluntary decision but in fact may have no other options for ensuring survival. Similarly, compulsory recruitment, which is presumably legal, often occurs illegally in African countries. Because few accurate birth records exist, it may be impossible to determine youths' actual age. Furthermore, troop-hungry commanders are often willing to overlook age and may recruit anyone who appears sufficiently large to carry a load or handle a weapon.

Aside from the logic of these categories, what matters most is how youth themselves perceive and understand their recruitment. Youth form cognitive schemata that frame their entry, define their position vis-à-vis the military force or armed group, influence their self-perceptions and identity, and activate a set of attributions regarding their own behavior. Perhaps the broadest schema is that of voluntary versus forced recruitment. For example, a youth recruited at gunpoint off the streets and forced to fight using a weapon may not identify himself as a military man and may attribute most of his fighting to avoidance of punishment and the necessity of obeying commanders to stay alive. In contrast, a youth who joins a liberation struggle without explicit coercion may see himself as a freedom fighter, perceive fighting as voluntary, and find meaning in aggressive behavior and commitment to a higher cause. In this sense, the youths' self-perceptions may be more important than the labels applied by adults and outsiders. With this in mind, various forms of forcible and voluntary recruitment are examined next, as told through the youths' own voices and perspectives.

Forced Recruitment

Few hard data are available regionally and globally on the percentage of youth recruits who enter the military by force. Across and even within countries, significant variety exists, reflecting the particular recruitment strategies used by government, paramilitary, and opposition groups as well as whether the local population views the fighting as worthwhile or necessary. Nevertheless, available evidence suggests that forced recruitment is widespread and that the majority of forced recruitment occurs through nonstate actors (Brett & McCallin, 1996; UNICEF, 2003; Wessells, 2002, 2006).

Abduction is one of the primary means of forced recruitment, as illustrated by the following testimonies.

> *A 13-year-old Ugandan boy:* Early on when my brothers and I were captured, the LRA explained to us that all five brothers couldn't serve in the LRA because we would not perform well. So they tied up my two younger brothers and invited us to watch. Then they beat them with sticks until two of them died. They told us it would give us strength to fight. My youngest brother was nine years old. (Human Rights Watch, 2003, p. 2)
>
> *A 19-year-old girl from Sierra Leone who had been abducted at age 16:* I was captured in Kono where I was with my aunt. Initially I escaped to the bush, but the RUF captured me and offered two options—kill or be taken. (Interview with M. Wessells, August 13, 2002)

An East Timorese boy who was forced to join an Indonesian militia at age 14: The militia first came to my village in early January. . . . They beat many people and killed some. They told us that if we did not join them we would die. When the militia came, my parents were very afraid and said to me, "If the militia ask you to do anything, just do it or they will kill us." The first time they took me from my house, we had to rape a woman and then kill anything we could find, like animals and people. They ordered us to rape. We did this together. . . . Everyday they came to get us and if we didn't want to go, they would threaten us with machetes. They beat me with a piece of wood everyday. (UNICEF, 2003, p. 17)

As these quotes indicate, the abduction experience is typically saturated with violence and fear of death, beginning a journey of forced servitude in which captors use terror to control their abductees.

Often, however, abduction occurs in more subtle, indirect ways that straddle the boundary with voluntary recruitment. In northern Afghanistan, for example, where Tajik and Uzbek peoples were eager to expel the Taliban, each village has a commander who mobilizes local people for fighting. This commander system, itself a vestige of the Afghan opposition to the Soviet invasion of the 1980s, creates strong pressures to go with the commander, who wields great power and controls access to food and basic services. Speaking of the fighting that occurred following September 11, 2001, a 15-year-old Afghan boy said, "The commander came to my house and told me to come with him. . . . If I had not gone with him, I would have been beaten or bad things could have happened to my family" (interview with M. Wessells, February 17, 2002). Many Tajik and Uzbek youth expressed mixed motives, saying they had gone with their commander because it had been their duty to protect their village and also because they feared the consequences of not going.

Abductions also occur through proxy (Brett & McCallin, 1996). In Angola, the opposition group National Union for the Total Independence of Angola (UNITA) used a quota system in which they told local village leaders to provide ten youth recruits or else the entire village would be destroyed (Wessells, 2002). Psychologically, this system highlighted local leaders' inability to protect the village, thereby weakening their prestige and ability to mobilize local resistance to UNITA. Similarly, in Taliban-controlled villages in northern Afghanistan, the Taliban required that the village turn over a quota of youths for military service, typically for a rotating tour of several months. The local selection process favored the wealthy, whose families sometimes protected their own sons by paying poorer families to send their sons instead (Wessells & Kostelny, 2002).

The disproportionate burden of youth soldiering on the poor is also visible in press ganging, a widely practiced form of group abduction and forced recruitment. In this method, groups of soldiers or militia arrive at a school, a marketplace, or any place where groups of youth congregate and take them away by force. In Myanmar, one youth described the process as follows: "We were leaving school at the end of the day and the . . . soldiers surrounded the school. . . . There were 30 or 50 of us all leaving together, and we were all arrested. We were all 15-, 16-, 17-years-old and we were all afraid of the soldiers. . . . Our teachers ran away in fear. Everything was in chaos . . . We were all terrified" (Brett & McCallin, 1996, pp. 84–85). Worldwide, armed groups often recruit by conducting round-ups in poor neighborhoods that may be less able to resist. Street children and separated children, including many orphans, are often favorite target groups because they lack adult protection.

Nonforced Recruitment

Even without explicit coercion, youth join military forces and armed groups for diverse reasons, one of the most important of which is ideology. In highly oppressive, conflict-torn societies, youth may learn to define themselves in part by opposition to the enemy. They may find meaning through participation in a liberation struggle, using violence as their means of achieving liberation (Garbarino, Kostelny, & Dubrow, 1991; Punamäki, 1996; Straker, 1992; Wessells, 2006). Within communities seeking liberation, adults typically use propaganda to politicize youth and make them willing to sacrifice for the cause. In Sierra Leone, a 17-year-old youth said, "When the RUF soldiers came, they took us . . . They taught us about social injustice and the need for armed struggle. I believed them—maybe I was brainwashed—but I believed them" (interview with M. Wessells, August 12, 2002). Many youth are attracted by ideologies that romanticize the struggle and portray martyrdom as the highest achievement. In Sri Lanka, girls who sacrificed their lives in battle or who took significant risks in battle were regarded as heroes and often received a "hero's welcome" back home (Keairns, 2002).

Extremist forms of religion play an increasingly prominent role in warrior ideologies, as is evident in militant forms of Islam. Radical ideologies that call people to engage in jihad have strong appeal to youth who are frustrated with the current situation, feel little hope for nonviolent change, and find meaning and identity in religious purification and struggle. In Pakistan, Afghan refugee youth received instruction in religious schools, known as *madrassahs*, that taught extremist forms of Islam and hatred toward Western countries. Thousands returned to Afghanistan to join the Taliban out of the belief that they were fighting a jihad and had a solemn obligation to expel the infidels (Rashid, 2000). Extreme religious ideologies often create strong, clear beliefs that the fighting is moral, divinely sanctioned, and an obligation to a higher power. In Afghanistan, as in other war contexts (such as Palestine), youths who sacrificed their lives were portrayed as martyrs; their stories often became part of communal memories and legends that invite more youth into the struggle.

Ideology, however, is only one of many factors that can lead youth to join armed groups. Young people may also join for reasons such as power, prestige, excitement, money, revenge, family or peer pressures, or escape from bad family or marriage situations. This diversity of reasons is best revealed through their own voices.

A 20-year-old boy from Myanmar who had joined at age 14: I left home in 1992 and traveled to the border, to a school in a Karenni village, with about 10 friends. I just wanted to be a soldier. I was attracted by the Karenni soldiers when I saw them in the village. I think soldiers are very beautiful. It makes me want to join the army. (UNICEF, 2003, p. 29)

A 25-year-old man from Sierra Leone who at age 15 had joined the CDF that fought the RUF: The RUF killed my father and also my mother. I had no way of getting anything— I joined the CDF to get food and water. (Interview with M. Wessells, August 10, 2002)

A 15-year-old from Philippines who had joined at age 7: I joined the movement to avenge my father's death in the hands of the military. When I was seven years old, I saw the military take away my defenseless father from our house . . . so I joined my grandfather who went to the mountains to join the movement. (UNICEF, 2003, p. 28)

   A girl soldier from Colombia: One of my mother's men tried to abuse me when I was younger. He tried to abuse me and because I didn't let him he got angry. He used to fight with my mum and he used to fight with me . . . so I didn't want to live with my mum anymore. (Keairns, 2002, p. 17)

   A 25-year-old young man from Papua New Guinea who had joined when he was 17: Realistically, if the enemy is approaching and destroying your community, how can you stand back? . . . Sometimes people were exploiting us . . . I want to save my island and my people . . . I have five brothers. Four joined the fighting, three joined before me. I want to defend my island and my people. My parents supported me. They know it's the right thing. (UNICEF, 2003, p. 26)

Two points stand clear in these and many other youth testimonies. First, youths' decisions to join are often bounded by victimization, difficult life conditions such as poverty, and desire to protect oneself and meet basic needs. It is in this respect that discussions of voluntary recruitment need to be contextualized. Second, youths' decisions are often influenced by important social ecologies, such as peers, families, and communities. For instance, in collectivist societies that place group welfare over that of the individual, it is particularly misleading to understand choice in the same individualized manner used in Western societies.

Roles and Experiences

Mapping the roles of youth soldiers is fraught with difficulty due to the enormous variety that exists in being a soldier and the fact that role multiplicity and change are the norm. Young women and men who become soldiers have diverse experiences that may vary according to the context, the norms of the armed group, and the culture, among others.

   To illustrate, enormous variety exists in regard to the sexual exploitation of young women and men (Mazurana et al., 2002; Wessells, 2006). In northern Sierra Leone and northern Uganda, many young girls who had been abducted by the RUF and the Lord's Resistance Army, respectively, were raped by their captors and served as "soldier's wives," a euphemism for the sex slavery that occurs (Wessells, 2002). In Angola, UNITA forced girls to dance and sing all night and respond to sexual demands (Keairns, 2002), presumably to entertain the men but in reality to maintain excitement and distract youth from thinking about home. In contrast, girl soldiers in armed groups such as the LTTE of Sri Lanka have not been abused sexually as part of their military experience, and some armed groups expressly forbid sexual exploitation (Keairns, 2002). Similarly, although sexual exploitation of girl soldiers has been reported more widely than the sexual exploitation of boy soldiers, the latter does occur (Thompson, 1999). In northern Afghanistan, where the soldiers were male, hospital physicians reported that it was not uncommon for an older, stronger soldier to sexually violate a new recruit, such as a smaller, weaker 14-year-old (Wessells & Kostelny, 2002). Unfortunately, such episodes are associated with strong taboos and stigmas and hence are underreported. As a result, little is known about the prevalence of the sexual exploitation of boy soldiers.

The variety of youth soldiers' experience is also evident in regard to drug use. In Sierra Leone, the RUF plied youth soldiers with drugs such as alcohol and amphetamines to prepare them for battle. A 16-year-old soldier reported, "When I went into battle, I felt no fear and no pain—I was so high . . . but NO FEAR!" (interview with M. Wessells, August 12, 2002). In contrast, youth soldiers in Afghanistan, a country that has massive opium production, did not report use of drugs, which would have violated their fervent Islamic beliefs.

Despite the enormous variety that exists in youth soldiers' roles and experiences, some generalizations are possible. Youth soldiers, girls as well as boys, perform multiple roles, such as combatants, cooks, porters, spies, bodyguards, and mine clearers. Within these roles, most youth soldiers experience attacks, witness killings, see dead bodies, and fear for their lives. Of those who are combatants, significant percentages report that they have fired their weapons at other people in battle, and many can recall having killed someone. No accurate statistics exist, however, regarding the frequency with which youth soldiers participate in combat or wound or kill people.

Often, roles evolve in accordance with youth soldiers' experience, level of competence, and trust of their commanders and peers. In Sri Lanka, for example, girl recruits initially receive a wooden dummy gun; they receive a real gun, an event viewed as a significant accomplishment, when they demonstrate comfort with the dummy gun and the desire to handle a rifle (Keairns, 2002). Similarly, youth soldiers who demonstrate valor or efficacy in combat may be rewarded by being made commanders. The armed groups that exploit youth as soldiers understand well the power of reinforcement and peer recognition and respect, and they use this to draw young people into increasing military responsibilities. These evolving roles reposition youth within their group and can change their perceptions regarding their identity. One 15-year-old youth in northern Uganda reported, "I was proud to be a commander, and my fighters looked up to me. I had never thought of myself as a military man, but that's what I became" (interview with M. Wessells, July 28, 1998).

Terror and Progressive Engagement in Violence

For many youth soldiers, extreme violence is a pervasive part of the soldiering experience. In contrast to the reward strategy described, many armed groups that abduct children ensure obedience and control by inflicting terror, pain, and fear, mixing these with indoctrination (Boothby & Knudsen, 2000; Cohn et al., 1994; Wessells, 2006). In many cases, the terror is linked with horribly brutal systems of training (Brett & McCallin, 1996). In Honduras, for example, commanders forced nearly naked youth recruits to roll on stony or thorny surfaces that stripped flesh off. In Paraguay, youth recruits suffered brutal initiation rites that included excessive exercise, hitting with sticks and rifle butts, burning with cigarettes, and being kicked in the legs or stomach. In such contexts, violence becomes normalized, thereby blunting one's emotional responsiveness to and questioning of it. To further the normalization process, some armed groups have forced youth recruits to engage in sadistic practices, such as cutting animals' throats and drinking their blood (Brett & McCallin, 1996).

In Sierra Leone, the terror had a strong gender component. When the RUF attacked a village, they frequently abducted and raped girls and women. Some were raped in open view of family and village members, apparently with the intent of defiling the girls, making them unacceptable to the community (Human Rights Watch, 1998). Abducted youth have also been forced to commit acts of violence and killing. In Sierra Leone, some youths who had been abducted by the RUF spoke of having been forced to commit atrocities, such as killing a neighbor or even a family member at the time of abduction as other village members watched. Apparently, this horrendous practice was calculated to break the bonds between the youth and his village, leaving no option to go home and thus sealing his fate as an RUF soldier.

Forced participation in killing, however, is often done in a manner calculated to reduce the moral qualms people usually have in regard to killing. One strategy is to force many young people to beat someone, thereby creating tacit peer pressure, diffusing responsibility, and making it nearly impossible to determine who actually killed the victim. A 15-year-old girl from northern Uganda reported:

> They came to our school in the middle of the night. We were hiding under the beds but they banged on the beds and told us to come out. . . . We waked and walked and they made us carry their property that they had looted. . . . On the third day a little girl tried to escape and they made us kill her. They went to collect some big pieces of firewood. Then they kicked her and jumped on her, and they made us each beat her at least once with the big pieces of wood. They said, "You must beat and beat and beat her." She was bleeding from the mouth. Then she died. (Human Rights Watch, 1997)

In many cases, youth soldiers are increasingly exposed to violence and killing to prepare them for their own participation. In northern Uganda, youth were initially forced to carry heavy loads with little food or water, and they watched as children who were too weak to continue were killed. Taken across the border into Sudan for military training, they were subjected to a brutal training regime in which the slightest mistake could result in a beating. When an abductee tried to escape, everyone had to beat the escapee. Subsequent escape attempts could bring orders for everyone to bayonet the escapee. This method, which gets youth to take small steps along a continuum of violence, desensitizes or numbs the youth to killing and reduces moral qualms about doing so. It also increases the likelihood that smaller steps, such as beating someone, will increase one's willingness to take larger steps, such as killing someone. Broadly, the principle is that normal people can be lead step by step to do horrendous things through progressive participation in violence (Staub, 2002; Waller, 2002).

Choices

The forcible recruitment, brutal treatment, and brainwashing of youth soldiers, coupled with the emphasis on compliance with orders of all armed groups, creates strong pressures for youth to obey. Some media images have portrayed youth soldiers as hapless victims who become mindless killers, "damaged goods" who are beyond rehabilitation. These simplistic portrayals fail to recognize that even when youths have been recruited forcibly, they are not passive victims who obey without question but agents who make choices and try to define their roles and pathways. Their choices may reflect long-standing values and help them resist complete identification with their captors and full integration into a system of violence. A young man from Sierra Leone whom the RUF had abducted at age 16 said:

> They [the RUF] captured me on my father's farm and took me away. I was forced to leave this area. They gave me a gun and forced me to go and loot. Also I was forced to carry all the loot, and if I refused [I] would be flogged or shot. We had food only sometimes. . . . The leader told us to beat women and saw it [watched us] with his eyes. Also the leader told us to have sex with women older than your mother. I told him "no" and was flogged and made to do hard work. (Interview with M. Wessells, August 11, 2002)

In a similar vein, a young woman who had been captured by the RUF at age 14 resisted sexual service to her captor, even though she knew her survival might depend on it. She said, "I told him I was too young. . . . He told the other soldiers, and they took me to Freetown. There, they cut off my left arm" (interview with M. Wessells, August 10, 2002). As these cases indicate, a largely untold story is of how youth soldiers make choices that do not compromise their values. Not infrequently, considerable emotional pain and ambivalence attends the choices they make. Not surprisingly, the young girl who had lost her arm reported that her life was very hard with only one arm and that if she had it to do again, she might have chosen differently.

A related point is that youth soldiers may actively define their own roles, with some managing to construct roles related to protection and caregiving. In Sierra Leone, one young woman reported that the RUF had abducted twenty-eight women, twenty-four of whom had been killed outright. Although they had also shot at her, the bullet had not entered her body. About to be bayoneted, a soldier nicknamed Rambo saved her. She decided she did not want to be a fighter and began looking after the children. The women in the company elected her the "mommy queen," the leader of the women and the caretaker who looked after women and girls. She proudly reported that 130 children had been in her care when the ceasefire had been achieved, and she had helped reunite them with their families. Although her choices may have depended partly on good fortune and circumstances, one should recognize that youths' agency may enable them to influence the nature of their roles and, correspondingly, the kinds of experiences they are likely to have.

Of course, youths' agency can be a double-edged sword, as some may choose to become assassins, executioners, or worse. In northern Sierra Leone, people in one village told of a youth soldier who, apparently without orders, had elected to terrorize local people and earn a reputation as a "bad man" by carving "RUF" into people's chests using a razor blade. Recognizing the bounded nature of decision making by youth soldiers, an important task for future research is to chart what factors lead youth to choose pathways leading toward increased violence or peace, respectively.

Psychosocial Impact: A Holistic Approach

To conceptualize the impacts of youth soldiering adequately, one must take a holistic approach that is temporally extended and grounded in local culture and the understandings of youth themselves (Wessells, 2006). A holistic conceptualization has numerous distinctive features. First, it integrates various dimensions of youth well-being—physical, emotional, cognitive, social, and spiritual—that are often considered separately in both theory and field practice. It recognizes that the psychosocial impact of soldiering cannot be reduced to individualized, clinical syndromes such as post-traumatic stress disorder (PTSD), depression, or anxiety (Bracken & Petty, 1998; Wessells, 2006). As will be outlined, youth soldiers' emotional well-being is inextricably linked with social, economic, physical, and spiritual well-being (Boothby, Crawford, & Halperin, 2006). Second, because it is culturally grounded, it reflects local understandings and reduces the tendency to impose outsider categories that fit neither the local culture nor youths' own perspectives. For example, Western clinical psychologists tend to focus on the impacts of violence, whereas youth soldiers may focus on other elements, such as inability to earn an income, fear of rejection by their community, or possible stigmatization as being unsuitable for marriage. Third, a holistic approach looks beyond a deficits focus that depicts only the negative impact of youth soldiering and portrays youth themselves as victims or as damaged individuals. In fact, youth themselves sometimes see soldiering as providing access to opportunities for training, leadership, and commitment to a meaningful cause that they might not have through other venues (e.g., Brett & Specht, 2004; Keairns, 2002; Peters & Richards, 1998). Fourth, because it is temporally extended, a holistic approach recognizes that the impact of youths' soldiering experiences do not stop when they have been demobilized but resonate in what happens afterward. Youth often report that the return to their village was as stressful as their experiences in the armed group had been.

To achieve a holistic conceptualization, it is necessary to analyze the main dimensions of impact while also noting their interrelationships.

Physical Impacts

The most visible physical impacts of youth soldiering are the death and physical injuries that occur in connection with shelling and firefights. The damage may be worse for children and youth who are forced to make frontal assaults or led into suicide bombing (Brett & McCallin, 1996). Landmines, which are widely used in armed conflicts, kill or maim significant numbers of youth soldiers. Many mine-affected youth become amputees and face disfigurement, stigmatization, social isolation, difficulty marrying, and reduced ability to earn a living in an environment already devastated by poverty. A 15-year-old Afghan soldier who lost his leg the previous week reported, "It was a trail I had walked many times. But this time, I hit a mine. Now I have no way of earning a living . . . What will I do?" (interview with M. Wessells, March 12, 2002). Even following release from an armed group, young soldiers continue to be at risk because they often have to travel on foot back to their village across both familiar and unfamiliar terrain that has been mined.

In addition to these visible physical impacts of wounding, youth report that the less visible physical ailments are the worst. In fact, many describe persistent hunger as the worst physical aspect of their soldiering experience. Furthermore, sexually transmitted infections, such as gonorrhea, syphilis, and HIV/AIDS, typically exact a heavy toll on youth soldiers, many of whom travel to different areas and engage in unprotected sex with numerous people, often through force. Health workers in Sierra Leone estimated a 70% to 90% prevalence rate for sexually transmitted infections among rape survivors (Mazurana et al., 2002). Conflict often helps HIV/AIDS spread due to the higher rates of sexually transmitted infections typical in armed forces. The resulting spread of HIV/AIDS, which occurs most rapidly among people between the ages of 10 and 24 years, leads to the birth of children who carry the disease or acquire it through breastfeeding from an HIV-positive mother (Machel, 2001). Because armed conflict devastates health infrastructure, few of these children or their young parents have access to proper health care. People who are HIV-positive often experience profound emotional and social trauma, such as stigmatization, shame, and hopelessness.

The physical impacts of soldiering are highly gendered (Mazurana et al., 2002). Young women who have been forced to engage in sex may sustain abdominal pain, bleeding, cervical tearing, and infection. Repeated rapes may lead to death, uteral deformation, menstrual complications, and premature births. These dramatic effects often mask quieter, daily affronts, such as the embarrassment and psychological anguish girls experience in military settings when trying to maintain personal hygiene in a context that affords no privacy. Birthing, too, is a risky process for young women in armed groups. In addition to the lack of health resources needed to handle complications, some armed groups use dangerous practices designed to force or delay birth according to the group's military needs. In Sierra Leone, RUF members reportedly jumped on the abdomens of girls in labor to force birth or, if the group needed to move, tied the girl's legs together to delay birth (Mazurana et al., 2002). Because of unwanted pregnancies, pregnant girl soldiers may induce abortions themselves, a practice that carries high risk of maternal death.

Emotional Impacts

Youth soldiers, like other war-affected children, may experience a complex constellation of emotional effects such as trauma, depression, and anxiety (Apfel & Simon, 1996; Danieli, Rodley, & Weisaeth, 1996). It is important to note, however, that how youth respond to traumatic experiences depends on temperament, whether they had preexisting problems, what kinds of emotional support they had while soldiering, and how they interpreted their experiences. Youth who believe they are fighting for a cause and see the violence as meaningful suffer less negative impacts than do those who experience random, meaningless violence (Punamäki, 1996; Straker, Mendelsohn, Moosa, & Tudin, 1996). In fact, research has shown that many youth soldiers exhibit remarkable resilience to the stressors of conflict (Cairns, 1996; Straker, 1992). This fact cautions against the simplistic depiction of traumatized soldiers that often accompanies discussion of youth soldiers. In addition, diagnostic categories such as PTSD (see Marsella, Friedman, Gerrity, & Scurfield, 1996) do not adequately reflect the reality that youth soldiers experience multiple, chronic stresses, such as separation from family, loss of home, death of loved ones, abduction, witnessing people being killed, and fighting and killing.

Most important, Western diagnostics may fail to capture what is most troubling to young soldiers themselves. In Sierra Leone, a 17-year-old former RUF soldier said, "When I came back [from the bush], my biggest feeling was fear. . . . I was so afraid . . . afraid someone might recognize me and remember what I had done, maybe try to kill me. People called me 'rebel' and I constantly feared rejection" (interview with M. Wessells, August 15, 2002). Similarly, youths' reactions to war experiences are mediated by cultural beliefs, including spiritual beliefs, which have no counterpart in Western psychology. In northern Sierra Leone, a 14-year-old girl soldier reported that her rape had made her impure and had given her a "heavy heart," meaning that she experienced great sadness. When asked what she needed, she replied "cleansing" by a traditional healer, whose cleansing ritual was believed to be capable of removing her spiritual impurity (interview with M. Wessells, August 13, 2002). As this example illustrates, the impact of rape is culturally constructed. The implications of rape and the emotional burdens it imposes differ according to whether the society understands rape as the girl's failure or as a dishonor to her family and community. Thus, emotional impacts can be understood only in social and cultural context.

Culture also must be taken into account in understanding problems such as nightmares, which potentially are symptomatic of PTSD. In Angola, for example, a former youth soldier complained that he could not sleep and felt too sad and worried to engage in his usual social activities. Asked why he did not sleep, he replied, "The man I shot . . . his spirit comes to me and asks 'why did you do this to me?'" In rural Angola, as in much of Sub-Saharan Africa, people believe that the visible world is intimately connected with the realm of the ancestors. An act such as killing someone is understood as destroying the harmony between the living community and the ancestors. According to local beliefs, the boy soldier is spiritually contaminated—haunted—by the unavenged spirit of the man he killed (Wessells & Monteiro, 2001). In contrast to Western psychology, which tends to view such issues as guilt and trauma as individual, rural Angolans understand the problem as collective. In particular, the boy's spiritual contamination is viewed as potentially causing bad things, such as poor health, misfortune, drought, and fighting to happen not only for the boy but also for his family and the wider community. Although such beliefs may appear superstitious to outsiders, they are very real to local people whose behavior they influence. That the emotional impacts are culturally constructed should make researchers eager to start by asking how local youth understand their experiences. Unfortunately, relatively few researchers have done so.

In contrast to images of hardened killers, youth soldiers often experience guilt and moral anguish, and many exhibit quite sophisticated moral reasoning (Straker, 1992). In some cases, youth soldiers who joined an armed group to support a movement feel guilty about being separated from their families and not being able to support them while they were away (Keairns, 2002). Often, the guilt relates to specific actions, including coerced actions. Boy soldiers from numerous countries have said that they killed to stay alive and to avoid being killed by their commanders, yet they nevertheless felt badly about having killed people. Interestingly, guilt sometimes emerges over time, becoming more prominent after the youth have reentered civilian life. It is as if they had used different moral frames while soldiering and afterward; the full weight of what they had done had become apparent only when they returned to an environment that prized life and in which violence was not normalized.

The adoption of military identity is among the most powerful psychological impacts of youth soldiering. These identity shifts change values, increase aggressive behavior, and may position young people to continue cycles of violence. As already discussed, armed groups use training regimens, prolonged brutality, reward structures, and propaganda calculated to remake youth as soldiers. That they may succeed is evident in the report of a 15-year-old boy from Mozambique who had been with the Mozambican National Resistance. "I was reborn in that base camp. Even if I could escape, I never could have gone home again. Not after what I had seen and done" (Boothby & Knudsen, 2000, p. 64). In Sierra Leone, the RUF assigned youth military names such as "Rambo" or "Cock and Fire," thereby cementing their military identity and inviting peer pressures to encourage "bad" behavior. Experience in many countries indicates that youth who take on a military identity are at risk of increased aggressive behavior. After the war has ended and demobilization has occurred, they may turn to banditry, using violence as a means of meeting basic needs and achieving a sense of personal power. Some evidence suggests that the amount of time a young person had spent with a group such as the Mozambican National Resistanceor the RUF determines whether they retain a military identity or transition back to a civilian identity (Boothby & Knudsen, 2000). Additional research is needed to ascertain the key turning points that lead to shifts toward military identity and what enables or blocks subsequent shifts back toward civilian identity.

The reification of identity should be avoided in discussions of youth soldiers. Popular writers in particular have tended to view youths' military identities as immutable, thereby creating a warrant for viewing the youth as damaged goods. A core principle of social psychology, however, is that situations exercise enormous influence on self-perceptions and behavior. In countries such as Guatemala, South Africa, Angola, Uganda, and Sierra Leone, many youth soldiers describe themselves as tough, determined freedom fighters with strong military identities. With appropriate changes in the situation, these individuals managed over a period of years to reconstruct a civilian identity and integrate back into civilian life. Careful longitudinal research is needed, however, to determine systematically the long-term identities and prospects of former youth soldiers.

Social Impacts

The impact of youth soldiering is best viewed from an ecological perspective that emphasizes the influence of diverse social ecologies, such as the family, the peer group, and the community (Dawes & Donald, 2000; Kostelny, 2006). Primary among the social impacts is separation from families, which puts youth at increased risk of such problems as abduction, sexual exploitation, and poverty (Machel, 2001; McCallin, 1998). Nearly universally, youth soldiers report that their family separation is very painful, a feeling that is amplified if their parents had been killed when the youth had been abducted.

Soldiering can also rupture relations between youth and their communities, whose adult members and leaders often regard them as troublemakers and fear them. Remembering bad things the youths had done, adults may be reluctant to allow them to reenter the community. In most cases, reentry occurs, but problems may continue. Isolation within the community may occur as youth themselves withdraw from normal activities, such as schooling. A 15-year-old former soldier from northern Uganda said, "I have been a commander and made many life and death decisions . . . How can I go back to school with children much younger than me and take orders from a teacher who has never faced death or been a commander?" (interview with M. Wessells, July 28, 1998). Peers may isolate the youth by keeping them at a distance or stigmatizing them by calling them names, such as "rebel." The sense of rejection and social isolation typically weighs heavily on youth and alters their perceptions regarding the future.

Exacerbating the weight of these problems is the lack of positive skills and their social role in the community. Having been with an armed group for years, in some cases a decade or more, many youth soldiers have little education and no job skills to use in earning a living. As a result, they may be viewed (and may view themselves) as a burden to others and as having little to offer the community. Having no positive role, youths' self-esteem and hope for the future typically plummets.

In many societies, the social effects of child soldiering have strong gender elements. Often, girls who have been soldiers are regarded as unsuitable for marriage. This sentiment is typically stronger in regard to a young girl who has been raped. If the girls' prospects for marriage are very low and marriage is a powerful cultural norm, girls who have left the armed group may not stay with their families and may see prostitution as the only means of earning a living (Brett & McCallin, 1996). Girl soldiers' situations may be even more difficult if they bore children as a result of their experiences. On return home, the children may be stigmatized as "rebel babies," and difficult questions arise regarding the girls' marital status. In Sierra Leone, some former youth soldiers who are also mothers regard their former captors as their husbands, although their parents may object. No matter how the children and girls are viewed, they face significant economic obstacles in meeting basic needs.

Economic Impacts

Closely intertwined with the social impacts are the economic impacts of youth soldiering. Although poverty has been identified as a cause for the inclusion of many youth into armed groups, becoming a soldier does little to mitigate these economic hardships. In fact, participation in an armed group often results in augmenting poverty by reducing social status and compromising the chance for success in civilian life. Particularly for youth who had been abducted and had seen their parents killed and their homes destroyed, soldiering marks the beginning of a downward descent into abject poverty. Poverty often continues while in the armed group, making it difficult to meet needs for such basic items as food. In addition, soldiering imposes significant opportunity costs because youth receive no education or job skills, making it difficult for them to earn enough money to obtain shelter, health care, and other necessities.

Following demobilization, youth often return to their communities with few belongings and feeling ashamed of their situation. In Sierra Leone, a 22-year-old whom the RUF had abducted at age 17 said, "When I came out, I had nothing, NOTHING! I was very, very hungry. . . . [I had] no clothes, not even a pair of shoes. I was too embarrassed to let anyone see me" (interview with M. Wessells, August 12, 2002). This young man's pain was grounded in the local reality that the poorest village members, particularly those who cannot even afford a pair of shoes or a shirt, have the lowest status and are stigmatized. In turn, low status and extreme poverty compromise one's marriage opportunities, which itself is very troubling in a context where being unmarried is isolating and may evoke ostracism. In some contexts, the combination of economic need, isolation, and shame leads young people to return to the bush or to take up the gun again. In northern Afghanistan following the Taliban's defeat, large numbers of youth continue to carry a gun, presumably as part of security forces but in fact under the control of their commanders. Nearly all of them report that they have stayed with their commander and carry a gun because they have no job or means of supporting themselves (Wessells & Kostelny, 2002).

To address this kind of problem, many countries have created disarmament, demobilization, and reintegration (DDR) programs that provide former soldiers with a small monetary dispensation and a kit containing such items as seeds and tools. Receipt of these kits and dispensation, however, may create additional social problems (Wessells, 2006). Returning youth soldiers may be stigmatized for having received benefits that are not available to other youth who were not soldiers but who are equally needy. In Sierra Leone, perceptions of favoritism led embittered noncombatant youth to ask, "Why should those who destroyed our communities be rewarded while we suffer?" (interview with M. Wessells, August 12, 2002). This question serves as a poignant reminder that well-being cannot be defined in strictly individual terms. Indeed, some of the greatest economic impacts on youth soldiers relate to the destruction of community infrastructure, such as markets, schools, health posts, wells, roads, and bridges.

Conclusion

This analysis has powerful implications for practice and policy. It indicates, for example, that because the impacts of youth soldiering are multifaceted and interconnected, programs that aim to assist former youth soldiers must be holistic. Rather than narrow psychosocial programs that emphasize trauma counseling, what are needed are integrated programs that enable youth well-being in all its dimensions—economic, social, spiritual, emotional, and so on—and that promote the well-being of communities (Ahearn, 2000; Wessells, 2006).

At the policy level, this analysis underscores the necessity of strengthening efforts to prevent youth soldiering and to protect youths' rights guaranteed under the CRC and related instruments such as the Optional Protocol on Children and Armed Conflict, which bans recruitment by nonstate actors and sets 18 years as the minimum age for combat participation. It also points out the need for effective DDR programs that include psychosocial components and orientation. Too often, such programs have focused exclusively on economic needs, and it has not been uncommon for youth to be excluded altogether. In Angola, which is just emerging from 40 years of war, the DDR program defined soldiers as people who are at least 20 years of age, thereby denying benefits to large numbers of younger soldiers. Perhaps most important, it underscores the need for preventing armed conflict, as it makes little sense for adults to allow wars to erupt and then try to pick up the pieces afterward. An important step in conflict prevention is to engage youth as peacebuilders and create positive, nonviolent life options for young people (Wessells, 2006).

It is also important to consider the wider social impacts of child soldiering, recognizing that the price of not preventing child soldiering is likely to be very high. The participation of children as actors in war only serves to normalize violence, politicize rising generations, and further militarize society. Additionally, children become the means for perpetuating cycles of violence that damage and devastate the supports for all children, worsen poverty and suffering, and leave in their wake divided societies that are ripe for further conflict. Following conflict in one country, child soldiers may become mercenaries in neighboring countries, adding to regional instability. Ultimately the price of children's exploitation in armed forces and groups must be measured in societal, regional, and international terms.

This analysis, however, is best regarded as an initial step toward the construction of an integrated, contextualized understanding of the impact of youth soldiering. It is very much in its preliminary stages, owing to a paucity of careful research regarding impacts. This framework will serve its purpose if it stimulates the integrated, multidisciplinary research that is needed.

References

Ahearn, F. (Ed.). (2000). *Psychosocial wellness of refugees.* New York: Berghahn.

Apfel, R., & Simon, B. (Eds.). (1996). *Minefields in their hearts.* New Haven, CT: Yale University Press.

Boothby, N., Crawford, J., & Halperin, J. (2006). Mozambican child solder life ooutcome study: Lessons learned on rehabilitation and reintegration efforts. *Global Public Health, 1*(1), 87–107.

Boothby, N., & Knudsen, C. (2000). Children of the gun. *Scientific American, 282*(6), 6–66.

Bracken, P., & Petty, C. (Eds.). (1998). *Rethinking the trauma of war.* London: Free Association.

Brett, R., & McCallin, M. (1996). *Children: The invisible soldiers.* Vaxjo: Rädda Barnen.

Brett, R., & Specht, I. (2004). *Young soldiers: Why they choose to fight.* Boulder, CO: Lynne Rienner.

Cairns, E. (1996). *Children and political violence.* Oxford: Blackwell.

Coalition to Stop the Use of Child Soldiers. (2002). *Child soldiers: 1379 report.* London: CSC.

Coalition to Stop the Use of Child Soldiers. (2004). *Child soldiers global report 2004.* London: CSC.

Cohn, I., & Goodwin-Gill, G. (1994). *Child soldiers.* Oxford: Clarendon Press.

Danieli, Y., Rodley, N., & Weisaeth, L. (Eds.). (1996). *International responses to traumatic stress.* Amityville, NY: Baywood.

Dawes, A., & Donald, D. (2000). Improving children's chances: Developmental theory and effective interventions in community contexts. In D. Donald, A. Dawes, & J. Louw (Eds.), *Addressing childhood diversity* (pp. 1–25). Cape Town: David Philip.

Erikson, E. E. (1968). *Identity: Youth and crisis.* New York: Norton.

Garbarino, J., Kostelny, K., & Dubrow, N. (1991). *No place to be a child: Growing up in a war zone.* Lexington, MA: Lexington Books.

Human Rights Watch (1997). *The scars of death: Children abducted by the Lord's Resistance Army in Uganda.* New York: Human Rights Watch. Human Rights Watch Web site, www.hrw.olrg/reports97/uganda.

Human Rights Watch (1998). *Sowing terror: Atrocities against civilians in Sierra Leone.* New York: Human Rights Watch.

Human Rights Watch (2003). *Stolen children: Abduction and recruitment in Northern Uganda.* New York: Author.

Keairns, Y. (2002). *The voices of girl child soldiers: Summary.* New York: Quaker United Nations Office.

Kostelny, K. (2006). A culture-based, integrative approach: Helping war-affected children. In N. Boothby, A. Strang, & M. Wessells (Eds.), *A world turned upside down* (pp. 19–37). Bloomfield, CT: Kumarian.

Machel, G. (2001). *The impact of war on children: A review of progress since the 1996 United Nations report on the impact of armed conflict on children.* New York: Palgrave Macmillan.

Marsella, A., Friedman, M., Gerrity, E., & Scurfield, R. (Eds.). (1996). *Ethnocultural aspects of posttraumatic stress disorder.* Washington, DC: American Psychological Association.

Mazurana, D., McKay, S., Carlson, K., & Kasper, J. (2002). Girls in fighting forces and groups: Their recruitment, participation, demobilization, and reintegration. *Peace and Conflict: Journal of Peace Psychology, 8*(2), 97–123.

McCallin, M. (1998). Community involvement in the social reintegration of child soldiers. In P. Bracken & C. Petty (Eds.), *Rethinking the trauma of war* (pp. 60–75). London: Free Association.

Peters, K., & Richards, P. (1998). Why we fight: Voices of youth combatants in Sierra Leone. *Africa, 68*(2), 183–189.

Punamäki, R. (1996). Can ideological commitment protect children's psychosocial well-being in situations of political violence? *Child Development, 67,* 55–69.

Rashid, A. (2000). *Taliban.* New Haven, CT: Yale University Press.

Singer, P. (2005). *Children at war.* New York: Pantheon.

Staub, E. (2002). The psychology of bystanders, perpetrators, and heroic helpers. In L. Newman & R. Erber (Eds.), *Understanding genocide: The social psychology of the Holocaust* (pp. 11–42). New York: Oxford University Press.

Straker, G. (1992). *Faces in the revolution.* Cape Town: David Philip.

Straker, G., Mendelsohn, M., Moosa, F., & Tudin, P. (1996). Violent political contexts and the emotional concerns of township youth. *Child Development, 67,* 46–54.

Thompson, C. (1999). Beyond civil society: Child soldiers as citizens in Mozambique. *Review of African Political Economy, 80,* 191–206.

UNICEF. (2003). *Adult Wars, child soldiers.* From page 8 East Timorese boy's testimony and add'l testimonies. Bankok: UNICEF.

UNICEF (2007). *The Paris principles: Principles and guidelines on children associated with armed forces or armed groups.* New York: UNICEF.

Waller, J. (2002). *Becoming evil: How ordinary people commit genocide and mass killing.* New York: Oxford University Press.

Wessells, M. G. (1997). Child soldiers. *Bulletin of the Atomic Scientists, 53*(6), 32–39.

Wessells, M. G. (1998). Children, armed conflict, and peace. *Journal of Peace Research, 35*(5), 635–646.

Wessells, M. (2002). Recruitment of children as soldiers in sub-Saharan Africa: An ecological analysis. In L. Mjoset & S. Van Holde (Eds.), *The comparative study of conscription in the armed forces* (Comparative Social Research, vol. 20) (pp. 237–254). Amsterdam: Elsevier.

Wessells, M. (2006). *Child soldiers: From violence to protection.* Cambridge, MA: Harvard University Press.

Wessells, M., & Kostelny, K. (2002). *After the Taliban: A child focused assessment in the Northern Afghan provinces of Kunduz, Takhar, and Badakshan.* Richmond: CCF International.

Wessells, M. G., & Monteiro, C. (2001). Psychosocial interventions and post-war reconstruction in Angola: Interweaving Western and traditional approaches. In D. Christie, R. V. Wagner, & D. Winter (Eds.), *Peace, conflict, and violence: Peace psychology for the 21st century* (pp. 262–275). Upper Saddle River, NJ: Prentice Hall.

Part II

SPECIFYING THE EFFECTS OF POLITICAL VIOLENCE

Following the general treatments of key aspects of the study of youth and political violence that were presented in Part I, the three chapters in Part II offer quite specific analyses intended to define more precisely the effects of political violence on young people. These chapters will be followed by Part III, which expands the scope of inquiry into this complicated topic.

As for the specific treatments in this part, Orla Muldoon, Clare Cassidy, and Nichola McCullough (Chapter 6) pay particular attention to both children's perception of political violence and socioeconomic variations in these perceptions. Through a series of data analyses, they illustrate the degree to which effects of political violence can be contingent on these types of variability. Focusing on the Bosnian experience, Christopher Layne and colleagues (Chapter 7) focus intensively on the critical area of adolescent-perceived social support during war and disaster. They detail the theoretically justified development of a new multisector measure of support and provide a series of tests to determine its reliability and validity. Finally, continuing the focus on Bosnia, Robert McCouch (Chapter 8) uses a policy lens to focus analyses of data from several hundred Bosnian youth. Extensive data analyses identify direct, indirect, and mediated effects between violence exposure and dimensions of youth postwar functioning.

Chapter 6

Young People's Perceptions of Political Violence
The Case of Northern Ireland

Orla Muldoon,
Clare Cassidy, and
Nichola McCullough

From the early days of the Northern Irish conflict, concern has been expressed for children and young people (Fields, 1980; Fraser, 1971, 1973). Over the years, researchers have attempted to identify the effects of such experiences (for reviews, see Cairns, 1987; Muldoon, Trew, & Kilpatrick, 2000). The variability in these researchers' conclusions has been considerable. This chapter reconsiders this issue by first examining the extent of young people's experience of political violence in Northern Ireland. It then goes on to consider young people's perceptions of these events. Perceptions of politically violent events among both young people and adults are interesting markers in and of themselves. However, they also inform our understanding of how young people experience and cope with political violence. Drawing on results that have examined children's ratings of the stress from encountering political violence, this chapter considers whether increased experience of political violence exacerbates the perceived stressfulness of these events and the impact these experiences have on coping and adjustment.

Children and the Northern Irish Conflict

Northern Ireland is a small region in the west of the European Union. It would be a relatively unknown and unremarkable place were it not for the armed political conflict of the past 30 years. Northern Ireland has a population of just under 1.7 million people, which is 2.84% of the total UK population. The population, however, is growing as a result of one of the highest birthrates of any region in the European Union. Northern

Ireland's population, therefore, is very young. Whereas 18% of the EU population are aged 15 or under, in Northern Ireland 26% of the population are in this age bracket. An additional 14% of the population are between 15 and 25 years of age. Because of these high numbers of youth, almost half of the population of Northern Ireland had never experienced peace until the onset of the recently negotiated ceasefires.

In the three decades since the start of the conflict, colloquially known as the Troubles, more than 3,300 people have been killed and 35,000 injured in Northern Ireland (Cairns & Darby, 1998; Hayes & McAllister, 2001). Exact figures as to the extent of child and adolescent casualties are difficult to obtain; police casualty figures are not broken down by age. Murray (1982) estimated that between 1969 and 1977, 103 people under the age of 17 had been killed as a result of the Troubles, representing 8% of all fatalities. Cairns (1987) subsequently estimated that between 1969 and 1983, approximately 150 children under the age of 14 had been killed or injured in Northern Ireland due to political violence. The most recent estimates suggest that between 1969 and 1998, 257 young people under the age of 17 (7.2% of all fatalities) and 1,019 young people between 18 and 25 years had been killed as a result of the Troubles (Smyth, 1998). At this level, children and young people in Northern Ireland have obviously paid a price for the political violence that has tainted the region.

Though the price for some children and young people has been high, young people's experience of political violence in Northern Ireland is highly variable. In terms of exposure to violence, the extent of young people's experience of the conflict in Northern Ireland appears to vary both within the region and across time. Available research illustrates this point. In one study using a random sample of preadolescents, one in five children reported they had been near a bomb or knew a relative or friend that had been injured as a result of the conflict (McGrath & Wilson, 1985). In a later study of a socially deprived community, 37% of young people of a similar age reported experience of bombings, and very high proportions of young people had witnessed many conflict-related events, including house searches (91%) and plastic bullets being fired (74%). The comparison of these sets of findings highlights an important issue. It would appear that children from deprived areas report greater experience of conflict-related events. This finding reflects the reality of the conflict in Northern Ireland and other regions torn by political violence; often, social deprivation and political violence coexist and exacerbate the pressures for those growing up in these circumstances (O'Connor, 1993).

In a number of related studies, we have examined children's experience and perceptions of political violence in Northern Ireland. In a large sample of 8- to 11-year-old Belfast children (Muldoon & Trew, 2000a), we examined children's experience of political violence. These data, collected prior to the current ceasefire (1994) and negotiated peace agreement, indicated that children had considerable experience of political violence. For instance, 13.6% of the sample had been picked up by the police, 23.8% had witnessed people shooting guns, 22.5% had been caught in a riot, 54.4% had been stopped at security checkpoints, 59.5% had experienced bomb scares, and 70.4% had encountered soldiers on the street. A primary aim of this study, then, was to provide an indication of children's current experience of political violence in Northern Ireland. The current chapter and the study reported here documents the extent of children's experience of political violence in Northern Ireland subsequent to the Belfast Good Friday Agreement—a period of relative peace.

The Current Study

In early 2003, data were collected from a comparable sample of 599 children attending eight primary schools in the greater Belfast area of Northern Ireland. The schools were selected so that a range of children across religious and socioeconomic backgrounds were represented in the sample. Overall, the sample was 42% male and 58% female; 34% of children were from state (Protestant) schools and 66% from maintained (Catholic) schools. Thirty-one percent of the sample received free school meals due to low family income, and 66% did not (for the remaining 3%, this information was not available). The larger Catholic sample was due to the fact that two of the Catholic schools that agreed to participate in the study had a much higher enrollment than the other schools. These two schools had middle-class catchment areas, and as a result, there was a disproportionate number of middle-class Catholic children in the sample (50% of the total sample). The mean age of children in the sample was 10 years, 4 months (standard deviation: 10 months).

The scale used to collect the data on children's experiences with and perceptions of politically violent events was originally devised by McWhirter and called the Stress Events Perception Scale. The original McWhirter (1984) instrument was adapted prior to use in 1994, hence only eighteen of the twenty-six items could be compared across time (see Muldoon, Trew, & McWhirter, 1998, for an account of this comparison). The scale used in this and the previous two studies was derived from other life events and fear schedules. Specific items were selected that were directly or possibly related to the conflict in Northern Ireland. Estimates of the scale's reliability were undertaken on the 1994 data, which suggested that the scale had adequate internal consistency across ages 8 to 11 years (Muldoon & Trew, 1995). The validity of the scale is supported by the developmentally appropriate changes in perceptions evident across middle childhood (Muldoon, 2003).

The instructions given to children on administration of the scale described the items as events or problems that children may experience, which can cause children to feel bothered, worried, or troubled. A 4-point rating scale ranging from not at all bothered (1) to an awful lot bothered (4) was used to indicate how children would feel if they experienced each of the events in the future. In addition each child also indicated whether they had experienced each of the events listed on the Stress Events Perception Scale.

Importantly, all the data presented in this chapter were collected in postceasefire Northern Ireland. Therefore, children in the study who were around 10 years old were infants at the time of the first Irish Republican Army (IRA) ceasefire and have lived half of their lives in postagreement Northern Ireland. As such, the sample represents children living through peacetime. Despite this, 65% of these children reported considerable experience with political violence (i.e., encountering soldiers on the street), only 5% less than in the preceasefire sample. Similarly, a smaller proportion of children reported experience of being stopped at checkpoints (41% versus 54%) and being picked up by the police (7% versus 14%) postceasefire than in 1994. However, a greater proportion of children (31% versus 22%) reported having been caught in a riot and seeing or hearing people shooting guns (37% versus 24%). Although the item relating to bombing would suggest less experience in 2003 (60% had experience of bomb scares in 1994 versus 38% reported having heard a bomb go off in 2003), this is likely to be related to the altered wording of this item. This comparison bears out police reports that suggest that the level of violence in Northern Ireland is again escalating to the levels seen prior to the ceasefires (McAuley, 2004). At a minimum, it suggests that children in Northern Ireland continue to be exposed to events associated with political violence.

Young People's Perceptions of Negative Life Events

Exploring young people's experience of conflict tells us little about how children view these experiences and their likely psychological impact. Lazarus and Folkman's (1984) transactional theory of stress and coping and the literature on childhood resilience to stressful life events point to the need to acknowledge individuals' personal or subjective experiences of negative events. Lazarus and Folkman argue that you can only understand the stress process by acknowledging an individual's own views of his or her experiences. Despite this, much of the research on childhood stress has failed to examine children's feelings or perceptions of their situation. In some cases, this omission has been because adults have sought to protect children from researchers (Cairns, 1987); in other cases, adults have assumed that they understand the meaning that stressful encounters have for children.

The importance of children's perceptions of negative events, which is a central tenet of Lazarus and Folkman's model of stress, should not be underplayed for a number of reasons. Research suggests that adult estimates of the stressfulness of events in childhood do not concur with children's own perceptions. In addition, perceptions of negative events are likely to be a key factor in determining children's coping responses and the ease of their adjustment to the event (Gore & Eckenrode, 1994; Rutter, 1994). Finally, perception of a negative event is likely to be a source of significant variation between children at an individual level as well as across cultures (Johnson, 1986). Importantly, therefore, this view of stress as hinging on individual perceptions of events allows for cross-cultural variability in children's perceptions. It can therefore be argued that perceptions are of such fundamental importance in determining how children process such stress that they must be examined to understand how children process violent experiences. This examination of children's perceptions of violent political events represents the second main goal of this chapter.

Available evidence indicates that children's perceptions are rarely consistent with adult estimates of the stressfulness of negative events in childhood (Yeaworth, York, Hussey, Ingle, & Goodwin,1980). In an empirical evaluation of the psychological adjustments made by adolescents to a range of experiences, Yeaworth and colleagues found that both youths' (8 to 11 years) and adults' ratings of stressful events differed significantly. In general, the adolescents rated events as more stressful than adults had perceived them to be. In particular, events related to peers, such as death of a close friend, were viewed much as more stressful than adults had believed them to be for children. Colton (1985) made a comparison of children's (aged 8–11) and teachers' ratings of the severity of various types of negative events. This study found that teachers tended to underestimate the severity of major life events for children. In addition, the study pointed to the importance of children's own experience in ameliorating the perceived stressfulness of many negative events.

Yamamoto and Felsenthal (1982) examined professionals' assessments of the stressfulness of children's negative experiences. Their study of 197 adult participants, all of whom were childcare professionals, found that there was close agreement between adults regarding the relative stressfulness of various negative events. However, the perceptions of these professionals did not correspond with the views of children obtained in a previous study (Yamamoto & Davis, 1982). Again, this comparison suggested that adults tended to underestimate the stressfulness of negative events for children. Rende and Plomin (1991) also examined the relationship between children's and adults' perceptions of negative events. Using Coddington's Social Readjustment Scale, 7-year-old children's perceptions of the events listed were compared with their parents' ratings of how stressful their children would perceive the events in question. The authors found that the relationship between parents' and children's perceptions of negative events was weak at best (correlation coefficient = 0.021) and that children were more likely to perceive major events as more stressful than parents believed them to be. On the other hand, more common or everyday events were perceived as less stressful by children than by their parents.

Young People's Perceptions of Politically Violent Events

Overall, this research would seem to suggest that adults are not accurate judges of the perceived stressfulness of negative events in childhood. Given the importance attached to the concept of appraisal and the subjective meanings of stressful experiences, this is a gap in our research knowledge. Further to this, along with the dearth of research on children's views of stressful events, children's views of political violence have rarely been sought or acknowledged. This can be attributed in part to adults' own difficulty of dealing with these experiences, coupled with a belief that they can insulate children from the conflict—a situation that bars adults from addressing these issues with children at all. Our studies of Northern Irish children attempt to redress this imbalance.

Table 6.1 indicates the perceived stressfulness of eleven negative events associated with the conflict in Northern Ireland. Interestingly, the rank order obtained in this

Table 6.1 Perceived Stressfulness of Eleven Events Associated with the Conflict in Northern Ireland

Event	Rank	Mean Rating	SD
One of my parents is going to jail.	1	4.57	0.98
Someone in my family is seriously ill or injured.	2	4.32	0.99
Getting put in jail.	3	4.30	1.23
A close friend is injured because of the Troubles.	4	3.73	1.20
Getting picked up by the police.	5	3.65	1.49
Hearing a bomb go off.	6	3.54	1.52
Seeing or hearing people shooting guns.	7	3.51	1.47
Getting caught up in a riot.	8	3.35	1.46
Getting stopped at a checkpoint.	9	2.26	1.30
Seeing soldiers on the street.	10	2.20	1.37
Seeing a march.	11	1.50	1.05

study differs from data collected in 1983, 1994, and 1998 (Muldoon, 2003; Muldoon et al., 1998). In a longitudinal study of a cohort of children aged 8 at time 1 and 11 at time 2 (Muldoon, 2003) and a larger sample of 8- to 11-year-old children (Muldoon et al., 1998), "people shooting guns" was ranked as more stressful than "bomb scares" and "being picked up by the police." In the current study, however, "people shooting guns," ranked seventh overall and was viewed as less stressful than "being picked up by the police" or "hearing a bomb go off." Perhaps the lower level of perceived stressfulness for this item reflects the lower threat of gun attacks in postceasefire Northern Ireland.

Social Factors and Perceptions of Political Violence

Developmental theorists have consistently pointed to the role social and external factors play in the development of children's social cognitions (Baumrind, 1980; Roopnarine, Colhran, & Mounts, 1988). From a Vygotskian perspective, children are believed to construct their social worlds through a process of internalization of social interactions (Woods, 1992). Consequently, social factors are likely to be strongly related to children's developing worldview, including their perceptions of negative events. This section reviews available research that explores the influence that three social factors—gender, socioeconomic status, and religious affiliation—have on children's perceptions of stressful events. The analysis undertaken examines children's perceptions of conflict-related stressful events in relation to gender, religious affiliation, and socioeconomic background. Given that the ratings for each event differed significantly [F (11, 545) = 309, $p < 0.01$], these relationship were examined for each event independently. A corrected significance level was used to prevent type I errors (interpretation of false positives). Thus, the conventional significance level was allowed family wise for each independent factor, namely, gender, religion, and socioeconomic background. No three-way or two-way interaction effects were evident.

Gender and Perceptions of Negative Events

Gender is one of the most fundamental categories to emerge in the social life of a child. From an early age, children are classified and subsequently classify themselves as male or female, and from then a whole set of sex-typed behaviors, attitudes, and cognitions develop (Yee & Brown, 1994). Maccoby (1988) suggests that the development of gendered identity is a result of three factors: biology, socialization, and cognitive categorizing. In addition, she argues that the power of gender identity is likely to be at its height between the ages of 6 and 12 when all three factors influence behaviors but the rigidity of social roles are not yet questioned.

Gender differences in the quality and intensity of self-reported emotions have been the topic of many research studies (see Brody, 1993, for a full review). Gender differences in children's fears and perceptions of stressful situations have been established previously (Brody, Lovas, & Hay, 1995; Gullone & King, 1992; Yamamoto, Soliman, Parsons, & Davies, 1987). Where differences are in evidence, females report greater negative effect in the face of stressful and fearful situations than their male counterparts.

Although this finding is well established, there are a number of problems in the research literature that remain unresolved.

First, the underlying cause of the gender differences in perceptions of stressful events has not been established. Some authors suggest that these differences represent a greater willingness on the part of females to disclose negative emotions. More recently, however, others have suggested that these differences may be related to gender differences in the interpretation of stressful events (Gore & Colten, 1991; Martin, 1989). A second unresolved problem in the literature is the fact that few studies have accounted for gender differences in perceptions of or responses to a variety of negative situations.

Brody et al. (1995), in attempting to address this latter problem, undertook a cross-sectional study of children (6–12 years), adolescents (14–16 years), and adults (over 30 years). They found that gender differences in perceptions of negative events did exist, but these were most marked where events provoked fear or anger. In addition, events that involved negative male stereotypical behavior were reported across all three age groups as significantly more stressful by females than males. This finding suggests that certain events may be interpreted as particularly stressful because of cultural stereotypes related to gender in both childhood and adulthood.

The current study examines gender differences in children's perceptions of each of the events. Gender differences were evident in relation to nine of the twelve events (see Table 6.2). In all cases, these differences showed that girls rated these events more negatively than boys. Importantly, however, the differences were evidenced in relation to those events that were perceived as least stressful overall. As such, it would not be true to say that those events that induce fear are perceived differently by males and females (Brody et al., 1995); rather, the distinction between events related and unrelated to gender differences in perceived negativity appears to relate to the impact the event may have on the young person's family. Events that impact on family life as a result of the conflict or other factors (e.g., death, a parent going to jail, or family members being injured) are rated as equally distressing by males and females. Events directly related to the political events in Northern Ireland, however, are viewed as less distressing by males than by females. Given that political violence and war has been

Table 6.2 Gender Differences in Children's Perceptions of Conflict-Related Events

Event	Boys Mean	Girls Mean	F
One of my parents is going to jail.	4.47	4.64	0.54
Someone in my family is seriously ill or injured.	4.25	4.37	2.3
Getting put in jail.	4.06	4.47	10.0**
A close friend is injured because of the Troubles.	3.37	3.99	20.9**
Getting picked up by the police.	3.27	3.94	6.4*
Hearing a bomb go off.	2.99	3.94	7.2*
Seeing or hearing people shooting guns.	2.82	4.01	66.5**
Getting caught up in a riot.	2.86	3.71	39.5**
Getting stopped at a checkpoint.	2.01	2.44	5.1*
Seeing soldiers on the street.	1.80	2.48	20.6**
Seeing a march.	1.36	1.60	3.7*

$*p < 0.05$; $**p < 0.01$.

constructed as an essentially male pursuit (Reilly, Byrne, & Muldoon, 2004), these gender differences can be seen as consistent with Brody et al.'s (1995) argument that events associated with stereotypically male behaviors are viewed as more threatening by girls than by boys.

Socioeconomic Status and Perceptions of Negative Events

Few of the available published studies on children's perceptions of stressful life events have examined these perceptions in relation to socioeconomic status (SES). SES has been linked to the extent of children's experience of negative life events. Children and adults of lower SES appear to experience greater numbers of stressful life events than do individuals from more affluent backgrounds (Chandler, Million, & Shermis, 1985; Dohrenwend, 1973; Garmezy, 1993; Trad & Greenblatt, 1990). This finding appears to be true regardless of whether uncontrollable or controllable life events are considered (Dohrenwend, 1973). As such, SES is likely to influence children's perceptions of negative events indirectly by being related to their experience of negative events (see section titled "Experience and Perceptions of Negative Events" for a fuller review of this literature).

The documented difference in exposure to stressful life events associated with lower SES has failed to explain adequately the differential vulnerability. This vulnerability relates to one of the most consistently documented associations in child and adult psychiatric epidemiology, that is, the association between SES and psychological distress (McLeod & Kessler, 1990). Research studies are increasingly sensitive to the fact that the impact of poverty in childhood can vary with other personal, family, or social factors (Huston & McLoyd, 1994) and that the vulnerability associated with lower SES may be a result of a combination of SES and other factors. For instance, Bolger, Patterson, and Thompson (1995) found that the effects of economic hardship on children's psychosocial adjustment were related to the persistence of the poverty as well as the gender of the child.

A number of authors have suggested that the effects of lower SES are felt by children and adolescents at least partly through their influence on parental emotional state and behaviors (McLoyd & Wilson, 1991). McLoyd and Wilson (1991) describe a model in which conditions of poverty increase parents' psychological distress, which diminishes their sensitivity and involvement in parenting. This in turn leads to impaired socioemotional functioning in children. If this is the case, SES is likely to be associated with perceptions of stressful life events (see Masten et al., 1988; Rossman & Rosenberg, 1992; Weigel, Wertlieb, & Feldstein, 1989).

The measure of SES employed in the current study was a child-centered measure, namely, whether children received free school meals (FSMs). In the United Kingdom, of which Northern Ireland is part, FSMs are provided in school for children of low-income parents. Children for whom these data were not available were excluded from this analysis (3% of total sample). As such, it is a crude but child-centered indicator of poverty.

Those in receipt of FSMs differed in relation to their perception of three events compared to those who did not receive such support. In all three cases, children in the lower income group rated these events as significantly more distressing than those who did not receive this benefit (Table 6.3). This finding is consistent with data obtained

Table 6.3 SES Differences in Perceptions of Stressful Conflict-Related Events

Event	Free School Meals		
	No	Yes	F
A close friend is injured because of the Troubles.	3.71	3.84	7.9**
Seeing or hearing people shooting guns.	3.46	3.69	13.2**
Getting stopped at a checkpoint.	2.15	2.53	3.6*

$*p < 0.05; **p < 0.01.$

in the 1994 study (Muldoon & Trew, 1995). Together, these findings suggest that children from lower socioeconomic groupings perceive some events associated with political violence as more threatening than their middle-class counterparts. Although this finding goes some way toward explaining the heightened vulnerability of lower SES children to the effects of conflict, it does not suggest an emotional insensitivity among this group (McLoyd & Wilson, 1991). If anything, the findings suggests the opposite: lower SES children have difficulty sensitizing themselves to the threat posed by political violence, perhaps because of their increased risk of being exposed to such violent events (see earlier section titled "Young People's Perceptions of Negative Life Events").

Ethnicity/Religion and Perceptions of Events

The two major religious groups in Northern Ireland may also be viewed as two different ethnic groups, because members of each conceive themselves as alike by virtue of their common ancestry and are so regarded by others. Ethnicity is more than ancestry, race, religion, or nationality. Ethnicity influences the development of children's perceptions, behavioral roles, and the rules of social interaction (Rotheram & Phinney, 1987). In Northern Ireland, the development of ethnic discrimination is delayed, probably because of the fact that ethnic discrimination there is based on stereotyped cues as against perpetual cues (Cairns, 1980). As a result, children in Northern Ireland take about 11 years to develop the ability to discriminate between the ethnicity of others, whereas in the United States the ability to discriminate between races develops at around 5 years of age (Cairns, 1980, 1989; Houston, Crozier & Walker, 1990). Although the ability to discriminate others' ethnicity is delayed, a study in Northern Ireland that examined children's knowledge of their own group affiliation suggested that by the age of 9, 75% of children can correctly identify their own group (McWhirter & Gamble, 1982).

Ethnicity is an acknowledged source of variation in children's perceptions of negative events (El-Sheikh & Klaczynski, 1993). Available studies, largely conducted in the United States on children's perceptions of negative events, have not examined religion as a source of variation related to these perceptions. Yamamoto and Byrnes (1984) compared 273 children's (aged 10–12 years) ratings of stressful events on the basis of ethnicity. There was agreement between the Anglo and Hispanic children regarding which events were perceived as most stressful. However, Hispanic children rated thirteen of the twenty events as less stressful than the Anglo children. Events that were rated as more stressful by the Anglo children included those in which Hispanic children had greater experience. For example, Anglo children rated academic retainment as more stressful than Hispanic children. Almost twice as many Hispanic (28%) than Anglo (14%) children had experience of this event. Again, this study suggests that children's perceptions of events are related to their experience of them together with other social factors. Newcomb, Huba, and Bentler (1986), in their study of the perceived undesirability of events in adolescents, compared four different U.S. ethnic groupings: Hispanics, Asians, blacks, and whites. This study found that the relative undesirability of events across ethnic goroups was quite consistent. However, numerous significant differences emerged regarding specific types of events. Overall, it appeared that black adolescents perceived two clusters of events as more stressful than the other ethnic groups. These clusters involved events that induced distress, such as illness, or those that resulted in deviant behavior, such as being in trouble with the law. Conversely, black adolescents perceived events necessitating relocation, such as changing schools, as less stressful than the other ethnic groups. The authors of this study concluded that the "event appraisal process is influenced by a person's ethnic background and must be considered an important mediator when evaluating the impact of life events" (Newcomb et al., 1986, p. 224).

Silverman, LaGreca, and Wasserstein (1995) interviewed 273 children (aged 7–12 years) regarding their worries in several areas, such as school, health, and family life. No differences were observed in the ratings of the frequency of event occurrences in relation to ethnicity across the three groups: African American, Hispanic, and white. However, African American children reported significantly more intense worries than their white peers in three areas relating to family life, war, and personal harm. The authors state that the reason for these differences is unclear but note the coincidence of lower SES and minority ethnic status in this U.S. sample and suggest that the increased worries of African American children may be related to social disadvantage rather than ethnicity.

In studies conducted in Northern Ireland, Gallagher, Millar, Hargie, and Ellis (1992) found that Roman Catholic adolescents (aged 15–18 years) expressed significantly more worries than Protestant adolescents across a number of areas. These included worries relating to school work, interacting with teachers, and decision making, among others. McWhirter (1984), in her study of the perceptions of negative events in 10- and 14-year-old children, also found a number of religious/ethnic variations in children's perceptions of these events. On analyzing the total of children's ratings, she found that Catholics reported higher levels of perceived stress than Protestants. However, an analysis of the individual item scores suggested that there were only five events that Catholics perceived as more stressful than Protestants. Also, the study suggested that religion or ethnicity interacted with factors such as gender and area of residence (a crude indicator of children's experience of political conflict) to influence perceptions.

Minority ethnic status is believed to have adverse psychological effects on children's self-worth and their sense of personal control (Simpson, 1993). Contradictory evidence is available relating to this issue in Northern Ireland. Hunter, Stringer, and Coleman (1993) found no differences in adolescents' (14–15 years) self-esteem in relation to religious affiliation, whereas two other studies suggested some differences in perceived self-competence in relation to religious affiliation in younger children (Muldoon & Trew, 2000b; Muldoon, 2000). Two more studies suggested that Catholic (minority group) young people are more ambivalent about their social identities and evaluate their group less positively than the Protestant majority group (Cairns, 1987; Stringer & Cairns, 1983). On the other hand, Trew and Benson (1996) and Cassidy and Trew (1998) suggest that higher levels of collective self-esteem exist among Catholics than Protestants in Northern Ireland. Given this diversity of findings, there has been some debate within the Northern Irish literature regarding how the majority and minority are defined. It is arguable that both groups represent majorities (Catholics in Ireland as a whole, Protestants in Northern Ireland) and minorities (Protestants in Ireland as a whole, Catholics in Northern Ireland).

Religious group affiliation may also represent another source of difference in children's perceptions of conflict events in Northern Ireland because of the history and nature of the conflict. Available research evidence suggests that a disproportionate number of the casualties (relative to the population as a whole) were Catholic throughout the course of the Troubles (Hayes & McAllister, 2001; Ruane & Todd, 2001). For this reason, ethnic status/religious affiliation is conceivably related to children's perceptions of negative events and their worries in Northern Ireland and beyond. The reasons that underlie any such variations remain unclear.

Table 6.4 indicates the differences in perceptions of events associated with religious affiliation in the current study. Eight of the eleven events were rated differently by Catholic and Protestant children. These events were rated as less stressful than those events where religious differences were not evidenced. In all cases, Catholic children rated these events as more distressing than their Protestant counterparts. This finding is consistent with previous studies (McWhirter, 1984; Muldoon et al., 1998), which also suggested differences in the same direction. Given that the difference is found in relation to some events and not others, it is unlikely that the underlying cause of the variation is related to differential psychological resources (e.g., self-esteem) in Catholic and Protestant children. Similarly, given that other research shows that children's perceptions of non–conflict-related events do not differ in relation to religious group

Table 6.4 Religion and Differences in Perceptions of Stressful Conflict-Related Events

Event	Protestant Mean	Catholic Mean	F
One of my parents is going to jail.	4.48	4.62	0.1
Someone in my family is seriously ill or injured.	4.34	4.31	0.34
Getting put in jail.	4.34	4.31	0.1
A close friend is injured because of the Troubles.	3.51	3.84	7.5**
Getting picked up by the police.	3.48	3.74	4.2*
Hearing a bomb go off.	3.09	3.77	14.6**
Seeing or hearing people shooting guns.	3.23	3.64	8.6**
Getting caught up in a riot.	3.17	3.44	4.5*
Getting stopped at a checkpoint.	2.04	2.37	11.1**
Seeing soldiers on the street.	1.68	2.46	20.6**
Seeing a march.	1.25	1.63	17.4**

$*p < 0.05; **p < 0.01.$

affiliation (Muldoon, 2003; Muldoon et al., 1998), it is fair to assume that these differences relate specifically to the aspects and the context of the events themselves. In short, it would appear that Catholic children are more threatened by the conflict around them than their Protestant counterparts. This increased perception of threat accurately represents the reality of the conflict in Northern Ireland, where Catholics have been more likely to be casualties of the conflict than Protestants (Hayes & McAllister, 2001; Ruane & Todd, 2001).

Multivariate Effects

Based on the literature that children's social circumstances may influence their social-cognitions, there was a need to examine the multivariate effects of SES, religion, and gender on perceptions of events. However, on this occasion few multivariate effects were evident within the data, and no three-way effects were obtained relating to any event. Two two-way effects were observed. Interestingly, these effects related to the two events rated least stressful by the cohort overall. The first related religion and SES to perceived stressfulness of seeing a march [$F = (1, 464)$ 5.8, $p < 0.05$]. Protestant children rated this event as less stressful than Catholics, with those Protestants in receipt of FSMs (low-income families) seeing it as least stressful of all. On the other hand, Catholics from low-income families rated this event as more stressful than those from more affluent families (see Table 6.5). The religious variation in perception of this event is not surprising. The majority of marches in Northern Ireland are associated with the Orange Order, an exclusively Protestant organization. These marches have been a contentious subject over the past decade. Protestants view the marches (of which there are about 2,000 annually) as a celebration of their culture and believe it is their right to parade through routes that dissect Catholic neighborhoods. Catholics, on the other hand, view the marches as threatening and triumphalist. The clashes that have resulted are most often seen in deprived areas. Indeed, the increased violence associated with Orange Order parades has meant that many Protestants have distanced themselves from the order. This group is likely to be disproportionately middle class, and their children's lack of contact with these events, except through negative media coverage, most likely explains the perceived differences in the stressfulness of this event for Protestant children. A heavily armed security presence often results from the clashes associated with these parades. Frequently, this presence is in or on the fringes of deprived Catholic areas where conflict flares when the marchers arrive. Furthermore, these areas have a traditional antipathy toward British security forces, hence, poorer Roman Catholic children are those that view these events as most stressful.

Table 6.5 Perceived Stressfulness of Seeing a March, Religious Affiliation, and Socioeconomic Status

	Not in Receipt of School Meals	In Receipt of Free School Meals
Protestant	1.34	1.07
Catholic	1.52	1.91

Table 6.6 Perceived Stressfulness of Soldiers on the Street Relative
to Gender and Socioeconomic Status

	Not in Receipt of School Meals	In Receipt of Free School Meals
Boys	1.84	1.73
Girls	2.36	2.67

A second multivariate effect was observed in relation to children's perceptions of soldiers on the street. Gender and SES interacted to effect this variable [$F = (1, 454)$ 8.23, $p < 0.05$]. Further examination of the data suggested that although boys rated this event as significantly less stressful than girls, those girls in receipt of FSMs rated this event as significantly more stressful than their counterparts from more affluent families (see Table 6.6). Perhaps what is surprising here is not the gender difference or the difference in perceptions related to social class among girls but the lack of such a significant difference among boys. This finding indicates that boys from lower income groups are not unduly upset by encountering soldiers on the street.

Experience and Perceptions of Negative Events

The relationship between children's perceptions of events and their prior experiences represents an important theoretical issue in this area. Few studies have considered this relationship with regard to political violence. However, there has been considerable attention to this issue in relation to stressful events related to family, school, and relationships. For instance, Lewis, Siegal, and Lewis (1984), in a large-scale study of 11-year-olds, compared event stress ratings made by children who had and had not experienced each event. They found that for a number of events, such as "parental separation" or "being forced to try something new," those who had not experienced the events rated them as more stressful than those who had experienced the events.

Colton's (1985) study also found that the perceptions of the event's upsetting nature varied in relation to children's experience of the events. Again, in this case, events were perceived as less stressful where the child had personal experience of the event. Brown (1986), in a study of 503 10- to 12-year-olds examined the relationship between perceptions and experience of six life events. The results indicated that children who had not experienced parental divorce rated this event as significantly more stressful than those who had experience of it. The author went on to conclude that "imagining or anticipating the event may be more upsetting than actually experiencing it" (Brown, 1986, p. 70).

Newcomb et al. (1986), in a study of 108 adolescents (15–18 years), also examined the desirability/undesirability of thirty-nine life-changing events. This study found that perceptions of twenty-seven of the events differed significantly in relation to adolescents' previous experience. In all cases except one (receiving medication from a doctor), adolescents who had experience of an event perceived it as less undesirable relative to those who had no previous experience.

Overall, therefore, the experience of stressful life events would appear to reduce the perceived stressfulness of them. However, the research evidence available in this area is limited, and the picture is far from complete. In a review of the available literature, Atkins (1991) points out that the least frequently occurring events are perceived as the most stressful. It appears that for children and adolescents, experience of certain or some events reduces their perceived negativity. Whether this reduction in perceived stressfulness applies for all children or all types of events is unclear, however. Given that individual differences in children's responses to psychosocial stress exist, it is unlikely that constancy across children and situations is the case. In addition, many other factors have been seen to influence perceptions of negative events, and none of these studies accounted for the influence of experience alongside other important predictors of children's perceptions of negative events.

Experience and Perceptions of Politically Violent Events

The need for people to cope and adjust to political violence, in situations where conflict is protracted, is readily apparent. In these contexts, the coping strategies employed are likely to be different from those necessitated by acute events. Indeed, the ongoing nature of the violence means that for many it must be integrated into the context of their lives. For this reason, some researchers have suggested that habituation or desensitization is likely to be a useful coping strategy.

There is some empirical evidence to support this case. For instance, Klingman (1992) studied the acute stress reactions in Israeli students over the first and fourth week of the 1992 Gulf War. Over this time, self-reported levels of psychological disturbance decreased significantly. Similarly, Gidron, Gal, and Zahavi (1999), in their study of Israeli bus commuters, found that commuting frequency was negatively related to anxiety about terrorist attacks, which the authors interpreted as a desensitization effect. In Northern Ireland, a longitudinal study by McIvor (1981) again emphasized the role of habituation. She asked recently arrived students about their first impressions of Northern Ireland on arrival and then again 1 year later. Reference to the political violence were prevalent in the accounts received following arrival but not a year later, again leading the author to conclude that these students had habituated to the conflict.

Similarly, such strategies as denial and distancing may be employed by individuals living in areas where violent conflict persists. Cairns and Wilson (1984) examined individuals' mental health and perceptions of levels of violence in two matched towns in Northern Ireland. One town had experienced relatively high levels of violence, and the second relatively low levels. Overall, levels of psychopathology appeared to be higher in the high-violence town. More important, however, those individuals living in the high-violence town that perceived the area to have little or no violence had better mental health. In effect, denying the existence of the conflict—or at least being able to tune it out—may facilitate psychological well-being. Other studies again support this contention. In a study comparing Israeli young people living in a violence-prone border town and in a more peaceful area, Rofe and Lewin (1982) found that the group living in the border town scored higher on a repression scale, fell asleep earlier, and had fewer dreams with violent themes than their counterparts in the more peaceful area.

The authors concluded that the residents of the border town, having experienced more political violence, have developed strategies to avoid thinking or ruminating about violent events.

However, the utility of habituation or distancing as a coping strategy may be limited to contexts where an attack has not been personally experienced and the threat from the conflict does not appear imminent. Some commentators have suggested that coping processes may be sensitive to the nature and salience of violent events (Cairns, 1994). Wilson and Cairns (1992) found in a community that had been devastated by a bomb attack in Northern Ireland that the majority of respondents did not deny the violence. The current data hopefully informs this debate. Examining children's perceptions of violent events relative to their previous experiences of such events allows us to consider whether habituation and desensitization can be used to adjust to conflict. Furthermore, by examining whether habituation is evident across high- and low-stress events, we can consider whether such a strategy is only useful when perceived threat is low.

Table 6.7 shows the perceived distress associated with each of the eleven conflict-related events contingent on young people's reported experience. Overall, children rated conflict-related events as less distressing when they had prior experience of them. Significant differences in perceptions of events related to experience were more frequently evidenced where events were ranked as less distressing overall. For instance, significant differences of ratings of events, such as seeing a march, soldiers on the street, getting stopped at checkpoints, getting caught in a riot, and getting picked up by the police, were found in relation to children's prior experience of events. This finding is consistent with the view that some level of habituation tends to occur in response to exposure to conflict events (Cairns, 1987).

Despite the desensitization or habituation evident in relation to the least distressing events, there is less evidence that this process occurs in response to events that children find most distressing or where perceived threat is high. For those events viewed as most

Table 6.7 Mean Stressfulness Ratings in Relation to Prior Experience of Each Event

Event	Prior Experience	No Prior Experience	% with Prior Experience	t
One of my parents is going to jail.	4.38	4.59	4.1	1.08
Someone in my family is seriously ill or injured.	4.39	4.19	66	−2.3
Getting put in jail.	3.73	4.31	1.8	−.1
A close friend is injured because of the Troubles.	3.60	3.75	18	1.1
Getting picked up by the police.	2.51	3.75	7	5.4**
Hearing a bomb go off.	3.56	3.54	38	−.2
Seeing or hearing people shooting guns.	3.21	3.67	37	3.7*
Getting caught up in a riot.	3.18	3.43	31	1.95
Getting stopped at a checkpoint.	1.91	2.50	42	5.4**
Seeing soldiers on the street.	2.00	2.57	65	5.0**
Seeing a march.	1.42	1.77	81	3.2*

*$p < 0.01$; **$p < 0.001$.

distressing (i.e., a parent going to jail or a friend being injured due to the Troubles), no significant differences were evidenced in relation to prior experience. Indeed, these variations in perceived stressfulness related to experience are intuitive. Habituation to threat in high-threat situations would not offer protection from danger or enhance safety. Unfortunately, this situation creates a catch-22 for many children growing up in violent societies where the greatest experience of violence tends to coexist with the highest level of perceived threat (see earlier section titled "Young People's Perceptions of Negative Life Events" and Table 6.3).

Conclusion

The literature reviewed and the study undertaken provide strong support for using the Lazarus and Folkman transaction model to enhance understanding of the impact of violence. An emphasis in the adult literature on the importance of the appraisal process in determining the impact of stressful and violent events has not been matched by a similar interest in children's perceptions. The absence of studies of this nature may be related to adults' discomfort as well as the ethical issues that arise when attempting to ascertain children's experiences and views of violence. However, researchers and those working with children directly affected by conflict must continue to solicit and acknowledge children's views of their experiences during times of war and political violence.

To understand the impact of violent events on young people, we first need to understand how these events are defined, viewed, and evaluated. Furthermore, we need to acknowledge that social grouping variables like gender, SES, and ethnicity are important moderators of the stress appraisal process in childhood, just as they are in adult life. Belonging to different social groups affects the nature and frequency of certain conflict-related events as well as how such events are appraised.

Children often show resilience in the face of political violence. Consistent with this suggestion are the data from this study indicating that children tend to rate some events as less stressful if they have prior experience of conflict-related events. On the other hand, minority groups and lower income children who have a higher risk of experiencing conflict-related events tend to perceive these events as the most stressful. Similarly, comparisons of children's perceptions across time indicate that particular forms of violence at a given historical point appear to be perceived as more threatening if they predominate at that time. Thus it can be said that children's fears regarding particular events to some degree represent the likelihood of the event occurring. Although anticipation of the event may be more negative than the actual experience itself, it is worth remembering two points. First, all children consider events related to political violence as negative when they are first experienced. Second, the fear of the events, in the absence of their occurrence, may represent a genuine concern and have its own negative effect. Finally, this fear is likely to affect disproportionately the groups that have higher exposure to violence.

Variability in young people's appraisal of events was the rule rather than the exception. Young people's views appeared to differ not only in relation to social factors but also in relation to temporal ones. Such changes in children's perceptions across time add to the difficulties of establishing the impact of conflict. Variations in the nature and intensity of the violence across time can necessitate alterations in the questions asked of young people and reduce the comparability of the available data. Furthermore, it can mean that findings may be specific to single cohorts. Indeed, the new data presented in this chapter represent a cohort with experience of the transitional phase from political violence to (hopefully) political agreement and peace. Importantly, however, they also represent a cohort of children whose parents also grew up during the Troubles. Any transgenerational effect of their parents' conflict experiences is unclear. Future research in this area would be worthwhile.

References

Atkins, F. D. (1991). Children's perspective on stress and coping: An integrative review. *Issues in Mental Health Nursing, 12*(2), 171–178.

Baumrind, D. (1980). New directions in socialization research. *American Psychologist, 7*, 639–652.

Bolger, K. E., Patterson, C. J., & Thompson, W. W. (1995). Psychosocial adjustment among children experiencing persistent and intermittent family economic hardship. *Child Development, 66*(4), 1107–1129.

Brody, L. R. (1993). On understanding gender differences in expression of emotion: Gender roles, socialization and language. In S. Ablon, D. Brown, E. Khnatzian, & J. Mack (Eds.), *Human feelings: Explorations in affect development and meaning* (pp. 87–121). New Jersey: Analytic Press.

Brody, L. R., Lovas, G. S., & Hay, D. H. (1995). Gender differences in anger and fear as a function of situational context. *Sex Roles, 32*(1–2), 47–78.

Brown, L. P. (1986). Stressful life events as perceived by children. PhD dissertation, University of Rochester, Rochester, NY.

Cairns, E. (1980). The development of ethnic discrimination in children in Northern Ireland. In J. Harbison & J. Harbison (Eds.), *A society under stress: Children and young people in Northern Ireland* (pp. 115–127). Somerset: Open Books.

Cairns, E. (1987). *Caught in crossfire.* Belfast: Appletree Press.

Cairns, E. (1989). Social identity and intergroup conflict in Northern Ireland: A developmental perspective. In J. Harbison (Ed.), *Growing up in Northern Ireland* (pp. 115–130). Belfast: Stranmillis College.

Cairns, E. (1994). Understanding conflict and promoting peace in Ireland: Psychology's contribution. *Irish Journal of Psychology, 15*(2 & 3), 480–493.

Cairns, E., & Darby, J. (1998). The conflict in Northern Ireland: Causes, consequences and controls. *American Psychologist, 53*(7), 754–760.

Cairns, E., & Wilson, R. (1984). The impact of political violence on mild psychiatric morbidity in Northern Ireland. *British Journal of Psychiatry, 145*, 631.

Cassidy, C., & Trew, K. (1998). Identities in Northern Ireland: A multidimensional approach. *Journal of Social Issues, 54*(4), 725–740.

Chandler, L. A., Million, M. E., & Shermis, M. D. (1985). The incidence of stressful life events of elementary school aged children. *American Journal of Community Psychology, 6*, 743–746.

Colton, J. A. (1985). Childhood stress: Perceptions of children and professionals. *Journal of Psychopathology and Behavioural Assessment, 2*, 155–173.

Dohrenwend, B. S. (1973). Social status and stressful life events. *Journal of Personality and Social Psychology, 2*, 225–235.

El-Sheikh, M., & Klaczynski, P. A.(1993). Cultural variability in stress and control: An investigation of Egyptian middle class, countryside and inner-city girls. *Journal of Cross-Cultural Psychology, 1,* 81–98.

Fields, R. M. (1980). *Northern Ireland: Society under siege.* Piscataway, NJ: Transaction Books.

Fraser, R. M. (1971). The cost of commotion: An analysis of the psychiatric sequelae of the 1969 Belfast riots. *British Journal of Psychiatry, 118*(544), 257–264.

Fraser, R. M. (1973). *Children in conflict.* London: Marin, Secker and Warburg.

Gallagher, M., Millar, R., Hargie, O., & Ellis, R. (1992). The personal and social worries of adolescents in Northern Ireland: Results of a survey. *British Journal of Guidance and Counselling, 3,* 274–290.

Garmezy, N. (1993). Children in poverty: Resilience despite risk. *Psychiatry, 56*(1), 127–136.

Gidron, Y., Gal, R., & Zahavi, S. (1999). Bus commuters coping strategies and anxiety from terrorism: An example of the Israeli experience. *Journal of Traumatic Stress, 12*(1), 185–92.

Gore, S., & Colten, M. E. (1991). *Adolescent stress: Causes and consequences.* New York: Aldine de Gruyter.

Gore, S., & Eckenrode, J. (1994). Context and process in research on stress and resilience. In R. J. Haggerty, L. R. Sherrod, N. Garmezy, & M. Rutter (Eds.), *Stress, risk and resilience in children and adolescents* (pp. 19–63). New York: Cambridge University Press.

Gullone, E., & King, N.J. (1992). Psychometric evaluation of a revised fear survey schedule for children and adolescents. *Journal of Child Psychology and Psychiatry, 6,* 987–998.

Hayes, B., & McAllister, I. (2001). Sowing dragons teeth: Public support for political violence and paramilitarism in Northern Ireland. *Political Studies, 49,* 901–922.

Houston, J. E., Crozier, W. R., & Walker, P. (1990). The assessment of ethnic sensitivity among Northern Ireland school children. *British Journal of Developmental Psychology, 8*(4), 419–422.

Hunter, J. A., Stringer, M., & Coleman, J. T. (1993). Social explanations and self-esteem in Northern Ireland. *Journal of Social Psychology, 133*(5), 643–650.

Huston, A. C., & McLoyd, V. C. (1994). Children and poverty: Issues in contemporary research. *Child Development, 65*(2), 275–282.

Johnson, J. H. (1986). *Life events as stressors in childhood and adolescence.* Beverly Hills, CA: Sage.

Klingman, A. (1992). Stress reactions of Israeli youth during the Gulf War: A quantitative study. *Professional Psychology: Research and Practice, 23*(6), 521–527.

Lazarus, R. S., & Folkman, S. (1984). *Stress appraisal and coping.* New York: Springer.

Lewis, C. E., Siegal, J. M., & Lewis, M. A. (1984). Feeling bad: Exploring sources of distress among pre-adolescent children. *American Journal of Public Health, 2,* 117–122.

Maccoby, E. E. (1988). Gender as a social category. *Developmental Psychology, 6,* 755–765.

Masten, A. S., Garmezy, N., Tellegen, A., Pellegrini, D. S., Larkin, K., & Larsen, A. (1988). Competence and stress in school children: The moderating effects of individual and family qualities. *Journal of Child Psychology and Psychiatry, 29*(6), 745–764.

Martin, C. L. (1989). Children's use of gender related information in making social judgements. *Developmental Psychology, 25*(1), 80–88.

McAuley, J. (2004). *Let Erin's trouble be over.* Inaugural Professorial Address, University of Huddersfield, UK.

McGrath, A., & Wilson, R. (1985). *Factor which influence the prevalence and variation of psychological problems in children in Northern Ireland.* Paper presented to the Annual Conference of the Developmental Section of the British Psychological Society, Belfast.

McIvor, M. (1981). *Northern Ireland: A preliminary look at environmental awareness.* Paper presented to the Biennial Conference of the International Society of Behavioural Development, Toronto, Canada.

McLeod, J. D., & Kessler, R.C. (1990). Socioeconomic status differences in vulnerability to undesirable life events. *Journal of Health and Social Behaviour, 31,* 162–172.

McLoyd, V. C., & Wilson, L. (1991). The strain of poor living: Parenting, social support and child mental health. In A. C. Huston (Ed.), *Children and poverty* (pp. 105–135). Cambridge: Cambridge University Press.

McWhirter, L. (1984). *Is getting caught in a riot more stressful for children than seeing a scary film or moving to a new school?* Paper presented to Annual Conference of the Northern Ireland branch of the B.P.S., Port Balllintrae.

McWhirter, L., & Gamble, R. (1982). Development of ethnic awareness in the absence of physical cues. *Irish Journal of Psychology, 5*(2), 109–127.

Muldoon, O. T. (2000). Self-perceptions in Northern Irish children: A longitudinal study. *British Journal of Developmental Psychology, 18,* 65–80.

Muldoon, O.T. (2003). Perceptions of stressful life events in Northern Irish school children: A longitudinal study. *Journal of Child Psychology and Psychiatry, 44*(2), 193–201.

Muldoon, O., & Trew, K. (1995). Patterns of stress appraisal in eight to eleven year old Northern Irish children. *Children's Environments, 12*(1), 49–56.

Muldoon, O. T., & Trew, K. (2000a). Children's experience and adjustment to conflict related events in Northern Ireland. *Peace Psychology: Journal of Peace and Conflict, 6*(2), 157–176.

Muldoon, O. T., & Trew, K. (2000b). Social group membership and self competence in Northern Irish children. *International Journal of Behavioural Development, 24*(3), 330–337.

Muldoon, O. T., Trew, K., & Kilpatrick, R. (2000). The legacy of the Troubles on the development of young people. *Youth and Society, 32*(1), 6–28.

Muldoon, O.T., Trew, K., & McWhirter, L. (1998). Perceptions of stressful life events in ten year old Northern Irish children: A ten year comparison. *European Child and Adolescent Psychiatry, 7*(1), 36–48.

Murray, R. (1982). Political violence in Northern Ireland: 1969–1977. In F. W. Boal & J. N. H. Douglas (Eds.), *Integration and division geographical aspects of the Northern Ireland problem* (pp. 309–331). London: Academic Press.

Newcomb, M. D., Huba, G. J., & Bentler, P. M. (1986). Desirability of various life change events among adolescents: Effects of exposure, sex, age and ethnicity. *Journal of Research in Personality, 20*(2), 207–227.

O'Connor, F. (1993). *In search of a state: Catholics in Northern Ireland.* Belfast: Blackstaff.

Reilly, J., Byrne, C., & Muldoon, O. T. (2004). Young men as victims and perpetrators of violence. *Journal of Social Issues, 60*(3), 469–484.

Rende, R. D., & Plomin, R. (1991). Child and parent perceptions of the upsettingness of major life events. *Journal of Child Psychology and Psychiatry, 4,* 627–633.

Rofe, Y., & Lewin, I. (1982). The effect of war environment on dreams and sleep habits. In N. A. Milgram (Ed.), *Stress and anxiety, 8* (pp. 59–75). New York: Hemisphere.

Roopnarine, J. L., Colhran, D., & Mounts, N. S. (1988). Traditional psychological theories and socialization during middle and early childhood: An attempt at reconceptualization. In T. D. Yawkey & J. E. Johnson (Eds.), *Integrative processes in socialization: Early to middle childhood* (pp. 5–22). Hillsdale, NJ: Erlbaum.

Rossman, B. B. R., & Rosenberg, M. S. (1992). Family stress and functioning in children: The moderating effects of children's beliefs about their control over parental conflict. *Journal of Child Psychology and Psychiatry, 4,* 699–715.

Rotheram, M. J., & Phinney, J. S. (1987). Definitions and perspectives in the study of children's ethnic socialization. In J. Phinney & M. Rotheram (Eds.), *Children's ethnic socialization: Pluralism and development* (pp. 10–28). Newbury Park, CA: Sage.

Ruane, J., & Todd, J. (2001). The politics of transition? Explaining political crises in the implementation of the Belfast Good Friday Agreement. *Political Studies, 49,* 923–940.

Rutter, M. (1994). Stress research: Accomplishments and tasks ahead. In R. J. Haggerty, L. R. Sherrod, N. Garmezy, & M. Rutter (Eds.), *Stress, risk and resilience in children and adolescents* (pp. 354–385). New York: Cambridge University Press.

Silverman, W. K., LaGreca, A. M., & Wasserstein, S. (1995). What do children worry about: Worries and their relation to anxiety, *Child Development, 66*(3), 672–686.

Simpson, M. A. (1993). Bitter waters: Effects on children of the stresses of unrest and oppression. In J. P. Wilson & B. Raphael (Eds.), *International handbook of traumatic stress syndromes* (pp. 601–624). New York: Plenum.

Smyth, M. (1998). *Half the battle: Understanding the impact of the troubles on children and young people.* Derry: INCORE.

Stringer, M., & Cairns, E. (1983). Catholic and Protestant young people's ratings of stereotype Catholic and Protestant faces. *British Journal of Social Psychology, 22,* 241–246.

Trad, P. V., & Greenblatt, G. (1990). Psychological aspects of child stress: Development of the spectrum of coping responses. In L. E. Arnold (Ed.), *Childhood stress* (pp. 23–49). New York: John Wiley & Sons.

Trew, K., & Benson, D. E. (1996). Dimensions of social identity in Northern Ireland. In G. Breakwell & E. Lyons (Eds.), *Changing European identities: Social-psychological analyses of social change* (pp. 123–143). Oxford: Butterworth-Heinemann.

Weigel, C., Wertlieb, D., & Feldstein, M. (1989). Perceptions of control, competence and contingency as influences on the stress behaviour symptom relation in school aged children. *Journal of Personality and Social Psychology, 56*(3), 456–464.

Wilson, R., & Cairns, E. (1992). Psychological stress and the Northern Ireland Troubles. *Psychologist, 5,* 347–50.

Woods, D. (1992). *How children think and learn.* Oxford: Blackwell.

Yamamoto, K., & Byrnes, D. A. (1984). Classroom social status, ethnicity and ratings of stressful events. *Journal of Educational Research, 77*(5), 283–286.

Yamamoto, K., & Davis, O. L. Jr. (1982). Views of Japanese and American children concerning stressful experiences. *Journal of Social Psychology, 116*(2), 163–171.

Yamamoto, K., & Felsenthal, H. M. (1982). Stressful experiences of children: Professional judgements. *Psychological Reports, 50*(3 pt. 2), 1087–1093.

Yamamoto, K., Soliman, A., Parsons, J., & Davies, O. L. Jr. (1987). Voices in unison: Stressful life events in the live of children in six countries. *Journal of Child Psychology and Psychiatry, 6,* 855–864.

Yeaworth, R., York, J., Hussey, M., Ingle, M., & Goodwin T. (1980). The development of an adolescent life change event scale. *Adolescence, 15*(57), 91–97.

Yee, M., & Brown, R. (1994). The development of gender differentiation in young children. *British Journal of Social Psychology, 33*(2), 183–196.

Chapter 7

Measuring Adolescent Perceived Support Amidst War and Disaster

The Multi-Sector Social Support Inventory

Christopher M. Layne, Jared S. Warren, Sterling Hilton, Dahai Lin, Alma Pašalić, John Fulton, Hafiza Pašalić, Ranka Katalinski, and Robert S. Pynoos

Recent wars and other mass casualty events, including terrorist attacks, have heightened scientists' and practitioners' concerns regarding the effects of war and disaster on youth, their families, and their communities—a focus that extends back well over a half century (Burlingham & Freud, 1949). This heightened concern has stimulated efforts to build both theories and measurement instruments that can assist in identifying, describing, and explaining the causal pathways that lead to "resilient" versus "nonresilient" child and adolescent postdisaster adjustment (Layne et al., 2006). This concern has stimulated efforts to develop prevention and intervention programs capable of identifying and assisting youth whose exposure to trauma, loss, and severe adversity significantly increases their risk for experiencing persisting distress, functional impairment, and developmental disruption (Saltzman, Layne, Steinberg, Arslanagić, & Pynoos, 2003). Social support has gained increasing prominence in these efforts over the past two decades, often being featured in studies of child and adolescent post-war or disaster adjustment (e.g., Kuterovac-Jagodić, 2003), and in interventions for youth exposed to trauma, traumatic bereavement, and severe adversity (Cox et al., 2007; Layne et al., 2001; Layne, Saltzman, et al., 2008; Saltzman, Layne, Steinberg, & Pynoos, 2006).

Appropriately designed measurement instruments (of social support and other constructs) are valuable tools for creating a theoretically sound foundation on which evidence-based prevention and intervention programs for youth at risk for exposure to severe stress can be built. A measure promotes theory building by elucidating how key variables—especially risk, vulnerability, and protective and promotive factors—interlink to form pathways of influence within the pre-, peri-, and postdisaster ecologies (e.g., by way of etiological, mediating, and moderating variables and their sequelae) (Layne et al., 2006). Of particular interest, pursuing rigorous measurement and modeling can facilitate the implementation of *primary prevention* and *early intervention programs* that seek to reduce exposure to and mitigate the adverse effects of risk and vulnerability factors, as well as augmenting the beneficial influences of protective factors (as in recently outlined wellness-oriented public health approaches; Layne, Beck, et al., 2008; Layne, Warren, Shalev, & Watson, 2007). Furthermore, more precision in identifying causal mechanisms and the processes through which they operate promotes *secondary interventions* that target trauma-exposed subgroups at high risk for severe persisting distress, functional impairment, and developmental disruption (Layne et al., 2007; Layne, Beck, et al., 2008). Examples include the development of assessment-driven, flexible intervention protocols with modules or components that target multiple risk, vulnerability, and protective and promotive factors (Layne, Saltzman, et al., 2008; Saltzman et al., 2003, 2006).

Fortunately, much has been learned about youth adaptation under non–war-related conditions of severe adversity that can be used to guide these efforts. The study of children's positive adaptation under adverse conditions has held the interest of psychological researchers for some five decades (e.g., Garmezy, 1974; Werner & Smith, 1982; see Luthar, 2006, for a recent review). Historically, the focus of resilience research has been on identifying protective factors—defined as characteristics, conditions, or person-environment transactions (such as social support) that mitigate or buffer the adverse influences of stressful life events, circumstances, or other disadvantages that place individuals at increased risk for unfavorable outcomes (Luthar, Cicchetti, & Becker, 2000; Masten & Coatsworth, 1998). Only recently have researchers begun to conceptualize stress resistance and resilience as extensions of normal adjustment processes that benefit youth facing more normative adversities, everyday hassles, and developmental challenges (Masten, 2001). This broader perspective has been accompanied by calls to move beyond merely identifying protective factors to "unpacking" the processes through which beneficial mechanisms operate as they confer protection (in the form of protective factors) against adversities and promote (in the form of promotive factors) wellness in general irrespective of the presence or absence of risk factors (Layne, Beck, et al., 2008; Luthar, Sawyer, & Brown, 2006).

Consistent with an unpacking approach to understanding beneficial causal mechanisms and the processes through which they promote positive youth adjustment, this chapter will describe efforts to conceptualize, develop, and evaluate the preliminary psychometric properties of a measure of perceived social support—the Multi-Sector Social Support Inventory (MSSI) using data collected from war-exposed adolescents. The MSSI is highly conducive to an unpacking approach because it is designed to unpack both youths' social support networks (into four network sectors) and the specific types of supportive "ingredients" (into eight social provisions) that youth exchange in interpersonal transactions with members of their social networks.

We begin with a brief methodological critique of the recent literature in which we underscore the benefits of an unpacking approach to the study of social support, in terms of both the specific network sectors from which support is received or perceived to be available and the specific types of social provisions that are interpersonally exchanged. We next present social provisions theory (Weiss, 1974) and discuss its role as the test's underlying theoretical framework. We describe the results of three empirical investigations drawn from two international samples of adolescents. The first study evaluated the MSSI's factor structure and provided guidelines for test scoring and interpretation. The second investigation, drawn from a subsample of that used in the first, examined the MSSI's criterion-referenced validity with respect to a widely targeted clinical outcome variable (depressive symptoms) to illustrate the test's utility for theory building and intervention planning. The third study evaluated the MSSI's associated psychometric properties, including test-retest reliability and convergent validity. We conclude by highlighting the implications of our findings for further test refinement and development, applied clinical research, and intervention.

Theoretical Justification for the MSSI

Relevance of Social Support to the Study of Youth Development in Stressful Contexts

Consistent with evidence that social support is a potent protective factor in trauma-exposed adult populations (Ozer, Best, Lipsey, & Weiss, 2003), social support is increasingly emerging within the scientific literature as a protective agent among youth living in highly stressful contexts, including war- and disaster-related settings. Social support appears to mitigate the adverse influences of war-related trauma and postwar adversities on adolescent psychosocial adjustment (Ekblad, 1993; Kuterovac-Jagodic, 2003). For example, Ekblad (1993) reported that social support was associated with a reduction in the adverse effects of war-related violence exposure, an apathetic or unstable mother, and other risk variables in children and adolescents housed in a Swedish refugee camp. Moreover, in their study of social support and psychological distress in Kuwaiti youth 2 years following the first Gulf War, Llabre and Hadi (1997) found support for a stress-buffering protective (i.e., moderated) effect of social support for girls only. Specifically, war-exposed girls who reported receiving high levels of social support also reported levels of post-traumatic stress disorder (PTSD), depression, and health outcomes comparable to those reported by control subjects with limited war exposure. In contrast, girls who reported the lowest levels of social support also reported experiencing the highest levels of psychological distress among all war-exposed and control groups.

Historically, the construct of social support is one of the most frequently examined correlates of stress exposure and psychosocial adaptation in the developmental psychopathology literature. It appears in a range of guises, including risk marker, correlate, mediator, moderator, protective factor, risk and/or vulnerability factor (if in deficiency), and outcome variable (e.g., Masten & Coatsworth, 1998). Although both perceived and received support have garnered attention in the literature, perceived social support has been the focus of greater research interest due to its close associations with a variety of mental and physical health outcomes and its theorized role as a buffer against the adverse effects of stress (Wills & Shinar, 2000). Unfortunately, although many studies have reported a reliable inverse association between social support and adverse outcomes in youth exposed to severe adversity (e.g., Dubois, Felner, Brand, Adan, & Evans, 1992; Dubow, Tisak, Causey, Hryshko, & Reid, 1991; Sandler, 1980; Werner & Smith, 1982), the particular ways social support has been conceptualized and measured in the majority of studies has shed only limited light on the mechanisms and processes through which it may exert its beneficial effects.

Some Methodological Shortcomings of the Child and Adolescent Social Support Literature

A significant impediment to unpacking the mechanisms and processes through which social support may promote positive youth adjustment is that studies do not adequately address the broad array of sources, types, and functions of this multidimensional and purportedly influential psychological construct. For example, in an early study, Sandler (1980) measured social support in children using simple network structure variables, including the presence versus absence of an older sibling and having one versus two parents, without measuring the child's perception of whether supportive interactions actually took place with these life figures or of their perceived helpfulness. In addition, Dubois et al. (1992) measured perceived social support from family members and friends, but did not assess support from extended family members or adult friends and mentors (e.g., teachers or coaches)—important sources of support for many youth (Cauce, Hannan, & Sargeant, 1992; Gottlieb, 1991). Similarly, studies by Dubow and colleagues (Dubow et al., 1991; Dubow, Edwards, & Ippolito, 1997) measured perceived social support from peers, family, and teachers. However, their measure was based on a conceptualization of social support that focused almost exclusively on esteem support (Cobb, 1976), thereby excluding other types of support commonly found in alternative conceptual frameworks.

Indeed, a review of the methods used by researchers to measure social support reveals nearly as many different tests of this construct as there are empirical studies (e.g., Cauce, Reid, Landesman, & Gonzales, 1990; Wolchick, Beals, & Sandler, 1989). Accordingly, although social support is conceptualized as a complex and multidimensional construct (Furman 1989; Weiss, 1974; Wolchik et al., 1989), empirical investigations of its precursors, correlates, and protective and promotive influences have generally not followed suit by using commensurately sophisticated measures—tests that gather information relating to the varying sources and types of support that youth receive or perceive to be available from their social networks. Moreover, although some studies have examined the relative importance of perceived support in relation to a number of types of interpersonal relationships (e.g., Dubois et al., 1992; Dubow et al., 1997; Parker, Cowen, Work, & Wyman, 1990), many have excluded important potential sources of support, particularly relationships within the extended family and with adult mentors and friends.

In addition to the consequences of these limitations for intervention programs discussed earlier, these methodological practices may also detract from the validity and clinical utility of tests designed to measure social support. To the extent that measures of social support do not adequately capture the full spectrum of both the social provisions that are exchanged and the sources of that support, the measures lack content validity and, by extension, construct validity (Haynes, Richard, & Kubany, 1995). When compared to more content-valid measures, such tests may yield less complete and accurate depictions of the structure of youths' social networks, the dimensionality of social support as an underlying theoretical construct, and the ways stressful events and social support intersect to influence specific psychosocial outcomes. Consequently, these deficiencies in test construction may result in less explained variance in outcomes, biased model parameter estimates, distorted or incomplete depictions of the composition of youths' supportive networks, and reduced capacity to elucidate the processes through which youths' interpersonal transactions function (see Layne & Larsen, 2008).

Benefits of Measuring Support Provided by Multiple Social Network Sectors: The Compensatory Hypothesis

Justification for a measure that assesses perceived social support from a suitably broad range of network sectors is provided by both theoretical and empirical sources. The concept that supportive social transactions may come from a wide variety of network sources is shared by many social support researchers (Furman, 1989; Weiss, 1974; Wolchik et al., 1989). For example, Masten, Best, and Garmezy (1990) emphasized the importance of extrafamilial sources of support in adolescence, because youth may be able to rely on these relationships to compensate for an adverse home environment. An important theoretical advancement underscoring the importance of measuring all relevant social network sectors was made by Bronfenbrenner (1977), who conceptualized human development and adaptation as occurring in the context of transactions between interacting subsystems (e.g., the child, family, peer group, school, and community), which are nested within larger cultural, economic, and societal spheres of influence within the social and physical ecology.

From this perspective, different sectors of social networks, including the nuclear family, extended family, peer group, and adult friends and mentors, lie within different subsystems of the broader social ecology and may potentially compensate for deficits found within one another—a proposition hereafter called the "compensatory hypothesis" as it applies to social support. The principle of interacting subsystems (including compensatory effects) is of such central import to Bronfenbrenner's theory as to induce the author to use a double entendre in proposing that "in ecological research, the principal main effects are likely to be interactions" (1979, p. 38). Stated more simply, assuming adequate methodological rigor, interactions between ecological sectors or subsystems (manifest via such moderator variables as protective, vulnerability, facilitative, or inhibitory factors) may arise more frequently across studies than direct, independent effects (manifest via causal risk or promotive factors; see Layne, Beck, et al., 2008).

The developmental psychopathology and mainstream social support literatures also emphasize the need to assess support from multiple sources in the social network. For example, Werner (1993) reported that support from sources outside the immediate family (including grandparents, neighbors, and other adult mentors) was a key determinant of long-term positive adaptation in disadvantaged youth. Similarly, Gottlieb (1991) reported that among adolescent males nominated by their peers as highly successful in a variety of domains, support from such authority figures as coaches played an important role in youths' ability to obtain useful advice and navigate challenging life circumstances.

Moreover, tests that assess multiple social network sectors may be more sensitive in detecting cultural differences in the ways that social support is perceived, transacted, and used. For example, support from extended family members may be particularly beneficial to youth belonging to cultural groups characterized by large, dense, extended family networks that possess positive attitudes toward support seeking (Wilson, 1989). Multisector measures of social support may thus assist in clarifying culturally linked differences in the sources, types, and amounts of support transacted within youths' social networks. Of equal importance, multisector measures may assist in discovering potential differences in the magnitudes of the sectors' beneficial effects in relation to specific configurations of risk, vulnerability, protective, and promotive factors and specific outcomes (Layne, Beck, et al., 2008).

The need for multisector measures of social support is also underscored by evidence of developmentally linked differences in the social networks of children and adolescents. Specifically, the composition and structure of support networks tend to change as a function of social development (Feiring & Lewis, 1989; Gottlieb, 1991). Similarly, the degree to which youth rely on different support sectors changes significantly from childhood through adolescence (Furman, 1989). Accordingly, measures of social support that do not adequately sample from a full range of potential support sectors are unlikely to capture important developmentally linked changes in youths' perceptions and use of their support networks. These changes may reflect differences not only in the specific sources of social support that youth perceive or receive from their networks, but also in the specific types of social provisions exchanged—a topic we now address.

Benefits of Measuring a Spectrum of Supportive Provisions: The Matching Hypothesis

As noted earlier, further clarification regarding the provisional "ingredients" exchanged in youths' supportive interpersonal transactions is needed to elucidate the ways social support promotes positive youth development in general (Benson, Scales, Hamilton, & Sesma, 2006), and enhances stress-resistant or resilient adaptation in stressful contexts (Furman 1989; Layne et al., 2007; Luthar et al., 2006; Weiss, 1974; Wolchik et al., 1989). Specific types of social support may have differential degrees of potency across different stressful contexts. Specifically, a popular proposition, called the matching hypothesis, posits that the degree to which social support mitigates the effects of stress depends on the specific match between the demands imposed by the stressor and the social provisions one receives (via received support) or perceives to be available (via perceived support) from one's social network (Cutrona & Russell, 1987; Wills & Shinar, 2000, p. 89; see Friedman, Resick, & Keane, 2007, for a discussion of the relevance of this approach to reducing vulnerability in populations at risk for trauma exposure). For example, facing a stressful choice may be best mitigated by guidance, whereas loneliness may be best alleviated by companionship. Conversely, less compatible pairings of provisions with stressors (e.g., offering advice to a lonely friend) may reduce their potency or generate adverse outcomes (e.g., a friend who feels misunderstood). By identifying the specific demands that stressors are likely to impose if they occur, prevention and early intervention programs can build up and replenish resources (including specific social provisions) that will reduce vulnerability by helping those exposed to cope with the stressor in adaptive ways (Layne, Beck, et al., 2008).

Underscoring the need for appropriate matching between social provisions and stressors, studies have suggested that the indiscriminant incorporation of social support–based skills into intervention programs may fall short if these efforts are not based on a theoretically and methodologically sound foundation. For example, Heller, Price, and Hogg (1990) speculated that the relative lack of effectiveness of some intervention programs that target social support may be due to their lack of adequate regard to the highly complex functions served by social networks, the possible roles of mediating or moderating variables, and the specific types of demands posed by varying stressful circumstances. Consequently, investigations that explore the interrelationships between specific support sources, support types, and stressful life events and circumstances may be necessary prerequisites to the development of effective intervention strategies. In their absence, practitioners are faced with a grab bag of techniques presumed to enhance support without an accompanying framework that suggests how specific types and sources of support may be optimally recruited and employed to cope with the demands generated by specific stressors.

In summary, studies that unpack social support networks and social provisions hold considerable promise for developing theoretically sound, evidence-based prevention and intervention programs that harness promotive and stress-protective processes. These studies will help to address such questions as the following.

- To what extent is support furnished within a given sector of the support network able to *compensate* for a lack thereof within other sectors? (the compensatory hypothesis).
- Are certain types of social provisions more beneficial in relation to specific stressors (e.g., traumatic bereavement, involuntary separations, economic strain, negotiating developmental tasks) than other types of provisions? (the matching hypothesis).
- "Do different social provisions 'specialize' in the specific types of beneficial resources (e.g., self-efficacy, self-discipline) that they foster or 'grow?' If so, how do we select which resources youth will need in their 'life resource caravans' and then create the circumstances needed to grow, sustain, and modify them over time so that they are a good match for youths' current life circumstances?" (Hobfoll, 1988).
- "Are meaningful *cross-trajectory* differences found between members of stress-resistant, resilient-recovery, and protracted-recovery trajectory groups in how social support is recruited and employed in coping efforts?" (Layne, Beck, et al., 2008).
- "What *knowledge, skills, and attitudes* do at-risk youth need to recruit and manage the type, source, timing, frequency, duration, amount, and/or quality of support required to cope with traumatic experiences, normative stressors, and developmental challenges, and how can we best disseminate them?" (Gottlieb, 1996).

All of these questions require expansive analyses, and therefore, all cannot be addressed here. This chapter concentrates primarily on assessing the psychometric properties of the MSSI and testing the first question regarding compensatory effects.

Importance of Assessing War-Related Disruptions to Youths' Social Milieus: The Case of the Bosnian Civil War

To address significant risks and vulnerabilities, clinically useful theories and measures of social support should also systematically address the damage and disruptions that war often wreaks on youths' social networks. Relevant dimensions include disturbances or losses in their composition (i.e., whom it contains), density (i.e., the extent and ways members interact and communicate with each other), accessibility, and ability to function. Youth are frequently exposed to some of the most extreme forms of war-related violence, often in the form of threats or actual deadly harm to their loved ones. As a case example, the 4-year (1992–1995) war in Bosnia and Herzegovina led to massive disruptions within youths' social networks, including traumatic deaths and disappearances; actual or threatened severe harm; the rape, torture, and other mistreatment of loved ones; and prolonged involuntary separations from loved ones (Milosavljevic & Savic, 2000). The war led to a massive loss of human life (close to 100,000 persons killed, approximately 41% of whom were civilians, including over 3,300 children) and the displacement of over two million people (Ahmetasevic, 2007). In a wartime study of Bosnian children aged 6 to 12, nearly two-thirds reported that a significant life figure had been killed in the war, approximately 40% reported witnessing the violent injury or death of a parent or sibling, and 93.8% met DSM-IV criteria for PTSD (Goldstein, Wampler, & Wise, 1997).

These war-related events also set in motion a protracted and stressful postwar period for Bosnian youth and their loved ones. Hundreds of thousands of Bosnians continue to live as internally displaced persons, war refugees, or returnees from foreign countries (see Chapter 11). Many more are exposed to the effects of overcrowding, domestic discord, poor caregiver physical or mental health, drug and alcohol abuse, ongoing separations from loved ones, unemployment, financial strain, inadequate living conditions and school facilities, and ongoing political tensions (Djapo et al., 1998). Of particular clinical concern, these adversities may exacerbate stressful features of close interpersonal relationships, especially interpersonal conflicts and burdens, thereby increasing both vulnerability to other stressors and the risk for adverse outcomes (Kaniasty & Norris, 1993, 2004). Interpersonal conflict and burdens may also increase due to the imposition of heavy domestic responsibilities (e.g., increased household duties following mothers' entry into the workforce necessitated by financial strain) that interfere with teenage participation in valued and developmentally important activities, including schoolwork, social activities, work, and romantic relationships.

Recommended Features of Social Support Measures Designed for War-Exposed Populations

Based on the foregoing observations, we suggest that clinically useful measures of interpersonal support and strain among stress-exposed youth may profitably assess at least six features. These include (1) the perceived availability of support; (2) multiple sectors of youths' social support networks; (3) multiple dimensions of supportive provisions; (4) damage and disruptions to youths' close interpersonal networks; (5) which supportive relationships and resources remain intact and available to furnish support; and (6) interpersonal stressors, particularly conflict and burdens, that may increase strain and undermine the availability or potency of support. The MSSI was constructed in a manner consistent with these recommendations. The test was originally designed as an applied clinical research instrument to accompany the Trauma and Grief Component Therapy program, a modularized intervention protocol implemented on a wide scale in postwar Bosnia and other regions of the world (Layne et al., 2001; Layne, Saltzman, et al., 2008; Saltzman et al., 2006). The MSSI assesses eight social provisions perceived to be available from, and in addition to, disruptions to four sectors of youths' social support networks, consisting of *nuclear family, extended family, same-age peers,* and *adult friends and mentors.*

As can be seen in Figure 7.1, MSSI items are not specifically referenced to war- or postwar war-related stressful life events and circumstances but instead describe general social provisions. There were two reasons for this choice. First, the MSSI is intended to capture the perceived *availability* of specific social provisions from different sectors of youths' social networks, not the perceived *utility* or *potency* of the social provisions in mitigating the adverse effects of specific stressors (we consider the latter question as best left to empirical study). Second, MSSI items were designed to measure social provisions theorized to collectively promote positive adjustment to a diverse array of stressors, including high-magnitude traumatic events, secondary adversities, normative developmental challenges, and daily hassles (see Seidman et al., 1995). Accordingly, the items are not referenced to any single type or magnitude of stressor.

Social Provisions Theory as a Guiding Conceptual Framework

The MSSI is based on Robert Weiss's (1974) six-dimensional framework of supportive provisions given its conceptual richness, precision, broad applicability, and relevance to promoting positive adaptation in youth whose social networks have been disrupted. Social provisions theory can guide effort to enhance youth's abilities to recruit and use social support due to three primary strengths. First, the framework possesses strong theoretical and clinical utility due to its designation of different social provisions (e.g., emotional connection, guidance, reassurance of worth) as the common currency of interpersonal support. This imbues the framework with both a precision and a concreteness that promotes test construction, theory building, and intervention efforts through the use of common denominator concepts and terms that youth, practitioners, and researchers can all understand. Second, social provisions theory sets the stage for using flexible interventions and coping strategies by proposing that a variety of life organizations (i.e., social network configurations) are capable of furnishing the support needed for positive adjustment: "an adequate life organization is one that makes available a set of relationships that, together, can furnish all the [needed] relational provisions . . . *quite different life organizations may potentially make available all needed relational provisions . . . an individual might require*" (Weiss, 1974, pp. 24–25, emphasis added).

NUCLEAR FAMILY MEMBERS

1. Are any members of your nuclear family *currently involved in your life?* (you live together, spend time together, write, or phone each other)

NO (skip to the next section, which is titled "My Extended Family")

YES First, think of which nuclear family members you can turn to for support, such as:

- affection
- talking about personal things
- companionship

- moral support
- advice
- favors and help with tasks

- supplies (food, clothing, tools)
- money (both gifts and loans)

Second, check everyone who provides you with some type of support:

Third, count how many you can turn to for support: (circle a number for each)

father/stepfather	1 2
mother/stepmother	1 2
brother(s)	1 2 3 4 5 6 7 8 9 10 11 12
sister(s)	1 2 3 4 5 6 7 8 9 10 11 12

My Relationships with my Nuclear Family (father/stepfather, mother/stepmother, brother, sister)

Type of Support	This Past Month I Felt:				
	Never	Rarely	Sometimes	Often	Always
1. I feel like I "fit in" and belong with the members of my nuclear family (father, mother, brother, or sister).	0	1	2	3	4
2. I have an understanding family member (father, mother, brother, or sister) who I can really talk to about personal things.	0	1	2	3	4
3. I have a family member (father, mother, brother, or sister) who I can turn to for good advice.	0	1	2	3	4
4. I can count on members of my nuclear family if I need help.	0	1	2	3	4
5. I feel like my nuclear family appreciates my abilities and helps me to believe in myself.	0	1	2	3	4
6. I feel like my nuclear family needs me.	0	1	2	3	4
7. I feel emotionally connected to the members of my nuclear family (we care about each other).	0	1	2	3	4
8. I have a nuclear family member who can help me in practical ways, like providing rides, helping with school assignments, or helping me with chores.	0	1	2	3	4
9. I have a nuclear family member who can help me in material ways, like providing food, clothing school supplies, and giving or loaning me money.	0	1	2	3	4
10. I have serious conflicts with member(s) of my nuclear family (father, mother, brother, or sister).	0	1	2	3	4
11. I have obligations or duties in my nuclear family that are burdensome and weigh me down.	0	1	2	3	4

[a]The same format is used for the three remaining network sectors (*Extended Family, Peers,* and *Adult Friends and Mentors*).

Figure 7.1. Sample of MSSI items: The nuclear family social network sector.

A third strength is Weiss's proposal that interpersonal relationships tend to specialize in the supportive provisions they provide, thus requiring that individuals form a variety of different types of relationships to meet their social needs. Indeed, Weiss posits that because humans are social animals for whom social provisions are essential to survival and well-being, they strategically form interpersonal relationships to meet needs for specific social provisions. This observation provides guidance in creating developmentally and contextually sensitive theories, models, and measurement instruments that can account for changes in the composition of youths' supportive networks. Just as a child's nutritional needs and eating habits change as he or she matures into adolescence or joins a sports team, youth and their caregivers may alter the composition of youths' social networks; the types of relationships they form, maintain, and end; and the ways they make use of social support. These alterations may reflect changes in youths' social needs driven by maturation and, equally as important, by changes (trauma-induced or otherwise) in their life circumstances.

Although this chapter focuses on the compensatory hypothesis, social provisions theory nevertheless sets the stage for evaluating and applying both the compensatory and matching hypotheses in youth exposed to severe stress (see Cutrona & Russell, 1987, for a test of the matching hypothesis). Regarding the compensatory hypothesis, youths whose social networks have been disrupted or damaged can strive to meet their support-related needs by modifying or reconfiguring their social networks. These reconfigured life organizations may differ substantially in composition and function compared to preexisting social networks, in that relationships within one sector (e.g., a grandfather or adult mentor) may be called on to at least partially compensate for deficiencies found within other sectors (e.g., loss of one's father). Regarding the matching hypothesis, social networks, even when modified into unusual configurations that furnish the social provisions needed for youths' positive adaptation and development within a given life context, can be considered "adequate." This matching perspective underscores the need for flexibility when intervening with at-risk youth. Specifically, the specific social provisions needed for positive adaptation and development—and by extension the specific configurations and operations of youths' social networks needed to furnish those provisions—will change as a function of life circumstances, developmental competencies, and developmental tasks. When paired with social support–focused interventions (e.g., Saltzman et al., 2006), tools like the MSSI can be used to collect information concerning the composition of each network sector and perceptions regarding the availability of specific social provisions therein.

MSSI Test Development

A search was first conducted for a social support measure that met the guidelines and was appropriate for war-related contexts. This search revealed that a multisector, multiprovision, clinically useful measure of perceived social support was not available (see Reis & Collins, 2000; Wills & Shinar, 2000). As an initial step in creating such a test, the first author reviewed both quantitative and qualitative pilot data collected from multiple sites throughout Bosnia and gathered information relating to social provisions and supportive exchanges from experienced local clinicians who served as supervisors and cultural experts in the UNICEF-sponsored program (Layne et al., 2001). These activities led to the decision to assess both the physical composition and perceptions of the availability of support from youths' social networks. Using social provisions theory as a guide (Weiss, 1974), MSSI items were generated following guidelines for the construction of ecologically valid tests (Smith, Fischer, & Fister, 2003). To enhance their cultural sensitivity (see Peña, 2007), test materials were translated and back-translated by expert translators with professional training in psychology or medicine. Items were then evaluated and modified in collaboration with the test author with respect to their cultural and developmental appropriateness.

As seen in Figure 7.1, sections of the MSSI were also developed to assess the structural composition of social support network sectors in terms of the nature, number, and losses of interpersonal relationships. The respondent places a checkmark next to the specific relationship categories within that sector (e.g., grandmother, grandfather, aunt, uncle, cousin) from which support is perceived to be available. Respondents also circle the number of relationships perceived as supportive within each checked relationship category (e.g., "If yes, how many uncles provide you with support?"). Optional loss-related items assess the nature and number of loved ones who were killed, disappeared, died of natural causes, or from whom the respondent is involuntarily separated due to the war. Due to their potentially evocative nature, these loss-related items should only be administered under clinically appropriate conditions.

Also as seen in Figure 7.1, a common set of nine items was generated to measure the perceived availability of each social provision as collectively furnished by the relationships within each of the four sectors. The question stems are identical across sectors, with the exception that the questions are referenced to members of the specific sector being assessed. All items are measured using a 5-point Likert-type frequency scale referenced to the past month ranging from 0, not at all; to 4, always. The nine items assess eight provisional dimensions of interpersonal relationships. To enhance clinical utility and brevity, each dimension is represented by one item per sector, except attachment, which is assessed by two items.[1] Seven items are drawn from Weiss's (1974) six-dimensional theory of social provisions, which include social integration, attachment, guidance and information, reliable alliance, reassurance of worth, and nurturance. To increase content validity and clinical utility, four additional dimensions extending beyond this framework were added to the final version of the MSSI. Each dimension was assessed by one item per sector, thus adding sixteen total additional items across the four sectors. Two social provisions, physical assistance and material support, were added based on their relevance in coping with adversities. Interpersonal conflict and burdensome obligations were also included to measure the stresses that social networks can impose, especially within stressful contexts (Kaniasty & Norris, 1993, 2004).

MSSI Test Validation

Psychometric Validation Procedures

Psychometric validation of the MSSI was undertaken in three studies. Analysis 1 was used to conduct both exploratory and confirmatory factor analyses to determine the internal structure of the MSSI and develop guidelines for test scoring and interpretation.

Analysis 2 examined the criterion-referenced validity of the newly derived MSSI sub-scales with respect to depression symptoms, a clinically relevant outcome variable often positively associated with exposure to war and its aftermath (e.g., Llabre & Hadi, 1997). To examine the MSSI's utility for research applications, this study tested a variety of hypothesized direct and interactive effects associated with the compensatory hypothesis. Analysis 3 employed a slightly expanded version of the MSSI (containing two additional items per sector measuring two additional relational provisions, instrumental and material support) to evaluate its test-retest reliability and convergent validity.

Analysis 1: Determining the MSSI Factor Structure and Scoring Protocol

The purpose of Analysis 1 was to determine the factor structure of the MSSI and develop recommendations for test scoring and interpretation. It was hypothesized that items designed to measure each of the social provisions, in addition to interpersonal conflict and burden, would load onto four sector-specific factors.

Participants and Procedure

Six hundred eighteen Sarajevo secondary school students (30% male, 63% female, 7% unreported; mean age = 16.85, range = 15–20; mean grade = 2.41, range = 1–4 in a 4-year school) completed the MSSI in combination with other measures not used in this study. Samples were collected in spring 1998 (approximately 2.5 years following the cessation of the Bosnian conflict) from eight secondary schools throughout the Republika Srpska, Bosnia, as part of the UNICEF Post-War Psychosocial Program for War-Exposed Adolescents (Layne et al., 2001). Following program protocol, school counselors who had received intensive training by the first author administered the questionnaire to participating students in a classroom setting.

Exploratory and Confirmatory Factor Analyses

MSSI test scores were first subjected to an exploratory factor analysis using SPSS 11.0 with principal axis extraction and oblimin rotation. Examination of scree plots, associated eigenvalues, and factor loadings suggested a six-factor solution comprised of the factors nuclear family support, extended family support, peer support, adult friend/mentor support, interpersonal conflict, and burden. Contrary to the hypothesis, the interpersonal conflict and burden items did not load onto their respective sector-specific factors, but loaded (across sectors) onto a fifth and a sixth factor, respectively. For this reason, the conflict and burden items were interpreted as indicators of constructs that were both distinct from and related to each other and to perceived social support. Given the focus of the study on measuring perceived social support, only the four social support factors were retained and tested in a structural equation model.

AMOS 4.0 (Arbuckle & Wothke, 1999) was used to conduct a confirmatory factor analysis of the four-factor perceived social support model, in which each test item was hypothesized to load its respective sector-specific factor. The four factors were hypothesized to covary with one another to a moderate to strong degree. Maximum likelihood estimation was used for all models. The independence model of no correlations among the observed variables was first rejected, $\chi^2(28) = 14,852.1$, $p < 0.001$. The hypothesized model was tested next, showing a significant improvement in model fit, $\chi^2(344) = 1,614.70$, $p < 0.001$, CFI (Comparison Fit Index) = 0.91.

Post hoc modifications were then conducted to develop a better-fitting model. Using standardized residual covariances and modification indices in conjunction with guiding theory, the error terms of the social provisions attachment (someone I can talk to about personal things) and advice were allowed to intercorrelate within each respective sector due to their close conceptual relatedness. This added four paths and resulted in an improved model fit, $\chi^2(340) = 1,312.23$, $p < 0.001$, CFI = 0.93. A χ^2 test of the difference between models indicated that the modified model constituted a significant improvement in fit compared to the original model, $\chi^2(4) = 302.47$, $p < 0.001$. In a second step prompted by many large standardized residual covariances among same-provision items across sectors, it was deemed reasonable to allow the error terms of each of the specific social provision items (reliable alliance, reassurance of worth, etc.) to intercorrelate across the sectors, thereby adding forty-two additional paths. The resulting model provided generally good fit, $\chi^2(298) = 827.92$, $p < 0.001$, CFI = 0.96, TLI (Tucker-Lewis Index) = 0.95; GFI (Goodness-of-Fit Index) = 0.91; AGFI (Adjust Goodness-of-Fit Index) = 0.88; RMSEA (Root Mean Square Error of Approximation) = 0.05. A χ^2 difference test indicated a significant improvement in fit compared to the first post-hoc model, $\chi^2(42) = 484.31$, $p < 0.001$. The second post hoc model was thus retained as the best approximation to the data and is presented in Figure 7.2.

Implications for Scoring and Interpreting the MSSI

These findings suggest that the MSSI should be scored by summing all items within each sector, thus generating four sector-specific subscale scores.[2] These subscale scores may be interpreted as reflecting the frequency with which all supportive provisions assessed are perceived to be available, as collectively furnished by the respondent's interpersonal relationships within each given sector. The lack of uniformly high structural intercorrelations among the four latent factors suggests that creating a perceived social support total scale score (across network sectors) is not empirically justifiable. As previously noted, the exploratory factor analytical results suggest that the conflict and burden items measure two separate underlying factors, each of which is distinct from perceived social support. With respect to the MSSI's structural items, network losses and the number and nature of existing supportive interpersonal relationships to date have been analyzed only at the descriptive level. This procedure is recommended, given that other factors that likely moderate the effects of support (e.g., network density, relationship quality; see Brissette, Cohen, & Seeman, 2000) are not assessed for the sake of brevity but can be assessed in conjunction with the measure.

Analysis 2: Social Support and Depression: A Test of the Compensatory Hypothesis

A primary purpose of Analysis 2 was to examine the criterion-referenced validity of the MSSI subscales with regard to a clinically relevant criterion variable—depression symptoms. Specifically, we hypothesized that inverse relationships would be found

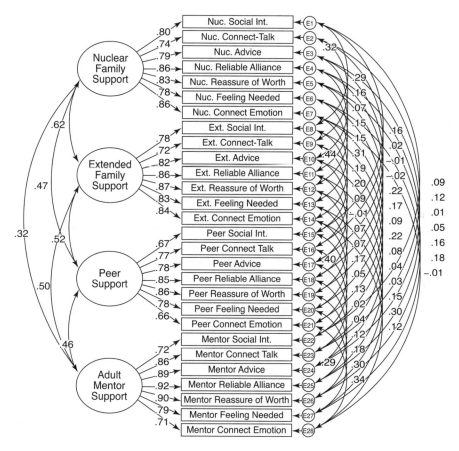

Figure 7.2. Results from the confirmatory factor analysis of the four-factor perceived social support model.

between depression and the levels of perceived social support within the four network sectors. A second purpose was to examine the flexibility and utility of the MSSI in testing questions relating to the compensatory hypothesis—that is, can support perceived to be available from one network sector compensate for perceived deficiencies in another? We theorized that perceived support from each social network sector would be inversely associated with depression (see Brajsa-Zganec, 2005). Because our focus was on the mean structure of these variables rather than the structure of the variances and covariances, we used multiple linear regression analysis in which DSRS (Depression Self-Rating Scale) scores served as the criterion variable and the four MSSI subscales served as predictor variables. We hypothesized that promotive factor–type main effects from each network sector would reach statistical significance. Furthermore, consistent with the compensatory hypothesis, we predicted three significant interactive effects between nuclear family support and extended family, peer, and adult friend/mentor support, respectively. If found, each interaction would suggest that the relationships between extended family, peers, and adult friends and mentors on depression, respectively, are moderated by nuclear family support—specifically, that the relationship between perceived support from these extra-nuclear family sectors and depression is of greater magnitude (suggesting greater beneficial impact) when nuclear family perceived support is low (suggesting deficiency) than when nuclear family perceived support is high (suggesting abundance).

Measure

The DSRS (Birleson, 1981) is a widely used eighteen-item self-administered scale for assessing children's depressive symptoms experienced within the past month. A modified 5-point frequency scale, ranging from never, 0, to almost always, 4, was used to increase variance and sensitivity to change and to standardize the scaling metric of measures contained in the questionnaire. The DSRS has demonstrated good internal consistency, reliability, and convergent validity in Bosnian adolescents using this metric (Djapo et al., 1998).

Participants and Procedure

A subsample of 530 students with complete data on the MSSI and the DSRS was selected for analysis from the larger Analysis 1 sample (subsample sex = 64% female, 30% male, 6% unreported; mean age = 16.8, SD = 1.66, age range = 15–20; mean grade level = 2.4, SD = 0.85, grade range = 1–4). DSRS scores ranged from 0 to 57 ($\overline{x}$ = 19.1, SD = 11.7). Although this DSRS data distribution tends toward the lower range of the scale, roughly 25% of the students possessed a DSRS score of at least twenty-eight, which served as an initial screening cut-off score used in Bosnia to classify students at risk for depression in need of further follow-up (Layne et al., 2001).

Analysis 2 examined hypothesized associations between student's perceptions of social support as measured by the four MSSI subscales and self-reported depression as measured by the DSRS. Because each MSSI subscale consists of seven items, each measured on a frequency scale ranging from 0, never, to 4, almost always, each subscale score ranges from 0 to 28 using the recommended summative scoring procedure. To increase interpretability and facilitate analysis of the study hypotheses, all subscale scores were partitioned into the following four categories, which corresponded (roughly) to sample quartiles across the four subscales.[3] These included low support (score of 0–17 out of 28 possible, = average subscale score between 0 and 2.5); medium-low support (score of 18–21, = average score of 2.5 to 3.0); medium-high support (score of 22–25, = average score of 3.0 to 3.5); and high support (score of 26–28, = average score of 3.5 to 4.0). Table 7.1 shows the number of students within each category for each of the four MSSI subscale scores. The distribution of perceived nuclear family support was negatively skewed and centered at the high end of the categories, with 60% of scores falling within high support and 20% falling within medium-high support. In contrast, the distributions of extended family and peer support were similar to each other, with fairly even distributions across the four categories. Adult mentors/friends support was positively skewed and centered at the low end, with 42% of scores falling within the low support category.

Table 7.1 Univariate Frequency Distributions for the Four MSSI Subscales

	Frequency of Students [n and (%)] in Each Supportive Category				
MSSI Subscale	Low Support (range = 0–17)	Medium-Low Support (range = 18–21)	Medium-High Support (range = 22–25)	High Support (range = 26–28)	Total *n*
Nuclear family support	65 (12)	40 (8)	108 (20)	317 (60)	530
Extended family support	148 (28)	120 (23)	117 (22)	145 (27)	530
Peer support	125 (24)	93 (17)	152 (29)	160 (30)	530
Adult mentor support	222 (42)	134 (25)	104 (20)	70 (13)	530

Bivariate Analyses and Results

Figure 7.3 is a graph of unadjusted (i.e., raw or unmodeled) mean DSRS scores, each plotted across the four MSSI categories. The standard deviations for these averages range from nine to twelve. These findings are generally consistent with the hypothesis that perceived social support is inversely associated with self-reported depression symptoms. Moreover, these findings raised questions pertaining to the comparative potency of perceived social support across network sectors.[4] That is, which subscale score, adjusted for the effects of the others, was most strongly (inversely) associated with depression symptoms?

In a first step, four separate multiple regression models were run in which DSRS scores were modeled using each of the four MSSI subscales in turn. Each model resulted

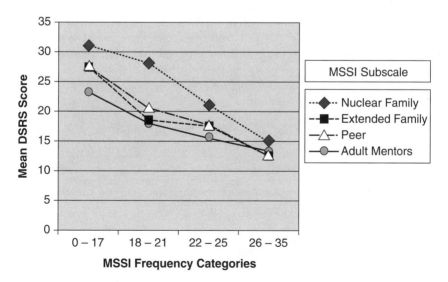

Figure 7.3. Average DSRS scores as a function of four MSSI frequency categories.

in statistically significant associations between the criterion and single predictor. Nuclear family support explained the most variability in DSRS scores ($R^2 = 25.5\%$); extended family support ($R^2 = 23.0\%$) and peer support ($R^2 = 21.5\%$) explained roughly similar proportions of variability; and adult mentors/friends support ($R^2 = 10.5\%$) explained a modest proportion.

Multivariate Analyses and Results

Although the preceding analysis found significant bivariate relationships between each MSSI subscale score and DSRS scores, the moderate to strong intercorrelations among the subscales observed in Analysis 1 suggested the need for modeling each predictive relationship after statistically adjusting for all other MSSI subscales. Three multiple regression models and their corresponding results are presented in Table 7.2. Model 1 included each MSSI subscale and all possible two-way subscale interactions (e.g., nuclear family × extended family, × peers, and × adult mentors/friends). Contrary to the compensatory hypothesis, no significant two-way interactions were found (all p's > 0.05).

Model 2 consequently dropped all interaction terms and estimated only main effects (see Table 7.2). Contrary to the hypothesis that all MSSI subscales would predict a unique proportion of criterion variance, one predictor, adult mentors/friends support, did not reach significance as a predictor of DSRS scores after adjusting for the predictive effects of the three other social sectors.

Model 3 consequently dropped the adult mentors/friends subscale scores while retaining the other three subscale scores, explaining a total of 37% of DSRS score variance. All three predictors reached significance at $p < 0.05$ or lower. Nuclear family support was most strongly associated with depression scores $F(3, 520) = 15.00$, followed by peer support $F(3, 520) = 12.90$, and extended family support $F(3, 520) = 8.90$ (see Table 7.2).

A next step involved the estimation of DSRS means for the main-effects model, which are presented in Table 7.3. This method of analysis is useful in understanding the unique relationship between DSRS scores and each MSSI subscale (including adult mentors/friends) after adjusting for the predictive effects of the three other MSSI subscales. These estimated means are also useful because they do not require

Table 7.2 Results from Three ANOVA Models Regressing DSRS Scores onto MSSI Subscales

Model	Model Components	DF	MSE	R^2
1	Depression regressed on nuclear family, extended family, peer, and adult mentors/friends support, plus all two-way subscale interactions	64	9.40	0.43
2	Depression regressed on nuclear family, extended family, peer, and adult mentors/friends support	12	9.36	0.37
3	Depression regressed on nuclear family, extended family, and peer support	9	9.34	0.37

Table 7.3 Estimated Average DSRS Scores Using the Main Effects Model

MSSI Subscale	Low Support (range = 0–17) A	Medium-Low Support (range = 18–21) B	Medium-High Support (range = 22–25) C	High Support (range = 26–28) D	Total N
Nuclear family support	34.4	33.3	28.3[a,b]	25.5[a,b,c]	530
Extended family support	34.4	29.8[a]	30.4[a]	27.6[a,b,c]	530
Peer support	34.4	30.2[a]	29.3[a]	26.6[a,b,c]	530
Adult mentor/ friend support	34.4	33.6	34.0	34.3	530

[a]Significantly lower ($p < 0.05$) than Low Support (category A).
[b]Significantly lower ($p < 0.05$) than Medium-Low Support (category B).
[c]Significantly lower ($p < 0.05$) than Medium-High Support (category C).

the assumption that the relationship between each subscale score and the criterion is strictly linear across all levels of perceived support. Because no between-subscale interactions were found, the predictive effect of each MSSI subscale was interpreted as independent of the predictive effects of the others. To facilitate interpretation, the estimated means in Table 7.3 assume that all respondents' scores on all MSSI subscales other than the one under examination fall in the lowest category (i.e., low support). This method provides a common reference point by which to evaluate whether incremental increases across a given subscale's support categories, starting from the lowest category, are associated with statistically reliable decreases in DSRS scores. This method also statistically isolates the predictive relationship between a given subscale score and the criterion variable by holding other subscale scores constant at their lowest value.

As viewed in Table 7.3, respondents whose scores fall in the low support category on each the four MSSI subscales have an estimated average DSRS score of 34.4. Increasing nuclear family support by one category increment to medium-low support (while remaining in the low support category on the other subscales) generates an estimated average DSRS score of 33.3, which is not significantly lower than that of the low support category, $p > 0.05$. In contrast, persons with medium-high or high levels of nuclear family support have estimated depression scores of 28.3 and 25.5, respectively. As indicated in the table, these means reliably differ from the lower two nuclear family support categories and from one other.

The extended family and peer support subscales are quite similar to each other in their relationships with DSRS scores. The estimated mean DSRS score for the lowest support levels are significantly higher than the other three support categories; the medium-low and medium-high levels of support are not significantly different from each other, and the estimated mean DSRS scores of the high support category are significantly lower than the three lower category levels. Consistent with the null findings of the previous analysis, no significant differences in estimated DSRS scores were found across levels of adult mentors/friends support, indicating an inert predictive effect.

Analysis 3: Evaluation of MSSI Test Reliability and Convergent Validity

Analysis 3 evaluated two main psychometric properties of MSSI data: reliability and convergent validity. Reliability was evaluated using estimates of internal consistency reliability and 2-week test-retest reliability. We theorized that although the construct of social support as measured by the MSSI changes over time, the construct was sufficiently stable that it would change negligibly over a 2-week period. Accordingly, 2-week test-retest reliability estimates reflect instrument reliability (i.e., freedom from unsystematic measurement error) rather than construct variability (i.e., variability in respondents' true scores on the construct across the assessment periods). Convergent validity was evaluated using correlations between the MSSI subscale scores and measures of clinically relevant criteria. Specifically, we hypothesized that the MSSI subscale scores would correlate strongly with an established measure of perceived social support and correlate moderately with measures of theoretically related constructs, including anxiety, somatic distress, grief, and post-traumatic stress reactions.

Measures

Measures included a gold standard criterion measure of perceived social support, the Provision of Social Relations Scale (PSRS; Turner, Frankel, & Levin, 1983), a fifteen-item widely used measure of perceived social support that, like the MSSI, is based on Weiss's (1974) social provisions framework. The scale includes two subscales, Family Support and Peer Support. Three widely used clinically relevant measures were included to gauge the MSSI's convergent validity. These included the UCLA Reaction Index-Revised (Steinberg, Brymer, Decker, & Pynoos, 2004), a seventeen-item measure of the frequency with which post-traumatic stress symptoms were experienced within the past month, and the Brief Symptom Inventory (BSI; Derogatis & Spencer, 1982), a twenty-four-item widely used self-report inventory of symptoms of psychological distress experienced during the preceding 7 days. Four BSI subscales were used in the present study, including Anxiety, Depression, Psychosomatic Symptoms, and Hostility. The DSRS, described in Analysis 2, was included as an additional clinical criterion measure. Last, the UCLA Grief Inventory (Layne et al., 2001), a self-report measure of maladaptive grief reactions, was used. Two subscales were used in the study: traumatic grief (in which distressing recollections of the death interfere with adaptive grief processes; six items), and existential grief (characterized by the loss of perceived purpose and meaning to one's life following bereavement; six items).[5]

Participants and Procedure

Participants were drawn from a different sample than those used in Analyses 1 and 2, and were comprised of 114 Sarajevo secondary school students (sex = 76.6% female, 14.5% male, 8.9% unreported; mean age = 16.67, SD = 0.93, age range = 15–18; mean grade = 2.56, SD = 1.04, grade range = 1–4). Students completed a battery of all tests on two separate occasions, separated by a 2-week interval, in a classroom setting in spring 2002 (more than 6 years postwar).

Test-Retest and Internal Consistency Reliability

Two-week test-retest Pearson correlation coefficients and Cronbach's α internal consistency reliability coefficients were calculated for all tests administered. The test-retest reliability coefficients of the MSSI subscales scores fell within the low-acceptable to very good range (values ranged between 0.59 for peer support to 0.81 for extended family support). In comparison, the test-retest reliability coefficients for the PSRS (values were 0.70 and 0.73 for peer and family support, respectively), and for the clinical criterion measures (values ranged between 0.64 to 0.84 for the reaction index, the DSRS, and the two grief subscales) generally fell within the acceptable range. Internal consistency coefficients of the MSSI subscales were also good to very good (α values ranged from 0.80 for peer support to 0.93 for adult mentors/friends). These values compared favorably to those of the PSRS (α values were 0.76 and 0.79 for the Family and Friends subscales, respectively), and to the clinical criterion measures (α values ranged between 0.74 to 0.89 for the reaction index, the DSRS, and the two grief subscales) in this validation sample.

Convergent Validity

In general, the MSSI subscales showed acceptable convergent validity with reference to the PSRS, as manifest by $r = 0.66$ between the MSSI and PSRS peer support subscales and $r = 0.60$ between the MSSI nuclear family support and PSRS family support subscales. In addition, the MSSI nuclear and extended family subscales showed generally good convergent validity in relation to theoretically related criterion measures (values ranged between a low of $r = -0.18$, $p < 0.03$ between extended family support and somatization, and a high of $r = -0.51$ between nuclear family support and DSRS depression scores, $p < 0.01$). Both nuclear and extended family support correlated -0.48 with the BSI depression subscale, $p < 0.01$. In comparison, criterion-referenced correlation coefficients ranged between 0.30 to 0.70 for the UCLA reaction index, 0.37 to 0.62 for the DSRS, and 0.23 to 0.58 for the two grief subscales in reference to the same set of intercorrelated measures.

Discussion

In this chapter, we describe the development and preliminary psychometric validation of a multisector measure of perceived social support—the MSSI—based on the proposition that psychometrically sound measurement instruments are indispensable tools for creating evidence-based, theoretically grounded, culturally relevant intervention programs and public policies that target youth exposed to severe stress. Accordingly, this chapter is a response to the child and adolescent trauma research agenda for the next decade proposed by Saigh, Fairbank, and Yasik (1998) in attempting to raise the standard of care for identifying and treating traumatized youth by increasing the soundness and clinical utility of the theories and tests used in designing, implementing, evaluating, and improving child and adolescent interventions. We further propose that the tragic and terrifying circumstances of war and disaster can be employed to develop, evaluate, and refine theories, measures, and interventions designed to benefit those exposed to its horrors. Because the study of stress resistance and resilient recovery involves examining adaptive functioning in stressful contexts, the study of youth exposed to war and disaster may lead to the identification of biopsychosocial mechanisms and processes that promote positive adaptation under conditions of extreme and often protracted stress (see Layne et al., 2007, and Layne, Beck, et al., 2008, for elaborations on this potential).

Summary of Findings

In Analysis 1, we used exploratory and confirmatory factor analysis to identify a good-fitting factor structure for the MSSI, which created four sector-specific summative perceived social support scales—namely, nuclear family support, extended family support, peer support, and adult friend/mentor support. Using this scoring procedure, Analysis 2 provided support for the convergent validity of the MSSI with respect to measures of depression symptoms and illustrated its flexibility and value in investigating questions relating to the compensatory hypothesis. Notably, the results of Analysis 2 only partially supported the study hypotheses, finding no support for the compensatory hypothesis in the form of interactive effects. Rather, main promotive factor–type effects were found for perceived support from the nuclear family, extended family, and peer network sectors, but not from the adult friend/mentor sector, in relation to depression symptoms. Our analyses also suggests that the relationships between levels of perceived support from the social network sectors and depression symptoms may depart from linearity. Last, results from Analysis 3 indicated acceptable to good test-retest reliability, internal consistency reliability, and convergent validity in reference to measures of a range of clinically relevant constructs.

Strengths, Weaknesses, and Caveats Pertaining to the Use of the MSSI

Strengths of the MSSI are found in its conformity to the recommendations of Wills and Shinar (2000) that social support measures should be of a length sufficient to measure a range of supportive functions and possess moderate to small intersubscale correlations to enhance sensitivity to differential effects for various supportive functions. The MSSI also conforms to Kaniasty and Norris's (1993) recommendations to measure both negative and positive dimensions of interpersonal interactions. Notably, the "negative" dimensions of interpersonal conflict and burden did not load on the same factors as the perceived support items and were thus excluded from the subsequent confirmatory factor analysis. Last, this study found an interpretable, adequately fitting factor structure for the measure and evidence supporting its construct validity.

With respect to drawbacks, the study design was cross-sectional, precluding causal inference. Significant associations found between variables should thus be interpreted as being consistent with but not reflective of causal relationships. Moreover, the MSSI possesses at least three notable weaknesses and associated caveats relating to its use. First, the measure uses a self-report format and thus is vulnerable to errors in measurement inherent in the use of this methodology. However, this is not necessarily an undesirable feature of the measure. As noted by Reis and Collins (2000), the use of self-report measures in perceived social support is indispensable because it reflects personal perspectives on matters that are "inherently subjective and idiosyncratic" (p. 165). Second, the MSSI imposes a trade-off noted by Wills and Shinar (2000) between breadth of measurement and precision with respect to the measurement of relationships and supportive provisions. Specifically, the MSSI is an aggregate measure of perceived social support within each network sector (e.g., "I can count on members of my extended family if I need help"), as opposed to referencing specific interpersonal relationships. Like many other measures, the MSSI consequently leaves room for subjectivity in how multiple interpersonal relationships within a given sector (e.g., grandfathers, grandmothers, aunts, uncles, and cousins) are appraised and integrated into an overall perceived availability score for a given social provision within that sector.

A third concern relates to the inclusion of items assessing social network size within each network sector. As noted by Brissette et al. (2000), the relationship between network size (a structural feature of social support networks) and health outcomes tends to be weak. Indeed, the authors suggest that measures of network density be used in studies of the links between social integration and psychosocial adjustment. Notwithstanding these concerns, a primary purpose of the MSSI's structural items is to conduct a postdisaster damage report by assessing which elements of the social network are compromised (due to deaths, involuntary separations, or disappearances) and which relationships remain intact and available for use in recruiting support.

In light of these considerations, it seems reasonable to infer that these study results provide promising initial evidence regarding the psychometric soundness of the MSSI as used with war-exposed youths and point to the benefits of conducting applied clinical research in field settings. Additional evaluation of the psychometric soundness and clinical utility of the MSSI is needed. These include replication studies of the full test's factor structure (containing all eight provisional dimensions) and evaluating construct validity, including convergent validity in reference to measures of a broader range of constructs and discriminant validity. Moreover, additional study is needed focusing on the stability of the MSSI's factor structure and its appropriateness and utility across different contexts, including stressor types (e.g., war versus disaster versus community violence versus everyday hassles), developmental periods, cultural groups, and genders. Longitudinal studies could also examine differences in the structure, composition, and supportive provisions provided by different network sectors over time and their comparative protective or promotive effects. Additional study is also needed in relation to investigating the test's clinical utility in such applications as triage to appropriate treatments, case conceptualization and treatment planning, and treatment outcome (Burns & Haynes, 2007). Finally, the adequate model fit indices obtained suggest the need for further examination of model specification, including identifying sources of method and error variance (Podsakoff, MacKenzie, Lee, & Podsakoff, 2003).

Directions for Future Research

Applied clinical research conducted under stressful circumstances may help elucidate which causal mechanisms impart beneficial or adverse effects, the processes through which they convey their influences, and their relative potencies (Layne et al., 2007;

Layne, Beck, et al., 2008). This knowledge, in turn, can assist in developing prevention and intervention programs, as recommended by Luthar et al. (2006), that target mechanisms prevalent in youths' environments, amenable to intervention that exert relatively enduring effects over youths' lives and facilitate the beneficial effects of other factors. We describe six research avenues that may promote these aims.

Avenue 1: Investigate the Intersection between Social Provisions Theory and Grief

Fruitful cross-pollination may come by exploring the intersection between social provisions and grief "tasks" or processes. Social provisions theory carries considerable explanatory power in accounting for what bereaved individuals are grieving the loss of as they grieve and what accommodation to the loss entails. Bereaved youth grieve not only the physical loss of a significant person but also the loss of what the relationship did for them—the provisions it furnished and the functions they served. As noted by Lieberman, Compton, Van Horn, and Ippen (2003), the more provisions and functions a relationship provides and serves (e.g., mothering in childhood), the more central and nonredundant a role it plays in one's life and identity and the more disruptive and devastating its loss will be. Due to their pervasively disorganizing consequences, the loss of central life figures may increase the risk for maladaptive existential grief reactions characterized by the perceived loss of a sense of life purpose, meaning, direction, and identity, and the adoption of a nihilistic outlook (e.g., "I feel like part of me has died"; "I've lost what I cared about the most, so nothing else matters"; Layne & Larsen, 2008). Moreover, many grief processes involve accommodating to the loss of social provisions, such as by forming or deepening relationships to furnish lost provisions, engaging in gratifying activities to compensate for lost provisions, or learning to do without (Worden, 1996).

Notwithstanding its utility, we caution that the injudicious application of social provisions theory to bereaved populations may both suggest a naiveté toward grieving processes and set the stage for superficially optimistic and insensitive "Pollyanna" interventions. For example, the suggestion that a grandfather or adult mentor can be invited to provide advice that a deceased father formerly gave may convey the assumption that exchanging "compensatory" provisions reflects interchangeable relationships and, by extension, replaceable people. The failure to honor the special and specific ways a close relationship furnished provisions, or the failure to acknowledge that most reconfigured social networks only partially compensate for lost provisions and that much of grief work involves often painful, difficult, uncomfortable, and protracted striving to recruit and accommodate to new sources, types, and ways of exchanging provisions, may be perceived as patronizing and devaluing toward both the deceased and the bereaved.

Avenue 2: Investigate Cultural Variations in the Definition, Expression, Use, and Effects of Social Support

Cultural sensitivity is integral to the appropriate conceptualization, measurement, and enhancement of social support in intervention efforts (Peña, 2007). A first step in constructing a given culturally valid test is the clear specification of the theoretical construct the test is intended to measure (Haynes et al., 1995). Culture may powerfully influence the ways social support manifests and "behaves" in specific populations and settings, how it is valued, how it is best measured, and its causes, correlates, and sequelae (Taylor, Welch, Kim, & Sherman, 2007). For example, a study of Somali refugees found that family units are integrated so completely that they cannot be meaningfully subdivided into distinct nuclear and extended family social network sectors (H. Ellis, personal communication, September 7, 2004). Cultural differences may also be found in the specific social network sectors to which youth turn for support. For example, Bosnian youth rarely turn to formal adult mentors, such as school counselors and teachers, for support because seeking mental health services is often stigmatized and because teacher-student roles tend to be highly prescribed and circumscribed. Rather, many youth reported that most support they receive from this network sector comes from adult neighbors and family friends who pay informal social visits.

Furthermore, although not the direct consequence of culture, the breakdown and disruption of social structures consequent to war and disaster can make conceptualizing and measuring youths' social networks (including the presence, structure, and composition of meaningfully distinct social network sectors) challenging. For example, if an orphaned child now lives with her aunt and uncle, is she still living with her extended family? What if a child is raised for an extended period by grandparents or a foster family? Although social provisions theory asserts that a variety of life organizations are adequate if they provide the requisite support, assessing the structural composition and functions of such varying life organizations is a formidable undertaking. Scores on the same social support measure may thus have substantively different meanings across varying cultural, developmental, and other contexts (Bolton, 2006).

Accordingly, efforts to develop or adapt measures of support-related phenomena should address factors likely to influence their conceptualization, measurement, utilization, and potency. It may thus behoove researchers to place higher priority on developing or adapting ecologically valid tests of social support for specific populations compared to the use of standardized, widely used social support measures. Although the latter strategy increases the possibility of (at least superficial) between-study comparisons, the use of "standardized" tests across disparate cultural and developmental contexts may introduce significant problems with ecological relevance and construct validity (Bolton, 2006; Layne & Larsen, 2008; Osterman & de Jong, 2007). Where appropriate, measuring both perceived and received social support will further elucidate the interrelationships between support perception processes and support enactment processes; measures of network density may also be profitably added.

Avenue 3: Clarify the Interrelationships between Negative versus Positive Processes in Interpersonal Relationships

Studies are also needed regarding how to conceptualize, measure, and therapeutically address the links between "negative" and "positive" features of interpersonal relationships. Kaniasty and Norris (1993) called for the inclusion of both stressful and supportive aspects of social relationships in studies of social support. Unfortunately, theories and instruments that can elucidate the structure and relationships between these dimensions (see Kaniasty & Norris's 2004 distinctions between altruistic helping, patriotism, and social bitterness) are in short supply in the literature. Pursuant to this end, our exploratory factor analytic findings that interpersonal conflict and interpersonal burden items loaded on two respective cross-sector factors, whereas the social provision items loaded on four within-sector factors, suggest that the conflict and burden items reflect factors that are theoretically and empirically related to but distinct from perceived social support in Bosnian adolescents.

Avenue 4: Develop Theories and Interventions that Facilitate Appropriate Support Seeking and Support Receiving

As noted by Hobfoll (1988), many social support studies are based on the implicit assumption that support receivers are passive recipients of support. By extension, "deficiencies" in support reflect inadequacies within individual's social network. Hobfoll criticizes this perspective for failing to account for the considerable influence that individuals exert over the sources, types, amounts, duration, quality, timeliness, and frequency of support that they recruit, receive, and use from their interpersonal relationships (see Gottlieb, 1996). Studies are thus needed to clarify the processes through which youth effectively recruit and utilize support from their interpersonal networks. For example, Saltzman et al. (2006) describe Trauma and Grief Component Therapy, a core component of which is learning support seeking and support giving skills. Youth learn to identify demands that stressful situations place on them, select a social provision to assist them in coping with those demands, and recruit support from sources of that provision. Participants identified this skill as one of the most valuable benefits of the program (Cox et al., 2007).

Moreover, attention should be given to clarifying cultural, developmental, and other factors that may moderate the effectiveness of support-focused interventions. For example, the finding in Analysis 2 that perceived support from the adult friends and mentors sector did not predict depression scores raises questions regarding whether this sector, commonly targeted in resilience-enhancing interventions, is an optimal intervention site with Bosnian youth at risk for depression. Rather, our findings suggest that the nuclear family sector where appropriate, in addition to the extended family or peer sectors, may yield a higher benefit. Furthermore, evidence of additive direct effects suggests that multipronged interventions targeting several network sectors may have incrementally beneficial effects in reducing risk for depression.

Avenue 5: Investigate and Therapeutically Harness Cognitive Mediators and Moderators of Social Support

Studies and interventions are also needed focusing on cognitive factors that may mediate or moderate the links between stress, perceived support, and psychosocial adjustment. Examples include rules, attitudes, and assumptions pertaining to support seeking (Reinecke, Dattilio, & Freeman, 2003) and efficacy-based expectations. Self-efficacy and collective efficacy are emerging as influential variables in the link between social support and psychosocial adaptation, assuming such roles as mediator, moderator, or independent promotive factor (see Benight & Bandura, 2004). Recent evidence indicates that social support, self-efficacy, and a sense of connection to one's broader community are associated (Vieno, Santinello, Pastore, & Perkins, 2007), suggesting that social support and efficacy may be linked to allegiance to the social contract (see Spencer et al., 2006). Moreover, youth with histories of exposure to high-magnitude and recurrent traumatic experiences during critical early developmental periods, including severe abuse, neglect, domestic violence, or armed conflict, may carry significant impairments in core capacities for self-regulation, secure attachment, and interpersonal relatedness (Cook et al., 2005). These youth may require significant preparatory work, such as building positive expectations concerning the safety and beneficial nature of interpersonal relationships (M. Cloitre, personal communication, September 2002) or acquiring foundational interpersonal and self-regulation skills (e.g., DeRosa et al., 2006) before they may benefit from learning support-recruiting skills.

Avenue 6: Investigate Links between Damage to Youths' Social Support Networks and the Networks' Abilities to Furnish Support

Studies have historically investigated the risks that war-inflicted damage to youths' social networks—including the violent death, disappearance, physical injury, persecution, detention of, or forced separations from loved ones—pose for developing PTSD and other mental disorders (e.g., Goldstein et al., 1997). Studies are now needed that focus on ways in which damage and disruptions to youths' social networks may influence youths' perceived or received social support. Such disruptions also constitute opportunities to test and apply the compensatory hypothesis—to what extent and how are youth and their caregivers able to reassemble, shape, and manage youths' support networks to provide the types of support they need over time?

Conclusion

We hope that the rigorous study of social support will assist in raising the standard of care for youth exposed to war, disaster, and other severe stressors. When furnished with theories and measurement tools that facilitate the gathering of reliable, valid, culturally appropriate, and developmentally sensitive information, practitioners, policy makers, researchers, humanitarian agencies, and advocacy groups will be better prepared to mount wellness-oriented public health prevention and intervention programs (Layne, Beck, et al., 2008). Thus empowered, these shareholders will be better able to progress from articulating what they want to accomplish to a concrete knowledge pertaining to why, with whom, where, how, and when to carry it out.

Acknowledgments   The MSSI is available free of charge for research or clinical use, pending the signing of a data-sharing agreement with the first author. Support for this work was provided by UNICEF Bosnia & Herzegovina; the Family Studies Center and the Kennedy International Studies Center, both of Brigham Young University; the UCLA Trauma Psychiatry Bing Fund; and Tony Bennett. The authors wish to thank participating Bosnian school counselors and their students, who generously contributed their time and effort to data collection. The authors are grateful to Drs. Heidi Ellis and Daniel and Lynda King, in addition to two anonymous reviewers and the editor, for helpful suggestions on earlier drafts of this chapter.

Notes

1. Consistent with Furman and Buhrmester's (1985) observation that individuals may have strong feelings of affection for others without necessarily engaging in intimate disclosures with them, *attachment* is represented by two items, one assessing feelings of affection; the other, intimate disclosure.
2. Because MSSI test items were clustered in the questionnaire by social network sector (e.g., nuclear family, extended family), and not by social provision (e.g., connection, social integration) or in random order (e.g., randomly intermixed with items from other tests), the possibility that item ordering may have significantly influenced the obtained factor structure cannot be ruled out. However, the finding that burden and conflict items respectively loaded on burden and conflict factors across network sectors argues against this possibility.
3. Because data distributions for each of the four MSSI subscales were centered towards the high end of the scale, divisions into these quartiles do not constitute equal intervals along the measurement scale used.
4. This investigation searched for markers of potency only. Given the cross-sectional nature of the design, causal inference is precluded.
5. A detailed description of these measures and their associated psychometric properties is available from the first author.

References

Ahmetasevic, N. (2007). Justice report: Bosnia's Book of the Dead. Retrieved October 16, 2007, from Balkan Investigative Reporting Network Web site, http://www.birn.eu.com/en/88/10/3377.

Arbuckle, J. L., & Wothke, W. (1999). *AMOS 4.0 user's guide*. Chicago: Smallwaters.

Benight, C. C., & Bandura, A. (2004). Social cognitive theory of recovery: The role of perceived self-efficacy. *Behaviour Research and Therapy, 42,* 1129–1148.

Benson, P. L., Scales, P. C., Hamilton, S. F., & Sesma, A. (2006). Positive youth development: Theory, research, and applications. In W. Damon & R. M. Lerner (Eds.), *Handbook of child psychology* (pp. 894–941). Hoboken, NJ: John Wiley & Sons.

Birleson, P. (1981). The validity of depressive disorder in childhood and the development of a self-rating scale: A research report. *Journal of Child Psychology and Psychiatry, 22,* 73–88.

Bolton, P. (2006). Challenges in international disaster mental health research. In G. Reyes & G. A. Jacobs (Eds.), *Handbook of international disaster psychology: Refugee mental health* (vol. 3, pp. 115–127). Westport, CT: Praeger Publishers/Greenwood.

Brajsa-Zganec, A. (2005). The long-term effects of war experiences on children's depression in the Republic of Croatia. *Child Abuse and Neglect: The International Journal, 29,* 31–43.

Brissette, I., Cohen, S., & Seeman, T. E. (2000). Measuring social integration and social networks. In S. Cohen, L. G. Underwood, & B. H. Gottlieb (Eds.), *Social support measurement and intervention: A guide for health and social scientists* (pp. 53–85). New York: Oxford University Press.

Bronfenbrenner, U. (1977). Toward an experimental ecology of human development. *American Psychologist, 32,* 513–531.

Bronfenbrenner, U. (1979). The ecology of human development: Experiments by nature and design. Cambridge, Mass: Harvard University Press.

Burlingham, D., & Freud, A. (1949). *Kriegskinder* [War children]. Oxford: Imago.

Burns, G. L., & Haynes, S. N. (2007). Clinical psychology: Construct validation with multiple sources of information and multiple settings. In M. Eid & E. Diener (Eds.), *Handbook of multimethod measurement in psychology* (pp. 401–418). Washington, DC: American Psychological Association.

Cauce, A. M., Hannan, K., & Sargeant, M. (1992). Life stress, social support, and locus of control during early adolescence: Interactive effects. *American Journal of Community Psychology, 20,* 787–798.

Cauce, A. M., Reid, M., Landesman, S., & Gonzales, N. (1990). Social support in young children: Measurement, structure, and behavioral impact. In B. R. Sarason, I. G. Sarason, & G. R. Pierce (Eds.), *Social support: An interactional view* (pp. 64–94). New York: John Wiley & Sons.

Cobb, S. (1976). Social support as a moderator of life stress. *Psychosomatic Medicine, 38,* 300–314.

Cook, A., Spinazzola, J., Ford, J., Lanktree, C., Bluestein, M., Cloitre, M., et al. (2005). Complex trauma in children and adolescents. *Psychiatric Annals, 35,* 390–398.

Cox, J., Davies, D. R., Burlingame, G. M., Campbell, J. E., Layne, C. M., & Katzenbach, R. J. (2007). Effectiveness of a trauma/grief–focused group intervention: A qualitative study with war-exposed Bosnian adolescents. *International Journal of Group Psychotherapy, 57,* 319–345.

Cutrona, C. E., & Russell, D. W. (1987). The provisions of social relationships and adaptation to stress. In W. H. Jones & D. Perlman (Eds.), *Advances in personal relationships* (vol. 1, pp. 37–67). Greenwich, CT: JAI Press.

Derogatis, L. R., & Spencer, P. M. (1982). The Brief Symptom Inventory (BSI): Administration and Procedures Manual-I. Baltimore, MD: Clinical Psychometric Research.

DeRosa, R., Habib, M., Pelcovitz, D., Rathus, J., Sonnenklar, J., Ford, J., et al. (2006). Structured psychotherapy for adolescents responding to chronic stress (SPARCS). Treatment manual. North Shore Hospital, New York.

Djapo, N., Kutlac, M., Layne, C. M., Pynoos, R. S., Gold, M., & Stuvland, R. (1998, August). School-based psychosocial interventions for adolescents exposed to war trauma. In R. Stuvland & S. Hessle (Chairs), *UNICEF psychosocial programs in Bosnia & Hercegovina.* Symposium conducted at the meeting of the International Association of Child and Adolescent Psychiatry and Allied Professions, Stockholm, Sweden.

DuBois, D. L., Felner, R. D., Brand, S., Adan, A. M., & Evans, E. G. (1992). A prospective study of life stress, social support, and adaptation in early adolescence. *Child Development, 63,* 542–557.

Dubow, E. F., Tisak, J., Causey, D., Hryshko, A., & Reid, G. (1991). A two-year longitudinal study of stressful life events, social support, and social problem-solving skills: Contributions to children's behavioral and academic adjustment. *Child Development, 62,* 583–599.

Dubow, E. F., Edwards, S., & Ippolito, M. F. (1997). Life stressors, neighborhood disadvantage, and resources: A focus on inner-city children's adjustment. *Journal of Clinical Child Psychology, 26,* 130–144.

Ekblad, S. (1993). Psychological adaptation of children while housed in a Swedish refugee camp: Aftermath of the collapse of Yugoslavia, *Stress Medicine, 9,* 159–166.

Feiring, C., & Lewis, M. (1989). The social networks of girls and boys from early through middle childhood. In D. Belle (Ed.), *Children's social networks and social supports* (pp. 119–150). New York: John Wiley & Sons.

Friedman, M. J., Resick, P. A., & Keane, T. M. (2007). Key questions and an agenda for future research. In M. J. Friedman, T. M. Keane, & P. A. Resick (Eds.), *Handbook of PTSD: Science and practice* (pp. 540–561). New York: Guilford.

Furman, W. (1989). The development of children's social networks. In D. Belle (Ed.), *Children's social networks and social supports* (pp. 151–172). New York: John Wiley & Sons.

Furman, W., & Buhrmester, D. (1985). Children's perceptions of the personal relationships in their social networks. *Developmental Psychology, 21,* 1016–1024.

Garmezy, N. (1974). The study of competence in children at risk for severe psychopathology. In E. J. Anthony & C. Koupernik (Eds.), *The child in his family: Vol. 3. Children at psychiatric risk* (pp. 77–97). New York: John Wiley & Sons.

Goldstein, R. D., Wampler, N. S., & Wise, P. H. (1997). War experiences and distress symptoms of Bosnian children. *Pediatrics, 100,* 873–878.

Gottlieb, B. H. (1991). Social support in adolescence. In M. E. Colten & S. Gore (Eds.), *Adolescent stress: Causes and consequences. Social institutions and social change* (pp. 281–306). Hawthorne, NY: Aldine de Gruyter.

Gottlieb, B. H. (1996). Theories and practices of mobilizing support in stressful circumstances. In C. L. Cooper (Ed.), *Handbook of stress, medicine, and health* (pp. 339–356). Boca Raton, FL: CRC Press.

Haynes, S. N., Richard, D. C. S., & Kubany, E. S. (1995). Content validity in psychological assessment: A functional approach to concepts and methods. *Psychological Assessment, 7,* 238–247.

Heller, K., Price, R. H., & Hogg, J. R. (1990). The role of social support in community and clinical interventions. In B. R. Sarason, I. G. Sarason, & G. R. Pierce (Eds.), *Social support: An interactional view* (pp. 482–507). New York: John Wiley & Sons.

Hobfoll, S. E. (1988). *The ecology of stress.* New York: Hemisphere.

Kaniasty, K., & Norris, F. H. (1993). A test of the support deterioration model in the context of natural disaster. *Journal of Personality and Social Psychology, 64,* 395–408.

Kaniasty, K., & Norris, F. H. (2004). Social support in the aftermath of disasters, catastrophes, and acts of terrorism: altruistic, overwhelmed, uncertain, antagonistic, and patriotic communities. In R. J. Ursano, A. E. Norwood, & C. S. Fullerton (Eds.), *Bioterrorism: Psychological and public health interventions* (pp. 200–229). New York: Cambridge University Press.

Kuterovac-Jagodic, G. (2003). Posttraumatic stress symptoms in Croatian children exposed to war: A prospective study. *Journal of Clinical Psychology, 59,* 9–25.

Layne, C. M., Beck, C. J., Rimmasch, H., Southwick, J. S., Moreno, M. A., & Hobfoll, S. E. (2008). Promoting "resilient" posttraumatic adjustment in childhood and beyond: Unpacking life events, adjustment trajectories, resources, and interventions. In D. Brom, R. Pat-Horenczyk, & J. Ford (Eds.), *Treating traumatized children: Risk, resilience, and recovery.* New York: Routledge.

Layne, C. M., & Larsen, L. C. (2008). Measuring child and adolescent maladaptive grief in the recent empirical literature: Methodological critique and recommendations. Manuscript under review.

Layne, C. M., Pynoos, R. S., Saltzman, W. R., Arslanagic, B., Black, M., Savjak, N., et al. (2001). Trauma/grief-focused group psychotherapy: School-based post-war intervention with traumatized Bosnian adolescents. *Group Dynamics: Theory, Research, and Practice, 5,* 277–290.

Layne, C. M., Saltzman, W. R., Poppleton, L., Burlingame, G. M., Pašalić, A. Duraković-Belko, E. et al. (2008). Effectiveness of a school-based group psychotherapy program for war-exposed adolescents: A randomized controlled trial. Manuscript under review.

Layne, C. M., Warren, J. S., Saltzman, W. R., Fulton, J., Steinberg, A. M., & Pynoos, R. S. (2006). Contextual influences on post-traumatic adjustment: Retraumatization and the roles of distressing reminders, secondary adversities, and revictimization. In L. A. Schein,

H. I. Spitz, G. M. Burlingame, & P. R. Muskin (Eds.), *Group approaches for the psychological effects of terrorist disasters* (pp. 235–286). New York: Haworth.

Layne, C. M., Warren, J., Shalev, A., & Watson, P. (2007). Risk, vulnerability, resistance, and resilience: Towards an integrative model of posttraumatic adaptation. In M. J. Friedman, T. M. Kean, & P. A. Resick (Eds.), *PTSD: Science & practice—a comprehensive handbook* (pp. 497–520). New York: Guilford.

Lieberman, A. F., Compton, N. C., Van Horn, P., & Ippen, C. G. (2003). *Losing a parent to death in the early years: Guidelines for the treatment of traumatic bereavement in infancy and early childhood.* Washington, DC: Zero to Three Press.

Llabre, M. M., & Hadi, F. (1997). Social support and psychological distress in Kuwaiti boys and girls exposed to the Gulf crisis. *Journal of Clinical Child Psychology, 26,* 247–255.

Luthar, S. S. (2006). Resilience in development: A synthesis of research across five decades. In D. Cicchetti & D. J. Cohen (Eds.), *Developmental psychopathology, vol. 3: Risk, disorder, and adaptation* (2nd ed., pp. 739–795). Hoboken, NJ: Wiley.

Luthar, S. S., Cicchetti, D., & Becker, B. (2000). The construct of resilience: A critical evaluation and guidelines for future work. *Child Development, 71,* 543–562.

Luthar, S. S., Sawyer, J. A., & Brown, P. J. (2006). Conceptual issues in studies of resilience: Past, present, and future research. *Annals of the New York Academy of Science, 1094,* 105–115.

Masten, A. S. (2001). Ordinary magic: Resilience processes in development. *American Psychologist, 56,* 227–238.

Masten, A. S., Best, K. M., & Garmezy, N. (1990). Resilience and development: Contributions from the study of children who overcome adversity. *Development and Psychopathology, 2,* 425–444.

Masten, A. S., & Coatsworth, J. D. (1998). The development of competence in favorable and unfavorable environments: Lessons from research on successful children. *American Psychologist, 53,* 205–220.

Milosavljevic, B., & Savic, J. (2000). *Children in and after the war.* Banja Luka, Bosnia: National and University Library of Republic of Srpska, and Centre for Development and Evaluation of Psychosocial Programmes, University of Banja Luka.

Osterman, J. E., & de Jong, J.T.V.M. (2007). Cultural issues and trauma. In M. J. Friedman, T. M. Kean, & P. A. Resick (Eds.), *PTSD: Science & practice—A comprehensive handbook* (pp. 425–446). New York: Guilford.

Ozer, E. J., Best, S. R., Lipsey, T. L., & Weiss, D. S. (2003). Predictors of posttraumatic stress disorder and symptoms in adults: A meta-analysis. *Psychological Bulletin, 129,* 52–73.

Parker, G. R., Cowen, E. L., Work, W. C., & Wyman, P. A. (1990). Test correlates of stress resilience among urban school children. *Journal of Primary Prevention, 11,* 19–35.

Peña, E. D. (2007). Lost in translation: Methodological considerations in cross-cultural research. *Child Development, 78,* 1255–1264.

Podsakoff, P. M., MacKenzie, S. B., Lee, J. Y., & Podsakoff, N. P. (2003). Common method biases in behavioral research: A critical review of the literature and recommended remedies. *Journal of Applied Psychology, 88,* 879–903.

Reinecke, M. A., Dattilio, F. M., & Freeman, A. (Eds.). (2003). *Cognitive therapy with children and adolescents: A casebook for clinical practice* (2nd ed.). New York: Guilford.

Reis, H. T., & Collins, N. (2000). Measuring relationship properties and interactions relevant to social support. In S. Cohen, L. G. Underwood, & B. H. Gottlieb (Eds.), *Social support measurement and intervention: A guide for health and social scientists* (pp. 136–192). New York: Oxford University Press.

Saigh, P. A., Fairbank, J. A., & Yasik, A. E. (1998). War-related posttraumatic stress disorder among children and adolescents. In T. W. Miller (ed.), *Children of trauma: Stressful life events and their effects on children and adolescents* (pp. 119–140).

Saltzman, W. R., Layne, C. M., Steinberg, A. M., Arslanagic, B., & Pynoos, R. S. (2003). Developing a culturally and ecologically sound intervention program for youth exposed to war and terrorism. *Child and Adolescent Psychiatric Clinics of North America, 12*(2), 319–342.

Saltzman, W. R., Layne, C. M., Steinberg, A. M., & Pynoos, R. S. (2006). Trauma/grief-focused group psychotherapy with adolescents. In L. A. Schein, H. I. Spitz, G. M. Burlingame, & P. R. Muskin (Eds.), *Group approaches for the psychological effects of terrorist disasters.* New York: Haworth.

Sandler, I. N. (1980). Social support resources, stress, and maladjustment of poor children. *American Journal of Community Psychology, 8,* 41–52.

Seidman, E., Allen, L., Aber, J. L., Mitchell, C., Feinman, J., Yoshikawa, H., et al. (1995). Development and validation of adolescent-perceived microsystem scales: Social support, daily hassles, and involvement. *American Journal of Community Psychology, 23,* 355–388.

Smith, G. T., Fischer, S., & Fister, S. M. (2003). Incremental validity principles in test construction. *Psychological Assessment, 15,* 467–477.

Spencer, M. B., Harpalani, V., Cassidy, E., Jacobs, C. Y., Donde, S., Goss, T. N., et al. (2006). Understanding vulnerability and resilience from a normative developmental perspective: Implications for racially and ethnically diverse youth. In D. Cicchetti and D. J. Cohen (Eds.), *Developmental psychopathology, vol. 1: Theory and method* (2nd ed.) (pp. 627–672). Hoboken, NJ: John Wiley & Sons.

Steinberg, A. M., Brymer, M. J., Decker, K. B., & Pynoos, R. S. (2004). The University of California at Los Angeles Post-traumatic Stress Disorder Reaction Index. *Current Psychiatry Reports, 6,* 96–100.

Taylor, S. E., Welch, W. T., Kim, H. S., & Sherman, D. K. (2007). Cultural differences in the impact of social support on psychological and biological stress responses. *Psychological Science, 18,* 831–837.

Turner, R. J., Frankel, B. G. and Levin, D. M., 1983. Social support: Conceptualization, measurement, and implications for mental health. *Research in Community and Mental Health, 3,* 67–111.

Vieno, A., Santinello, M., Pastore, M., & Perkins, D. D. (2007). Social support, sense of community in school, and self-efficacy as resources during early adolescence: An integrative model. *American Journal of Community Psychology, 39,* 177–190.

Weiss, R. S. (1974). The provisions of social relationships. In Z. Rubin (Ed.), *Doing unto others* (pp. 17–26). Englewood Cliffs, NJ: Prentice Hall.

Werner, E. E. (1993). Risk, resilience, and recovery: Perspectives from the Kauai Longitudinal Study. *Development and Psychopathology, 5,* 503–515.

Werner, E. E., & Smith, R. S. (1982). *Vulnerable but invincible: A study of resilient children.* New York: McGraw-Hill.

Wills, T. A., & Shinar, O. (2000). Measuring perceived and received social support. In S. Cohen, L. G. Underwood, & B. H. Gottlieb (Eds.), *Social support measurement and intervention: A guide for health and social scientists* (pp. 86–135). New York: Oxford University Press.

Wilson, M. N. (1989). Child development in the context of the black extended family. *American Psychologist, 44,* 380–385.

Wolchik, S. A., Beals, J., & Sandler, I. N. (1989). Mapping children's support networks: Conceptual and methodological issues. In D. Belle (Ed.), *Children's social networks and social supports* (pp. 191–220). New York: John Wiley & Sons.

Worden, J. W. (1996). Children and grief: When a parent dies. New York: Guilford.

Chapter 8

The Effects of Wartime Violence on Young Bosnians' Postwar Behaviors
Policy Contours for the Reconstruction Period

Robert J. McCouch

Armed conflict has received increasing attention as an international development issue in recent years as the proportion of civilians among its casualties has risen (Garbarino, Kostelny, & Dubrow, 1991; Machel, 1996). The increasing civilian involvement in conflict raises questions about how to cope with the mounting number of humanitarian relief crises and how to reduce the inequalities that both lead to and result from conflicts that occur within and across societies. These concerns take on added urgency in an increasingly interconnected world, where conflict in one region can have a ripple effect on populations far beyond its borders—for example, when wars in Iraq and Afghanistan and incursions into the West Bank and Gaza spur increased risk of terrorist acts elsewhere, when targeted sanctions on diamond or timber trading in many African conflicts affect the economy of key trading partners, and so on.

Young people play a central role in the day-to-day reality of armed conflict—and in its aftermath—and yet to date little if any research has examined the policy ramifications of their experience. This chapter attempts to fill this void. Young people are of particular policy interest in this study of armed conflict for two main reasons. First, they make up an ever larger share of conflict's casualties. Worldwide, more than six million were injured and more than two million children died during the 1990s as a direct result of combat (Ladd & Cairns, 1996; Machel, 2001). Their age renders them more vulnerable to becoming victims of the violence, as combatants attempt to destroy their enemies' "best and brightest." As these and other authors (e.g., Brett & Specht, 2004; Rosenblatt, 1983) note, young people, because of their age, are increasingly becoming participants in the violence, either voluntarily or through physical and economic coercion. The violence can also rob them of important family, community, peer, and school supports through death, disability, and displacement.

Second, adolescence is a bridge between childhood and adulthood when one gradually assumes one's political, social, and economic responsibilities (Hawley & Little, 2002; Lerner, 1993; Morch, 1983). Adolescence therefore represents a period of heightened opportunity to enhance young people's ability to become healthy, productive, and engaged members of their families and communities (Yates & Youniss, 1998). It also represents a period of heightened risk—from substance use to unprotected sex—that can thwart their transition (Ward, 1998). These risks often come at great cost to the individual, to his or her family and community, and to society in the form of increased social outlays, lost productivity, and weakened social fabric. As populations attempt to rebuild, it is critical that we determine whether and how youths' experience of violence affects their ability to navigate this transition and become functional members of society.

As noted throughout this volume, the literature on youth and political violence has focused primarily on conflict's mental health effects. Several of the limitations of this narrow focus were summarized in Chapter 1. What is more, these limitations also have important policy implications. Specifically, their concrete applications are limited largely to humanitarian questions of whom to treat and with what treatments (Punamäki, Qouta, & El-Sarraj, 2001; Sagi-Schwartz et al., 2003). Although these questions are undoubtedly critical and relevant, policy interests would be more fully served if analyses reached farther and included the implications of mental health functioning for the broader ability of young people to function—behaviorally—in their burgeoning political, social, and economic roles as adults postconflict. Successful performance of these roles is critical to key policy objectives, not least of which is the manifold goals of societal reconstruction.

Given that there has been very little explicit attention to policy concerns in the research literatures on youth and political violence, a general contribution of this chapter is its attempt to focus a policy lens on data collected from youth who have been directly involved in political conflict (in Bosnia). This effort has been both challenging and illuminating in its task of framing and testing policy-relevant concerns in data that were not explicitly produced with a policy focus. The success of this effort has been encouraging in forging a needed integration between research and policy; it has also been instructive as to the limitations of research data as they are commonly collected in this realm of inquiry. Before a description of the study itself, the chapter discusses some key policy parameters so that the questions asked in this study and the answers accorded to them by the findings can be understood in terms of their relevance to and implications for policy making.

The Policy Context

Policy, within the context of modern governance, is typically thought of as the measure or set of measures that legitimate authorities of state take to achieve their desired objectives for their societies (see Larsen & Møller, 2004; Müller & Surel, 1998). As such, the policy process serves to clarify objectives and systematically identify and compare alternative policies for achieving these objectives. Typically, the policy or policies selected for deployment and implementation are those shown in some systematic way to achieve the greatest output (e.g., jobs created, likelihood of terrorist event reduced, smokers who quit, and so forth) per unit of input (i.e., typically financial resources, but also physical and human resources).

In the case of child and youth development policy, these objectives vary widely, and generally center on easing youths' transition from childhood to the social, political, and economic roles of adulthood in the society. They include the reduction of youth risk behaviors in adolescence (e.g., substance use, gang activity) and increasing more positive alternatives to these behaviors (e.g., youth employment, after-school programs, volunteerism) directly to creating the conditions in which this transition can occur successfully (e.g., parent literacy and employment, paid family leave, treatment of family pathology, community safety). The policies to achieve these ends vary equally widely (see Shonkoff & Phillips, 2000).

The Goals of Youth Development Policy in Postconflict Settings

The shape taken by this overarching objective of positive youth development in postconflict settings is a long-neglected but urgent area of investigation. This neglect is due at least in part to the nebulous state of affairs of many postconflict scenarios. As the definition suggests, policy, whether enacted through statutory law, judicial fiat, or executive order, assumes more or less functioning sovereign political entities with the legitimacy to set goals through some aggregation of the polity's shared values, and articulate, implement, and enforce the vehicles through which to achieve these goals. This assumption is certainly untenable in many conflict and postconflict settings where the legitimate and sovereign power is elusive, the polity is undefined or in open conflict, and the key objective is a more immediate humanitarian one: to stop the fighting, minimize youths' (and nonyouth civilians') exposure to it, and simply save lives.

That said, there is a growing international consensus that the postconflict setting can and should be a forum in which to pursue policies more generally conducive to forging more stable, peaceful, and sustainable societies. The postconflict reconstruction process consists of at least three more or less sequential phases: (1) fundamental stabilization (e.g., cessation of violence, provision of emergency humanitarian relief, etc.), (2) greater capacity (e.g., physical and economic reconstruction, meeting basic social welfare needs, etc.), and (3) sustainability (e.g., continued support for reconstruction, heightened support for civil society to strengthen gains, etc.) (Center for Strategic and International Studies, 2002). Within this overarching framework of postconflict policy goals, it is possible to assimilate the goals of youth development. The body of youth development policy turns on the notion of youth transitions: the progression from the dependency of childhood to the growing agency of adolescence and finally to the responsibilities of adulthood (as family members, members of the community, voters, economic providers, and so on). Both transitions, therefore, present opportunities to enhance young people's ability to become healthy, productive members of society. But they also present heightened risks, from substance abuse to sexually transmitted disease, that can thwart their transition to adulthood. This can come at a great cost to themselves, their families, and society in the form of increased social outlays, lost productivity, and weakened social fabric.

This focus on boosting young people's resilience by maximizing their assets while simultaneously minimizing their risks both directly (within the individual child) and indirectly (within the child's family, peer, school, and community systems) constitutes the crux of youth development policy (Earls & Buka, 2000; Werner, 2000). Indeed, a failure to address the notion that risk and resilience accrue differently to different young people—whether defined by race or country of origin in many Western industrialized countries, or sex or ethnicity in many developing countries—constitutes a key social justice concern. How to redress these inequalities in youths' healthy transition is thus a key consideration of policy makers.

In postconflict settings, this overarching goal of successfully transitioning young people into their adult roles and responsibilities, both in youths' own interest and the interest of society, does not change. As populations attempt to rebuild, it is critical that we determine whether and how youths' experience of violence affects their ability to navigate this transition and function in society. In this respect, armed conflict might first and foremost be seen as one potential risk to healthy youth development that can hamper the positive progression to becoming fully functional adults able to take on their social, political, and economic responsibilities; however, the society in question might define these. Thus, one goal of youth development policy in postconflict societies is to minimize the potential injury inflicted on youth by the experience of the conflict, be it physical or mental, clinical or nonclinical, or direct to the individual or indirect via injury to his or her family, peer, community, or school systems.

Purpose of the Current Study

The study described herein sets out to assess—to the extent that the selected, existing data set permitted—the degree to which a group of youth exposed to long and severe conflict were functioning several years postconflict in areas that are directly relevant to the existing policy values and approaches, and specifically, with the three inter-linked phases of reconstruction mentioned above (fundamental stabilization, greater capacity, and sustainability). Thus, for example, the study considered political and community-based forms of participation postconflict, behaviors that are strongly associated with the last stage of reconstruction, the central objective of which is to create and strengthen local political and social structures—structures that redouble the gains of peace and prosperity fostered in the two earlier phases and ensure their sustainability after international peacekeepers and technical experts are gone. Second, the study tested the effect of violence exposure on the level of postconflict criminality. Youth criminality is a phenomenon of interest to policy makers (to say nothing of peacekeepers) attempting to establish and maintain the peace, particularly during the initial reconstruction phase of stabilization period that lays the groundwork for all subsequent reconstruction.

Finally, the study focused on the employment efforts and patterns of youth post-conflict. Working or searching for work is one indicator of economic activity of keen interest during the second phase of reconstruction, focusing as it does on the type of fundamental capacity building of primary interest during this phase. Furthermore, youth ability and willingness to work can reinforce the gains of stabilization and peace forged in earlier stages of reconstruction while laying the groundwork for the type of social and political sustainability (e.g., through productive gainful engagement, the acquisition of economic assets one wishes to protect through the rule of law, and so on) dominating the last stage of reconstruction).

Beyond considering the direct impact of living amid political conflict on postconflict functioning in these policy-relevant domains, the analyses conducted in this study sought to understand more precisely why such effects would obtain. Thus, the main question that the study addressed—"Do heightened levels of exposure to the violence of armed conflict diminish young people's ability to thrive in their burgeoning political, social, and economic roles as adults postconflict?"—was refined by also asking, "If so, what psychological responses account for their diminished postconflict functionality?"

With regard to this latter refinement, qualitative work in Bosnia by Barber (Chapter 12) and McCouch (2006) suggests what these psychological responses might be. They include a turn away from others (in the form of diminished relationships to peers and adults), coupled with a turn inward toward the self (in the form of depression and perceived loss of their childhood), ostensibly to shield oneself from threats to survival. In tandem with this dynamic, Bosnian youth expressed developing negativity toward the future and one's place in it, an adaptive response to war when day-to-day survival is paramount and the longer term future is uncertain. It was hypothesized that each of these factors would account for any negative effects of exposure to violence on postconflict participatory, risk, and labor-related behaviors. In addition, it was posited that the often referred to "fight" response to violence—young people's increased feelings of aggression that is also adaptive during wartime—was responsible for heightened postconflict criminal behaviors among those who had experienced more violence (van der Kolk, 1994; see Chapter 3 in this volume for a thorough treatment of the theoretical bases and qualifications of the link between violence exposure and aggression).

Methods

Data Collection

Data were from the Bosnia Young Adult Survey (BYAS; N = 623), a youth-reported survey that was administered to a cross-sectional sample of youth in Sarajevo, Bosnia. The youth, ages 13 to 24 years by war's end, had lived through at least 2 years of the war. Data were collected in 2002, 6 years after the end of fighting. The BYAS was part of the larger Adolescents in Political Violence Project (APVP; see Chapter 12 for a description of the overall project). The BYAS included a range of information surrounding respondents' past war experiences, demographic information, and their feelings and behaviors over a number of periods spanning from the time before the war to the time of data collection.

Data were collected from both college-attending (approximately 60% of the sample) and non–college-attending youth (approximately 40%) to conform with the previous phase of the APVP in ensuring that the samples were not unduly biased by youth who had opportunity or means to pursue higher education. Permission was obtained from the department heads of a variety of departments (faculties) at the University of Sarajevo, and the survey was administered in classes until the target sample was reached (i.e., approximately 400 youth of the appropriate age). No incentives were offered to respondents. Non–college-attending respondents were enlisted using a snowball sampling procedure, whereby interested youth referred the research team to other youth until the target subsample was achieved (i.e., approximately 200 youth of the appropriate age). These respondents were paid 10 DM each for their participation in the survey, which they completed independently at a variety of locales throughout Sarajevo.

These nonprobabilistic or convenience samples (although often used in research in conflict zones) are not representative of Bosnia's youth population on a variety of key demographic characteristics, such as sex, ethnoreligious identification, and region of residence during the war. The present analysis partially attenuated this limitation ex post facto by constructing poststratification weights that adjusted for the sample's nonrepresentativeness. (See McCouch, 2006, for details on the statistical procedures pursued to account for the nonrepresentativeness of the sample.)

Data Analysis

The variables selected for presentation here represent a subset of a broader group of variables from the BYAS, given that space considerations did not permit a full presentation. Nor was space adequate to fully describe the very detailed analyses that were conducted on these variables. Relevant details are available in McCouch (2006). The set of variables and analyses presented here are nonetheless illustrative and exemplary of the ways the full data set has been useful at testing basic policy-relevant issues.

The basic plan of analyses included a series of three simultaneous equations for each specific exposure-psychological-behavioral pathway postulated. Logistic regression was employed, rather than ordinary least squares (OLS) regression, because exploratory analyses of the data recommended the creation of noncontinuous dependent variables (see following discussion), for which logistic regression is most appropriate. Each set of equations aimed to uncover the potential mediating role of posited psychological factors in the relationship between violence exposure level and the behavioral outcome in question. Thus, as one example, depression was tested for the degree to which it mediated the relationship between neighborhood violence and work and work search—that is, whether neighborhood violence lowered young people's work and work search by way of increasing their levels of depression.

Testing mediation effects involves four steps spread over three simultaneous equations (e.g., Baron & Kenny, 1986). In the first step, the independent variable needs to predict the dependent variable in a statistically significant way. In the second step, the independent variable needs to predict the proposed mediator in question in a statistically significant way. A final simultaneous equation concurrently tests the last two steps for concluding a mediating relationship. Here, the dependent postconflict behavioral measure is regressed on both the independent measure and the proposed mediator. Mediation is determined when the coefficients between the independent variable and the mediator and between the mediator and the dependent variable are both significant and when the direct association between the independent and dependent variables is reduced statistically in strength (partial mediation) or if it disappears (complete mediation).

Measures

Violence Exposure Level

For each of four periods, "before the war," "first three 3 of the war (1992–1994)," "last 2 years of the war (1995–1996)," and "after the war," BYAS respondents were asked to report the frequency with which soldiers subjected them to each of nineteen exposure items. The response scale for all items was: 1, never; 2, once; 3, 2–10 times; 4, 11–20 times; 5, 21–50 times; and 6, more than 50 times. After inspecting the distribution of these items across the four time periods, it was decided to focus initially only on the latter war period, last 2 years of the war (1995–1996).

Exploratory factor analysis with varimax rotation produced four factors whose statistical properties were superior to that of a single-factor solution resulting from a validation test, as well as two distinct indicators that did not load highly onto any factor.[1] Only one of these factors, however, possessed sufficient variance in this sample to warrant further analysis. This factor was labeled neighborhood violence, and it included four items: "close your school," "shoot at you with bullets," "kill a neighbor," and "demolish the home of a neighbor."[2] A composite measure of respondents' averaged standardized scores of these four measures was constructed and recategorized to conform to the OLS normality assumption.[3] This final composite measure was recategorized to adjust for its own nonnormal distribution. This process resulted in a 5-point ordinal Likert scale, anchored at the low end by 0, lowest level of exposure, and at the high end by 4, highest level of exposure, ($\alpha = 0.72$).

Postconflict Behaviors

The BYAS includes a variety of items that gauge the type and frequency of political, social and economic behaviors youth engaged in after the conflict.

Participatory Behaviors   Respondents reported whether they engaged in a variety of participatory activities in the year prior to data collection according to the following response scale: 0, never; 1, rarely; 2, occasionally; 3, often; 4, very often. The political participation area includes two closed items for participation: "attended meetings or musical events at a political group's headquarters" and "attended seminars about political issues." The civic participation area includes three items: "volunteered as a teacher," "volunteered to help the disabled," and "helped teach the Koran or the Bible to others." Both the political and civic forms of participation also include an open-ended "other activity" category.

Exploratory factor analysis using varimax rotation, followed by a validity-lending confirmatory single-factor solution, distinguished behavioral patterns along the political and civic lines rather than on a single participation factor. As with the independent measure, the composite measure incorporating those items loading most highly on each of these three factors was computed as the averaged z-score across all of these items, recategorized to conform to the OLS and maximum likelihood estimation (MLE) assumption of univariate normality. This recategorization resulted in a dichotomous scale for each of these participatory behaviors as 0, lower participation, and 1, higher participation.

Risk Behaviors   The BYAS instrument contains seven items describing a range of antisocial behaviors, referenced to the 6 months prior to data collection. These items include several criminal or protocriminal behaviors of both a violent nature (i.e., "purposely damaged or destroyed property," "hit or threatened to hit someone") and nonviolent nature (i.e., "stolen or tried to steal something of high value," "stolen or tried to steal something of low value"), and two related to substance use (i.e., "used alcoholic beverages" and "used tobacco"). Factor analysis produced a solution that separated the items along a typology of criminality and substance use. Composite variables for each of these two factors were calculated in the same way as all other measures: as averaged, recategorized z-scores. The composite criminality variable resulting from this analysis was dichotomous as 0, lower criminality, and 1, higher criminality. The recategorized composite substance use variable, for its part, was ordinal in nature, with the following categories: 0, lower substance use; 1, moderate substance use; and 2, higher substance use ($\alpha = 0.75$).

Labor Behavior   For each of 5 years since the war's end, the BYAS asked respondents to report their level of participation in the labor force. These included four nuanced measures of work—"worked full-time for pay in Bosnia," "worked full-time for pay abroad," "worked for a family business for pay," and "worked for a family business with no pay"—and one measure of work search, "looked for paid work." It did so by asking respondents to indicate how often they engaged in these activities on a 5-point Likert scale ranging from 1, never, to 5, very often.

The multiyear retrospective nature of these items within a cross-sectional design lent a level of complexity to a factor analysis. Factor analysis generated a factor onto which all years for both work search (i.e., "looked for paid work") and one work behavior (i.e., "worked full-time for pay in Bosnia") loaded highly. These eight items formed the basis for a single work and work search (1996–2000) dependent measure. This composite variable was computed using the same average-of-standardized-scores method used elsewhere. After recategorization, the work and work search measure possessed a 3-point Likert scale: 0, lower work and work search; 1, moderate work and work search; and 2, higher work and work search ($\alpha = 0.94$).

Socioemotional/Psychosocial Mediators

All told, the BYAS contains sixty-three socioemotional and psychosocial items, alternately measured on any one of five different Likert scales. Such high diversity of scales across items slated for combination into the same composite measure underscored the necessity of basing any combination strategy on respondents' standardized scores rather than their raw scores.

Exploratory factor analysis revealed a set of seventeen socioemotional and psychosocial factors. These factors, the composite measures for which were calculated in the same way as the independent and dependent measures, revealed both dichotomous and ordinal scales when recategorized. Those selected for presentation here are depression (under which were subsumed the individual items "I feel sad," "I feel lonely," "I feel inclined to feel that I am a failure, "I certainly feel useless at times," "I am more depressed," and "I am not getting anywhere"; $\alpha = 0.87$) (see Achenbach &

Edelbrock, 1987, and Rosenberg, 1979, for the original source of these items); social initiative (under which were subsumed the individual items "[I] share feelings/ideas with friends," "[I] express liking/caring for my friends," "[I] help friends who might need assistance," "[I] ask questions of adults when I need advice," and "[I] share feelings/ideas with older adults in the community"; $\alpha = 0.88$) (see Barber, Stolz, & Olsen, 2005, for the source and cross-cultural reliability and validity of this scale); a negative sense of the future (under which were subsumed the individual items "I am more pessimistic about the future" and "I am confused about the future"; $\alpha = 0.84$), and aggression (summarizing the indicator "I am more violent").

Control Covariates

The analysis also included standard demographic variables that could be correlated with the independent, dependent, or mediating measures. These included variables associated with the poststratification weights: sex, ethnoreligious identity, and geographic location during the war. It also contained a range of others: urban versus nonurban residence during the war, respondent education, and mother's and father's educational attainment.

In addition to these, there were a number of socioemotional and psychosocial items in the BYAS that pertained to the conflict and early postconflict period (i.e., pre–data collection), that might serve as confounders of the relationship between violence exposure levels and the mediators and between the mediators and the behavioral outcomes. These controls included "negative meaning attached to the war/one's own participation" and, alternately, "positive meaning attached to war/one's own participation" (both on a recategorized agreement scale from 1, low agreement, to 6, high agreement); having "felt frightened," "felt social pressure to participate," "felt depressed," and "felt self-confident" (all on an agreement scale from 1, strongly disagree, to 6, strongly agree); and felt "worried about the future" (on a recategorized scale from 1, low agreement, to 4, high agreement).

Several additional covariates were also used in the analyses. With regard to the dependent work and work search measure, these included items or combinations of items that might explain some of the variance in this outcome. These include "worked for a family business for pay (1996–2000)," "worked for a family business for no pay (1996–2000)," and two separate composite measures for "worked abroad for pay," one for the years 1996 through 1998 and one for 1999 and 2000, possibly denoting a conceptual split in young people's emigration patterns. These covariates were computed using the same average-of-standardized-scores method used elsewhere.

One other outcome, criminality, also entailed model-specific confounders observed in the BYAS. Here, higher violence neighborhoods might have been more likely "hot spots" in the war, providing a preexisting source of higher violence levels during the conflict as well as higher postwar violent tendencies in the youth who reside there. A recent study in Bosnia has supported this presumption (Jones & Kafetsios, 2005). The BYAS offers a series of neighborhood-level indicators of social disorganization (Sampson, Raudenbush, & Earls, 1997). These included four items concerning the frequency of various forms of neighborhood disorganization "in the past few months." A single factor emerged onto which all but the last item loaded highly. Possessing a 4-point

Likert scale after recategorization, this covariate ranged from 1, lowest neighborhood disorganization level, to 4, highest neighborhood disorganization level ($\alpha = 0.72$).

Results

The Impact of Neighborhood Violence on Youth Behaviors

The initial step of Baron and Kenny's (1986) test of mediation involved the regression of the key behavioral outcomes of interest on neighborhood violence exposure levels.[4] In preliminary bivariate tests, neighborhood violence was associated with four out of the five postwar behavioral outcomes in a statistically significant way. These included political participation ($F = 4.29$, $p = 0.014$), civic participation ($F = 4.44$, $p = 0.012$), criminality ($F = 5.53$, $p = 0.004$), and work and work search ($F = 7.56$, $p = 0.001$). Substance use constituted the only exception to this pattern ($F = 0.67$, $p = 0.513$) and was dropped from further analysis. Of the variables that neighborhood violence predicted in a statistically significant way, the direction of these relationships was consistent with those hypothesized (i.e., with odds ratios of <1 associated with positively scaled outcomes and >1 associated with negatively scaled outcomes), with the exception of work and work search. Here, higher neighborhood violence was more (not less), likely to lead to higher work and work search.

For each of these statistically significant bivariate relationships, multivariate stepwise regressions were performed to test the robustness of the neighborhood violence measure in the face of the controls described earlier. These multivariate tests showed that neighborhood violence predicted all key outcomes in the face of these controls. Its predictive value did not change with respect to political participation ($F = 4.29$, $p = 0.014$), civic participation ($F = 6.83$, $p = 0.001$), criminality ($F = 3.02$, $p = 0.050$), or work and work search ($F = 5.43$, $p = 0.005$). That said, this statistical significance did not extend to individual category-by-category contrasts in any uniform way. T-tests of the β coefficients associated with each level of the neighborhood violence regressor yielded mixed results, with neither the lower nor higher contrast categories of neighborhood violence being statistically significant with respect to political violence ($b = 0.58$, $t = 0.78$, $p = 0.436$, and $b = -0.96$, $t = -1.48$, $p = 0.139$, respectively) and to criminality ($b = -0.56$, $t = -0.91$, $p = 0.365$, and $b = 0.67$, $t = 1.03$, $p = 0.302$, respectively). In MLE, the overall test of significance indicates that the independent variable in question is a significant predictor of the dependent variable in some way; it does not, however, indicate whether it influences the dependent variable in the expected direction (i.e., positively or negatively), nor does it pinpoint exactly which specific levels of the independent variable are statistically significant. Thus, it is possible to have a statistically significant independent measure with only some of its individual levels showing statistical significance as well. In these cases, it is possible to look at trends in these category contrasts to determine the direction of the relationship while being careful to note only those individual categories in the independent variable that demonstrate statistical significance. In this test, one of neighborhood violence's two contrast categories was statistically significant with respect to civic participation ($b = 0.45$, $t = 0.54$, $p = 0.592$, and $b = -1.73$, $t = -2.01$, $p = 0.045$, respectively) and work and work search ($b = -2.20$, $t = -2.47$, $p = 0.014$, and $b = 0.38$, $t = 0.53$, $p = 0.593$, respectively).

The odds ratios associated with neighborhood violence offered additional confirmatory evidence of the direction of this variable's effects on outcomes. As in the bivariate tests, neighborhood violence was associated with the outcome in question in the expected direction for three out of four outcomes. Those at one unit of neighborhood violence above baseline were only 21% as likely as those at baseline to fall into the higher political participation category, with lower and upper confidence intervals both bounded by numbers falling below 1 ($CI_L = 0.07$, $CI_U = 0.63$). Although the same level of precision was not evident for those at two units above baseline, these respondents possessed a similar point estimate, suggesting that they were less likely than those at baseline to fall into the higher level of political participation (that is, they were 56% as likely to report higher political participation than those at baseline; $CI_L = 0.13$, $CI_U = 2.43$). An identical pattern inhered in the relationship between neighborhood violence and civic participation. Respondents at one level above baseline were only 11% more likely to report higher civic participation as those at baseline ($CI_L = 0.07$, $CI_U = 0.63$), as were those at two levels above baseline (i.e., 63% less likely than those at baseline), albeit with less statistical precision ($CI_L = 0.12$, $CI_U = 3.31$).

The odds ratios associated with neighborhood violence's association with criminality were similarly confirmatory and similarly mixed in their statistical precision. Respondents at one unit above baseline neighborhood violence levels were 3.44 times as likely to fall into the higher criminality category ($CI_L = 1.28$, $CI_U = 9.22$). Those at two levels above baseline were also more likely than those experiencing the lowest level of neighborhood violence to exhibit higher criminality, at 1.76 times the rate, but with less statistical precision ($CI_L = 0.52$, $CI_U = 5.97$).

Finally, the odds ratios surrounding neighborhood violence's effect on work and work search ran counter to the expectation that neighborhood violence would have a negative impact on these behaviors and with a greater statistical precision than its impact on other outcomes. At one elevation above baseline exposure level, respondents were 7.99 times as likely as those experiencing the lowest exposure to report greater work and work search ($CI_L = 2.73$, $CI_U = 23.34$). At two levels above baseline, respondents were 11.67 times as likely to do so ($CI_L = 3.21$, $CI_U = 42.41$).

Overall, work and work search was most strongly predicted by neighborhood violence. Thus, when averaging the three standard approximations of the adjusted R^2 in weighted MLE models, neighborhood violence, together with its key covariates, explained approximately 47.5% of the variance in work and work search, compared to approximately 10.8% of the variance in political participation, 17.5% of the variance in civic participation, and approximately 18.8% of the variance in criminality. Furthermore, the design effects associated with each point estimate—that is, the "cost" to inferential precision of using the poststratification weights—generally fell well below the acceptable threshold of 3.

Psychological Mechanisms Underlying the Association between Neighborhood Violence and Youth Outcomes

With the relationship between neighborhood violence and the key outcomes established, it was possible to test the effects of the proposed mediators of interest. In bivariate testing, neighborhood violence significantly predicted all four of the potential mediators selected for presentation here. Three of these relationships retained significance after controlling for key covariates in multivariate stepwise models: depression ($F = 3.02$, $p = 0.003$), social initiative ($F = 2.56$, $p = 0.010$), and negative sense of the future ($F = 2.17$, $p < 0.001$). Neighborhood violence explained a moderate to high degree of the variance in these socioemotional and psychosocial mediators as well, ranging from roughly half of the variance of the depression and social initiative to roughly three-quarters of the variance in the negative sense of the future measure. Moreover, although bracketed by confidence intervals often spanning 1, the odds ratios surrounding neighborhood violence exposure levels' effects largely followed expected patterns.

In the final stage of hypothesis testing, each of the four behavioral outcomes obtained in the first stage was regressed separately in stepwise models on neighborhood violence, the proposed mediators, and all relevant covariates. Three are reported here.[5]

Political Participation

Table 8.1 summarizes the results associated with the political participation outcome. As for social initiative, there was no longer a significant association between it and political participation, and thus, the level of social initiative reported by youth did not explain any of the effect of neighborhood violence on political participation.

With respect to depression and negative sense of the future, both retained a significant association with political participation ($F = 2.74$, $p = 0.028$, and $F = 2.40$, $p = 0.049$, respectively). With very few exceptions, notwithstanding the statistical precision of individual confidence intervals, cell-by-cell contrasts associated with each mediator were directionally correct. In general, higher levels of depression and a negative sense of the future were associated with lower political participation.

However, given that there remained also highly significant associations between neighborhood violence and political participation in both equations, it is not clear that these two psychosocial characteristics mediated (i.e., explained any of) this effect. Rather, it can be said that in addition to having a direct association with political participation, neighborhood violence also was indirectly associated with political participation through its significant associations with depression and negative sense of the future. Thus, it appears that in this sample, two of the consequences of experiencing political violence were higher levels of depression and feeling negative about the future, both of which predicted lower levels of involvement in political issues.

It should be noted that the amount of variance in political participation explained was relatively moderate, with various estimates of pseudo R^2's hovering around about 33%. Clearly, factors other than those proposed here are partially responsible for variance in rates of political participation. Furthermore, because separate equations were tested for depression and negative sense of the future, it is not yet known what a saturated model containing both measures (and their covariates) would reveal relative to the statistical significance of neighborhood violence, or how much of the variance in political participation it would explain.

Table 8.1 Summary of Political Participation Regressed on Neighborhood Violence, Psychosocial Variables, and Covariates

	Overall Model Effects (IV)		*Log Likelihood*			
	Wald F	*p*	IV Category Contrast	Odds Ratio	Lower 95% CI	Higher 95% CI
Neighborhood violence	7.95	0.000	1 vs. 0	0.18	0.07	0.43
			2 vs. 0	0.67	0.22	2.08
Social initiative	2.27	0.061	1 vs. 0	1.19	0.21	6.70
			2 vs. 0	1.77	0.35	8.98
			3 vs. 0	5.27	1.00	27.69
			4 vs. 0	3.88	0.57	26.23
Sarajevo residence	4.82	0.029				
Wartime family SES	20.19	0.000				
Postwar family SES	11.47	0.001				
PC4: social pressure	6.99	0.008				
PC7: self-confident	3.86	0.050				
Neighborhood violence	7.91	0.000	1 vs. 0	0.16	0.06	0.41
			2 vs. 0	0.49	0.15	1.53
Negative sense of the future	2.40	0.049	1 vs. 0	0.30	0.07	1.33
			2 vs. 0	0.15	0.04	0.56
			3 vs. 0	0.29	0.07	1.12
			4 vs. 0	0.10	0.02	0.62
Sarajevo residence	4.13	0.043				
Postwar family SES	11.37	0.001				
Wartime family SES	16.90	0.000				
PC4: social pressure	20.75	0.000				
PC7: self-confident	10.59	0.001				
Neighborhood violence	6.85	0.001	1 vs. 0	0.16	0.06	0.44
			2 vs. 0	0.41	0.12	1.48
Depression	2.74	0.028	1 vs. 0	2.66	0.72	9.89
			2 vs. 0	5.17	1.65	16.22
			3 vs. 0	1.68	0.45	6.32
			4 vs. 0	4.09	0.86	19.45
Sarajevo residence	4.70	0.031				
Postwar family SES	8.95	0.003				
Wartime family SES	11.78	0.001				
PC4: social pressure	2.76	0.097				
PC7: self-confident	3.81	0.051				

Note: Whether estimates are based on binomial or multinomial logistic regression depends on the number of categories in the dependent measure. DE denotes design effects associated with using poststratification weights. For social initiative, the average DE across all individual independent-dependent cell tests was 2.72; for negative sense of the future, the average DE was 2.36; and for depression, the average DE was 2.56. Measures of variance in the dependent measure explained by each model in question consisted of three separate pseudo R^2 statistics: the McFadden, the Cox and Snell, and the Nagelkerke R^2. For social initiative, these ranged from 0.300 (McFadden) to 0.337 (Cox and Snell) to 0.451 (Nagelkerke). For negative sense of the future, these ranged from 0.322 (McFadden) to 0.356 (Cox and Snell) to 0.478 (Nagelkerke). For depression, these ranged from 0.292 (McFadden) to 0.330 (Cox and Snell) to 0.443 (Nagelkerke).

Civic Participation

Table 8.2 summarizes the results of the analyses with respect to the civic participation measure.

Unlike with political participation, social initiative retained a significant association with civic participation ($F = 3.28$, $p = 0.011$), but depression did not ($F = 1.50$, $p = 0.201$). As was the case with political participation, however, negative sense of the future was still significantly associated with civic participation ($F = 3.80$, $p = 0.005$). With very few cell-by-cell exceptions and several odds ratios with confidence intervals enveloping 1, overall higher levels of negative sense of the future were generally associated with lower civic participation, and higher levels of social initiative were associated with higher civic participation overall.

Because once again neighborhood violence retained highly significant associations with civic participation, there is evidence for indirect effects and not mediation. Thus, although it cannot be said that social initiative and negative sense of the future explained any part of the effects of neighborhood violence on civic participation, it is evident that they were additional pathways through which the violence was channeled. In other words, two of the ways exposure to political violence impacted youth civic involvement postconflict in this sample were by lowering the level of perceived social competence and heightening the level of perceived negativity about the future. The amount of variance explained by each full model was moderate with respect to civic participation, although the pseudo R^2's averaged slightly higher than their counterparts related to political participation. Once again, given that separate models were tested, presently it is unknown whether the cumulative effects of all three psychometric measures would jointly draw down the statistical significance of neighborhood violence in a saturated model (thus constituting partial mediation) or render the effect between neighborhood violence and civic participation nonsignificant (thus indicating full mediation).

Criminality

Table 8.3 summarizes the results of the analyses associated with the criminality measure.

As was the case with civic participation, both social initiative ($F = 3.61$, $p = 0.008$) and negative sense of the future ($F = 5.09$, $p = 0.000$) retained significant associations with criminality. However, although social initiative can be considered an indirect path from violence to criminality as before, in this case, there is evidence that negative sense of the future actually mediated the effects of political violence on criminality, and fully so. This is seen by the drop to nonsignificance of the direct effect between political violence and criminality ($F = 2.27$, $p = 0.105$). In other words, in this sample, having acquired a negative sense of the future fully explains how exposure to violence was associated with higher levels of criminality.

Once again, it should be noted that the pseudo R^2's associated with each psychosocial variable were still only moderate (0.230 for social initiative and 0.254 for negative sense of the future). How much additional variance would be explained by a model including all of these factors, or what alterations in the mediating properties of the variables, was not assessed.

Table 8.2 Summary of Civic Participation Regressed on Neighborhood Violence, Psychosocial Variables, and Covariates

	Overall Model Effects (IV)		Log Likelihood			
	Wald F	p	IV Category Contrast	Odds Ratio	Lower 95% CI	Higher 95% CI
Neighborhood violence	4.82	0.008	1 vs. 0	0.17	0.06	0.53
			2 vs. 0	0.50	0.15	1.72
Social initiative	3.28	0.011	1 vs. 0	1.82	0.23	14.30
			2 vs. 0	8.41	1.53	46.31
			3 vs. 0	10.55	1.55	71.63
			4 vs. 0	17.95	2.67	120.79
Age	14.46	0.000				
Wartime family SES	6.79	0.009				
PC7: self-confident	3.00	0.084				
Peer/adult rels × age	5.66	0.000				
Social initiative × PC7: self-confident	2.94	0.020				
Neighborhood violence	5.66	0.004	1 vs. 0	0.19	0.07	0.50
			2 vs. 0	0.46	0.14	1.51
Negative sense of the Future	3.80	0.005	1 vs. 0	0.17	0.03	0.92
			2 vs. 0	0.06	0.01	0.29
			3 vs. 0	0.16	0.03	0.75
			4 vs. 0	0.04	0.00	0.31
Age	9.30	0.002				
Respondent sex	1.80	0.181				
Respondent education	4.58	0.033				
Wartime family SES	3.52	0.061				
PC5: worried about future	5.48	0.020				
PC7: self-confident	4.51	0.034				
Neighborhood violence	5.00	0.007	1 vs. 0	0.17	0.06	0.51
			2 vs. 0	0.60	0.13	2.77
Depression	1.50	0.201	1 vs. 0	1.81	0.41	7.93
			2 vs. 0	2.20	0.52	9.27
			3 vs. 0	0.53	0.07	4.30
			4 vs. 0	0.44	0.06	3.12
Wartime family SES	5.04	0.025				
PC5: worried about future	4.15	0.042				
PC7: self-confident	7.27	0.007				

Note: Whether estimates are based on binomial or multinomial logistic regression depends on the number of categories in the dependent measure. DE denotes design effects associated with using poststratification weights. For social initiative, the average DE across all individual independent-dependent cell tests was 1.42; for negative sense of the future the average DE was 2.35, and for depression the average DE was 3.09. Measures of variance in the dependent measure explained by each model in question consisted of three separate pseudo R^2 statistics: the McFadden, the Cox and Snell, and the Nagelkerke R^2. For social initiative, these ranged from 0.393 (Cox and Snell) to 0.429 (McFadden) to 0.571 (Nagelkerke). For negative sense of the future, these ranged from 0.350 (Cox and Snell) to 0.375 (McFadden) to 0.512 (Nagelkerke). For depression, these ranged from 0.276 (Cox and Snell) to 0.277 (McFadden) to 0.401 (Nagelkerke).

Table 8.3 Summary of Criminality Regressed on Neighborhood Violence, Psychosocial Sariables, and Covariates

	Overall Model Effects (IV)		Log Likelihood			
	Wald F	p	IV Category Contrast	Odds Ratio	Lower 95% CI	Higher 95% CI
Neighborhood violence	3.54	0.030	1 vs. 0	3.64	1.39	9.57
			2 vs. 0	2.23	0.71	6.97
Social initiative	3.51	0.008	1 vs. 0	0.24	0.08	0.78
			2 vs. 0	0.16	0.04	0.66
			3 vs. 0	0.12	0.03	0.41
			4 vs. 0	0.11	0.02	0.69
Respondent sex	5.19	0.023				
Respondent education	5.74	0.017				
Neighborhood violence	2.27	0.105	1 vs. 0	2.74	0.98	7.63
			2 vs. 0	1.10	0.36	3.31
Negative sense of the future	5.09	0.000	1 vs. 0	0.52	0.12	2.16
			2 vs. 0	2.31	0.51	10.44
			3 vs. 0	1.27	0.33	4.84
			4 vs. 0	7.74	1.77	33.86
Respondent sex	8.91	0.003				
Respondent education	2.74	0.099				

Note: Whether estimates are based on binomial or multinomial logistic regression depends on the number of categories in the dependent measure. DE denotes design effects associated with using poststratification weights. For social initiative, the average DE across all individual independent-dependent cell tests was 3.53; for aggression the average DE was 2.63; and for negative sense of the future the average DE was 2.28. Measures of variance in the dependent measure explained by each model in question consisted of three separate pseudo R^2 statistics: the McFadden, the Cox and Snell, and the Nagelkerke R^2. For social initiative, these ranged from 0.197 (Cox and Snell) to 0.204 (McFadden) to 0.299 (Nagelkerke).

Discussion

Focusing a policy lens on existing empirical data, this study sought to understand the relationship between young people's wartime experiences and their postconflict behaviors. Notwithstanding a number of methodological limitations associated with these data, it found wartime exposure levels to neighborhood violence, a common form of violence that young people experienced during the war in Bosnia, to be associated with lower political and civic participation as well as higher criminality in the postconflict period. Neighborhood violence exposure levels were not, however, associated with increased substance use, a nonconfirmatory finding that might stem from measurement error in the survey instrument: the illicit substances most likely to be abused in postwar Bosnia from qualitative work leading up to these analyses, such as heroin, were not measured in the BYAS. All told, however, these findings are quite consistent with much other work that has been done on Bosnian populations (e.g., Freedman & Abazovic, 2006; Jones, 2002; Jones & Kafetsios, 2005; Kerestes, 2006), as well as other populations of children and youth (see Chapter 2 for a review of such studies).

Those young people experiencing the most violence during the war in Bosnia appeared to withdraw from positive, prosocial investment in the collective and its future after the conflict, and instead tended to engage in more antisocial criminal behaviors.

The findings of this study also documented some of the possible socioemotional or psychosocial processes whereby violence exposure might lead to these negative outcomes. Thus, to varying degrees, it was evident that the degree to which the youth reported feeling depressed, having a negative sense of the future, and their social competence were pathways whereby violence exposure was predictive of negative functioning. Given the moderate proportion of variance on any given behavioral outcome explained by these models, further analysis should determine other unobserved factors that might additionally add explanatory value and estimate multivariate models.

In the meantime, the findings of these analyses suggest potential implications for the realm of postconflict reconstruction policy. As noted earlier, the behavioral outcomes were selected to align (to the extent that the data set permitted) with the overarching youth development goals associated with three interlinked phases of reconstruction: fundamental stabilization, greater capacity, and sustainability. Youth criminality was selected for its relevance to the policy goal of establishing and maintaining the postconflict peace, particularly during the initial reconstruction phase of stabilization period that lays the groundwork for all subsequent reconstruction. Labor behavior (i.e., work and work search) was selected to indicate economic activity that is of interest during the second phase of reconstruction, focusing as it does on the type of fundamental capacity building of primary interest during this phase. As suggested, youth ability and willingness to work can reinforce the gains of stabilization and peace forged in earlier stages of reconstruction, while laying the groundwork for the type of social and political sustainability (e.g., through productive gainful engagement, the acquisition of economic assets one wishes to protect through the rule of law, and so on) dominating the last stage of reconstruction. Political and community-based forms of participation were selected because of their relevance to the last stage of reconstruction, the central objective of which is to create and strengthen local political and social structures—structures that redouble the gains of peace and prosperity fostered in the earlier phases and ensure their sustainability after international peacekeepers and technical experts are gone.

In this respect, the findings of these analyses—namely, that higher levels of violence exposure might dampen participatory behaviors while raising criminality—are consistent with a narrative that these youths' wartime experiences of violence can thwart their ability to thrive in postconflict society. That said, the key unexpected finding that higher levels of wartime violence exposure might serve to increase rather than decrease work and work search suggests a possible positive entry point for policies that meet the need for economic reconstruction while serving as an antidote to otherwise negative behaviors associated with higher violence exposure. These findings, viewed jointly, speak to the potential promise of a two-pronged policy approach: one that lowers these youths' likelihood of antisocial tendencies (e.g., criminality that threatens the peace, lowered investment in the collective institutions that make the gains of reconstruction sustainable) while harnessing the drive to work, steering them away from these negative tendencies and toward more positive pursuits while hastening much-needed economic recovery.

Rooted in the findings related to the possible intervening effects of some socio-emotional and psychosocial characteristics of youth—downturns in young people's relationships to peers and adults (i.e., lower social initiative), a negative sense of the future, and depression—this discussion hones in on policies that specifically target these socioemotional and psychosocial antecedents of postconflict functionality problems, rather than surveying the full gamut of possible but ultimately peripheral policies aimed at these same behaviors (e.g., for criminality, greater policing; for participation, civics lessons; and so forth). These policies include cost-effective, direct supports that address young people's need for healing, programs that build bridges between youth leaders from across the fault lines of the conflict, and educational reform that better prepares young people for postconflict social, economic, and political success. Each of these policy areas is reviewed in turn.

Direct Socioemotional and Psychosocial Supports to High-Exposure Youth

In deciding among a range of possible policy alternatives through which to achieve their desired objectives, all societies are subject to fiscal constraints that force difficult choices about how to achieve maximal impact with the least amount of resources possible. This perennial problem is even direr in postconflict societies. Owing to the large-scale destruction of the economic base conflicts typically entail, coupled with the sheer number and magnitude of the social challenges the society faces afterward, postconstruction societies face a unique catch-22 situation in which they desperately need to stabilize the population to begin rebuilding but lack the rebuilt infrastructure with which to amass and distribute the resources to do so. The findings of the present study suggest that interventions aimed at short-circuiting the etiology of postconflict psychological distress might have considerable social dividends. However, the case of Bosnia, where qualitative analyses to triangulate these findings revealed that low- or no-cost interventions were not available on a large scale for prolonged periods or were inappropriate to the local operating context, suggests that such interventions be rapidly deployable in postcrisis settings, cost-effective, sustainable, and context-appropriate. A number of such cost-effective interventions have been deployed with high-risk youth populations in post-trauma settings to target these young people's socioemotional and psychosocial needs effectively and in nonstigmatizing ways. (For sample interventions and a review of best practices, see Macy, 2003; Noam, 2003.)

Creating Meaning out of the Past and Building Bridges for the Future

In Bosnia, as in many postconflict zones, what was once a thriving multiethnic society is now an internally balkanized collection of ethnoreligious pockets that defined this conflict in the first place. Thus, the ethnoreligious patchwork of postwar Bosnia and the simmering tensions across groups poses additional challenges to the project of nation building.[6] The findings of the present analysis suggest a further social fault line, namely, that youth might turn away from the other and inward toward the self, regardless of in-group or out-group membership, with ramifications for the rebuilding effort. Policies aiming for more positive postconflict life trajectories could therefore address this added challenge of reconnecting the nation's young people to each other cognitively and affectively, both within their own group (i.e., social capital of the "building" variety) and across the ethnoreligious divide (i.e., social capital of the "bridging" variety).

By virtue of the Bosnian conflict's overt ethnoreligious overtones, and data from the BYAS that indicate a sustained uptick in religiosity among youth of all confessions, this first prong of intervention might need to embrace (at least in part) the religious facet of reconciliation. One such program that has successfully done so, notwithstanding the vicissitudes of communal violence and ceasefires that have characterized the overall movement to peace, has been the Corrymeela Community in Northern Ireland. Open to all ages but particularly focused on youth, the Corrymeela Community has become a beacon of interfaith reconciliation throughout Ulster (for a review, see Brennan, 1997; Morrow, 1995).

Education for Democracy

Education provides both the "hard" academic skills and the "soft" interpersonal skills that heighten one's prospects in the labor market. As with many of the interventions noted above, schools can also serve as a catchment area for identifying and treating young people's barriers to such prospects. In postconflict societies like Bosnia, it would be worthwhile to consider education reform that is better suited to creating sustainable economic development. Such reform would entail a shift away from authoritarian structures and rote memorization toward more critical and creative thought that encourages young people to question and innovate. Achieving critically important economic milestones can help undo the negative sense of the future born out of the war experience, but to do so, young people must be prepared for the workforce.[7]

But education does not only serve an economic role. Rather, it imbues youth with the knowledge and sense of responsibility for contributing in meaningful ways to the collective. It does this directly through civics and history lessons and indirectly through the social relationships (e.g., peer relationships, pupil-teacher relationships, teacher-administration relationships) and institutional structures (e.g., nonhierarchical with high student agency, hierarchical with low student agency, and so on) to which pupils are exposed. Schooling can thus be viewed as a social and moral project as much as it is an individual one geared toward one's own economic security (Blomkvist & Inkinen, 2004; Kohlberg, 1995).

The argument for education as a force of positive social change is not new (Broström, 2005). What this analysis underscores is the critical need for education to attend to its role as political, social, and economic training ground. By educating young people in the lessons of the violent past, by expanding their cognitive and affective horizons surrounding who "belongs" in their society, and by instilling in them a sense of responsibility to the collective both within and across ethnoreligious lines, a nation helps ensure its own long-term sustainability.

With political and civic participation shown to be low overall in the BYAS sample (see univariate statistics), cultivating young people's ability to dissect arguments, come to their own conclusions, and devise and share their own ideas might help reverse the historical passivity and lack of informed decision making much bemoaned in postwar Bosnian society (European Stability Initiative, 2004). Above and beyond this skills-based curriculum reform, what students in postconflict transitional societies arguably need is the cultivation of critical, analytical, and creative thought. Cultivating these faculties can help the young and vulnerable postconflict population take fuller advantage of its newfound political and economic freedoms that are frequently assumed by economic development and democratic theorists to be happening perforce (Sen, 1999). On the political front, this type of thinking might not only help inoculate young people against political ideologies that, as in the past, proffer a return to violence but over time can help create a polity more conversant with the process of defining policy goals, debating alternative policy vehicles for achieving them, and weighing the relative merit of competing values and evidence pursuant to sound policy making. Finally, more circumspect thinkers can force greater transparency in economic, social, and political institutions, creating a culture of accountability on which the functioning of free institutions rests (e.g., Fischer-Rosenthal, 2000).

The emphasis on democracy-enhancing cognitive skills, infused as it is with a penchant for individual freedoms, poses yet another challenge to a democratic postconflict society in light of the findings of this analysis. The singular focus on the needs of the individual suggested here signals a bellwether for democracy itself if institutions do not temper this solipsistic trend with a concomitant focus on communal concerns. As noted earlier, there are several other policy mechanisms for promoting greater bridge building from the self to the other. But the educational system, in its role not just of skills builder but also of socializing agent, must match its task of promoting greater individuality in cognitive development with a concomitant commitment to (re)establishing young people's connection to the collective. In part, the school-based psychosocial interventions mentioned earlier can help reestablish these bonds, but the educational system can play an even more direct role in fostering these values. Democracy-enriching educational reform, therefore, might include a shift toward greater experiential learning in the form of group activities and projects, closely mentored by instructors who reward cooperation and mutual respect (Flam, 2000).

This recommendation stems from the notion that education can have a role not only in the skills-based and cognitive development of youth but in their moral development as well (Kohlberg, 1995). It can do so in a variety of ways. First, as the drop-off in political and civic participation suggests, schools play an active role in conveying key civics lessons—the rituals, rights, and responsibilities of a democratic society—in an engaging and experiential way. Second, in addition to promoting bridge building through interethnoreligious encounters and constructive conflict resolution through socioemotional and psychosocial interventions, schools can also achieve this through curricula that foster tolerance. By extension, third, policy makers can play an active role in promoting national unity through curricula that give meaning to the past while contextualizing it in a larger narrative of a more hopeful future. One such curriculum is the Facing Our History and Ourselves program (Schultz, Barr, & Selman, 2001), which harnesses the lessons of history to cultivate young people's mutual tolerance and respect, their cognitive complexity, and their ability to confront society's difficult moral dilemmas in a constructive way. Through curricula such as these, postconflict policy makers might help counter young people's negativity about the past and the future and their apathy and even contempt for the political and social realm with a greater sense of positivity, engagement, and self-efficacy.

Harnessing the Drive to Work for Positive Social Change

Relying on evidence-based models, policy makers can garner funding for interventions such as those described and bring them to scale locally in a cost-effective way. The assumption underlying their long-term sustainability, naturally, is that the foundations of physical security and economic stability—the key goals of the first and second phases of reconstruction described earlier—are in place for these further gains to occur.

The present study suggested that young people who experienced the highest levels of exposure to violence appear to be more likely to work and search for work. This finding, though unexpected and pending replication, bodes well for postconflict efforts at economic reconstruction—if, that is, policy makers seize this energy to work for positive social gain rather than allowing the market forces to dictate demand for labor.

By creatively engaging this drive, whatever its sources, to work and search for work—the present study does not reveal whether it stems from positive socioemotional states such as increased self-efficacy from one's adult role during the war, negative socioemotional states such as a neurotic obsession with survival, or neither—policy makers can torque the pace of economic recovery and the physical reconstruction on which it is based. In so doing, they stand to reinforce the physical security gained in the earliest phases of reconstruction while providing the tax base to support the costs of basic services and governance (not least of all the policies described earlier in this section). Creatively engaging this drive could also steer young people away from some of the more antisocial responses to their war experiences—criminality and social detachment—and toward more positive, constructive, gainful pursuits. With the appropriate programmatic undergirding, a youth work program can help young people deal with socioemotional and psychosocial scars of the past, reconnecting them to peers and adult mentors while enabling them to feel good about themselves, their work, and their contribution to society. Most important, perhaps, a youth work policy can help restore in youth a more positive sense of the future, one that ripples throughout society as the economic gains of the program are realized. Considering all of the positive potential associated with work and the typical destruction of conflict, this might hypothetically take the form of a nationwide youth employment program explicitly aimed at rebuilding the nation's industrial and agricultural production capacity as well as its physical infrastructure.

The notion of collective youth work as a nation-building tool is not new; New Deal policies of the post–Great Depression United States serve as one of the most familiar precedents. Judt (2005) additionally posits work as an important component of post–World War II Europeans' almost maniacal fervor to process (or in the case of Germans, temporarily erase) the past and embrace the future. Even more immediate to the notion of a youth work scheme is the pivotal economic, social, and political role that the kibbutz movement has historically played throughout the history of the State of Israel. This model simultaneously sought to steer the large influx of post-Holocaust immigrants toward the productive pursuit of work, rapidly rebuilding an economic base out of the devastation they had experienced in their countries of origin while developing a common national ethnoreligious and linguistic identity (Gavron, 2000).

This recommendation embodies a distinct nation-building appeal as well. Working on collective Bosnia-building endeavors across the ethnoreligious divide, young people might also help reweave the social fabric of their peer relationships and of Bosnia as a multiethnic society. Other Eastern European countries offer some evidence in this regard, having relegated the hardships of the communist past and the transitional present as secondary to the goal of national freedom, openness to Europe and the rest of the world, and prosperity. By extension, such a narrative in Bosnia might place the past within a larger narrative of Bosnia's quest for autonomy as a historically unique, multiethnic, tolerant, and egalitarian society after decades of outside political machinations to squelch this unique feature of the nation. Ultimately, the precise form this nation-building, meaning-bestowing motto would take in Bosnia is best left to the local population to decide. On this note, these findings pose another policy implication: the need to resocialize young Bosnians for a more deliberative society.

Promoting Social Justice in the Aftermath of Conflict

Having offered up a range of policy propositions to respond to this problem, it is beneficial to take stock of what these findings are really saying (or not saying), about the state of postconflict youth in postwar Bosnia. In point of fact, although this study makes correlational linkages between violence exposure and postconflict functionality problems, the actual incidence of these problems is quite low, as indicated in the univariate statistics associated with each mediating and dependent variable.

But the low incidence of postconflict distress should not be taken as a justification for neglecting the needs of those who suffer from it. From a rational standpoint alone, it is clear—judging from our experience with a host of other social problems, from domestic violence to substance abuse to HIV/AIDS—that social ills experienced by a minority do not occur in a vacuum but reverberate throughout society. Viewed in this light, the minority of young Bosnians experiencing the most distress in postconflict society can entail disproportionately high costs for their families, communities, and society as a whole.

But there is another normative policy lens through which to view this minority of postconflict young people: that of equity. Their postconflict plight poses a social justice issue for the larger society and for the international actors taking responsibility for reconstruction. These young people, for no other reason than having had the ill fortune of being exposed to higher levels of violence, appear to embark on the path of reconstruction on an unequal footing with their peers who experienced lower levels of exposure to violence. This unequal footing entails lowered quality of life—from higher depression to lower quality of social relationships and a dimmed sense of the future—that actually impedes their ability to move on with their lives, let alone thrive in meeting the opportunities that a more stable society and freer institutions might bring. Provided there is some modicum of consensus around the injustice of this state of affairs, the overarching policy narrative from which all policy objectives and specific policy mechanisms are derived should be relatively straightforward: all else held constant, policies that enhance these young people's ability to catch up should be acceptable, while those that lower their ability to catch up should be unacceptable.

The reality of postconflict reconstruction in Bosnia suggests that the exact opposite has been the case. In short, rather than addressing the needs of youth that this study's findings and those of many other studies speak to, the prevailing model of postconflict reconstruction, a neoliberal model focused on rapid economic liberalization, has not met these needs and in many ways has exacerbated them. Rather than reweaving the social fabric, economic liberalization has further fractured society by introducing competition between the haves (defined narrowly as those who were lucky enough to flee before or during the war, those lucky enough to get a job with the occupying forces, and those engaged in illegal economic activities) and have-nots (defined as those who stayed behind, and among these, those of interest in this study who experienced the worst violence). Rather than offering them a better future in real and symbolic terms by providing for youths' and their families' material needs (e.g., in the form of reduced negative sense of the future, a sense of a future worth investing in, and so on), economic liberalization has provided 10 years of economic depression.

A main hindrance in this regard has been the lack of large-scale, sustainable improvement in the country's physical infrastructure. This lack of improvement speaks to a wider, more systemic weakness in the current paradigm of economic reconstruction. The Western-style free-market reforms summed up by the Washington Consensus reforms have led to chronically high unemployment and stagnant to declining household income, the ensuing social dislocations between very few haves and a large reservoir of have-nots, and the attendant social problems like crime and illegal economic activities.[8] It is not difficult to see the moral precariousness of the free-market approach, whatever long-term benefits it might offer, when in the short term underemployed or unemployed families desperate to erase the war's physical scars from their bullet-riddled homes take out home improvement loans they can never afford to repay from a newly deregulated financial services industry eager to lend them money at high interest rates. Or when unemployment leads young girls to prostitute themselves and young boys to take part in organized or petty crime to feed their siblings and widowed mothers. Or when young people whose families were either lucky enough, smart enough, or wealthy enough to get them safe passage abroad during the war return to their home country with superior education and receive the best jobs. These and many other examples were raised in qualitative exercises aimed at triangulating the findings of the present analysis. They not only call into question the market's ability to aid human recovery but also suggest the potential for the reconstruction process itself to be undermined in populations' hearts and minds when they see far more of its nefarious effects than its benefits.

Many of the sources of Bosnia's economic woes are related to factors outside the scope of this inquiry. In large part, they are a feature of many societies that, like Bosnia, have embarked on the transition from socialist institutional arrangements to post-socialist liberal institutional arrangements. But Bosnia, as a singular example of a war-ravaged transitional society, presents special challenges. The standard bitter pill approach applied elsewhere in the transitional societies of Eastern Europe—where it resulted in massive social and economic dislocations that in some cases persist even today—seems out of place entirely in a vulnerable society where the stakes of failure are much higher (a higher number of human dislocations in an already war-ravaged population and a possible a return to war itself).

What might instead be fitting here is a more fundamental paradigm shift in how economic reconstruction is "done" in postconflict settings. Specifically, this shift would entail a move away from the current bitter pill mode and toward a more buffered pill approach. This approach, in addition to relying on the type of demand-side employment projects that spur recovery (e.g., such as a youth employment scheme), would also move more actively to protect and cultivate the recovering nation's industries of comparative advantage and focus on rebuilding the infrastructure to get them to regional and international markets. Until a modicum of economic stability has been achieved, this approach would also entail loan forgiveness, low-interest rate economic aid packages, and a host of trade privileges from key trading partners.

The critical importance of these postconflict institutional arrangements, whether in their bitter or buffered pill form, should not be underestimated. We know, for example, from the developmental literature that a young person's resilience level is neither dichotomous nor static. Rather, there is a continuum of resilience, and the place a young person occupies on this continuum can change over time due to shifts in his or her life at either an individual level (e.g., diagnosis with a disease, flunking a grade in school) or a social ecological level (e.g., caregiver job loss, increase in crime in the surrounding neighborhood). In this scenario, it is not only the violence of armed conflict that embodies individual and ecological determinants of resilience (i.e., individual trauma as well as destruction of schools, communities, and families). The postconflict period can also serve as an additional source for change, posing both an opportunity to heal the individual and enhance his or her sources of resilience, as well as a risk of exacerbating the war's scars. This latter risk might further alienate individuals from one another and compromise their future prospects while aggravating the ecological sources of healing through protracted economic depression, decreased likelihood of social and economic success, and failed political institutions.

The extent to which the postconflict period actually affected the young people could not be addressed in this study, given that the predictive variables were (retrospective) conditions that occurred during the conflict. Thus, we do not know whether otherwise resilient young people deteriorated psychologically and functionally as the postconflict chaos in Bosnia continued. But it is clear from the low level of variance explained in the dependent variables of this study (part of which, naturally, is a function of inadequate measurement of the constructs and processes of interest) that something else is affecting young people's postconflict functionality other than the dynamics investigated here. The qualitative comments of young people conducted separately from this study's survey, however, underscore the notion that the postconflict period is at least as important as what happens during the war in predicting young people's longer term trajectories.

Pending further preventive policies such as these, the plight of young people enduring the violence of armed conflict remains a problem that affects their ability to thrive in the aftermath of fighting. As this discussion suggests, their plight is not only a humanitarian and moral problem but also a policy problem as well. The findings suggest that these young people's postconflict difficulties can in turn affect their societies' ability to rebuild stronger, more stable, and prosperous societies. To borrow from a familiar if somewhat clichéd maxim, in an interdependent world, what happens to young people in these settings affects us all.

The postconflict scenario does not occur in a vacuum, however, and sometimes the reconstruction period is witness to a wider societal transition. This is certainly the case in Bosnia, which, like many of its Balkan neighbors and indeed most of Eastern Europe, has seen much greater economic and political freedoms, this to the presence of occupation forces firmly rooted in Western notions of social, economic, and political development. (Thus, Bosnia's mode of greater capacity-building, described as being the cornerstone of the second phase of reconstruction, is marked by a move away from its prewar socialist past and toward greater economic and political liberalization in the aftermath of the war.) Aside from their war experience, therefore, young people in Bosnia and settings like it are faced with the additional risks and opportunities associated with a full-scale societal transition. Among the manifold risks are greater economic insecurity, greater access to drugs and other behavioral risks, and greater potential for social alienation. Among the many opportunities, by contrast, are greater freedom to exercise political voice, greater individual control over their own futures, and greater variety of social opportunities.

The postconflict period therefore embodies a separate set of factors influencing young people's transition to a functional adulthood, factors that can wield their effects on young people and their systems separately, while at the same time exacerbating the effects of the conflict on their postconflict trajectories. An analysis of youth policy should take into account the additional sources of risk and resilience associated with the postconflict period when examining young people's development after the fighting has ceased. These effects might exert their influence on youth development directly, or they might exacerbate the effects of the war.

Notes

1. Full details of this and all other analyses are available from the author on request.
2. All three remaining factors, as well as the two individual indicators that did not load highly onto any factor, possessed face validity in light of young Bosnians' qualitative accounts (McCouch, 2006). The three factors included direct nonlethal violence toward oneself and one's family (under which were subsumed the indicators "hit or kick you," "beat or humiliate your father in front of you," "verbally abuse you," and "torture you"), tear gas (under which were subsumed the indicators "shoot at you with tear gas" and "shoot tear gas into your school"), and raids/incursions (under which were subsumed the indicators "raid your school," "raid your home," "raid the home of a neighbor," and "demolish your home"). The two indicators not loading highly on any factor, meanwhile, included "hit you with bullets" and "kill a family member."
3. Scores were averaged to account for missingness in individual items. Thus, if a respondent only registered scores for three out of four items, his or her end score would be the average of these three data points, rather than averaging a total sum by four possible responses or dropping the person from the analysis altogether. Scores were based on standardized scores, meanwhile, to account for the nonparity of item responses on the scale. Specifically, on the original scale a response of 1 on item 1 and 3 on item 2 averages to 2, as does a 2 on item 1 and a 2 on item 2. These two averages are not comparable to each other. Standardizing the original indicator scores as z-scores before averaging them remedies this problem of comparability.

4. As the discussion suggests, the process of factor analyzing these indicators and constructing composite measures out of them resulted in factors bearing little resemblance to an easily interpretable scale. Thus, because most of the dependent measures, once recategorized, were dichotomous or ordinal rather than continuous, the simultaneous equations in this analysis used MLE methods instead of OLS regression. But this recategorization, as well as the use of standardized rather than raw scores in constructing composite variables, also leads to a challenge of interpretability. Because almost all measures at all levels are either dichotomous or ordinal rather than continuous, and because their scales are no longer conceptually rooted, the next section detailing the study's results speaks of elevations or unit increases in the independent measure leading to elevations or unit increases/decreases in the dependent measure at hand, rather than in more concrete measures of unit-to-unit change. It is hoped that in this process what was lost in interpretability is gained in robustness.

5. The work and work search outcome was subjected to a single mediation test. Its proposed mediator—positive identity development—was not shown to be a robust mediator.

6. Other recent conflicts, such as the war in Iraq (with its ethnoreligious fault lines—largely geographically delimited—of Shiites, Sunnis, and Kurds) and the genocide in Rwanda (with its communally defined ethnic rift between Tutsis and Hutus) come immediately to mind.

7. In fact, economic planners have bemoaned young Bosnians' lack of preparedness for these jobs, not least of all entrepreneurial, service-based, and white-collar jobs (European Stability Initiative, 2004). Many young Bosnians, especially those who stayed behind instead of fleeing to refugee camps or abroad, missed out on critical years of education during the war. For those young adults who have outgrown the primary and secondary educational systems but need remedial skills training, civil society organizations should help meet these needs through skills-based retraining programs.

8. The Washington Consensus reforms are summed up as follows: fiscal policy discipline; redirection of public spending toward education, health, and infrastructure investment; tax reform (specifically a regressive tax system, with lower taxes for higher income brackets); moderate interest rates; competitive currency exchange rates; trade liberalization; openness to foreign direct investment; privatization of state enterprises; deregulation of most industry; and the rule of law to protect property rights (see Williamson, 2000).

References

Achenbach, T. M., & Edelbrock, C. (1987). *Manual for the adolescents self-report and profile.* Burlinton: University of Vermont, Department of Psychiatry.

Barber, B. K., Stolz, H. E., & Olsen, J. A. (2005). Parental support, psychological control, and behavioral control: Assessing relevance across time, method, and culture. *Monographs of the Society for Research in Child Development, 70*(4).

Baron, R. M., & Kenny, D. A. (1986). The moderator-mediator variable distinction in social psychological research: Conceptual, strategic and statistical considerations. *Journal of Personality and Social Psychology, 51,* 1173–1182.

Blomkvist, H., & Inkinen, M. (2004, April). Transforming political culture? Democracy, primary education and group relations in Bosnia. Paper presented at the ECPR Joint Sessions, Uppsala, Sweden.

Brennan, P. (1997, July 15). Hopes of peace, fears of conflagration. The post-election line-up in Northern Ireland. *Le Monde Diplomatique.* Retrieved November 27, 2005, from http://mondediplo.com/1997/07/.

Brett, R., & Specht, I. (2004). Young soldiers: *Why they choose to fight.* Boulder, CO: Lynne Rienner.

Broström, S. (2005). *Social kompetence og samvær.* Copenhagen: Systime.

Center for Strategic and International Studies. (2002). *Post-Conflict Reconstruction Framework.* Retrieved October 8, 2006, from CSIS Web site: http://www.csis.org/isp/pcr/framework.pdf.

Earls, F. J., & Buka, S. (2000). Measurement of community characteristics. In J. P. Shonkoff & S. J. Meisels (Eds.), *Handbook of early childhood intervention* (pp. 309–324). New York: Cambridge University Press.

European Stability Initiative. (2004). *Governance and democracy in Bosnia and Herzegovina: Post-industrial society and the authoritarian temptation.* ESI Publication No. 10/11/04. Berlin and Sarajevo: European Stability Initiative.

Fischer-Rosenthal, W. (2000). Was bringt die Biographieforschung der Transformationsforschung? In I. Miethe & S. Roth (Eds.), *Politische Biographien und sozialer Wandel* (pp. 27–39). Gießen: Psychosozial-Verlag.

Flam, H. (2000). Entry und Exit: Zwei zentrale Momente in der Begegnung zwischen, Ich' und, Kollektiv. In I. Miethe & S. Roth (Eds.), *Politische biographien und sozialer wandel* (pp. 191–204). Gießen: Psychosozial-Verlag.

Freedman, S. W., & Abazovic, D. (2006). Growing up during the Balkan wars of the 1990s. In C. Daiute, Z. Beykont, C. Higson-Smith, & L. Nucci (Eds.), *International perspectives on youth conflict and development.* New York: Oxford University Press.

Garbarino, J., Kostelny, K., & Dubrow, N. (1991). What children can tell us about living in danger. *American Psychologist, 46*(4), 376–383.

Gavron, D. (2000). *The kibbutz: Awakening from utopia.* Lanham, MD: Rowman & Littlefield.

Hawley, P. H., & Little, T. D. (2002). Evolutionary and developmental perspectives on the agentic self. In D. Cervone & W. Mischel (Eds.), *Advances in personality science* (pp. 177–195). New York: Guilford Press.

Jones, L. (2002). Adolescent understandings of political violence and psychological well-being: A qualitative study from Bosnia Herzegovina. *Social Science & Medicine, 55,* 1351–1371.

Jones, L., & Kafetsios, K. (2005). Exposure to political violence and psychological well-being in Bosnian adolescents: A mixed method approach. *Clinical Child Psychology and Psychiatry, 10*(2), 157–176.

Judt, T. (2005). *Postwar: A history of Europe since 1945.* New York: Penguin.

Kerestes, G. (2006). Children's aggressive and prosocial behavior in relation to war exposure: Testing the role of perceived parenting and child's gender. *International Journal of Behavioral Development, 30,* 227–239.

Kohlberg, L. (1995). *Die Psychologie der Moralentwicklung.* Frankfurt: Suhrkamp Verlag.

Ladd, G. W., & Cairns, E. (1996). Children: Ethnic and political violence introduction. *Child Development, 67,* 14–18.

Larsen, J. E., & Møller, I. H. (Eds.). (2004.) *Socialpolitik.* Copenhagen: Hans Reitzels Forlag.

Lerner, R. M. (Ed.). (1993). *Early adolescence: Perspectives on research, policy, and intervention.* Hillsdale, NJ: Erlbaum.

Machel, G. (1996). *The impact of war on children.* New York: Palgrave.

Machel, G. (2001). *The impact of war on children: A review of progress since the 1996 United Nations report on the impact of armed conflict on children.* New York: Palgrave Macmillan.

Macy, R. D. (2003). Community-based trauma response for youth. *New Directions for Youth Development, 98,* 29–49.

McCouch, R. J. I. (2006). *Destruction and reconstruction in the aftermath of armed conflict: Assessing risk, resilience, and youth behaviors in post-war Bosnia.* Ph.D. diss., Brandeis University.

Morch, S. (1983). Er ungdomsproblemet et socialisationsproblem? Spørgsmål og svar. *Udkast, 11*(2), 152–181.

Morrow, J. (1995). *Journey of hope.* Dublin: Columba Press.

Müller, P., & Surel, Y. (1998). *L'analyse des politiques publiques.* Paris: Montchrestien (Clefs).

Noam, G. G. (2003). Learning with excitement: Bridging school and after-school worlds and project-based learning. *New Directions for Youth Development, 97,* 121–138.

Punamäki, R.-L., Qouta, S., & El-Sarraj, E. (2001). Resiliency factors predicting psychological adjustment after political violence among Palestinian children. *International Journal of Behavioral Development, 25*(3), 256–267.

Rosenberg, M. (1979). *Conceiving the self.* New York: Basic Books.

Rosenblatt, R. (1983). *Children of war.* New York: Anchor Press.

Sagi-Schwartz, A., van IJzendoorn, M. H., Grossmann, K. E., Joels, T., Grossmann, K., Scharf, M., et al. (2003). Attachment and traumatic stress in female Holocaust child survivors and their daughters. *American Journal of Psychiatry, 160*(6), 1086–1092.

Sampson, R. J., Raudenbush, S., & Earls, F. (1997). Neighborhoods and violent crime: A multi-level study of collective efficacy. *Science, 277,* 918–924.

Schultz, L. H., Barr, D. J., & Selman, R. L. (2001). The value of a developmental approach to evaluating character development programmes: An outcome study of Facing History and Ourselves. *Journal of Moral Education, 30*(1), 3–27.

Sen, A. (1999). *Development as freedom.* New York: Anchor Books.

Shonkoff, J. P., & Phillips, D. A. (Eds.). (2000). *From neurons to neighborhoods: The science of early childhood development.* Washington, DC: National Academies Press.

van der Kolk, B. A. (1994). The body keeps the score: Memory and the emerging psychobiology of post traumatic stress. *Harvard Review of Psychiatry, 1,* 253–265.

Ward, J. (1998). Changing youth transitions: New risks and vulnerabilities. *Drugs: Education, Prevention & Policy, 5*(1), 105–108.

Werner, E. (2000). Protective factors and individual resilience. In S. J. Meisels & J. P. Shonkoff (Eds.), *Handbook of early childhood intervention* (pp. 115–132). Cambridge: Cambridge University Press.

Williamson, J. (2000). What should the World Bank think about the Washington Consensus? *World Bank Research Observer, 15*(2), 251–264.

Yates, M., & Youniss, J. (1998). Community service and political identity development in adolescence. *Journal of Social Issues, 54*(3), 495–512.

Part III

EXPANDING THE SCOPE OF INQUIRY INTO YOUTH AND POLITICAL VIOLENCE

Following the general treatments of youth and political violence in Part I and the specific attempts to refine understanding of its effects in Part II, the four chapters in Part III contribute by illustrating how the scope of inquiry into adolescents' experiences with political violence can be expanded to provide a more comprehensive understanding of its effects. In Chapter 9, Brian Barber and Joseph Olsen analyze data from several hundred Palestinian youth. In addition to measuring conflict exposure, they included detailed assessment of adolescent activism, as well as an array of long-term psychological, social, and civic functioning. Analyses revealed some evidence of impaired functioning associated with conflict exposure (particularly for females), but also evidence of enhanced functioning for both males and females associated with their degree of activism. In Chapter 10, Neil Boothby and colleagues present the first long-term follow-up of a group of Mozambican child soldiers. Their study highlights the role of community reintegration, spiritual cleansing, and family and intervention program support in enabling most of the soldiers to become trusted and productive members of society. In Chapter 11, Steven Weine and colleagues focus on a group of Bosnian refugee youth living in the United States. Their interview data teach us that a narrow focus on violence-related trauma misses the complexity of challenges that many postconflict youth can face, including displacement, exile, the varied challenges of urbanization, and so on. Finally, in Chapter 12, Barber uses interview data from Bosnian and Palestinian youth to illustrate the variability with which adolescents process their experiences with political violence and how the availability of explanatory meaning during conflict can shape their identity.

Chapter 9

Positive and Negative Psychosocial Functioning after Political Conflict
Examining Adolescents of the First Palestinian Intifada

Brian K. Barber and
Joseph A. Olsen

wo of the limitations of the current research on adolescents and political violence have to do with narrowness of the scope of inquiry. The first of these—attention predominantly to individual psychological functioning (mostly psychopathological functioning)—has been discussed throughout this volume. Essentially, that concentrated focus has not produced a representation of adolescent functioning in the context of war that adequately captures the complexity of personal and social experiences. The second form of narrowness has to do with the predominant focus on adolescent exposure to the violence of political conflict. This preoccupation with discerning the effects of exposure to stress and trauma associated with war is understandable and critical. It does not, however, adequately capture the complexity of adolescent experiences with political conflict. Although it is the case, for example, that in some conflicts adolescents are passive victims of the violence of war (e.g., in Bosnia; see Chapters 7, 8, 11, and 12), it is also often the case that adolescents are active participants in political conflict. Boothby et al. (Chapter 10) and Wessells and Kostelny (Chapter 5) thoroughly discuss child soldiers, for example, one type of active participation in conflict—albeit coerced—participation. Another form of active participation is voluntary activism on the part of youth, such as in the classic cases of the South African and the Israeli-Palestinian conflicts. Given that many adolescents play active roles in political conflict, some attention should also be placed on that dimension of their experience and not solely on assessing the extent of violence they have experienced.

This chapter addresses both limitations by assessing a broad array of indicators of both positive and negative functioning as they are predicted by thorough assessments of both victimization and activism in a large sample of Palestinian adolescents from the First Intifada. That uprising is a particularly useful case study for adolescent experience in political conflict because of the uniquely high rates of adolescent participation in the conflict, as will be elaborated.

The First Intifada

Scores of volumes have been written about the Israeli-Palestinian struggle, and dozens of books have been written in particular on the First Intifada (Arabic for "uprising" or "shaking off"), one of the critical stages in the overall conflict. Thus, a comprehensive treatment of the century-old conflict between the two peoples and the historically unique movement of the First Intifada (hereafter referred to as simply "the Intifada" for simplicity) are neither possible nor necessary to provide here. However, some brief historical background is important to set in context the distinctive involvement of adolescents in this particular struggle.

Essentially, the Intifada (1987–1993) was an extension of a century-long, periodic though increasingly severe conflict between Arabs and Jews. This conflict began at the turn of the twentieth century when Jews from Europe and Russia fled intense persecution, and under the political banner of Zionism began successive waves of immigration to establish a homeland in the region of the world that for previous centuries had been referred to as Palestine, a region of critical historic importance to them. Initially, relations among Jews and indigenous Arabs (i.e., Palestinians) were harmonious, but it was not long before tensions related to economics, identity, and nationalism surfaced on both sides. The succeeding decades brought a series of skirmishes and wars between the two peoples that resulted progressively in increasing economic and political control over the area by Jewish residents and culminated in the creation of the state of Israel in 1948. Accompanying this significant change in the formal political landscape were displacements of hundreds of thousands of Arab Palestinian residents, primarily to the neighboring countries of Egypt, Jordan, Lebanon, and Syria.

This Palestinian refugee situation was expanded by the 1967 seizure by Israel, again via war with Arab states, of the three territories that hosted the densest groupings of Palestinian refugees—the West Bank (then held by Jordan), the eastern portion of the city of Jerusalem, and the Gaza Strip (then held by Egypt). Israel annexed East Jerusalem and declared the other regions occupied territories. That designation persists today, modified by a partial and inconsistent granting of Palestinian self-governance via the Palestinian National Authority (PNA) that was established at the end of the Intifada through the Oslo Declaration of Principles (see e.g., Tessler, 1994, for a full treatment of the Israeli-Palestinian conflict).

Although the Intifada had an ostensibly spontaneous ignition in December 1987 with the deaths of four Palestinian workers returning to Gaza from their day labors in Israel, there were assorted local conflicts and broader political events that immediately preceded it and gave it sense and momentum (see e.g., Hunter, 1993, for a full treatment of the Intifada). Most important for the purposes of this analysis, the Intifada was understood clearly by adolescents—through both formal education and through oral histories passed on by fathers and grandfathers—as a logical and key extension of the historic conflict, a juncture in the struggle that adolescents seized to make their own significant and highly visible contribution to the fight (see Chapter 12 for an analysis of the meaning Palestinian youth attached to the struggle).

Adolescents, Activism, and Political Violence

Social science literatures have not prepared us particularly well for understanding why people as young as adolescents choose to participate in war and political violence—and surely not to the high degree that Palestinian adolescents did during the Intifada. Whereas historically not more the 25% of a population of youth have participated in a political movement (Cairns, 1996), Palestinian adolescents participated in large majorities in the Intifada (see following discussion). Nevertheless, insights from both theory and empirical evidence from a variety of literatures can be gathered to provide some understanding of why adolescents might engage in political conflict (see Barber & Olsen, 2006. for a fuller discussion of potential explanations for adolescent engagement in political conflict).

As mentioned in Chapter 1, perhaps most distal in focus yet most current in time is the contemporary wave of interest in "youth development," a concentrated effort on the part of scholars (largely developmental psychologists), practitioners, and policy makers to shift from negative characterizations of adolescents in favor of acknowledging and strengthening their considerable competencies (see, e.g., Brown & Larson, 2002; Eccles & Gootman, 2002; Villarruel, Perkins, Bordern, & Keith, 2003). Even newer subareas of the youth development movement that are more proximal in focus to voluntary involvement in political conflict are the "youth civic engagement" (e.g., Lerner, 2004; Yates & Youniss, 1999) and "youth activism" (e.g., Sherrod, Flanagan, & Kassimir, 2005) efforts, both of which incorporate the decidedly competence-based approach in endorsing adolescents' capacity to consider and participate in efforts to effect change in social, environmental, civic, and political arenas. Most recently, Daiute, Beykont, Higson-Smith, and Nucci (2006) focus on youth and a variety of conflict types, including political conflict. They also share the competence approach. In short, some of the most current thinking about the capacity of adolescents in general would recommend that adolescents would or could engage themselves in the social and political issues that often define war.

Longer standing social science literatures also offer some insight into why adolescents might participate in durable and severe political conflicts. The well-established sociology and political science literatures on social movements and collective action have given some attention to young populations, typically to young adults (e.g., college students). Although a definition of adolescents is inherently elusive given cultural variations in conceptions of the life course and, more specifically, if and to what degree in a given culture there is a critical period of adolescence between childhood and adulthood (e.g., Larson, 2002; Rogoff, 2003; see Chapter 1 for an elaboration of the problems in defining adolescence), generalizations from college-aged (and even more so, college-attending) youth to younger adolescents may be problematic. Furthermore, the movement literatures speak only indirectly to youth involvement in the durable and violent political conflict of wars, focusing mainly on social and political movements that may well include instances or strategies of violence, but much more episodically.

These movement literatures of sociology and political science have vacillated over the decades between internal and external explanations of collective action, ranging from explanations of frustration and aggression associated with perceived grievances (e.g., isolationist, marginalization, and relative deprivation theories; Brinton, 1956, Davies, 1962; Gurr, 1970) to more rational and strategic mobilization of resources at politically opportune times by organized networks and groups in responding to perceived deprivations (e.g., resource mobilization theory; McAdam, 1982; McCarthy & Zald, 1977; Oberschall, 1973; Tilly, 1978).

In addition to these group-oriented approaches, there is ample information in psychologically oriented literatures that pertains (directly or indirectly) to an individual's involvement in political conflict. Victoroff (2005), for example, recently reviewed an array of theories that might bear on defining the profile of individuals who engage in political violence (in his case, "terrorism"). These include psychoanalytically driven theories that invoke explanations of narcissism (a pathologically exalted self resulting from deficits in maternal empathy) or paranoia (assigning intolerable internal feelings of damaged self-concept to an external object); nonpsychoanalytic theories that, for example, implicate cognitive limitations; and more development-oriented theories that credit presumed adolescent affinity for risk and thrill seeking for engagement in violent behavior. Along this line, Stagner (1977) focused on adolescent age-specific egocentrism, equating it with the ethnocentrism he felt was at the root of nationalism that also facilitated group violence by attributing undesirable features to members of the out-groups.

Having been unable to identify any psychological profile, these and other deficit or psychopathology approaches have not been very helpful in explaining political violence, even for terrorists, who, arguably because of the extremity of their behavior, would evidence most clearly this symptomatology (Cairns, 1987; Victoroff, 2005). With specific regard to Palestinians, the same absence of a deficit or psychopathological profile is being consistently found in the rapidly accumulating writings on suicide bombings, a strategy that was absent in the First Intifada but one that has characterized the Second Intifada (2000–2005; see Argo, 2006, for a review).

Palestinian Activism

There are a variety of ways of attempting to understand the unusual level of Palestinian adolescents' activism during the Intifada. Demographically, half of the population of the West Bank and the Gaza Strip was 14 years old or younger during the Intifada. These children and adolescents were born during the Israeli occupation and therefore had no personal recollection of the previous failed attempts at resistance. The occupation and resistance to it served as a model of aggressive behavior for them. In particular, they were firsthand witnesses to some of the most intrusive elements of the occupation, such as house raids, home demolitions, and deportation of fathers. The Islamic groups (e.g., Hamas and Islamic Jihad) also recruited among the youth. Furthermore, the prominence of schools as a location for violence inevitably involved young people in the resistance. Finally, because of the confiscation of prime agricultural land and restriction on water usage that reoriented the structure of production in the occupied territories, many youth sought employment in Israel and the oil-producing Arab peninsula. However, with the end of the oil boom era in 1982, employment opportunities in the Gulf states dried up, leaving many Palestinian youth frustrated in not being able to find employment (see, e.g., Farsoun & Landis, 1991; Roy, 1995; Tessler, 1994, for more comprehensive discussions of these issues).

As for research, Khawaja (1993, 1995) has found some support for both relative deprivation and resource mobilization perspectives in studying the Intifada, albeit using macro-level analyses that were not focused explicitly on youth. He noted, moreover, that true tests (of the deprivationist perspective) need to be done with attitudinal and individual-level data. In this regard, interview data with Palestinian youth from the Intifada supports the relevance of both perspectives, given the adolescents' widespread perception of severe economic, political, and human rights deprivation at the hands of the occupation and the sophisticated networking and organization of resistance by multiple political factions that characterized the Intifada (Barber, 1999a, in press).

As for developmental approaches, Braungart (1984) advanced a generational hypothesis that youth movements arise out of natural conflict that occurs between the young and the old. This might have some minor bearing on the Palestinian experience—given anecdotal and occasional interview reports from youth that implicate their parents' (read: fathers') failure to remove the occupation as a motivation for their own involvement (e.g., Barber, in press), but his finding that historically youth movements carry a clear theme of nationalism and self-determination is soundly supported in Palestinian adolescent involvement in the Intifada. Unequivocally, Palestinian adolescents of the Intifada cited the morality and urgency of replacing the occupation with an integral Palestinian political entity as the prime motive for their involvement (Barber, in press).

Consistent with Murphy's (1974) examination of youth movements, then, the Palestinian adolescent experience might be less well explained by aggression and generational conflict as by attempting to meet psychological and emotional needs— importantly, needs that are tied specifically to their perceptions of the inequities experienced by their collective people, by related moral and political ideologies, and by their belief that they could be active agents of change (see Braungart, 1984, for a review of similar perspectives explaining youth activism; see Daiute, 2006, and Turiel, 2006, for discussions of children's capacity to identify and react against injustices). Consistent with this socioemotional focus are suggestions from sociologists and political scientists that protracted conflict is importantly informed by national- or ethnic-sourced emotions of alienation, resentment, and rage (e.g., Petersen, 1993; Scheff, 1994, 1997; see also psychologist Frijda, 1987, for the emotion of revenge).

It appears more relevant developmentally, however—at least for adolescents or youth who voluntarily engage with other elements of their society in collective political activism, such as in South Africa and Palestine—to consider the identity component of social-psychological theories. Establishing a coherent identity was the primary task that Erikson (1968) originally assigned to adolescence, and cases of conflicts involving the struggle for self-determination and nationalism appear to be exemplars of the sociohistorical-political realm that Erikson and others always viewed as important to the achievement of this identity. Importantly, there is no clear distinction between the formation of a personal identity and the collective identity that the solidarity and close social ties of critical movements generate (Farsoun & Landis, 1991; McAdam & Paulsen, 1993). This might be particularly so for Palestinians, whose existence has always been a question of both cultural and political identity (Khalidi, 1997). That Palestinian adolescents quite consciously and authentically participated in these identity battles is clear from their own narratives (Barber, 1999a, in press); indeed, some scholars have viewed the Intifada as a renaissance of Palestinian identity (Usher, 1991) during which identity was particularly enhanced given the respect, responsibility, and status they achieved through their active participation (Darweish, 1989). Thus, their willingness to engage in the political conflict of the Intifada was driven by a desire to contribute to the achievement of an overall Palestinian identity (culturally, geographically, politically), an engagement that appears to have also substantially enhanced their own sense of identity and competence (Barber & Olsen, 2006). This is in line with Carmines (1991), who noted the growing recognition that an adolescent's sense of personal competence is critical to understanding engagement in political violence.

As to actual rates of participation, Palestinian adolescents appear to have participated to a considerably higher degree in the Intifada than the maximum 25% of youth (including older, college-aged young people) recorded in other historical examples of social or political movements (e.g., Cairns, 1996). There are ample anecdotal reports of this, by individuals and by media; there is also some empirical documentation of these very high rates of youth activism during the Intifada. One large-scale study just after the Intifada ended (1994–1995) collected survey data from 7,000 14-year-old Palestinian refugee adolescents from the West Bank, East Jerusalem, and the Gaza Strip. Included in the inventory were four items assessing activism during the Intifada: distributing leaflets, protecting someone from the Israeli Defense Force (IDF), demonstrating, and throwing stones. Interview data collected thereafter from several dozen Gazan youth also confirm the high rates of participation (e.g., Chapter 12; Barber, 1999a, 2002).

Furthermore, this chapter presents confirming data collected in 1998 from a representative sample of 900 Gazan youth who had lived at least 3 of their teen years during the time of the Intifada. Those data add to the record of Palestinian adolescent activism in the Intifada in several ways. First, the study concentrated on the Gaza Strip, an area that despite its small size (an average of 5 miles across and 25 miles long) experienced generally the heaviest doses of the occupation's constraints, by virtue of its geographic isolation, extremely taxing economic circumstances, and its role as the center of both militant movements and nascent Palestinian political efforts. It also had much of the most intense conflict during the Intifada. Second, the sample was selected carefully to represent the broad diversity of the population in Gaza (e.g., multiple political factions, dwelling types [camps, villages, towns], etc.). Third, the assessment of activism was quite thorough (e.g., seventeen specific forms of activism), detail that was learned through substantial interaction with Gazan youth themselves (see Chapter 12 for an elaboration of that interaction).

Effects of Political Activism and Victimization

The theme of competence also emerges when attempting to understand the effects political activism has on adolescents (consistent with Boyden's 2003 conclusions relative to the competence of children in facing war adversities). Students of youth social movements have regularly concluded that activism can have long-term effects on social and civic competence (e.g., maintaining liberal beliefs, continued participation in movements, pursuit of lifestyles in concert with beliefs; see Fendrich, 1993; McAdam, 1989; Whalen & Flacks, 1989 for evidence from studies of U.S. civil rights activists; active in politics, committed to needs of minorities, etc.; see Flanagan & Syvertsen, 2005, for evidence from multiple cultures). There is relatively little evidence, however, for competence effects in the literatures on adolescents and political violence, but this is largely because few measures of positive functioning have been included in study designs. Elements of competence that have been noted or empirically found include: active and "courageous" coping skills (Punamäki, 1989, 1996, 2000); moral development (Coles, 1987; Straker, Mendelsohn, Moosa, & Tudin, 1996); self-esteem (Baker, 1990); education, work status, and marital status (Sack et al., 1993); and civic reintegration, employment, and family formation (e.g., Chapter 10). (See Chapter 2 for a full overview.)

Most recently, in summarizing a set of studies of youth in various parts of the world (Daiute et al., 2006), Daiute (2006, pp. 13–14) notes several "important ironies of conflict," whereby, in addition to negative consequences, participation in conflict appears to also have promotive psychosocial effects, including self-determination, social determination, flexibility and tolerance to enemies, and cooperation toward a collective future. This duality of negative and positive effects from experience in conflict (even exposure absent active participation) is consonant with theoretical and in part empirical expositions of "post-traumatic growth" (e.g., Calhoun & Tedeschi, 2006). Thus, for example, Powell, Rosner, Butollo, Tedeschi, and Calhoun (2003) noted that Bosnian refugee and displaced youth—besides suffering from psychological and medical symptoms—perceived positive changes in themselves after the war.

In the case of Palestinian adolescents of the Intifada, there are two additional types of data that speak directly to competent functioning during and after involvement in political activism. First, the interview data of Gazan youth already mentioned reveal that despite conflicting political views on the legitimacy or validity of the peace agreement that ended the struggle (temporarily) in 1993, the clear self-perceived impact of their activism was heightened maturity, self-awareness, and civic responsibility, achievements that by their own report involved the complex management of a challenging host of emotions (e.g., fear, exhilaration, guilt, passion, loyalty, etc.; Barber, 1999a, in press). In the 1994–95 survey, multivariate modeling discerned the common finding that higher rates of Intifada involvement were correlated with higher reported feelings of depression (particularly for females) and antisocial behaviors (particularly smoking tobacco), but involvement was unrelated to academic achievement, educational aspirations, or family values. The link found between Intifada involvement and antisocial behavior was further specified to hold only for those adolescents who had poor relationships with their parents and/or had deviant peers (Barber, 1999b, 2001). One limitation of that work was that assessments of activism were aggregated with the assessment of frequency of victimization associated with the conflict into an Intifada involvement scale, a limitation of the analytic design that might help explain why there were only some negative correlates of involvement in the conflict.

To avoid this ambiguity, analyses of the 1998 Gazan youth data done for this chapter treated activism and victimization separately (although conjointly in multivariate modeling). This was also done in an initial analysis of the same data set that revealed that activism over the full course of the Intifada, net of its covariation with victimization, was significantly correlated with youth's perceived growth and maturity during the movement (e.g., feelings of maturity, happiness, and being an important part of history; concern about social issues; more political involvement; and having discovered identity; Barber & Olsen, 2006). This perceived growth was in turn correlated significantly with stated willingness to reengage in the conflict should it ignite again, which, of course, it did via the 2000–2005 Second (Al-Aqsa) Intifada. Rather than focus on social-psychological experience during the conflict, analyses for this current chapter concentrated on the perceived long-term effects of conflict, assessing psychological, social, religious, political, and civic activities or behaviors at the time of assessment (1998, 5 years after the end of the Intifada).

Methods

Sample

Data for these analyses came from a 1998 survey of 20–27-year-old youth in the Gaza Strip. Because the intent of the study was to assess adolescents' (retrospective) experience in the Intifada, this age range ensured that the participants would have lived at least 3 years of their adolescence during the 1987–1993 uprising. The survey built on a previous survey (Barber, 1999b, 2001) and interview work (Barber, 1999a, in press) on Palestinian adolescents in the West Bank, East Jerusalem, and the Gaza Strip. It was written first in English and then translated into Arabic. Three evolving versions of the Arabic instrument were pilot-tested on groups of appropriately aged youth in the Gaza Strip. The final version was then administered to 917 youth from two sampling frames. First, 67% (N = 614) of the sample were youth who were participants in the nine United Nations Development Program (UNDP) training programs operating throughout the Gaza Strip. Permission to conduct the survey was granted by the UNDP leadership in the Gaza Strip, and participation was solicited by the individual training center program leaders. The surveys were completed at the training centers. Second, 33% of the sample (N = 303) were students in randomly selected classrooms at the two major universities in the Gaza Strip: Al Azhar University (n = 193) and Islamic University (n = 110). Permission to conduct the survey was granted by the respective university presidents. Palestinian project staff administered the survey in classrooms. Every effort was made to include adequate representation of the diversity that exists in the Gaza Strip, including sex, region of residence, type of residence (e.g., camp, village, town), political affiliation, education, employment, and so on. Relevant sample characteristics are reported in Table 9.1.

Measures

Activism

The survey included a list of seventeen specific forms of activism that had been identified in past literature on the Intifada and in extensive interviews with youth in Gaza

Table 9.1 Sample Characteristics

Characteristics	Range	Average
Age (years)	20–27	22.4
Family size		
Brothers		4.3
Sisters		3.4
Sex		
Male		59%
Marital status		
Single		82%
Religious affiliation		
Muslim		99%
Geographic distribution		
Gaza Strip north		16%
Gaza Strip central		47%
Gaza Strip south		36%
Residence		
Camp		55%
Village		9%
City/Town		36%
Standard of living		
"Poorer than most"		17%
"Richer than most"		13%
Father employed 1997		42%
Educational attainment		
Finished secondary school		98%
Completed university		20%
Currently enrolled in university		61%
Employment		
Employed "never" in 1997		48%
Employed "very often" in 1997		33%
Political affiliation		
No political affiliation		41%
Fatah		33%
Hamas		13%
PFLP		7%
Islamic Jihad		2%
Other		4%

(see Barber, 1999a, in press; and Chapter 12 for a discussion of the interview data). For each of four discrete time periods—before the Intifada, first 2 years of the Intifada (1988–1989), last 3 years of the Intifada (1990–1993), and after the Intifada—respondents were asked to mark the appropriate level of participation in the forms of activism according to the following 5-point response scale referring to "how often did you do the following things in the conflict with the Israelis?": 1, never; 2, once; 3, occasionally; 4, often; 5, regularly. Responses for the second and third time periods were used for the present analysis because during these two periods most of the political violence occurred. Means and standard deviations are presented in Tables 9.2 and 9.3, respectively.

Table 9.2 Means and Standard Deviations for Activism Items Reported during the First Two Years of the Intifada, by Sex of Youth

"How often did you do the following things in the conflict with the Israelis?" (first two years)	Mean			N			SD		
	Male	Female	Total	Male	Female	Total	Male	Female	Total
a. Demonstrate	3.53	2.31	3.03	510	362	872	1.326	1.250	1.427
b. Distribute leaflets	2.50	1.23	1.97	497	355	852	1.533	0.742	1.412
c. Obey leaflets	3.44	2.82	3.19	493	344	837	1.592	1.589	1.619
d. Protect someone from IDF	2.52	2.23	2.40	500	362	862	1.496	1.431	1.476
e. Write slogans	2.46	1.05	1.87	503	359	862	1.515	0.326	1.364
f. Follow instructions from slogans	3.64	3.19	3.45	502	364	866	1.463	1.516	1.501
g. Burn tires	2.85	1.14	2.14	509	361	870	1.471	0.532	1.448
h. Erect barricades	3.08	1.36	2.36	504	361	865	1.421	0.852	1.482
i. Throw stones	3.84	2.12	3.12	507	359	866	1.384	1.330	1.603
j. Erect Palestinian flag	3.18	1.89	2.65	508	354	862	1.517	1.261	1.552
k. Throw Molotov cocktails	1.64	1.09	1.41	495	356	851	1.155	0.464	0.969
l. Wear a mask	2.56	1.08	1.94	493	352	845	1.575	0.423	1.432
m. Deliver supplies to participants	3.25	2.34	2.87	503	358	861	1.439	1.394	1.490
n. Care for wounded	2.84	1.86	2.43	505	360	865	1.442	1.226	1.439
o. Try to distract soldiers	2.85	2.16	2.56	504	360	864	1.467	1.390	1.475
p. Bring onions to help with tear gas	3.21	2.72	3.00	512	365	877	1.453	1.395	1.449
q. Visit the family of a martyr	3.39	2.01	2.82	510	364	874	1.409	1.304	1.525

Table 9.3 Means and Standard Deviations for Activism Items Reported during the Last Three Years of the Intifada, by Sex of Youth

"How often did you do the following things in the conflict with the Israelis?" (last three years)	Mean			N			SD		
	Male	Female	Total	Male	Female	Total	Male	Female	Total
a. Demonstrate	3.78	2.33	3.18	513	362	875	1.301	1.362	1.507
b. Distribute leaflets	2.90	1.27	2.22	500	354	854	1.608	0.821	1.560
c. Obey leaflets	3.56	2.89	3.29	497	344	841	1.527	1.614	1.596
d. Protect someone from IDF	2.69	2.33	2.54	506	358	864	1.554	1.498	1.541
e. Write slogans	2.85	1.07	2.11	503	358	861	1.556	0.397	1.501
f. Follow instructions from slogans	3.75	3.23	3.53	501	359	860	1.380	1.519	1.461
g. Burn tires	2.95	1.14	2.21	514	358	872	1.508	0.579	1.506
h. Erect barricades	3.21	1.37	2.45	508	357	865	1.422	0.914	1.534
i. Throw stones	3.90	2.08	3.15	513	357	870	1.368	1.341	1.624
j. Erect Palestinian flag	3.30	1.94	2.74	511	355	866	1.516	1.333	1.589
k. Throw Molotov cocktails	1.81	1.10	1.51	497	356	853	1.254	0.513	1.071
l. Wear a mask	2.86	1.10	2.14	502	350	852	1.601	0.504	1.540
m. Deliver supplies to participants	3.49	2.34	3.01	504	358	862	1.413	1.398	1.516
n. Care for wounded	3.08	1.88	2.58	508	359	867	1.439	1.272	1.493
o. Try to distract soldiers	2.99	2.17	2.65	503	360	863	1.492	1.386	1.504
p. Bring onions to help with tear gas	3.25	2.79	3.06	514	364	878	1.451	1.460	1.472
q. Visit the family of a martyr	3.65	2.12	3.02	516	364	880	1.310	1.358	1.526

Although the full, continuous response scales were employed in all analyses, for insight into the degree of participation, percentages of males and females who "ever participated" during the second and third time periods are presented in Table 9.4. The proportions reveal remarkably high levels of involvement, with large majorities of males and in many cases substantial percentages of females engaged in the variety of forms of activism across the course of the Intifada. For males, over 75% of the sample reported participating in many forms of activism, with proportions higher than 85% for some behaviors (e.g., demonstrating, throwing stones, etc.). Even for the highest risk behaviors (e.g., distributing leaflets and writing slogans on walls to encourage protests, and participating to a degree that wearing a mask to hide one's identity was deemed necessary), over half of the sample reported involvement. The relatively low percentage (29%) of male youth who threw Molotov cocktails indicates the comparatively low incidence of this more volatile form of activism during the movement.

Although participation rates were regularly lower than those of males, female activism was remarkably high, especially given the orthodox nature of Muslim culture in Gaza that under normal conditions restricts women to the private spheres of life (e.g., Fronk, Huntington, & Chadwick, 1999; Huntington, Fronk, & Chadwick, 2001; Moghadam, 1993; Sharoni, 1995). Thus, for example, half to two-thirds of the females reported having demonstrated and thrown stones. Females followed instructions (via leaflets and slogans) at nearly the same high level as males, and as many as 40% of females reported engaging in numerous other forms of activism, including protecting a combatant from soldiers (e.g., warning the combatant), erecting flags, and several

Table 9.4 Percent of Males and Females Who Ever (One or More Times) Participated during Time 2 (First Two Years of the Intifada) and Time 3 (Last Three Years of the Intifada)

"How often did you do the following things in the conflict with the Israelis?"	Percentage	
	Male	Female
a. Demonstrate	88, 89	63, 57
b. Distribute leaflets	57, 65	12, 12
c. Obey leaflets	78, 81	65, 65
d. Protect someone from Israeli soldiers	60, 62	49, 50
e. Write slogans on a wall	57, 66	3, 4
f. Follow instructions from slogans	85, 88	77, 76
g. Burn tires	72, 71	8, 7
h. Erect barricades	78, 79	19,17
i. Throw stones	88, 88	50, 47
j. Erect a Palestinian flag	77, 77	40, 40
k. Throw Molotov cocktails	29, 36	4, 5
l. Wear a mask	57, 64	4, 5
m. Deliver supplies to participants	80, 85	56, 57
n. Care for the wounded	72, 78	40, 39
o. Try to distract soldiers away from the participants	70, 73	49, 49
p. Bring onions to help with tear gas	79, 79	71, 69
q. Visit the family of a martyr	84, 89	46, 49

service functions such as caring for the wounded, visiting the family of slain *shabab* (martyrs), and bringing onions to help with the effects of tear gas (71%) (see Peteet, 1991, for a full-length treatment of women in the Palestinian resistance).

For both males and females, the rates of activism were quite similar across the two time periods of the movement.

Victimization

The survey included nineteen specific forms of victimization from the IDF that, likewise, were identified in past work with Palestinian adolescents. For the same time periods, respondents were asked to mark the appropriate level of exposure to victimization according to the following 6-point response scale referring to "how often did Israeli soldiers do the following": 1, never; 2, once; 3, 2–10 times; 4, 11–20 times; 5, 21–50 times; 6, more than 50 times. As for the activism variables, data reported for the second and third time periods were used in the present study, employing the full, continuous response scale. Means and standard deviations are presented in Tables 9.5 and 9.6, respectively.

Table 9.7 lists percentages of males and females who reported "ever" (the aggregation of response categories 2 to 6) being victimized during the two time periods of the movement. Like for activism, very high proportions of males and females reported experiencing numerous personal and nonpersonal forms of victimization during the Intifada.

Between 70% and 92% of both males and females reported experiencing IDF raids of their own home, homes of neighbors, and schools, and being shot at with tear gas in and outside of school. Of males, two-thirds to three-quarters reported having been verbally abused, hit or kicked, witnessed the beating/humiliation of a neighbor's father, and the killing of a neighbor; one in five reported having one or more of his bones broken and having a family member killed; one in four was hit with a bullet and imprisoned; and nearly half reported some form of torture. With the exception of the killing of family members, all of these severe forms of victimization were reported much less frequently by females—given that the actions were likely in part retaliatory responses to the more frequent and front-line activism of males.

As was the case with the activism variables, there does not appear to be much change across the course of the movement; whatever change did occur varied by type of victimization, with some types increasing over time (e.g., verbal abuse, being hit by bullets, imprisonment, etc.), and other types decreasing (e.g., home demolition, humiliation of fathers, etc.).

Psychosocial Indicators

Initial exploratory factor analyses (here and elsewhere, such analyses were conducted using principal components extraction and both varimax and oblimin rotation) were conducted on eight separate item sets that were included in the survey to measure the longer term psychosocial functioning of Intifada youth: respect from others, social competence, empathy, self-esteem/depression, antisocial behavior, civic/religious engagement, and identity. Finally, a single item was used to assess one aspect of the parent-youth relationship.

Table 9.5 Means and Standard Deviations for Victimization Items Reported for the First Two Years of the Intifada, by Sex of Youth

"How often did Israeli soldiers do the following?" (first two years)	Mean			N			SD		
	Male	Female	Total	Male	Female	Total	Male	Female	Total
a. Verbally abuse you	2.98	1.69	2.45	507	360	867	1.714	1.100	1.619
b. Hit or kick you	2.41	1.30	1.94	497	365	862	1.338	0.703	1.242
c. Break one or more of your bones	1.33	1.05	1.21	493	358	851	0.792	0.318	0.651
d. Shoot at you with bullets	2.41	1.35	1.96	495	357	852	1.528	0.802	1.378
e. Hit you with bullets	1.43	1.08	1.28	488	358	846	0.885	0.377	0.735
f. Shoot at you with tear gas	3.79	2.73	3.35	501	356	857	1.665	1.599	1.717
g. Imprison you	1.37	1.04	1.23	497	361	858	0.782	0.309	0.648
h. Torture you	1.87	1.12	1.55	500	362	862	1.183	0.589	1.047
i. Raid your home	3.49	3.04	3.30	504	365	869	1.479	1.527	1.515
j. Raid the home of a neighbor	3.68	3.32	3.53	494	355	849	1.506	1.523	1.522
k. Demolish your home	1.13	1.07	1.11	497	353	850	0.619	0.437	0.551
l. Demolish the home of neighbor	1.44	1.36	1.41	490	355	845	0.818	0.863	0.838
m. Beat/humiliate your father in front of you	1.71	1.60	1.67	492	351	843	0.993	1.050	1.018
n. Beat/humiliate the father of a neighbor in front of you	2.21	2.06	2.14	496	353	849	1.227	1.282	1.252
o. Kill a family member	1.29	1.22	1.26	499	360	859	0.728	0.534	0.654
p. Kill a neighbor	2.10	1.82	1.98	489	347	836	1.081	1.084	1.090
q. Raid your school	3.40	2.71	3.11	498	351	849	1.548	1.499	1.565
r. Shoot tear gas into your school	3.99	3.18	3.65	501	362	863	1.607	1.558	1.636
s. Close your school	2.86	2.50	2.71	502	365	867	1.398	1.429	1.421

Table 9.6 Means and Standard Deviations for Victimization Items Reported for the Last Three Years of the Intifada, by Sex of Youth

"How often did Israeli soldiers do the following?" (last three years)	Mean			N			SD		
	Male	Female	Total	Male	Female	Total	Male	Female	Total
a. Verbally abuse you	3.44	1.86	2.78	505	360	865	1.716	1.348	1.754
b. Hit or kick you	2.61	1.29	2.06	493	358	851	1.482	0.732	1.388
c. Break one or more of your bones	1.34	1.09	1.24	493	359	852	0.838	0.456	0.714
d. Shoot at you with bullets	2.58	1.33	2.05	497	362	859	1.626	0.838	1.485
e. Hit you with bullets	1.55	1.09	1.35	489	360	849	1.005	0.443	0.847
f. Shoot at you with tear gas	3.91	2.69	3.40	498	360	858	1.720	1.605	1.777
g. Imprison you	1.52	1.06	1.33	492	363	855	0.919	0.378	0.774
h. Torture you	2.09	1.16	1.70	499	362	861	1.367	0.698	1.225
i. Raid your home	3.62	3.17	3.43	498	359	857	1.540	1.518	1.546
j. Raid the home of a neighbor	3.79	3.36	3.61	495	355	850	1.511	1.514	1.526
k. Demolish your home	1.15	1.12	1.14	493	355	848	0.614	0.578	0.599
l. Demolish the home of neighbor	1.38	1.36	1.37	488	352	840	0.817	0.885	0.846
m. Beat/humiliate your father in front of you	1.72	1.61	1.67	490	349	839	1.141	1.139	1.141
n. Beat/humiliate the father of a neighbor in front of you	2.29	2.05	2.19	497	355	852	1.351	1.387	1.371
o. Kill a family member	1.33	1.23	1.29	498	358	856	0.756	0.614	0.702
p. Kill a neighbor	2.12	1.82	2.00	489	350	839	1.207	1.148	1.192
q. Raid your school	3.48	2.64	3.13	494	350	844	1.647	1.496	1.638
r. Shoot tear gas into your school	4.07	3.11	3.67	499	362	861	1.684	1.622	1.723
s. Close your school	2.84	2.43	2.67	500	363	863	1.431	1.438	1.448

Table 9.7 Percent of Males and Females Who Were Ever (One or More Times) Victimized by IDF Soldiers during Time 2 (First Two Years of the Intifada) and Time 3 (Last Three Years of the Intifada)

	Percentage	
"How often did Israeli soldiers do the following?"	Male	Female
a. Verbally abuse you	73, 82	38, 40
b. Hit or kick you	67, 70	19, 17
c. Break one or more of your bones	20, 20	4, 5
d. Shoot at you with bullets	62, 63	21, 19
e. Hit you with bullets	27, 32	6, 6
f. Shoot at you with tear gas	88, 87	70, 68
g. Imprison you	25, 34	2, 3
h. Torture you	47, 53	6, 7
i. Raid your home	89, 91	81, 85
j. Raid the home of a neighbor	93, 93	87, 88
k. Demolish your home	6, 7	3, 6
l. Demolish the home of your neighbor	30, 25	22, 21
m. Beat/humiliate your father in front of you	43, 38	34, 31
n. Beat/humiliate the father of a neighbor in front of you	66, 62	55, 50
o. Kill a family member	19, 22	18, 15
p. Kill a neighbor	66, 61	48, 44
q. Raid your school	87, 84	74, 71
r. Shoot tear gas into your school	92, 89	85, 81
s. Close your school	83, 79	69, 64

Respect from Others

Four items were written for this study to measure the degree of respect youth reported having experienced during the Intifada from their parents, friends, and teachers, respectively. These items constituted a single factor that we labeled *Respected*. Specifically, youth responded on a 5-point response scale from 1, never, to 5, always/almost, to the following items: "I felt respected by my father," "I felt respected by my mother," "I felt respected by my friends," and "I felt respected by my teachers." Cronbach's α for these items (averaged across the second and third time period of the Intifada) was 0.93.

Social Competence

Social competence was measured by the degree to which youth reported engaging in and initiating social interaction with peers and adults, using a five-item subset of the thirteen-item Social Initiative scale (Barber & Erickson, 2001). This scale has been shown to be reliable and valid in studies of adolescents from numerous cultures (Barber, Stolz, & Olsen, 2005, using the full thirteen-item set, including two samples of adolescents in conflict zones—Sarajevo, Bosnia, and in a different sample from the Gaza Strip, Palestine). Additionally, the same five-item subset was demonstrated to be both reliable and valid in an older population (youth retrospecting on their adolescence) from Sarajevo (see Chapter 8). Like for that study, in the data for the present study these five items formed a single factor. Specifically, youth responded on a 5-point scale from 1, never, to 5, very often/always true, as to the truth of the following statements for them now: "I share feelings and ideas with friends," "I share feelings and ideas with older adults in the community," "I help friends who might need assistance," "I ask questions of adults when I need advice," and "I express liking and caring for my friends." Cronbach's α for this scale was 0.76.

Empathy

Three items were selected from Davis's (1996) empathy scale for use in this study. One of them—"When I see someone being treated unfairly, I sometimes don't feel very much pity for them"—was relatively uncorrelated with the other two and was therefore omitted from analyses. The other two items were "I often have tender, concerned feelings for people less fortunate than I" and "I feel very sorry for other people when they are having problems." Youth responded on a 5-point response scale ranging from 1, does not describe me well, to 4, describes me very well. The correlation between these two items was 0.49 ($p < 0.001$).

Self-Esteem

Five items from Rosenberg's (1965) Self-esteem Inventory and two items from the depression subscale of the Child Behavior Checklist—Youth Self Report (Achenbach & Edelbrock, 1987) were factor analyzed together, producing a three-factor solution. For the self-esteem factors, one consisted of two items referring to positive self-esteem and one consisted of two items referring to self-derogatory feelings. This two-factor structure is consistent with several past analyses, in which, additionally, the self-derogatory items were particularly useful in predicting adolescent psychosocial functioning in multiple cultures (e.g., Openshaw, Thomas, & Rollins, 1984; Shagle & Barber, 1993; Stewart, Bond, Abdullah, & Ma, 2000). Therefore, we focused on the two items reflecting self-derogation. Specifically, youth responded to the following items on a 5-point scale ranging from 1, strongly disagree, to 5, strongly agree, relative to how they felt about themselves now: "I certainly feel useless at times" and "All in all, I am inclined to feel that I am a failure." The correlation between these two items was 0.40 ($p < 0.001$).

Depression

To the two items measuring depression ("I feel lonely," "I feel sad"), youth responded on the same 5-point scale from 1, strongly disagree, to 5, strongly agree, relative to how they felt about themselves now. The correlation between these two items was 0.63 ($p < 0.001$).

Antisocial Behavior

Factor analysis of seven items adapted from commonly used scales to measure antisocial behavior (e.g., Elliott, Huizinga, & Ageton, 1985) or written to apply specifically to the Gaza culture produced two separate factors. Youth responded to all items on a 5-point scale ranging from 1, never, to 5, often, with reference to "how many days during the past 6 months have you done the following things?" The three-item scale was labeled *Substance Use/Partying* and consisted of the following items: "used alcoholic beverages," "used tobacco," "attended parties with female dancers at the beach." Cronbach's α for this scale was 0.55. The four-item scale was labeled *Theft/Vandalism* and consisted of the following items: "purposely damaged or destroyed property," "stolen or tried to steal something of low value," "stolen or tried to steal something of high value," "hit or threatened to hit someone." Cronbach's α for this scale was 0.64.

Civic/Religious Engagement

Nine items were written to measure community (civic, political, religious) engagement, to which youth responded on a 5-point scale ranging from 1, never, to 5, very often relative to how often they engaged in that activity during the past year. An additional four items were written to more precisely define religious involvement (i.e., public and private religiosity; Thomas & Carver, 1990) during each of the four time periods. For these analyses, we used data referring to the last time period (after the Intifada); youth responded to these items on a 5-point response scale ranging from 1, not at all, to 5, every day. Because of the overlap in orthodox Muslim culture of civic, political, and religious participation, the combined set of fourteen items were factor analyzed together. This produced four factors.

The first factor, labeled *Public Religiosity,* contained four of the five religious involvement items: "Go to mosque/church to pray," "Helped teach the Koran or the Bible to others," "Listened to religious tapes," "Did other religiously oriented activities, such as _____." Cronbach's α for this scale was 0.72.

The next factor, labeled *Political Involvement,* consisted of the following three items: "Attended meetings or musical events at a political group's headquarters," "Attended seminars about political issues," "Participated in other political events, such as _____." Cronbach's α for this scale was 0.72.

The third factor, labeled *Volunteering,* also consisted of three items: "Volunteered as a teacher," "Volunteered to help the disabled," "Did other civic service voluntary work, such as _____." Cronbach's α for this scale was 0.61.

The fourth factor, labeled *Private Religiosity,* had four items: "Pray alone," "Read in the Koran/Bible," "Think seriously about religion," "Talk about religion with my friends." Cronbach's α for this scale was 0.67.

Identity

Nine items reflecting identity development were selected from the Measures of Psychosocial Development Scale (Hawley, 1988) for inclusion in this study. However, seven had very low intercorrelations as well as low correlations with the remaining two items: "I consider myself to be an adult" and "I feel I have matured fully." We labeled this pair of items *Maturity*. The correlation between these two items was 0.63 ($p < 0.001$).

Relationship with Parents

Finally, a single item labeled *Arguments with Parents* was used to assess one aspect of the parent-youth relationship. For each of the four time periods, youth responded to the question: "How often did you have disagreements with your parents?" on a 6-point scale from 1, never, to 6, almost every day. We used the report for the fourth time period (after the Intifada) in these analyses to index the postconflict parent-youth relationship.

Results

Initial Analyses

Activism

Based on parallel exploratory factor analyses of the seveteen activism items each at time 2 and time 3, three sets of items were identified that had high factor loadings on three primary factors. One set, labeled *Supportive Activism,* consisted of items d, m, n, o, p, and q, all of which describe activities that were not direct protest behaviors but served important supportive functions, such as protecting protestors, distracting soldiers from protestors, caring for the wounded, and delivering various supplies. Another set of items, labeled *Direct Activism,* consisted of items a, b, e, g, h, i, j, k, and l, all of which pertain to more direct forms of protest, such as demonstrating, throwing stones, erecting barricades, and so on. A third set, labeled *Follow* consisted of just two items, c and f, dealing with following instructions from slogans written on walls and obeying the directives contained in the leaflets often distributed on behalf of the Intifada leadership. Scales were created by calculating the average for each of these sets of items at time 2 and at time 3. Reliabilities (Cronbach's α) for each of the scales at each of the time periods were: Supportive Activism: 0.84, 0.85; Direct Activism: 0.88, 0.88; Follow: 0.82, 0.80. In the final structural equation model, we used the averages of the corresponding scales across both time periods.

Victimization

Based on parallel factor analyses of the nineteen victimization items each at time 2 and time 3, four sets of items were identified that had high factor loadings on each of four primary factors. One set, labeled *Personal Victimization,* consisted of items a, b, c, d, e, g, and h, mostly dealing with specific IDF actions experienced personally by the adolescents, for example, being hit, kicked, shot at, and so on. Another set of items, labeled *School Victimization,* was comprised of items q, r, and s, all related to IDF activities conducted at schools (raiding and closing schools, shooting tear gas into schools). A third set of items, labeled *Intrusion,* consisted of items i, j, m, n, and p and consisted mostly of IDF actions that were particularly intrusive (e.g., home raids, humiliation of fathers, etc.). The fourth set of items, labeled *Destroy,* consisted of items k, l, and o, representing house demolitions or killing of a family member. Scales were created by calculating the average for each of these sets of items at time 2 and at time 3.

Reliabilities (Cronbach's α) for each of the scales at each of the time periods were: Personal Victimization 0.83, 0.83; School Victimization 0.82, 0.84; Intrusion 0.78, 0.78; Destroy 0.58, 0.54. In the final structural equation model, we used the averages of the corresponding scales across both time periods.

Modeling Activism and Victimization

Based on examination of the correlations among the activism and victimization scales and on exploratory factor analyses of these scales, we developed a model to represent the basic constructs of Activism and Victimization. Personal Victimization was treated as separate construct, and School Victimization and Intrusion were treated as indicators of a more general, neighborhood and community Victimization construct. Direct Activism and Supportive Activism were treated as indicators of a more general Activism construct. The Follow activism scale was less related to Supportive Activism and Direct Activism than those two forms of Activism were to each other, and therefore, Follow was omitted from further consideration. A similar pattern was observed with respect to the Destroy victimization scale. It was less strongly related to community and neighborhood Victimization than that general measure's components were to each other. We think that part of the reason for this was its low reliability, given that it produced a worsened fit when we attempted to include it as an indicator of Victimization. Eventually, we would like to build a more comprehensive model that would include both Follow and Destroy, but we felt that this model would be an adequate rendering of Activism and Victimization for our present purposes.

Each of the three major constructs—Activism, Personal Victimization, and neighborhood/community Victimization—was substantially intercorrelated. Activism and neighborhood/community Victimization were correlated at 0.77, and Personal Victimization was correlated at 0.75 with Activism and at 0.62 with neighborhood/community Victimization. In addition, the residuals for the Direct Activism and Intrusion indicators were strongly negatively correlated (–0.64). Thus, it appears that the part of personal participation in Intifada activities that is not part of general Activism is negatively related to the part of highly intrusive IDF behavior that was not part of general neighborhood/community Victimization. This might reflect an intimidation factor in that although Activism and Victimization were highly positively correlated generally, some very highly intrusive behaviors may actually have lead some youth to reduce certain forms of activism. It will be instructive to pursue at a later time which specific behaviors are accounting for this relationship.

Predicting Psychosocial Functioning

The thirteen psychosocial outcome measures were treated as multiple dependent variables in a multivariate latent variable regression model with the previously described activism and victimization variables as predictors, using analysis of moment structures (AMOS) (Arbuckle, 1994). Models were run separately for males and females. The fit of both models was good: males—χ^2 (30) = 71.10, $p < 0.001$, CFI = 0.979, RMSEA = 0.051; females—χ^2 (30) = 81.69, $p < 0.001$, CFI = 0.960, RMSEA = 0.067. The standardized regression coefficients for these models are shown in Tables 9.8 and 9.9,

Table 9.8 Regression Coefficients between Activism/Victimization Measures and Psychosocial Outcome Measures from Structural Equation Analysis for Males

Psychosocial Outcome Measures	Activism	Personal Victim	Neighborhood Victim
Civic Involvement			
Volunteering	0.20*	0.07	–0.02
Politics	0.45***	0.13*	–0.29**
Religious Commitment			
Private religiosity	0.05	–0.05	0.09
Public religiosity	0.05	0.06	0.02
Antisocial Behavior			
Substance use/partying	0.19*	0.05	–0.08
Theft/vandalism	–0.29**	0.16*	0.21*
Social Competence			
Social initiative	0.50***	–0.11	–0.12
Relationship with Parents			
Arguments with parents	0.28**	–0.07	–0.20*
Orientation to Others			
Respect from significant others	0.17	–0.10	0.10
Empathy for others	0.29**	–0.06	–0.15
Identity			
Maturity	0.17	0.00	–0.12
Mental Health			
Depression	–0.03	–0.05	–0.03
Self-derogation	–0.16	0.07	0.01

$*p < 0.05$; $**p < 0.01$; $***p < 0.001$.

respectively. For ease of presentation, we grouped the outcome variables into eight categories: Civic Involvement, Religious Commitment, Antisocial Behavior, Social Competence, Relationship with Parents, Orientation to Others, Identity, and Mental Health.

Civic Involvement

For both males and females, past activism significantly predicted both measures of civic involvement, such that the higher the reported activism during the Intifada, the higher the 5-years-later level of volunteering and involvement in political activities. The degree of personal victimization also significantly predicted higher later political involvement for males but not for females, such that the more males reported having been harshly treated personally during the Intifada, the more likely they were to be involved in political activities later. In contrast, the more both males and females experienced harsh events in their neighborhoods during the Intifada, the less likely they were to be involved in political activities later. Neither form of victimization was related to the level of later volunteering in the community for either males or females.

Table 9.9 Regression Coefficients between Activism/Victimization Measures and Psychosocial Outcome Measures from Structural Equation Analysis for Females

Psychosocial Outcome Measures	Activism	Personal Victim	Neighborhood Victim
Civic Involvement			
Volunteering	0.42**	0.04	–0.18
Politics	0.77***	0.05	–0.46**
Religious Commitment			
Private religiosity	0.15	–0.21***	0.07
Public religiosity	0.47***	–0.02	–0.17
Antisocial Behavior			
Substance use/partying	–0.01	0.21***	0.03
Theft/vandalism	–0.15	0.30***	0.01
Social Competence			
Social initiative	0.37**	–0.15*	–0.21
Relationship with Parents			
Arguments with parents	0.30*	–0.09	–0.23
Orientation to Others			
Respect from significant others	0.23	–0.08	–0.13
Empathy for others	0.04	–0.08	0.01
Identity			
Maturity	0.16	–0.14*	0.06
Mental Health			
Depression	–0.17	0.13	0.17
Self-derogation	–0.18	0.02	0.07

*$p < 0.05$; **$p < 0.01$; ***$p < 0.001$

Religious Commitment

Neither activism nor victimization was related significantly with either form of religiosity for males. For females, past activism was associated positively with public religiosity, such that the more females were actively involved in the Intifada, the more they were involved in public religious activities later, such as going to mosque, helping teach the Koran, and so on. Harsh experiences during the Intifada were unrelated to later levels of females' religiosity, with the exception that the more females reported being treated harshly personally, the less they were later involved in private religious activities, such as praying, reading the Koran, and so on.

Antisocial Behavior

There were countervailing associations between Activism and antisocial behavior for males, depending on the type of antisocial behavior. The more active males were (1) the more likely they were later to report using substances (i.e., tobacco, alcohol) or attending beach clubs, but (2) the less likely they were to report involvement in theft or vandalism later. For females, Activism was not associated with either form of antisocial behavior. Personal Victimization was associated with higher levels of later Theft/Vandalism for both males and females, and it was additionally associated with higher levels of Substance Use/Partying for females. Neighborhood Victimization was only associated (positively) with higher Substance Use/Partying and, furthermore, only for males.

An inspection of the individual items making up the Substance Use/Partying variable revealed that, consistent with the 1994–1995 study (Barber, 1999b, 2001), Activism was associated particularly strongly with the use of tobacco. There was no differentiation in patterns of prediction from victimization to the specific items making up the Substance Use/Partying variable.

Social Competence

For both males and females, Activism during the Intifada was significantly associated with later Social Initiative, such that the more active the youth were during the struggle, the higher they reported their later social competence in the form of initiating relationships and interaction with peers and adults.

Neither form of victimization predicted social competence for males, but Personal Victimization was significantly associated negatively with Social Initiative for females, such that the more they recalled experiencing harsh treatment during the Intifada, the lower they rated their social competence.

Relationship with Parents

There was a significant association between reported Activism and Arguments with parents for both males and females, such that the higher they recalled having participated in the struggle, the more they later recalled having arguments with their parents. Neither form of victimization was related to arguing with parents for either males or females.

Orientation to Others

For males, there was a significant association between Activism and Empathy, such that the more active the males were during the Intifada, the higher they rated their later concern for others. Activism was unrelated to Empathy for females, and for neither males nor females was there an association between either form of victimization and the degree to which they felt respected by significant others in their lives.

Identity

Neither activism nor victimization was related to self-perceived maturity in males. For females, Personal Victimization was significantly negatively associated with Maturity, such that the higher the females reported suffering personally, the less they self-reported feeling mature.

Mental Health

For neither males nor females was any measure of Activism or Victimization associated with perceptions of later self-derogation or depression.

In sum, the long-term effects of reported Activism on numerous assessments of psychosocial functioning for both male and female youth were largely positive. For both males and females, Activism (net of its covariation with Victimization) was associated with higher reported Civic Involvement (both volunteering and political activities) and Social Competence, as it was also for higher reported Empathy for males and higher reported Religiosity (public devotion) for females. Also for both males and females, higher reported Activism was associated with more disagreements with parents, presumably reflecting either the heightened autonomy that activism asserted or differing views as to the political outcomes of the Intifada. Finally, for males, although Activism was associated with higher involvement in one form of Antisocial Behavior (e.g., "status offenses," like tobacco/alcohol use, beach parties), it predicted lower levels of theft and vandalism.

There were relatively fewer psychosocial effects of Victimization (net of its covariation with Activism). Consistent with the majority of other studies (see Chapter 2), effects were mostly negative, such that Victimization was related to poor psychosocial functioning. For males, only one index of psychosocial functioning—the more serious form of Antisocial Behavior—was predicted by both Personal and Neighborhood Victimization. The effects were more widespread for females: Personal Victimization was associated with lower (private) Religiosity, higher Antisocial Behavior (both measures), lower Social Competence, and lower Maturity. In addition, for females, Neighborhood Victimization was also associated with lower Civic Involvement (political activities).

Discussion

This study attempted to contribute to the growing literature on adolescents and political violence in two fundamental ways, both of which were pursued by broadening the typical scope of inquiry. First, as is evident in the review presented in Chapter 2, most studies have not attended to the degree to which adolescents have participated in political conflict, focusing instead on exposure to political violence. To address this deficit, the current study included a detailed assessment of the numerous specific types of activism Palestinian adolescents recalled engaging in during the first Intifada. As far as we are aware, this is the first systematic assessment of adolescent activism in political conflict. It provided windows into the variety of types of behaviors in which adolescents have engaged, the degree to which they participated in these behaviors (and how levels of participation did or did not change over the long course of the conflict), and importantly, how this activism was correlated with later psychosocial functioning.

The second broadening of the typical scope of inquiry had to do with the assessment of psychosocial functioning itself. As noted in detail in Chapter 2 and referred to elsewhere throughout this volume, the predominant focus of empirical assessments of youth and political conflict has been on identifying the negative psychological correlates of political violence. That focus can be justified in part because the majority of the studies have concentrated on exposure to stresses and trauma of war or political conflict (what we have labeled in this study as victimization). Not surprisingly, most studies have found correlations between exposure and negative psychological (and to a less frequent degree, behavioral) functioning, a finding that was also partly confirmed in this study.

Even so, the narrow focus on negative functioning has proven inadequate given the evidence of successful or adaptive functioning by youth confronted with grief and many types of traumatic experiences (e.g., see Bonanno, 2004; Masten, 2001; see Chapter 12 for an elaboration of the growth potential from hardship), including war (e.g., Powell et al., 2003). In addition to noting the failure of many studies to identify significant associations between conflict and negative functioning of adolescents, the review of the empirical literature on adolescents and political violence presented in Chapter 2 also indicates that approximately half of those few studies that did include measures of competent functioning found them to be regularly and positively predicted by the adolescents' experiences with conflict. The inclusion in the current study of positive elements of psychosocial functioning was particularly appropriate given its parallel assessment of the active participation of adolescents in political conflict. As noted earlier in this chapter, although limited, the available research on activism in social and political causes regularly invokes positive outcomes of the types assessed here (e.g., civic participation, social competence, etc.) (See also Blattman, 2008 for similar findings from a UNICEF study among youth from Uganda.)

There is a synergistic benefit from expanding both the assessments of experience with political violence and psychosocial functioning in that multiple components of each can be tested simultaneously for their unique roles in the conflict-to-outcome equation. This was facilitated by the relatively large size of the sample, which permitted advanced multivariate tests of the associations among the multiple dimensions of conflict involvement (i.e., activism and victimization) and psychosocial outcomes (i.e., civic involvement, social competence, antisocial behavior, etc.). The result was that the unique associations among the modeled variables were assessed. Thus, the portions of activism and victimization that did not overlap in their prediction of the outcome variables (due to their own, in this case, substantial intercorrelation) were tested for associations with the portions of the multiple forms of psychosocial functioning that themselves were not shared with each other. This rendered a more refined (i.e., "purer" or less redundant) set of linkages among the variables than has been available from most other studies that have tested only the simple correlations between violence exposure and a single outcome, or a set of outcomes that have significant intercorrelations (e.g., multiple assessments of negative psychological function, for example, anxiety, depression, post-traumatic stress disorder, etc.).

Naturally, this study has its share of limitations. Many researchers are understandably concerned about relying strictly on youth reports of all variables in any study, for reasons of possible under- or overreporting and systematic response bias. Furthermore, retrospective reflections on behaviors that carry such heavy symbolic value (i.e., personal contributions to the struggle through activism and the harsh treatment experienced in the process) are subject to memory inaccuracy and reconstruction. Unfortunately, it is extremely difficult to collect data during political conflicts because of risk and restricted access, and thus there is little option other than to assess experiences retrospectively. Similarly, even if there were some more objective source of information (which is unlikely in many political conflicts such as the Israeli-Palestinian conflict and the Northern Ireland conflict because of how polarized the general world population appears to be in attributing blame to one side or the other in the conflict), participants are likely still the best source of data on their activism, especially in the nuanced detail with which this study assessed it.

Although it is not clear how substantially better data could be collected on experiences with conflict (except, perhaps, validations from close peers), it is the case, however, that other types of data on psychosocial functioning could have enhanced the reliability and validity of its measurement. This is all the more important in the current case, given that some of the scales had low reliabilities. Ideally, two or more sources of information on reliable scales would be used to validate social and perhaps some forms of psychological functioning (e.g., parallel reports from parents, peers, teachers, or employers; official records from school, police, or court, etc.).

That said, it is important once again to highlight the vicissitudes of doing research in conflict zones, particularly those that long after the conflict subsides remain unstable, impoverished, and without reliable or persistent governmental structures. In Gaza, widespread unemployment renders that domain not useful to assess youth functioning. No more available or reliable would be official police or judicial records given the precarious existence or operation of those systems (and in some cases also educational systems), particularly given the fought-for but nevertheless disrupted and incomplete transfers of authority over those domains from the Israeli government to the Palestinian Authority that occurred after the First Intifada. Nevertheless, except for some internal variables, such as self-esteem and depression, that are best reported subjectively, any replication of this study would benefit at least from the validating perspectives of parents, peers, and perhaps instructors for those enrolled in school or university.

With these methodological limitations in mind, the present study produced useful findings in three areas. First, was the validation of the remarkably high levels of Palestinian adolescent involvement in the Intifada. Our earlier survey of several thousand Palestinian adolescents indicated similarly high prevalence (of both activism and victimization), but with much cruder measures (Barber, 1999b, 2001). The current study thus validated these high rates on another fairly representative sample, but most important, with very detailed assessments of adolescent activist behaviors. Similarly, the detailed assessment of the many and varied forms of victimization adolescents experienced in the course of their participation in the struggle has offered a more complete appraisal of the harshness, stress, or trauma that is often part of political conflicts of this type. Importantly, these specific forms of both activism and victimization were derived from substantial interaction with the participants themselves (see Chapter 12; Barber, in press).

Beyond inspecting the prevalence rates (across two time periods) of activism and victimization, in this study we did not exploit the specificity of measurement past their grouping into more general factors: for activism—supportive functions, direct involvement in tactical behaviors, and following instructions from movement leaders—and for victimization—personal victimization, school victimization, intrusion, and destruction. This dimensional modeling was necessary to parsimoniously represent the variables in a complex model, and it proved useful in distinguishing the independent effects of activism and victimization on several forms of psychosocial functioning, the essential purpose of the study. We look forward to future analyses of these data that take advantage of the specificity of measurement, such as testing for unique effects of discrete forms of activism and victimization, assessing the temporal ordering of the variables (over the four time periods covered in the data), examining higher order relationships (e.g., additive and/or interactive properties), as well as person-centered analyses to identify profiles and trajectories of involvement in the Intifada.

Flowing from this finding of very high rates of activism is the second area of this study's contribution, namely, the comment it makes on the broader issue of competence that is driving much of the recent research on adolescents generally (see Chapter 1 for an elaboration). In this case, the findings presented here reveal a clear commitment on the part of adolescents to a broad and demanding sociopolitical cause via their activist behaviors, even when (or perhaps in part because of being) exposed to very harsh treatment. Substantial interview data with a smaller sample of same-aged Gazan (predominantly male) youth reveals that this dedication was fueled by the fundamental and urgent moral and ethical meaning Palestinian youth ascribed to the legitimacy of their people's struggle against what they perceived to be an unjust and debilitating oppression—emotions and ideologies that also inform the positive outcomes reported here and discussed shortly (Barber, 1999a, 2002, in press; Chapter 12).

The extension of the adolescent competence argument into political activism brings much complexity with it, because by definition, the activism involves blatant and provocative challenges to authority, which in some cases take on violent forms. Neither disrespect of authority nor violence lends itself easily to value-free analyses. Even though philosophical and moral deliberations about youth behavior during the First Intifada are spared the vexing problem of Palestinian suicide bombings that were rampant in the Second Intifada (the first Palestinian suicide bombing did not occur until 1993 as the First Intifada was ending), there are still diverse views on youth behavior during that uprising. Some who have commented informally on these findings, for example, have preferred to view all forms of insurrection and violence as morally unacceptable and antisocial. Others have concluded that extreme adversity and perceived oppression require opposition and therefore, defiance, even if violent, is self-respectful, self-preserving, and prosocial. Naturally, there are other value configurations somewhere in between these poles, but in the end, all are judgments and here is not the place to debate their multifaceted complexity and ambiguity (e.g., questions of what is resistance and what is insurrection, which parts of war and political conflict are more or less acceptable, who and what is a freedom fighter and who and what is a terrorist, etc.). Our own judgment to view the commitment of Palestinian adolescents as an indicator of competence is driven by the research findings: first, the youth share with all segments of their society the view that their contributions to the struggle were honorable, dutiful, and valuable toward moral purposes; second, they themselves perceive it to have contributed to their growth as individuals and members of society; and, third, activism was associated almost uniformly with later psychosocial competence (using generally accepted concepts of psychological health and positive social and civic behavior).

This latter point on the effects of activism represents the third area of contribution of this study. The contribution is valuable both because the finding is novel (i.e., systematic analyses of prevalence and effects of youth activism during political conflict have not been done previously) and because of the relative clarity, strength, and valence of the finding: higher rates of activism associated with more competent functioning years later. This finding extends the limited yet consistent evidence of long-term growth from involvement in social movements into the highly violent and extended conflict that was the Intifada. It is not difficult to understand how committed (and recognized) service in behalf of a valued social agenda would enhance a youth's sense of efficacy, worth, and value and otherwise promote commitment to social conformity and service. (Insight from the youths themselves relative to the salience of this social identity, and how it was facilitated by the meaning they were able to attach to the conflict and their involvement in it, is developed in Chapter 12.) Here it is worth noting that this growth occurred in the context of regular, durable, intense, and violent interactions.

We were able to technically distinguish between activism and victimization in the empirical analyses conducted for this study, but their high correlation makes clear that activism carried with it not just youth's own violent activity (e.g., throwing stones and less regularly Molotov cocktails) but also the fierce and often crushing response it received. Thus, the evidence of competence assessed years later must be recognized to have emerged from the identity-enriching sacrifice for the social good, despite the presence of high and intense levels of violence.

This was particularly the case for males, for whom also there were few negative effects of victimization. The competence effects were also evident for females, but these were more widely spread negative effects of victimization. This could be explained in part by their relatively lower levels of activism, particularly in the more assertive forms that might particularly embolden a buffering sense of identity and contribution. Relatedly, their cultural assignment to the private sphere (i.e., the home, except to attend school, and bouts of participation in the case of the Intifada) gave them less opportunity to feel the binding cohesion and reinforcement afforded males by their regular activity and communion about it.

Acknowledgment This chapter was supported in part by a grant to Brian K. Barber from the United States Institute of Peace.

References

Achenbach, T. M., & Edelbrock, C. (1987). *Manual for the child behavior checklist and revised child behavior profile.* Burlington: University of Vermont, Department of Psychiatry.

Arbuckle, J. L. (1994). AMOS: Analysis of moment structures. *Psychometrika, 59,* 135–137.

Argo, T. N. (2006). The role of social context in terrorist attacks. *Chronicle Review, 52*(22), 15.

Baker, A. (1990). The psychological impact of the Intifada on Palestinian children in the Occupied West Bank and Gaza: An exploratory study. *American Journal of Orthopsychiatry, 60,* 496–505.

Barber, B. K. (1999a). Youth experience in the Palestinian Intifada: Intensity, complexity, paradox, and competence. In M. Yates and J. Youniss (Eds.), *Roots of civic identity* (pp. 178–204). New York: Cambridge University Press.

Barber, B. K. (1999b). Political violence, family relations, and Palestinian child functioning. *Journal of Adolescent Research, 14,* 206–230.

Barber, B. K. (2001). Political violence, social integration, and youth functioning: Palestinian youth from the Intifada. *Journal of Community Psychology, 29,* 259–280.

Barber, B. K. (2002). Politics, politics, and more politics: Youth life experience in the Gaza Strip. In D. L. Bowen & E. Early (Eds.), *Everyday life in the Muslim Middle East* (pp. 209–226), Indianapolis: Indiana University Press.

Barber, B. K. (in press). *One heart, so many stones: The story of Palestinian youth.* New York: Palgrave/Macmillan.

Barber, B. K., & Erickson, L. D. (2001). Adolescent social initiative: Antecedents in the ecology of social connections. *Journal of Adolescent Research, 16,* 326–354.

Barber B. K., & Olsen, J. A. (2006). Adolescents' willingness to engage in political conflict: Lessons from the Gaza Strip. In J. Victoroff (Ed.), *Tangled roots: Social and psychological factors in the genesis of terrorism* (pp. 203–226). Amsterdam: IOS Press.

Barber, B. K., Stolz, H. E., & Olsen, J. A. (2005). Parental support, psychological control, and behavioral control: Assessing relevance across time, method, and culture. *Monographs of the Society for Research in Child Development, 70*(4).

Blattman, C. (2008). From violence to voting: War and political participation in Uganda. HiCN Working Paper, 42.

Bonanno, G. A. (2004). Loss, trauma, and human resilience: Have we underestimated the human capacity to thrive after extremely aversive events? *American Psychologist, 59,* 20–28.

Boyden, J. (2003). Children under fire: Challenging assumptions about children's resilience. *Children, Youth and Environments, 13*(1). Retrieved July 2, 2006, from http://www.colorado.edu/journals/cye/13_1/index.htm.

Braungart, R. C. (1984). Historical generations and youth movements: A theoretical perspective. *Research in Social Movements, Conflict and Change, 6.*

Brinton, C. (1956). *The anatomy of revolution.* New York: Vintage Books.

Brown, B. B., & Larson, R. W. (2002). The kaleidoscope of adolescence: Experiences of the world's youth at the beginning of the 21st century. In B. B. Brown, R. W. Larson, & T. S. Saraswathi (Eds.), *The world's youth: Adolescence in eight regions of the globe* (pp. 1–20). Cambridge: Cambridge University Press.

Cairns, E. (1987). *Caught in the crossfire: Children and the Northern Ireland conflict.* New York: Syracuse University Press.

Cairns, E. (1996). *Children and political violence.* Cambridge: Blackwell.

Calhoun, L. G., & Tedeschi, R. G. (2006). *Handbook of posttraumatic growth: Research & practice.* Mahwah, NJ: Erlbaum.

Carmines, E.G. (1991). Psychological antecedents of adolescent political involvement: Personal competence and political behavior. *International Journal of Adolescence and Youth, 3,* 79–98.

Coles, R. (1987). *The political life of children.* Boston: Houghton Mifflin.

Daiute, C. (2006). General introduction: The problem of society in youth conflict. In C. Daiute, Z. F. Beykont, C. Higson-Smith, & L. Nucci (Eds.), *International perspectives on youth conflict and development* (pp. 3–20). New York: Oxford University Press.

Daiute, C., Beykont, Z., Higson-Smith, C., & Nucci, L. (Eds.). (2006). *International perspectives on youth conflict and development.* New York: Oxford University Press.

Darweish, M. (1989). The Intifada: Social change. *Race and Class, 29,* 47–56.

Davies, J. C. (1962). Toward a theory of revolution. *American Sociological Review, 27,* 5–19.

Davis, M. H. (1996). *Empathy: A social-psychological approach.* Boulder, CO: Westview Press.

Eccles, J. S., & Gootman, J. (2002). *Community programs to promote youth development.* Washington, DC: National Academies Press.

Elliott, D., Huizinga, D., & Ageton, S. (1985). *Explaining delinquency and drug use.* Beverly Hills, CA: Sage.

Erikson, E. E. (1968). *Identity, youth and crisis.* New York: Norton.

Farsoun, S. K., & Landis, J. M. (1991). The sociology of the uprising: The roots of the Intifada. In J. R. Nassar & R. Heacock (Eds.), *Intifada: Palestine at the crossroads* (pp. 15–36). Birzeit, West Bank: Birzeit University Press and Praeger Publishers.

Fendrich, J. M. (1993). *Ideal citizens: The legacy of the civil rights movement.* Albany: State University of New York Press.

Flanagan, C., & Syvertsen, A. K. (2005). Youth as a social construct and social actor. In L. R. Sherrod, C. A. Flanagan, & R. Kassimir (Eds.), *Youth activism: An international encyclopedia. Vol. 1.* Westport, CT: Greenwood Press.

Frijda, N. (1987). *The emotions.* New York: Cambridge University Press.

Fronk, C., Huntington, R. L., & Chadwick, B. A. (1999). Expectations for traditional family roles: Palestinian adolescents in the West Bank and Gaza. *Sex Roles, 41,* 705–735.

Gurr, T. R. (1970). *Why men rebel.* Princeton, NJ: Princeton University Press.

Hawley, G. MPD: Measures of psychosocial development. Lutz, FL: Psychological Assessment Resources, Inc.

Hunter, F. R. (1993). *The Palestinian uprising: A war by other means.* Berkeley: University of California Press.

Huntington, R., Fronk, C., & Chadwick, B. A. (2001). Family roles of contemporary Palestinian women. *Journal of Comparative Family Studies, 32,* 1–19.

Khalidi, R. (1997). *Palestinian identity: The construction of modern national consciousness.* Chicago: University of Chicago Press.

Khawaja, M. (1993). Repression and popular collective action: Evidence in the West Bank. *Sociological Forum, 8,* 47–71.

Khawaja, M. (1995). The dynamics of local collective action in the West Bank: A test of rival explanations. *Economic Development and Cultural Change, 44*(1), 146–179.

Larson, R. W. (2002). Globalization, societal change, and new technologies: What they mean for the future of adolescence. *Journal of Research on Adolescence, 12,* 1–30.

Lerner, R. T. (2004). *Liberty: Thriving and civic engagement among America's youth.* Thousand Oaks, CA: Sage.

Masten, A. (2001). Ordinary magic: Resilience processes in development. *American Psychologist, 56*(3), 227–238.

McAdam, D. (1982). *Political process and the development of black insurgency.* Chicago: University of Chicago Press.

McAdam, D. (1989). The biographical consequences of activism. *American Sociological Review, 54,* 744–760.

McAdam, D., & Paulsen, R. (1993). Specifying the relationship between social ties and activism. *American Journal of Sociology, 99,* 640–667.

McCarthy, J., & Zald, M. N. (1977). Resource mobilization and social movements. *American Journal of Sociology, 82,* 1212–1241.

Moghadam, V. M. (1993). *Modernizing women: Gender and social change in the Middle East.* Boulder, CO: Lynne Reiner.

Murphy, H.B.M. (1974). Theories of youth unrest in cross-cultural perspective. *Australian and New Zealand Journal of Psychiatry, 8,* 31–40.

Oberschall, A. (1973). *Social conflict and social movements.* Englewood Cliffs, NJ: Prentice Hall.

Openshaw, D. K., Thomas, D. L., & Rollins, B. C. (1984). Parental influences of adolescent self-esteem. *Journal of Early Adolescence, 4,* 259–274.

Peteet, J. M. (1991). *Gender in crisis: Women and the Palestinian resistance movement.* New York: Columbia University Press.

Petersen, R. (2003). *Explaining ethnic violence.* Cambridge: Cambridge University Press.

Powell, S., Rosner, R., Butollo, W., Tedeschi, R. G., & Calhoun, L. G. (2003). Posttraumatic growth after war: A study with former refugees and displaced people in Sarajevo. *Journal of Clinical Psychology, 59,* 71–83.

Punamäki, R. L. (1989). Factors affecting the mental health of Palestinian children exposed to political violence. *International Journal of Mental Health, 18,* 63–79.

Punamäki, R. (1996). Can ideological commitment protect children's psychosocial well-being in situations of political violence? *Child Development, 67,* 55–69.

Punamäki, R. L. (2000). Personal and family resources promoting resiliency among children suffering from military violence. In L. van Willigen (Ed.), *Health hazards of organized violence in children* (vol. 2, pp. 29–41). Utrecht: Pharos.

Rogoff, B. (2003). *The cultural nature of human development.* New York: Oxford University Press.

Rosenberg, M. (1965). *Society and the adolescent self-image.* Princeton, NJ: Princeton University Press.

Roy, S. (1995). *The Gaza Strip: The political economy of de-development.* Washington, DC: Institute for Palestine Studies.

Sack, W. H., Clarke, G., Him, C., Dickason, D., Goff, B., Lanham, K., & Kinzie, J. D. (1999). A six-year follow-up study of Cambodian adolescent refugees traumatized as children. *Journal of the American Academy of Child & Adolescent Psychiatry, 32,* 431–437.

Scheff, T. J. (1994). *Bloody revenge: Emotions, nationalism, and war.* Boulder, CO: Westview Press.

Scheff, T. J. (1997, September). *Alienation, nationalism, and inter-ethnic conflict.* Retrieved from University of California, Santa Barbara, Sociology department Web site, http://www.soc.ucsb.edu/faculty/scheff/5.html.

Shagle, S. C., & Barber, B. K. (1993). Effects of family, marital, and parent-child conflict on adolescent suicidal ideation. *Journal of Marriage and the Family, 55*(4), 964–974.

Sharoni, S. (1995). *Gender and the Israeli-Palestinian conflict.* Syracuse, NY: Syracuse University Press.

Sherrod, L. R., Flanagan, C. A., & Kassimir, R. (Eds.). (2005). *Youth activism: An international encyclopedia.* Westport, CT: Greenwood Press.

Stagner, R (1977). Egocentrism, ethnocentrism, and altrocentrism: Factors in individual and intergroup violence. *International Journal of Intercultural Relations, 1,* 9–29.

Stewart, S. M., Bond, M. H., Abdullah, A. M., & Ma, S.S.L. (2000). Gender, parenting, and adolescent functioning in Bangladesh. *Merrill-Palmer Quarterly, 46,* 540–564.

Straker, G., Mendelsohn, M., Moosa, F., & Tudin, P. (1996). Violent political contexts and the emotional concerns of township youth. *Child Development, 67,* 46–54.

Tessler, M. (1994). *A history of the Israeli-Palestinian conflict.* Bloomington: Indiana University Press.

Thomas, D. L., & Carver, C. (1990). Religion and adolescent social competence. In D. L. Thomas (Ed.), *Developing social competency in adolescence* (pp. 195–219). Newbury Park, CA: Sage.

Tilly, C. (1978). *From mobilization to revolution.* Reading, MA: Addison-Wesley.

Turiel, E. (2006). Social hierarchy, social conflicts, and moral development. In C. Daiute, Z. F. Beykont, C. Higson-Smith, & L. Nucci (Eds.), *International perspectives on youth conflict and development* (pp. 86–99). New York: Oxford University Press.

Usher, G. (1991). Children of Palestine. *Race and Class, 32,* 1–18.

Victoroff, J. (2005). The mind of the terrorist: A review and critique of psychological approaches. *Journal of Conflict Resolution, 49,* 3–42.

Villarruel, F. A., Perkins, D. F., Borden, L. M., & Keith, J. G. (2003). *Community youth development: Programs, policies, and practices.* Thousand Oaks, CA: Sage.

Whalen, J., & Flacks, R. (1989). *Beyond the barricades: The sixties generation grows up.* Philadelphia, PA: Temple University Press.

Yates, M., & Youniss, J. (Eds.). (1999). *Roots of civic identity: International perspectives on community service and activism in youth.* New York: Cambridge University Press.

Chapter 10

Mozambican Child Soldier Life Outcome Study

Neil Boothby,
Jennifer Crawford, and
Agostinho Mamade

It is estimated that every day some 5,000 children are newly displaced due to conflict somewhere in the world (United Nations High Command for Refugees [UNHCR], 1999). Many may be able to flee the violence with their families, but an increasing number become separated from their families and are recruited into armed groups as a result of erupting wars. Whether victims or perpetrators of violence, during a conflict children see the protective fabric around them collapse as homes are destroyed, families are uprooted, schools and health services are ransacked, and communities become consumed by violence.

Over the past decade, the number of child soldiers has increased. Children are becoming more involved in conflicts due to the prevalence of easy-to-carry and operate small arms and lightweight weapons and the continuance of conflicts in forgotten corners of the post–cold war world (Machel, 2001). An estimated 250,000 boys and girls under the age of 18 currently participate in ongoing conflicts in Asia, Africa, Europe, the Americas, and the former Soviet Union (Child Soldiers, 2004). Fortunately, the problem of child soldiering has not gone unnoticed. Increased human rights attention has led to new international legislation to protect children against armed recruitment.[1] Additionally, the protection and welfare of child soldiers is now being included in the international community's peace and security agenda through several United Nations Security Council resolutions (United Nations Security Council, 1999, 2000, 2001, 2002). These resolutions have led to a range of operational initiatives, including the deployment of child protection professionals in UN peacekeeping missions and the earmarking of significant funds from government donors for child soldier prevention and rehabilitation programs. In light of these recent developments, it is important to learn more about how children are affected by soldiering experiences and what kinds of assistance enable their psychological recovery and social-economic reintegration over time.

238

This chapter offers initial findings on the first longitudinal study of life outcomes of former child soldiers.[2] Between 1988 and 2004, information was prospectively collected on thirty-nine male former child soldiers in Mozambique. Our research began at the Lhanguene Rehabilitation Center in Maputo, continued after the subjects were reintegrated into families and communities, and culminated most recently in 2004 with a study to discover how these former child soldiers now fare as adults.[3]

Journalistic accounts in 1988 and 1990 labeled Mozambique's children as a "lost generation" and "future barbarians." Our research suggests that this is not the case. To the contrary, the vast majority of the group of former child soldiers we followed for the past sixteen years has become productive, capable, and caring adults. Most have regained a foothold in the economic life of rural Mozambique, are perceived by their spouses to be "good husbands," are taking active steps to ensure their own children's welfare, and are engaged in the collective affairs of their communities. Only a few continued their violent ways, or are so traumatized that they have been unable to take hold of their lives.

At the same time, none of these former child soldiers are truly free from their pasts. All continue to struggle with psychological distress linked to their experiences. When troubling memories from the past reappear, these former child soldiers rely solely on themselves, their families, and friends for comfort and support. Many have managed to reduce the frequency of post-traumatic distress by identifying situations that have promoted painful thoughts and feelings in the past and avoiding them. They try not to dwell on troubling memories when they do emerge; rather, they consciously think about more positive aspects of their lives, reengage in day-to-day work activities, or seek solace in religious institutions, prayers, rituals, and texts. Wives, for the most part, are aware of their husbands' struggles. They tend to encourage their husbands not to become overwhelmed by invasive thoughts and feelings and to compensate in other ways when they become despondent. Extended family members and neighbors also are aware of these tendencies and typically respond with patience, advice, or support.

Our research also identified specific interventions that were important in enabling these former child soldiers' substantial recovery and reintegration. Activities that were identified as important were those that supported and strengthened individuals' coping skills for anticipated trauma and grief as well as those that supported normative life cycle milestones (explained shortly). Additionally, activities that instilled a sense of social responsibility and promoted safe codes of conduct, self-regulation, and security-seeking behavior were helpful. Over and above all this, however, was the need of the former child soldiers to be accepted by their families and communities after the war. Thus, apprenticeships, as well as community sensitization campaigns, community works projects, and outward support of traditional community rites, were some of the most important activities related to the successful recovery of many of the former child soldiers.

War Overview

Mozambique's armed conflict lasted for almost 30 years. In 1964, FRELIMO (Mozambique Liberation Front) launched an armed insurgency for national liberation from the Portuguese colonists. Portugal bitterly resisted liberation efforts but acquiesced after a 10-year war. In 1975, the minority regimes in South Africa and Rhodesia looked on in alarm when Mozambique declared itself an independent nation. Rhodesia particularly viewed this as a threat because it shared its eastern border with Mozambique and feared its own indigenous population would similarly fight for independence (Vines, 1991). The Rhodesian secret police organized, trained, and armed anti-FRELIMO groups and disgruntled ex-FRELIMO soldiers into an organization called the Mozambique National Resistance (RENAMO) (Hanlon, 1984). In 1977, after Mozambique gave sanctuary and support to guerrillas fighting the Rhodesian regime, RENAMO infiltrated Mozambique and began its own brutal guerrilla operations.

In 1980, RENAMO lost its sponsorship in Rhodesia after the minority regime fell and the country became Zimbabwe. South Africa intervened and offered its territory as a sanctuary and training ground. With South African support, RENAMO returned to Mozambique and continued to wage a guerrilla campaign to undermine both the country's infrastructure and the government's ability to govern by destroying factories, schools, health clinics, and stores (Morgan, 1990).

Intervention/Organized Assistance

In 1988, Save the Children began its Children and War Program in Mozambique. The program's initial focus was on thirty-nine boy soldiers (between 6 and 16 years of age), all of whom had been abducted from their families by RENAMO. They were trained to fight and in many instances encouraged to kill other humans. Eventually, these boys escaped or were liberated from rebel strongholds. After brief stays in prisoner of war camps, the government decided to place them in the Maputo Center, and Save the Children was asked to provide psychological and social assistance.

Rehabilitation efforts at the Lhanguene Center focused on four interrelated components that were integrated into all center activities: establishment of safety and appropriate codes of conduct, reestablishment of self-regulatory/impulse control processes, promotion of security versus survival-seeking behavior, and support of meaning making. Additionally, a family tracing and reunification program, community sensitization campaigns, traditional ceremonies, and apprenticeships were set up to assist the reintegration of these boys into their communities.

Methods

Any research done in a war-torn setting is fraught with practical and ethical constraints (Jensen, 1996). Such is the case here. The boy soldiers who were the subjects of this study were not randomly selected; rather, they were pulled from detention centers in southern Mozambique by the government to draw international attention to RENAMO's abuse of children.[4] Between 1989 and 1990, three members of our research team undertook a parallel study of 504 separated children (reported shortly). The results from this study reveal that the Lhanguene child soldiers' experiences were similar to those of other abducted children in RENAMO base camps. Girls were also abducted and forced to take on different roles with RENAMO, but unfortunately, they were not selected by the government to be in the Lhanguene Center.[5]

When the Lhanguene Center opened in 1988, culturally sensitive assessments were conducted to guide the rehabilitation and reintegration efforts. War-related experiences (events, severity, and duration) were recorded using a life events profile. Children's ecologies were assessed using a Documentation, Tracing, and Reunification (DTR) protocol.[6] A Child Behavior Inventory Form (CBI) was also established to assess aggression, traumatic symptoms, and high-risk to prosocial behavior. Follow-up assessments were conducted in 1988, 1989, and 1990 in the boys' communities. A number of these visits were videotaped.

For the 2003–2004 phase of research, former Lhanguene staff led research teams and conducted interviews because it was not possible to gain access into rural communities without the presence of these trusted individuals. Between the initial phase of the study in 1988 and the most recent phase in 2003–2004, the Harvard Trauma Questionnaire (HTQ) had become a standard in the literature on international trauma assessment. We found that many items from one section of the HTQ matched a number of the items on the original CBI (and were also mentioned by key informants in free listing exercises) (Boothby, Sultan, & Upton, 1991).[7] Thus, we adapted this section, called the Trauma Symptoms Checklist (TSCL), for use in the 2003–2004 phase of the study.[8]

We piloted the TSCL with key informants from the more accessible communities where the Lhanguene boys had been reunited. As a result of the pretests, several modifications were made, as many nuances in the English-language variables proved redundant when translated into local languages. We also used free listing to identify relevant social functioning tasks important to local people (Bolton & Tang, 2002). The aim was to ensure that our definition and measures of adult social functioning matched local perceptions of Mozambican adult social functioning.

None of the former child soldiers declined to be interviewed, nor did any terminate the interview once it started. If conversations digressed from the questionnaire forms, notes were taken on the back of the questionnaire. Additionally, if any outstanding physical or situational circumstance presented, a note was made.

To triangulate the data, focus groups with families, community members, and community leaders were also conducted. Our overall aim was to gain as accurate a picture as possible of how the former child soldiers have adapted over time, paying particular attention to their psychosocial well-being as well as their roles as husbands, fathers, economic providers, and neighbors.

Results

Children in War

Mozambique's conflict had a devastating impact on children. Surveys during this time revealed that a third of Mozambique's children died before they reached the age of 5 years through starvation, malnutrition, and preventable illnesses that paralleled the continuing conflict (UNICEF, 1987).

What happened to Mozambican children who did survive beyond the age of 5? In 1989, in an effort to answer this question, members of our initial research team interviewed 504 children in forty-nine districts comprising seven of Mozambique's ten provinces (covering a broad geographical range from Maputo in the south to Nampula in the north).[9] Mozambican nationals asked a randomly selected sample of 227 boys and 227 girls between the ages of 6 and 15 years to describe their war-related experiences in detail. The results were staggering:

- 77% had witnessed murder, often in large numbers.
- 88% had witnessed physical abuse and/or torture.
- 51% had been physically abused or tortured.
- 63% had witnessed rape and/or sexual abuse.
- 64% had been abducted from their families.
- 75% of the abducted children were forced to serve as porters or human cargo carriers.
- 28% of the abducted children (all boys) were trained for combat.

In addition to these statistics, children's descriptive accounts provided considerable insight into how RENAMO socialized children into violence. Adults relied on physical abuse and humiliation as the main tools of indoctrination. In the first phase of indoctrination, RENAMO members attempted to harden the children emotionally by punishing anyone who offered help or displayed feelings for others, thus conditioning them to not question the group's authority. Children were encouraged to become abusers themselves. A progressive series of tasks—taking a gun apart and putting it back together, shooting rifles next to their ears to get used to the sound, killing cows—culminated in requests to kill unarmed humans. Children were expected to assist adult soldiers without question or emotion. Those who resisted were often killed. Those that did well became junior chiefs or garnered other rewards, such as extra food or more comfortable housing. On reaching the final stages of training, normally after their first murder, RENAMO marked the occasion with ceremonies that resembled traditional rites of passage. The process of mimicking traditional ceremonies appeared to be aimed at usurping children's ties to their families, communities, and traditional ideas of right and wrong. As one 15-year-old boy put it: "I was changed in that base camp. Even if I could have escaped, I never would have gone home again. Not after what I had seen and done."

The Lhanguene Boys

The Lhanguene boys' child combatant experiences were similar to those reported by other abducted boys. The length of time spent in base camps ranged from 2 months to 3 years, and their functional roles varied from spies, to cooks, cleaners, porters, combatants, and leaders of combatants. Their survival depended on RENAMO leaders who were unpredictable, suspicious, and quick to react to the slightest provocation. According to the boys, drugs and alcohol were a regular staple of life, adding to the unpredictability of life in base camps.

One of the most striking initial observations at the Lhanguene Center was the range of behaviors the boys exhibited when they first arrived. Some appeared listless and numb, unable or unwilling to talk or engage in organized activities. Others were talkative, anxious, and active. A number of younger boys interacted with adult caretakers, whereas many older ones avoided contact or communication with others altogether.

Some did not interact with peers; others engaged openly with one another. A few older boys bullied younger ones, and some engaged in fights and high-risk behavior.

Mozambican volunteer caretakers recorded their observations of the boys' behavior while they were at the Lhanguene Center. The following synthesizes one volunteer's observations during the first 3 months at the center:

> We [the caretakers] were frightened of the boys, too. None of us wanted to work with them at first. We thought they were going to hurt us. But day by day, each side began to get to know the other better. After about a month, the situation improved. I think the boys realized that we were different than RENAMO. I guess we realized they weren't going to hurt us either. After a while, we just started treating them like our own children. We joked with them, watched their football games, encouraged them to do their homework, made the younger ones sit in our lap. It was difficult because some of them insulted us at first, and argued when they did not get what they wanted.

Save the Children program staff used the CBI protocol to record observations of the boys' behavior at the center at 1- and 3-month intervals. These observations roughly parallel the descriptive account just provided (see Table 10.1).

Considerable normalization of individuals' behavior took place during the initial 3 months of intervention at the Lhanguene Center. Some program staff reported that overall aggressive behaviors subsided and prosocial behaviors increased as the boys became increasingly comfortable and attached to their adult caretakers.

The length of time spent with RENAMO impacted these boys' adjustments at the center. In general, boys who spent 6 months or less as a child soldier (72%) appeared to emerge with their basic trust in human beings and social values more or less intact. Although all of these boys had been exposed to severe trauma, and some had also participated in abuse and violence, they described themselves as victims rather than members of RENAMO.

A different picture emerged for boys who spent 1 year or longer as child soldiers (28%). This group continued to exhibit disobedient and uncooperative behaviors during the first 3 months at the center. Despite their ability to articulate the belief that violence was wrong, these boys continued to use aggression as a principal means of exerting control and social influence. Their self-image also appeared to be bound up

Table 10.1

Behavior Sometimes/Frequently	First Month	Third Month
Aggressive with other children	56%	17%
Aggressive with adults	34%	9%
Withdrawn	44%	29%
Disobedient	66%	27%
Lying	32%	15%
Sexually provocative	7%	2%
Playfully engages in structured activities	7%	41%
Obeys rules	46%	90%
Cooperates with other children	27%	76%
Cooperates with adults	29%	83%

with the persona of their captors. They rarely described themselves as victims; rather, they tended to identify themselves as members of RENAMO:

- "I could have escaped but didn't because I had a good position."
- "I was a leader and others respected me."
- "I first served as his [a base camp leader's] personal servant. Then he made me chief of a group of other boys. I had power."
- "They used to follow my orders. Now [at the Lhanguene Center] they don't."

Traumatic Symptoms over Time

All of the boys experienced recurrent thoughts of past traumatic events while at the Lhanguene Center; all still do so 16 years later. Although other symptoms persist, the number of former child soldiers experiencing them as adults is considerably lower than those who experienced them as children. Six common elements in the 1988 and 2003 assessments are found in Table 10.2.

To date, we have identified two variables that are linked to decreases in post-traumatic stress symptoms over time: the individual's use of cognitive strategies and avoidance to manage their symptoms, and duration of time as a child soldier. As already shown, five symptoms decreased in frequency over time and one (avoidance activities) increased over the course of the past 16 years. Avoidance, as described by the former child soldiers, included actively identifying social situations, physical locations, or activities that had triggered an emergence of post-traumatic stress symptoms in the past and making efforts to avoid them in the future. This rise in avoidance activities, when further probed in interviews, proved to be adaptive, as these former child soldiers were actively managing their symptoms more consciously and effectively. Moreover, those who reported using avoidance as a coping mechanism scored lower on the TSCL (i.e., had fewer symptoms) than those that did not employ these same strategies.

One of the strongest traumatic reexperience triggers was physical location, with some former child soldiers avoiding places where they witnessed or participated in

Table 10.2

Question	Percentage of FCSs that Responded either "Sometimes" or "Frequently"	
	Lhanguene CBI (1988)	TSCL (2003)
Recurrent thoughts or memories of the most hurtful or traumatic events	100%	100%
Feeling as though the traumatic event(s) is happening again	63%	45%
Recurrent nightmares	52%	36%
Sudden emotional or physical reaction when reminded of the most hurtful or traumatic moments	48%	36%
Inability to remember parts of the most hurtful or traumatic events	61%	45%
Avoid activities that remind you of the most hurtful or traumatic events	35%	63%

violent and inhumane events. For one boy, it was a large tree in his village where
RENAMO thugs killed his father and abducted him. For another subject, it was a
village footpath where, as a 12-year-old boy, he came across a row of decapitated
heads impaled on poles. Four former child soldiers cited social drinking with other
male companions as a traumatic reexperience trigger. Boisterous drinking rekindled
memories of rowdy, drug and alcohol–induced RENAMO base camp experiences.
All four of these former child soldiers now actively avoid social drinking. Two young
men reported that they no longer slaughter animals because this routine chore "reminds me of the war." Their wives assumed this function. Several found they could no
longer use machetes or other farming tools because they had been used as instruments
of torture and death during RENAMO's reign of terror.

Moreover, the severity of post-traumatic stress symptoms is reduced by conscious
efforts not to dwell on troubling thoughts and feelings when they emerge. Former
child soldiers with lower TSCL scores described a kind of cognitive "change of menu"
strategy to ward off painful thoughts and memories:

- "Thinking about what I did in the war is wasting time because it [the war] helped
  nothing."
- "When I start to think about the war, I go to church and read the Bible. I keep
  reading until the bad thoughts disappear."
- "I try to think about the present and the future, not the past."
- "When bad thoughts enter my mind, I replace them as quickly as possible with
  better ones."
- I think about my children or my wife."

Conversely, former child soldiers with higher TSCL scores do not actively use
avoidance or employ other identifiable cognitive coping strategies. Instead, when confronted with painful memories, they tend to become consumed by them, often with-
drawing from daily activities and routines. The following comments are indicative of
these less adaptive tendencies:

Wife: "Sometimes he is fine and sometimes he is not. I can tell when things are bad for
him because he stops working and spends time alone. Sometimes he tells me about what's
bothering him, but most of the time he does not. I try to do my best to help him forget,
like doing more work and selling things [normally the husband's responsibility] so when
he returns from his bad thoughts things will be in order. Eventually, he goes to work,
forgets, and gets better."

(Mother): "He will suddenly get irritated and then very quiet. He'll go into the house
and refuse to leave. We all know that his mind is back in the past. I tell everyone that we
must be patient with him, but sometimes this is difficult. We all know he has suffered.
We talk to him about the war, how it is over, and how he must also get over it. We try to
do this with a good attitude and patience. Sometimes he threatens us when we talk to him
this way, but so far nothing bad has happened. We will continue [to] live as we have and
accept him as part of the family. He can change, it is just a matter of perseverance."

As noted above, former child soldiers who spent 6 months or less as a child soldier
exhibited less severe symptoms and behavioral problems at the Lhanguene Center than
those who spent a year or longer with the guerilla group. This trend continued into

adulthood. Adults who spent 6 months or less as a child soldier scored lower on the TSCL than those that spent 1 year or longer. Moreover, the three former child soldiers who continue to suffer significantly as young men were with RENAMO for 2 years or longer.[10]

Although all of these former child soldiers continue to experience post-traumatic stress symptoms, only three suffered significantly impaired social functioning. These subjects were not able to curb their violent behavior or live peacefully among others in their communities. All three were deemed to be "troubled children" while at the center and had been a child soldier for 2 years or longer. Two were youth leaders, and one was only 6 years old when abducted.

Returning Home

All of the Lhanguene boys were reunited with relatives (parents, grandparents, aunts, uncles, or older siblings). Assessment reports and videotapes of initial reunifications reveal both overt and reserved joy and excitement as well as tears and words of sorrow over time spent apart. Subsequent family follow-up visits in 1989 and 1990 found that all of the Lhanguene boys continued to be well received by their relatives. Only one required an alternative placement. The following comments from 1988–1989 are indicative of how these boys viewed family acceptance a year after their reunifications:

- "I was well treated; no one ever said anything bad about my participation in the war."
- "I was well received by my family, they made me part of the family and they shared their food with me."
- "They were glad to see me because they knew that I had suffered.
- "They paid lots of attention to me."
- "I was well received, they made a traditional ceremony of welcoming to inform and thank the ancestors for protecting me."

No negative comments regarding family reunification were recorded at that time.

In 1989 and in 1990, all of these former child soldiers reported feeling accepted by their communities, with only two exceptions. One boy reported that the community was not happy with his return and accused him of having killed their relatives. A second boy described how his lack of money led to a poor reception by his community; he had nothing to offer anyone when they asked for help. All other subjects reported that they were received without problems or discrimination:

- "I have been well received by the community."
- "People came to speak with me and welcome me."
- "They received me well because the government brought me and they respected me."
- "The community treated me well, they even sacrificed a hen to commemorate my return and inform the spirits of my arrival."

Our 2003–2004 follow-up employed a feeling of acceptance scale to gauge these former child soldiers' perceptions of community acceptance today.[11] The overwhelming majority reported that as adults they feel respected by their neighbors, that their families care for them very much, and that their friends lookout for them.

- "I can rely on my friends."
- "When I need something, I ask my neighbors and friends, and if they can help me, they will."
- "If I die tomorrow, I think that people would miss me."
- "Members of my community rely on me and I rely on them. It is how we live here."

All of the Lhanguene boys went through traditional ceremonies on returning to home villages. The traditional ceremonies afforded individuals a chance to be cleansed from their acts during the war as well as provided protection for the community from ancestral rebuke that may be brought on because of what the child had done (Chicuecue, 1997).

In our 2003–2004 interviews, most former child soldiers stated that these ceremonies helped them return to civilian life, allowing them to attend to many issues they faced during their initial reintegration. The traditional ceremonies helped repair social ills, cleansing those that came home "contaminated" from the atrocities of war and resolving social conflict in cases where normal social roles had been perverted. Not only were these ceremonies important for these former child soldiers as individuals, they were also reported to be vital for rebuilding community trust and cohesion.

Traditional ceremonies also reportedly endow those returning from war with the ability to forget their experiences and begin a normal life again:

- "Yes, it was helpful because today I am leading a normal life."
- "There is a definite difference between before and after the ceremony."
- "The war memories never came back after the ritual."
- "Before there was something missing in my body and in my life, but after, I am okay. I came back to normal life and now I feel like the others."
- "It was helpful because it removed the evil that I was bringing with me. I was able to forget easily all the evils that I had, even though I still dream about it."

Although former child soldiers used the word *forgetting* to describe the benefits of traditional ceremonies, subsequent discussions revealed that they were referring to the shame associated with their war-related experiences rather than the actual experiences per se. *Forgetting*, in this case, was in reference to varying degrees of absolution of painful stigma associated with their participation in the war. Many reported that this internal transformation helped them become "just like everyone else."

Family members and neighbors also reported that the traditional ceremonies—which are simply local beliefs put into practice—were important because they gave the community a form of defense or protection against problems that returning child soldiers could bring with them. During the war, children were forced to violate social hierarchies, sometimes killing elders and commanding their peers into battle. The righting of these wrongs and the reestablishment of social hierarchies with deceased ancestors was a priority. Social stigma based on one's participation in the war appeared to be minimal, but family and community members still were concerned that the Lhanguene boys might be disruptive due to their previous indoctrination into violence. To be sure, as the locus for issues between the returning individual and his or her society, communities fulfill an important role in the reintegration of former child soldiers and, coupled with traditional ceremonies, help facilitate the realignment of individual, family, and communal relationships.

Community sensitization campaigns also had a positive impact on community acceptance of former child soldiers. Sensitization campaigns were designed to enable community members to understand that former child soldiers were victims, too, even though they may have perpetrated violence against that very community. Local military, police, teachers, and community leaders were encouraged to support the reintegration of former child soldiers by taking collective responsibility for the fate of the returnees. Community projects, such as reparation of hospitals, water systems, and other needs identified by community members, were initiated in these areas as a way of supporting collective child welfare efforts. During the course of our 2003–2004 focus group discussions, community members reported that they remembered government officials coming and talking to them about the children returning and that it made an impact on them.

- "I remember the government people coming to tell us that our sons were going to come home and that we should treat them like everyone else. That is what we have done."
- "We listened to the advice of the people that came from Maputo. We have accepted these boys and they live with us now. There is no difference."
- "The big men came and told us what to expect from our boys. Now we eat what they eat, we live together. We are all the same."
- "They are our sons; what they did they were forced to do, so we cannot blame them for such bad things."

Making Up for Lost Time

A major facet of successful reintegration was the ability to return to a normal life and resume daily activities. Going to the fields and working to help one's family allowed respondents "to leave behind the traumatic experiences." They emphasized the need for everyone to "be the same." Most reported that their greatest wish in returning home was to "be like everyone else." Other research suggests that the main element of suffering the young men taken in by RENAMO experienced was being removed from their homes and suspending the pursuit of their life plans (Schafer, 2001). This theme was repeatedly identified in our 2003–2004 interviews.

Additionally, boys reported that one of the most devastating legacies of child soldiering was the years of lost economic opportunity that, in turn, made the key life cycle tasks of choosing a wife and building a family difficult. Many of these former child soldiers reported these challenges to be more problematic than the actual war experiences themselves.

- "I had no problems choosing a wife, but I have had problems because of a lack of money."
- "I had no resources; I had to begin everything from the beginning."
- "Those who did not go to the war had the time to earn some money, but I had nothing after the war."

- "I had to go to the swamp and cut reeds [one of the lowest forms of work in rural Mozambique] to build my house."
- "It is difficult because we had to search in many different places for a place to live. It took much longer to build my house and family."
- "If I had not gone to war I could have made money, and I would be living nicely now, but I am not."
- "I think the war was evil. It delayed my life. I lost 10 years."
- "I would have gone to work in the mines in South Africa. This would have helped me, but I didn't have an opportunity."

To what extent has this group of former child soldiers overcome these obstacles and regained a foothold in the normative life cycle of rural Mozambique? Several indicators were employed to explore this question, such as household income, securing adequate housing and food, and their own children's health and educational status.

Despite disruptions to their life trajectories, this group of former child soldiers is faring as well as (and often better than) national averages for these socioeconomic and child welfare indicators. The national average for household ownership is 91.7%, which matches the average of the former child soldiers (91%). Although 100% of these former child soldiers are engaged in farming, 63% of them also earn additional income from wage labor endeavors. The national average for off-farm activities of rural inhabitants in Mozambique is estimated at 38% (Amimo, Larson, Bittencourt, & Graham, 2003). Unfortunately, Mozambique is in the midst of a serious food crisis in its rural areas. General estimates suggest a third of the population is classified as chronically food insecure, mostly coming from the south and central regions, where this study took place (World Food Programme, 2001). All of these former child soldiers and their families are affected by this crisis. Eighty percent reported that they are not always able to eat or provide balanced meals to their children. Nine out of 10 also said that the adults in their households reduced portion sizes or skipped meals almost every month during the past year. Despite this food shortage, the weight of their children (under 5 years of age) in relation to their height is above the national average. All scored above the median using the World Health Organization/National Center for Health Statistics (NCHS) normalized referenced weight for height scale (WHO, 1994).[12]

We asked our Mozambican interviewers to provide general observations about the parenting styles of these former child soldiers. In light of socioeconomic and cultural differences in parenting styles and the risk of misinterpretation, this was a simple exercise in which the interviewers provided either a "supportive" or a "nonsupportive" rating in those situations where parent-child interactions could be observed as they were naturally taking place. These generalized observations, although falling far short of addressing the complexities of parent-child relationships, indicated that former child soldiers were generally far more supportive and engaging in interactions with their children than they were harsh and punitive. Moreover, all of the former child soldiers who were parents (62%) spoke, often at length, about their desires for their children to experience a better childhood than they had had. Most, in turn, indicated that the schooling they had been denied due to their child soldiering experiences was the "best way" to ensure a "good future" for their children. Indeed, 75% of this group's school-aged daughters and sons were attending primary school, which is considerably higher than the national average of 52% (UNICEF, 1987).

Eighty percent of these former child soldiers were married in 2003. The overwhelming majority of their spouses perceive them to be "good husbands." Wives concurred with the economic hardships in these areas of Mozambique, noting that jobs are scarce for everyone. They also indicated that they appreciated their husbands' efforts to earn extra income.

- "I am happy with my husband. Even though he was in the war, he is just like everyone else."
- "My husband helps me with the children. When I ask for money, he gives it to me if he has any. He doesn't spend it on drinking like some other husbands."
- "He often looks for work. Usually, he does not find any, but when he does it helps us a lot."
- "I can't complain. I am fortunate."
- "He is a good man. He is kind to me and takes good care of our daughters."

Individual welfare in Mozambique is linked to informal sector enterprise and collective help networks. The extended family normally provides a form of social security to its members that follow long-standing patterns of personal and kinship relationships. Community support is also expected for significant life events such as childbirth, initiation ceremonies and weddings, personal crises such as sickness and death, and external crises such as draught, flood, crop failure, and war. Social harmony and responsibility are key attributes in rural communities, where the outcome of many activities is a function of teamwork.

In 2003–2004 interviews, the majority of the former child soldiers were able to cite specific incidences when they provided money, food, or other forms of assistance to needy family members or neighbors. They also actively participate in community activities that center on the church, the school, or the community infrastructure and, in doing so, tend to be leaders of group activities rather than solely members. Additionally, the percentage of former child soldiers that voted in the national presidential election was higher than national averages in rural communities. When questioned about leadership roles, many former child soldiers said that since the war they have made a concerted effort to fit in to their communities by doing "everything I can to help my family and community" to prove themselves worthy.

- "If people ask for something, I try to give it them. It is important to help someone who is in need."
- "I try to be good, and lend things to people when they need them. I take part in community work because in this way everyone benefits."
- "I want to feel like normal people, so I work hard to help others."
- "I visit friends, share things with them, and do the same things others do."
- "The church tells me God wants me to help others and I believe this is true. When I do help someone, I feel good about myself. I am paying back others for the bad things I did with RENAMO."
- "I try to not refuse anything to anyone. Helping people helps me feel like I belong here. That I am important."

All of these former child soldiers spoke positively about their Lhanguene experiences, and twelve of them cited these experiences as factors that contributed to their involvement with people in need and in broader community affairs. Spending time with responsive adults (role models) at the center and learning specific life skills also were identified as factors that contributed to their current sense of social responsibility. Two former Lhanguene staff members accompanied interview teams into these former child soldiers' villages. Both were received with hugs, tears and exclamations of disbelief: "We can't believe that you remembered us after so long!" "It is very important that you are here because it shows that you have not forgotten about us." Where proximity allowed, Lhanguene boys were still actively involved in each other's lives.

Discussion

In the same way an oyster transforms a raw irritant into a valued pearl over time, so have most of these former child soldiers emerged from violent childhoods to become trusted and productive adult members of their communities and nation. Their life stories suggest that human resiliency is too dynamic and complex to be conceptualized as merely the ability to ward off or bounce back from traumatic adversities. These young men's resiliency involves active quests to derive existential meaning from violent events; to be cleansed from their pasts and forgiven for their wrongdoings; to regain their true identity by being like everyone else; to find their place in community by helping others; and to manage intrusive thoughts and reveries in ways that enable them to continue their day-to-day lives. Family and community acceptance and spiritual and religious beliefs and practices—so entwined with individual well-being in rural Mozambique—are the wellsprings of this resiliency.

The next phase of our research in Mozambique is to compare the Lhanguene boys to the adult outcomes of a similar group of child soldiers who were not provided organized assistance. Until then, we are not in a position to comment on the efficacy of specific organized interventions. Nonetheless, we do believe it useful to offer some preliminary findings based on these young men's observations, as well of those offered by their wives and neighbors.

Neither the Lhanguene Center interventions nor the work of traditional healers and spiritualists put an end to traumatic symptoms. Indeed, is a "cure" even possible in the aftermath of severe and chronic child soldiering? We are not in a position to answer that question, but our findings do suggest that supporting and strengthening coping skills for anticipated trauma and grief responses are key intervention objectives. Moreover, in the absence of formal mental health or psychosocial support programs (the norm in most of today's war-affected countries), avoiding situations and activities that remind former child soldiers of troubling experiences may be among the most adaptive coping skills they should be encouraged to employ.

A number of interventions aided these former soldiers' transitions into society. Most of these young men described the time they spent with adult caretakers and other former child soldiers at the Lhanguene Center as positive. Program efforts to promote safe codes of conduct, self-regulation, and security-seeking behavior appear to have engendered a sense of social responsibility among these former child soldiers that is evident today.[13]

Traditional cleansing ceremonies played key reconciliation roles. They helped repair relationships with their families and communities and to realign the boys' well-being with the spirit world. The rituals enabled these boys to feel "like everyone else" and deepened their sense of acceptance. This, in turn, ameliorated degrees of guilt and shame over past misdeeds and represented a form of protection for community members who worried about what these boys might do once they came home. Numerous community members recalled the government-led sensitization campaigns organized 16 years earlier by Save the Children. They, too, helped foster community acceptance and forgiveness.

Other forms of assistance that supported normative life cycle milestones, such as employment, housing, farming, and marriage, were viewed by these former child soldiers as helpful. Apprenticeships, income-generation projects, provisional seeds, and tools were cited as positive forms of support. In contrast, educational stipends (for fees, books, and clothes) were not deemed helpful. Instead, they tended to cause tensions in several families because they singled out one child for support over the others. Also, most of these boys were not motivated to stay in school but felt compelled to earn money, find a wife, and build a house. Understanding the normative life cycle—including key developmental milestones and how the social systems that support them have been affected (and may be assisted to become realigned)—proved to be a pragmatic framework for assessing, designing, and evaluating this child soldier reintegration program.

Notes

1. The UN General Assembly adopted an optional protocol to the Convention on the Rights of the Child establishing 18 as the minimum age for participation of children in conflict. The Rome Statues for the International Criminal Court, the International Labour Organization, and African Charter on the Rights and Welfare of the Child also have addressed child soldiering.
2. Preliminary results on the intervention findings of this study were reported in Boothby (2006). This chapter represents a fuller, more detailed account focused more on the study outcomes themselves.
3. For the purposes of this study, we refer to a child soldier as any child under the age of 18 years who was in RENAMO base camps, regardless of their particular role as porters, servants, or combatants.
4. Given the small sample size and the lack of a comparison group, these findings represent a somewhat culturally specific context and may not be generalizable to child soldiers in other contexts. Further comparison would be needed to strengthen the representativeness.
5. Descriptions of girls' experiences who spent time with RENAMO have been included in McKay and Mazurana (2004).
6. The DTR Protocol was used to document over 25,000 separated children nationwide, including former child soldiers (Boothby, 1993).
7. The free listing exercise revealed that the local population described a state of existence very similar to post-traumatic stress disorder that they called *npfuka*. Much of the symptomatology, including nightmares, violent outbursts, and restlessness, are the same; however, the

etiology is quite different. One becomes infected or possessed by npfuka by killing another human being. The perpetrator of the violent act is thought to become possessed by the spirit of the person(s) he or she killed, and the physical manifestations are a result of the spirit's anger at being killed. To be freed from this condition, the perpetrator and his or her family must submit to traditional ceremonies that call on the spirit of the victim for forgiveness. The ceremonies are designed to calm the spirit and send it away, essentially exorcising it from the body of the killer. For the purposes of this chapter, the authors use "post-traumatic stress" to describe this varied set of behaviors exhibited by the Lhanguene boys and described locally as npfuka.

8. Scoring for the TSCL scale followed the recommended procedures. Cronbach's α calculation was used to assess TSCL internal consistency and reliability. Bivariate analysis using independent sample t-tests was used for one-way analysis of variance for continuous variables that were measured. We used logistic regression analysis with the TSCL score as the dependent variable, and the potential confounders of age at abduction and length of time spent with RENAMO were entered in the model as control variables.

9. Children from Manica, Niassa, and Cabo Delgado were not included because Save the Children was not working in these provinces at the time.

10. On the TSCL, the scores ranged from 32 to 77, with a mean score of 47 out of a possible range of 28 to 112 for twenty-eight questions. Chronbach's α coefficient was 0.8849. Statistical significance for all tests, including logistic regression analyses, was set at $p < .05$, and were two-tailed without adjustment for multiple comparisons. Boys that spent less than 6 months with RENAMO scored between 32 and 40 on the TSCL, and those that spent over 6 months scored between 42 and 77 with only five exceptions.

11. On a scale from 13 to 52 (13 being the best score and 52 being the worst score), respondents scored between 16 and 35. The mean score was 23.1597, and the α coefficient for reliability was 0.7185.

12. The 1996 World Food Summit defined food security as "a situation in which all people at all times have physical and economic access to sufficient, safe, and nutritious food to meet their dietary needs and food preferences for an active and healthy life" (Rome Declaration on Food Security, 1996).

13. Although the government of Mozambique established the Lhanguene Center for political reasons, the intervention program's activities could have been implemented in rural communities. Decentralized approaches are generally more cost-effective and are also capable of reaching larger numbers of affected individuals. Undertaking such efforts in the communities themselves is also conducive to maintaining supportive child-adult and peer-to-peer relationships for longer periods of time. The challenge in decentralized programming is the selection of caring adults and maintenance of quality training, supervision, and support.

References

Amimo, O., Larson, D., Bittencourt, M., & Graham, D. (2003). *The potential for financial savings in rural Mozambican households*. Plenary session paper presented at the 25th International Conference of Agricultural Economists, Durban, South Africa.

Bolton, P., & Tang, A. M. (2002). An alternative approach to cross-cultural function assessment. *Social Psychiatry and Psychiatric Epidemiology, 37,* 537–543.

Boothby, N. (1993). Healing the wounds of war. *Duke Magazine*, Duke University, Spring Issue.

Boothby, N. (2006). When child soldiers grow up. In N. Boothby, A. Strong, & M. Wessells (Eds.), *A world turned upside down: Social ecological approaches to children in war zones.* Bloomfield, CT: Kumarian Press.

Boothby, N., Sultan, A., & Upton, P. (1991). *Children of Mozambique: The cost of survival.* Washington, DC: U.S. Committee for Refugees.

Chicuecue, N. M. (1997). Reconciliation: The role of truth commissions and alternative ways of healing. *Development in Practice, 7*(4), 483–486.

Child Soldiers. (2004). *Some facts.* Retrieved April 4, 2004, from Child Soldiers Web site, http://www.child-soldiers.org.

Hanlon, J. (1984). *Mozambique: The revolution under fire.* London: Zed Books.

Jensen, P. S. (1996). Practical approaches to research with children in violent settings. In R. J. Apfel & B. Simon (Eds.), *Minefields in their hearts: The mental health of children in war and communal violence* (pp. 206–217). New Haven, CT: Yale University Press.

Machel, G. (2001). *The impact of war on children.* London: Hurst.

McKay, S., & Mazurana, D. (2004). *Where are the girls? Girls in fighting forces in northern Uganda, Sierra Leone, and Mozambique: Their lives after the war.* Montreal: International Centre for Human Rights and Democratic Development.

Morgan, G. (1990). Violence in Mozambique: Towards an understanding of Renamo. *Journal of Modern African Studies, 28*(4), 603–619.

Rome Declaration on Food Security, World Food Summit, Rome, 13–17 November, 1996 (http://www.fao.org/docrep/003/w3613e/w3613e00).

Schafer, J. (2001). Guerrillas and violence in the war in Mozambique: De-socialization or re-socialization? *African Affairs, 100,* 215–237.

UNHCR. (1999). *State of the World's Refugees.* Cambridge: Oxford University Press.

UNICEF. (1987). *Children on the front line: The impact of apartheid, destabilization and welfare on children in southern and South Africa.* New York: UNICEF.

United Nations Security Council. (1999). Security Council resolution 1261. Available at www.child-soldier.org.

United Nations Security Council. (2000). Security Council resolution 1314. Available at www.child-soldier.org.

United Nations Security Council. (2001). Security Council resolution 1379. Available at www.child-soldier.org.

United Nations Security Council. (2002). Security Council resolution 1460. Available at www.child-soldier.org.

Vines, A. (1991). *Renamo: Terrorism in Mozambique.* London: Villiers.

World Food Programme. (2001). Visit of WFP Executive Board to Mozambique, June 2–9, 2001. www.wfp.org/eb/docs/2001/wfp006158N1.pdf

World Health Organization. (1994). *Assessing nutritional status and recovery.* From WHO Web site, http://www.who.int/child-adolescent-health/publications/referral_care.

Chapter 11

Tasting the World
Life after Wartime for Bosnian Teens in Chicago

Stevan Weine,
Alma Klebic,
Adana Celik, and
Mirela Bicic

This chapter focuses on Bosnian adolescents and young adults who survived ethnic cleansing and war, became refugees, and were resettled in Chicago. The work is a collaborative effort between several Bosnian adolescents and young adults and an American psychiatrist and ethnographer to document and analyze the subjects' life experiences related to political violence. The youths' accounts underscore the point that refugee trauma for resettled adolescent refugees encompasses not only prior exposure to political violence but also current experiences with other adverselife changes associated with forced displacement, exile, immigration, and urbanization. Teen refugees' first-person accounts call for a broader conceptualization, whereby refugee trauma is viewed as part of an interacting bundle of historical, social, cultural, economic, political, and familial processes. A *trauma bundle* perspective is described that can assist in understanding the enormous changes that teenage refugees and their families endeavor to manage.

"I really believe that we do not know how to teach these kids. We have to be much more sensitive to what they are going through. What does trauma do to a child? I have kids who have come in to my room telling me stories about one or both of their parents being killed. What does that do to you?" (Alan Berkson, bilingual teacher, Amundsen Senior High School, Chicago). Because the authors are not high school bilingual educators, we cannot offer a professional opinion on what Berkson asked about teaching teen refugees. But we very much respect his observations and reflections on educational practices. He questioned both how educators formulate teen refugees and how they act to help them. His concerns and questions also apply to those of us who provide psychosocial services to teen refugees. Berkson was the former bilingual coordinator at Amundsen, the school with the largest number of Bosnian teens in Chicago. For the past 10 years, Weine's program of research has been conducting fieldwork for an ethnography of Bosnian adolescent refugees in Chicago, which included participant-observation at schools as well as interviews with many Bosnian adolescents and their families throughout the city. We, the researchers spent time with Berkson, as well as several Bosnian bilingual teachers, because the teachers knew these teens very well. We shared many of the same concerns regarding how these youth were adjusting and coping after having experienced genocide and war in Bosnia-Herzegovina.

There are more than 35,000 Bosnian refugees in Chicago, which is the second highest total of any city in the United States (St. Louis surpassed Chicago several years ago). Bosnian refugee families started coming to the city in 1992 after the first liberations of concentration camps in northeastern Bosnia-Herzegovina. Most families were displaced to a third country first, some for several years, before coming to the United States. Many teen refugees spent their childhood in the war, early teen years temporarily residing in Croatia or Germany, and then later teen years resettled in the United States.

Most Bosnians initially settled on the near North Side of Chicago. Unlike other immigrant groups, there has not yet been a mass exodus to the suburbs; rather, at least for the first 15 years, the Bosnian community stayed put in the city. Nearly all of these families begin their lives in the United States in poverty. "Work comes first," parents often say. Most adults become laborers, some become managers, and a few become professionals. Most families have multiple wage earners and pay a high price in terms of diminished family time and low parental involvement with their youth's school life. Most teenagers attend their neighborhood public schools. Some then move on to junior or community colleges in the Chicago metropolitan area.

As part of an ongoing interest in survivors' testimonies, the researchers looked for teenagers and young adults who would volunteer to tell their trauma stories (Weine, 1999). But in comparison with the many parents who have freely told their stories, relatively few teenagers were prepared to do so. Certainly, a great many of them were exposed to extreme violence; suffered terrible losses; witnessed the destruction of their country, communities, and homes; and had to leave against their will. However, most teens did not appear to regard themselves as trauma survivors or victims. The vast majority did not exhibit or speak of the symptoms of post-traumatic stress disorder (PTSD). This is consistent with a previous study that found little PTSD among Bosnians adolescent survivors of ethnic cleansing (Weine et al., 1995). It is also reflected in the existing psychiatric literature on adolescent trauma, which suggests that one is more likely to see acting out behaviors than full PTSD (Cohen et al., 1998). The researchers have seen cases of attentional problems, hyperactivity, oppositional and disruptive be-havior, alcohol and substance abuse, learning problems, and school failure among teen refugees. This is often regarded by them and their teachers as a consequence of the war, but conclusions should not be reached without systematic investigation.

If trauma is not being expressed in symptoms or identity, could it manifest in other ways? When we started to do documentary work with teenage refugees from Bosnia-Herzegovina, we found that instead of telling their war stories, they primarily wanted to focus on their lives now in the Bosnian community in Chicago. What interested them was "Why do some Bosnians want to forget everything?" "Why do some Bosnians turn their back to us?" "Why do others not like us?" Yet as these questions indicate, even when some talked about the difficulties that they were currently facing concerning adjustment to school life and city life, the shadow cast by political violence was still present, even if it was not explicitly named. In their accounts, the war and its sequelae interacted with multiple other factors related to forced displacement, exile, immigration, and urbanization.

This sequence of factors illustrates a central intellectual and practical challenge for helping professionals involved with refugee youth. Helping professionals, especially those in the mental health field who are informed by traumatic stress theory, have learned to focus on trauma as a discrete cognitive phenomenon that comes from exposure to particular types of events. These professionals have also come to prioritize the idea of survivors telling their stories as a way of ridding themselves of traumatic memories. For teen refugees, trauma may be one component of an interacting bundle of broader historical, social, cultural, economic, political, and familial processes that shape their worldview, beliefs, ethics, choices, dispositions, and actions. Because trauma in this sense becomes something that is neither discrete nor given but is continually constructed, negotiated, merged, amplified, transformed, and distributed through interactions, it becomes far more difficult to describe, analyze, measure, or intervene. The overall aim of this chapter is to share several teen refugees' narrative accounts of their everyday experiences and engage in theoretical reflection focused on clarifying this broader conceptualization of refugee trauma. This calls for methods of study that are focused on first-person narratives.

Listening in Difficult Spots

Much of the existing literature on refugee mental health takes the existence of individual psychological trauma as a given. This reflects the approach of the traumatic stress field, which claims that certain types of experiences are traumatic, will lead to "trauma related symptoms and disorders," and will or should be recognized by the person as traumatic (Marsella, Friedman, Gerrity, & Scurfield, 1996). The validity of these assumptions regarding psychological trauma has been questioned by social scientists, humanists, and clinicians (Becker, 1995; Bracken, 2002; Hacking, 1998; Kleinman, Das, & Locke, 1997; Weine, 2006; Young, 1995). This inquiry did not begin with the presumption that these youth were traumatized. In listening to the teens, the researchers did not attempt to frame or lead their narrative in a direction focused on trauma. Rather, we listened to what the teens were talking about when they talk about the changes in their lives (Weine, 1999, 2006). This chapter is concerned with what meanings these teens find, how these meanings change, and how such changes might matter in the lives of individuals, families, communities, and societies. First-person accounts and conversations offer valuable ways to get at meanings, but because people (especially teens) do not always say what is expected, it also requires an open attitude on the part of the researcher. The researchers found it helpful to turn to several engaged scholars from outside of the field of trauma mental health who have listened to persons involved in or after catastrophes.

The situation presented by teenage refugees in urban America is what French sociologist Pierre Bourdieu (1993) called a "difficult spot . . . difficult to describe and think about." Bourdieu found it necessary to depart from dominant professional discourses because they did not adequately address the problem of a person's social and cultural marginalization. He specifically did not want the person's accounts to be framed by objectifying professional language or concepts. With regards to teen refugees, his concerns seem appropriate given the tendency to depict refugees as one-dimensional pathetic caricatures reflected in mental health professionals' psychopathological approach and journalists' pathos-filled approach. What is also helpful is the form of textual inquiry presented by Bourdieu, loosely based on the Bakhtinian concept of the polyphonic novel, which brings together multiple voices and presumes no particular outcome. Bourdieu's majestic *Weight of the World* is precisely that kind of unwieldy, exciting text.

In his book, Bourdieu provides multiple perspectives via multiple interviewers and multiple interviewees who practice what is called "non-violent communication" (pp. 608–609). Interviewers selected subjects through personal contacts, so that those involved are more known to one another, permitting greater exchange and mutual understanding of the purposes of the research and greater symmetry in the exchanges. The aim is to "reduce as much as possible the symbolic violence exerted through that relationship" (p. 609). Bourdieu was concerned with both avoiding representations that would fail as "objectification" of the subject and representations that failed to take into account "the objective conditions common to an entire social category" (p. 609).

This chapter uses a *Weight of the World* approach with some of the Bosnian teenagers and young adults whom we came to know through our work in the Bosnian community in Chicago. There were many individuals that could have been chosen; five were selected for this chapter. This research did not employ sampling methods that allow anyone to claim that these five are representative of either Bosnian refugees or refugees in general. However, although each of these person's story is unique, the themes identified through these narratives and conversations are experienced by many teen refugees resettled in Chicago.

What these young people all had in common is that they were committed to self-expression and trusted the interviewer as a confidant and collaborator. As it turned out, some of them wanted to write their narratives; after reading their texts we decided that their writings could be their contributions. Before they wrote, however, we had several open conversations regarding the life experiences of Bosnian refugees in Chicago. It is important to emphasize that these conversations were not conducted from the vantage point of any particular theory, including psychological trauma. We consciously tried to limit ourselves from framing or interpreting what they were saying in exchanges with them. All conversations and writings were conducted in English, and transcriptions were prepared for inclusion in this text. We made minor edits to the text to make them more readable and concise. No substantive changes were made.

Responding to these texts, the researchers drew on several concepts of trauma that go beyond the clinical approach. A central concept in Bourdieu's book is that of "positional suffering." *Positional suffering* refers to those whose suffering is compounded because they "occupy an inferior position in a prestigious and privileged universe" and because "they participate just enough to feel their relatively low standing" (p. 4). Bourdieu found this to be a useful construct for linking the individual's subjective experience with objectively definable external conditions. Similarly, Das, Kleinman, Lock, Ramphele, and Reynolds (2001) proposed the notions of "social trauma" and the "remaking of everyday life" to guide comparative ethnographic investigations of communities that suffered political violence of various forms. They described how after experiencing the extremities of atrocity and loss, survivors try to reassert the normal in their lives, and this necessarily involves their efforts at narration. Das and colleagues contrasted the attempts of individual survivors and communities to remake everyday life with professionals' often heavy-handed efforts to claim those experiences as a part of the clinical enterprise. Their expressed faith in survivors' ways of working things out in their lives is close in spirit to Bourdieu's approach. To Das and colleagues, survivors converse, share, and exchange in ways that facilitate healing, and their text documents, (rather than engineers) those processes. The ethnographic studies that Bourdieu and Das et al. present specifically look at the movement toward healing, both individually and collectively, for experiences of social suffering resulting from political violence. As far as we know, these notions have not been applied to the situation of teen refugees.

The researchers were interested in seeing how teen refugees from Bosnia-Herzegovina talk about their experiences and use their statements as a basis for considering a broader formulation about refugee trauma in teens that fits both their sensibilities and the conditions of their lives. This approach to inquiry also draws from the qualitative research methodology of Harry F. Wolcott, especially his article on "Adequate Schools and Inadequate Education: The Life History of a Sneaky Kid" (in Wolcott, 1994). His approach emphasizes using narratives from case material to let the person tell his or her story in his or her own words. Wolcott believed that the advantage of this approach was that it offered new perspectives on professional practices and beliefs by helping place them into broader contexts and seeing them from several different perspectives.

Mirela: This New Life

Mirela is a 16-year-old girl from Sarajevo whom we met when she was a sophomore at Amundsen High School. She had been in Chicago for a little over 1 year. Mr. Berkson introduced her, and she was invited to be a part of a Bosnian teen documentary project under way. After several conversations, she chose to write a text (for which she also got credit for her ESL class) that explained her thoughts and feelings about life in Chicago after wartime.

> Life here in Chicago for me is very difficult. This major change in my life happened because I came from a small country, Bosnia, where everything was different—traditional way of life, music, food, education, leisure time, working conditions, and many more. A Bosnian teenager living in a big city like Chicago usually has a hard life. Still, life is much easier for me if I don't have much time to reflect about the horrible things in Bosnia, such as war, devastating famine, and especially death.
>
> One of the biggest problems for immigrants living in big cities in the United States is language. When I started school, all my Bosnian "so-called friends" didn't help me with the language. Instead of giving me help, they didn't even pay any attention to me. It seems that most teenage boys today can only think about cars.
>
> I don't feel the kind of respect I think that I truly deserve in a "free" country. I should be given that respect in this country. I also believe that Bosnia is a free country and has always been.
>
> My mission is to finish school here in the United States and to become someone who can help people all around the world, especially my people, the Bosnians. In my opinion,

only the Bosnians who fought in the war can appreciate the extreme sadness that comes with the death of relatives and loved ones and also the conditions brought about by extreme famine and poverty.

I hope that this above-mentioned dream will someday come true because I'm not used to living in a big city with so many different kinds of ethnic groups. It is hard for me to trust anyone in this country. Coming here, not knowing anyone, was like experiencing a brand-new life from the very beginning. Trying to figure out whom I could be friends with was much more difficult because of so many American teenagers [are] taking drugs and alcohol and having unprotected sex. To come here and to have my whole life change so drastically was a shock to me.

I'm not quite sure yet if my life has changed for the better or for the worse. For me in my life, time goes very quickly and I'm becoming more mature and grown-up each day because in this country I have so many different kinds of responsibilities and many matters to worry about.

Adults, such as parents, relatives, teachers, and more mature people that have had diverse experiences, can help us teenagers. There needs to be good, strong communication between Bosnian teenagers and older people of this generation from Bosnia. To survive and to be endowed with the gifts of love, concern, tolerance, and understanding are important steps for us. That is why we need people who are close to us and who really care about us.

Mirela expresses worries and doubts that are commonly felt by teen refugees in the United States as they struggle to remake their lives amid the conditions of refuge in urban America. She says that what has been most difficult is the experience of emigrating from a more traditional society to a more modern society. She carries with her memories and feelings associated with political violence in Bosnia-Herzegovina; like most teen refugees, she would prefer to avoid them. She finds that everyday life in the United States does not always provide a suitable distraction because it presents difficulties that often resonate with the memories of violence. For example, she speaks of the betrayal of "friends" who turned away or exploited her family when their help was needed to learn English. This was a reminder of the betrayal by neighbors in Bosnia-Herzegovina. Even though she tries not to recall those memories, they come back.

Instead of seeing herself as a war survivor, Mirela sees herself as a girl from a small town trying to adjust to life in the big city. She approaches this adjustment by making a comparison between Bosnia-Herzegovina and the United States regarding the issue of freedom. As documented in other ethnographic studies (Weine, Ware, & Lezic, 2004), what Bosnian teen refugees say remarkably often and intently is that life as a whole in America is not as free as they imagined it would be: "There is not a lot of freedom here"; "In America, we have lots of opportunities but we are not as free as we are supposed to be. In Europe, we had few opportunities but we were actually more free than we thought we were." In their expressions regarding freedom are traces of several important historicopolitical concerns, although these are rarely made explicit. One is the sense of having been forced to leave Bosnia-Herzegovina. Another is a kind of critique of American urban life and its highly regulated approach to social spacing (Bauman, 1993). The teen refugees' stories and behaviors suggest that the desire for freedom penetrates deeply into their tastes, habits, and beliefs.

Mirela has a dream that comes from the experience of living through political violence. She believes she has an obligation to help others, and she sees education as a necessary step to getting there. The emphasis that she places on education is common among Bosnian families. So is the shock, confusion, and frustration she experiences when she sees how different (and often inferior) some American public schools are in comparison with the schools she knew in Bosnia-Herzegovina. Our clinical and research work has found that there is often little help out there for teen refugees and their families to adjust to a new education system and modify their attitudes about schools and education in a way that might bring more parental involvement and greater academic achievement for the teens.

Mirela sees herself as a citizen of the world, but like many other teen refugees, she often finds that it's not easy living in neighborhoods with people from other ethnic and racial groups. In particular, Bosnians struggle because they find that their idea of multiculturalism does not map well onto the realities of American life. The American ideals of multiculturalism that the schools and other institutions prefer are not helpful to them in guiding their social and cultural integration (Baumann, 1999). Mirela wants and needs help with this cultural adjustment. To help her with these and other problems, she appeals to the adults in her life, namely, her parents and teachers. We hear many teen refugees asking these questions, and it makes us wonder who is listening and who is helping the teens.

Paltalk: Re-Creating Everyday Life

Mirela introduced the researchers to her friend Nadina in an ESL class at Amundsen High School in July 2002. Nadina is a 19-year-old senior from Bugojno. We decided to have some conversations that were audio-recorded. After we explained our interests in teen refugees, what they wanted to talk about was Paltalk, an Internet site of chat rooms where they connect with other Bosnian kids from all over the United States and Europe. That made sense, because we knew how much the issue of computers came up in field observations. Nearly all kids have Internet access and use it regularly. Walking into the computer lab at the high school, one is likely to find Bosnian kids in Bosnian chat rooms or on other Bosnian Web sites (i.e., Nostalgia). We did not know how this related with our concerns about teen refugees, but it seemed like it might. To give an adequate sense of what was learned that day, this conversation is excerpted at some length.

STEVAN: What is a chat room and what do you do on it?

NADINA: I'm always in the chat room. It's very nice for me. To speak with Bosnian people. To talk with them. There I find many Bosnian people. We have different rooms there with different headlines.

MIRELA: We have Bosnian people coming from lots of different places in Bosnia.

S: Are the chat rooms organized from where you are from?

N: No, it's all mixed.

M: I am always walking.

N: I escape.

M: Me, too.

N: Sometimes I'm in Bosansko Sjelo. Sometimes I'm in other room.

M: Wherever there is cool music, I stay there.

M: I have three rooms that are mine. The music is cool. There are many people. It is friendly. I like people that are Bosnian. I like the Bosnian language.

M: We have many rooms. In different rooms are different people. In one of my rooms there are forty people.

S: It's a room you started?

M: Yes, I have three rooms.

S: What are the names?

M: Ludara.

S: Can you tell me what that means?

M: Ludara is like crazy room. . . . That's special music. And it's like a cool room. Something like that.

N: I don't have my room. I am always with her.

S: Those are the rooms that you go to the most? When you don't like one you escape to another?

M: Yeah. I like Urnubes soba a lot. There's a lot of people there. Anytime. P.M., A.M.

N: In that room there are always the same people. We know each other. We gather.

S: Where are the people from?

N: Different spaces in Bosnia. Sarajevo, Tuzla, Bugojno.

S: Did you ever meet them in person?

N: No, maybe only those in Chicago.

M: Mostly its people in America. Because in Bosnia there are not too many computers.

s: What other parts of America?

n: Different.

s: How does it work? Tell me about last night.

n: Last night, for me, was not cool. I don't know what happened to me. I was sad.

m: I was there. But there were none of my friends. I didn't meet somebody who I know. I don't know what was happening.

n: She has a new screen name. That's like 9/11. It's a crazy screen name.

m: I like that. I am a crazy person. Its Hitna Pomoc.

s: So do people know you?

m: Nobody.

s: So now you're like a new person.

m: I change my screen name and nobody knows who I am.

n: Me, too.

s: What did you become?

n: I have ten screen names. Last night is SARAJKAmm.

s: Do you remember what you were talking about together?

m: Yes, about her, she's crazy.

n: I'm not.

m: Just fun conversation.

n: Fun, always I have fun. Nothing . . .

s: I saw there were lots of making sounds with hitting the key.

m: Like TOOOOO and OPAAAAAA. That's like when we have a good song and everybody likes that song and everyone is happy for that song, so we dance like for dance. TOOOOO is like for dancing.

s: It was all Bosnian music?

M: Last night was cool music. I'm serious. Such cool music.

N: My song was one singer, Sinan Sakic. That song was for her, but she left.

S: How do you do the song? You have it on your computer?

M: No, like I have a Winmax and I assign singer and that song, my choice go with my music, and I put microphone and that song is there.

S: Can anybody choose the music?

N: Everyone.

S: Do people take turns?

M: Everybody listens and after mine finishes, other people choose.

S: So, you played that song last night, this Bosnian singer. Did people like that?

M: It's a new and good song.

S: From Sarajevo?

M: No from Serbia. Serbian music is such good music. I'm serious. So much better than Bosnian music. Everyone likes that. Serbia has such good singers.

S: Does that bother any people from Bosnia to listen to Serbian music?

M: No, we don't have problem with that.

M: Oh, I had a problem. Five nights ago, in my room some Serbian people came and they bothered us Bosnian people. Like his screen name is Serbian 5, Serbian 3, and Serbian 4, and I'm so angry.

N: That's not fair. She kicked them [out]. They're Serbian.

S: It's not fair?

M: Yes to bother Bosnian people. I don't know why.

S: Did they ever do that before?

M: First time.

S: What did they say?

M: Very bad words. And I kicked them out.

s: What bad words?

m: I don't know. Many bad words. Too much.

s: How do you kick them out?

m: I don't know how you explain. I have an op that is like crazy a.

n: She oversees the room, so nobody can bother somebody else.

s: You just made them go. You decided by yourself.

m: Yes. People were angry. My friends say, hey what are you doing Mirela?

s: They are angry because they stayed there before you kicked them out?

m: Yeah.

s: How long did they stay?

n: 5 minutes.

m: What the hell you doing, Muslim people? That's not fair. Who are you? Something like that.

s: I can see why that would bother you. That's like your space. Your place and then they come in.

m: Yeah.

n: 24 hours they don't come again. If she kicks them out they can't come for 24 hours.

s: Did they come back again?

m: No.

s: So last night how many hours were you on for?

m: Not too much. Four. It's a little time.

s: How about you?

n: I was on 3 P.M. to 5 P.M. and I make some break, then came again 7 to 10.

m: After school to 8 o'clock, then break till 9, then 9 till 1.

s: You have a computer in your room?

m: Yeah.

s: So nobody else cares? It's no problem?

m: Sometimes my mom says, "What are you doing? Do you need a clock? Go to bed Tomorrow is school. Look at your eyes." "Oh, mom!" Yesterday she says, "Look at your eyes, you are like grandmother." "Oh, mom!"

s: Sounds like you really have a good time when you do that.

n: Oh, yeah.

s: Why don't each of you say something about like if you were explaining to somebody who doesn't know anything about Paltalk, why it's such an important [site].

m: For me it's good because I live in America and my wish is not to forget the Bosnian language. My wish is to have many Bosnian friends.

n: Yes, we need that.

s: So you get those things on Paltalk?

m: Uh huh.

n: I don't know it's the same things. I like my Bosnian people. I can't forget them. I know them just through Paltalk, but I feel that in my heart. It's Bosnian, so I like them. I don't want to forget them, never. Never.

s: So it really helps you to stay connected to Bosnia? Bosnian things? People? Language?

m: Yes.

s: Can you imagine what it would be if you didn't have that?

m: Nothing, I don't have idea.

s: Do you know kids who don't use Paltalk?

m: I know, yeah, my cousin, he's first. Lives in my building. "I hate Paltalk." "Okay, I hate you! I'm just kidding."

s: Some people don't like it?

m: People who came from Bosnia 5 years ago, 6 years, or 7 years. They don't like that. I don't know. Don't like Bosnian people. They act like such big people. Like I'm here 10 months and I am there on floor. And they are there.

s: They have an attitude?

м: They left Bosnia as a child. One year. Seven years. They can't remember too much about Bosnia. Maybe that's the problem.

s: They were little kids. Okay.

n: Now they are 18 years old, but they can't remember everyone. They didn't have a life in Bosnia. Nothing.

м: Okay, Nadina, I understand you, but what about people who are here 2 years and don't like Bosnian people. What about them?

n: I don't know what is happening with those people. I meet people coming here before 10 years. They don't like Bosnians. They grow up here in America.

м: They are more Americanized. And so they don't feel the same need that you feel to stay connected.

n: In this school I know people who hate Bosnia, who don't speak [the] Bosnian language, only English. I hate that.

м: And I hate people who say, "I don't go back in Bosnia never." I hate that.

s: People who say, "I don't ever want to go back to Bosnia"?

м: I don't like that.

s: A lot say that?

м: Uh huh.

s: I'm just trying to think about how your days work. Aside from Paltak, you see kids in school, but you don't have much contact with other Bosnians outside of school except on the computer. You don't go to other people's houses or have people over, or don't go to club or café or park?

м: No, it's just on computer.

s: Why is that?

n: Some of my friends are busy, some are working, some are having some problems, with parents, with kids. Some need to stay home with brothers and sisters. And at night, together in Internet conversation that's time for it.

Mirela's and Nadina's words suggest that Paltalk is being used by some teen refugees as a creative solution for what Das and colleagues (2001) call the "remaking of everyday life" after political violence. These teenage girls want to be normal, have a normal life, and a normally crazy good time. Naturally, they want to do so by using the Bosnian language and by listening to Bosnian music with Bosnian friends. What Paltalk offers is a virtual community at a point in their lives where there is little other sense of community. They find themselves in Chicago, the city that offered them refuge, without many friends, stuck in their apartments, and separated from their long-time friends and family members. American society is unable to offer a community in any way like what they had in Bosnia-Herzegovina. But their new home compensates by providing the technological tools to establish a virtual community. Through the creativity and resourcefulness of these girls and their Bosnian friends around the globe, a new communal space comes alive. Although this space on Paltalk is geared to remedy some of the consequences of political violence, it is certainly not being experienced by them as a political activity. Even so, it retains connections with the political that are potentially important.

What they want is freedom of self-expression, identity, and also movement ("I escape"). Lots of teens in Western countries want freedom from constrictions of parents and teachers and anything that obstructs or entangles their movements. But teen refugees' desire for these freedoms are shadowed by the fact that their families came (against their will) from Bosnia-Herzegovina, where these freedoms were denied because of extreme ethnic nationalism. This desire is also impacted by their refugee resettlement experiences in the United States, the "land of the free," where these freedoms were promised but from their perspective were not quite realized. In other words, apart from their daily experiences of life in Chicago, they carry within them a sense of freedom as a social imaginary, which is being expressed in these girls' use of Paltalk. For teen refugee boys, it shows in other ways, such as their love of cars. Instead of seeing these activities as only social problems, we regard them as resources that might possibly be put to good use—akin to what Bourdieu (1998) calls "cultural capital." It also begs the question: what kind of leadership, guidance, or support from adults could help teen refugees nurture and develop the social imaginary of freedom into attitudes and behaviors that would enhance their social and cultural adjustment in cities of refuge?

It is important to note that there are several troubling aspects to the search for community on the Internet. It says something about the lack of opportunities for community in public life for teen refugees in locations of urban refuge in the United States. Is there more that state or community institutions could be doing to create social spaces where a sense of community could grow? Is there more that parents could be doing?

Another troubling aspect is that the girls' desires for community run up against obstacles and antagonisms. They recognize that not all Bosnians are alike. There is, for example, a rather large tension between those who came to the United States in their childhood and have already become Americanized and those who came in adolescence and are still more like "real Bosnians." These girls cannot readily understand or accept how Bosnian refugees become Americanized so fast. To them, it seems like a betrayal of tradition, ethnicity, religion, and their native country. Can these girls learn something from their chat room contacts that will help them make the right choices about their identity and relationship with others in their community? Again, who else will help them? Can they do it alone?

There is also the problem of a shared Bosnian communal space being invaded by others who pose as their enemy. These girls are fairly open to Serbians and Serbian culture, far more so than many in their parents' generation. This presents opportunities for contact across ethnonational communities that may be something to build future reconciliation efforts on. When these girls are assaulted in virtual space, they are served with a reminder that for teen refugees, the reestablishment of community, no matter how local, remains connected with the political. This is also a reminder that teen refugees are still highly vulnerable to the ethnonationalist politics of their parents' generation, which in this case were by no means resolved by the 1995 Dayton Accords.

Alma: Living with Memories

Alma was the first Bosnian teen refugee in Chicago to graduate from an American college. She received a bachelor's degree in international relations in May 1998, and worked for over 5 years with our CAFES (Coffee and Family Education and Support) project. She conducted survey and qualitative interviews with Bosnian families and youth and facilitated multiple-family groups. When she wrote this text, it happened to be the 10-year anniversary of her father's killing, an event that she does not like to talk about. She was subdued and said, "That day in May is always the most awful day of the year." Weine offered to speak with her about it, but she declined. She was asked if she wanted to write about it, but again she declined. This is what she wrote instead.

> There are certain questions that you wanted me to answer. One of them is what does the younger generation want to tell the older generation about what they need and want?
>
> When the war started we were too young to understand what was going on and why, but not too young to feel pain, to be scared and hopeless. Maybe we were not too young to understand but we did not have anyone to teach us more about our neighbors, about history, about who we are.
>
> My Serbian classmates, kids that I grew up with, were carrying weapons. In one day they became complete strangers. In some ways I became a stranger to myself, too. My life and the lives of my family members were in danger because of our names and religion. I never knew those things mattered, which means that I did not know many things about myself, too. That is what made me a stranger to myself.
>
> What I want from the older generation is to teach us and the next generations about history, religion, and identity. To speak up and not to be afraid. What is there to lose since you already lost everything?
>
> One of my friends told me not too long ago, "I blame our parents and their generation for being so silent, for not educating us about something as good as religion. Even now after all of this some people still don't know about religion, and that's one of the reasons why our youth is getting in trouble not only in the U.S. but throughout the world. What helped many people in difficult, hard situations during the war and in life in general is believing in God."
>
> What we need from the older generation is to work with us on saving memories, good or bad, to help us build strong characters as individuals and as a community. We owe it to the ones that didn't make it and to our second chance at life.
>
> It is known that communities get stronger when they share the same struggles and when they have common goals and that can happen only when they know history and know who they are.

Serbs and Croats knew about history, not only from books—even the ones that were not educated knew a lot because they talked about it at homes, they were singing about great "heroes," they worked hard and are still doing the same at teaching new generations and refreshing memory of older generations.

What we need the older generation to understand is that is that we were silent observers; we witnessed genocide, ethnic cleansing, and human behavior at its worst. We were witnesses and now we are one of reminders to the whole world that genocide happened again.

We are not silent observers anymore, we have tools now to help us speak up, express ourselves. We speak several languages and we know different cultures. Those are also things that can be used to build strong community in diaspora and help rebuild Bosnia.

How do young people manage to imagine the future among such hardships, memories, and struggles? Americans have one good saying and it goes like this: "What does not kill you only makes you stronger." I see my generation as a strong generation. We learned a lot about people, life, and survival through this war and after the war, in the process of adjusting to different environments.

We missed many things in the past. That is why we are looking forward to the future. Our families and friends mean a lot to us. We learned the hard way to appreciate and cherish every moment with them.

Our memories are part of who we are. We have to save them and preserve them so we or the next generation don't forget.

Alma wrote about memory and its impact on present life, a theme she is sensitive to in her own family and has observed in a great many Bosnian teens and families. She is troubled by the gap between young persons' recollections of political violence and the lack of articulation about those experiences in the daily life of the family. Although these adolescents certainly experience memories and emotions associated with political violence, Alma feels that these teens are not finding a sufficient place in their lives to talk about such memories and emotions and consider their meaning. She recalls that unlike her Serbian classmates, Bosnian youth were never taught by their families to organize their memories in terms of a Bosnian Muslim identity. She does not want to respond with an extreme ethnic nationalism for Bosnian Muslims, but she does recognize that rebuilding some kind of legitimate political identity is necessary.

What Alma's comments suggest is that there is something welling up from within this younger generation of teen refugees concerning memories and politics. What bothers her is that she and other young people cannot help this something take form on their own. She cannot find leaders, organizations, or adults who are prepared to help the younger generation work with their memories and feelings. She feels that the adults of her parents' generation are not stepping up to this challenge either. This is no surprise given that they were for the most part complicit in the quieting down of Bosnian identity in the second Yugoslavia (Weine, 1999). The kind of leadership Alma desires could possibly be found in Muslim faith, but she recognizes that religious communities also have difficulty engaging youth and families in the conditions of exile.

Alma expresses both optimism and pessimism. Because her generation carries the memories, she believes that they recognize their special obligation. Without help in determining what exactly that obligation is, she is worried that little will come of such responsibility. It is possible that nothing will come of this for some time, or one might predict something like a belated politicization or a return to tradition in the years to come.

The family is an important place where teens can expect some sort of dialogue about these matters. Alma has been living with her single mother. Those kinds of arrangements are never easy and often do not provide young people with the kind of dialogue that they seek. Alma and the author see similar patterns in many Bosnian families.

Alma recently married a young man from Bosnia-Herzegovina, and they are starting a family of their own. She thinks about what she will tell her son about what happened in Bosnia-Herzegovina and whom she wants him to grow up to be.

Maid: Return to Religion

Maid is a serious and hard-working 20-year-old man living with his family in Chicago. He came from Mostar by way of Germany, where his family went after hostilities erupted in 1992. When Weine first met him, he was a freshman at Wright Community College in Chicago and was planning to go to pharmacy school. Maid is living that call to tradition that was heard in Alma's text. He is deeply committed to Bosnia-Herzegovina and to Islam. He tries to reconcile living both the American and Bosnian ways of life. We had a long conversation that turned to the topic of religion.

M: I go every Friday to pray. To the Dzuma. Northbrook is too far. [Note: This is the location of the Islamic Community Center. Northbrook is a suburb of Chicago, which is difficult for most Bosnians in the city to reach.] There's one here in the basement. We have a mosque in the basement. Many people come here. There's a *hodza*.

S: What is that like for you?

M: It helps in your life to make a decision. What's good and what's bad. It keeps your mind clean. Don't do bad stuff. Keeps you very clean.

S: Were you involved in religion before coming here?

M: In Germany I had many Turkish friends. I was always with them. They were my best friends. We went always to mosque. I learned very much from them. They are also very religious people.

S: Are you friends with other young people interested in Islam here?

M: I didn't make contact with others here. Fifteen to twenty people come to pray on Fridays. We just pray together. I don't really know them. They are mostly old people. There are only a few young people.

S: What about other young people from Bosnia?

M: They go to the mosque only sometimes. They drink. They do lots of bad stuff. They are behaving like some gang members. They just believe in Islam when they have a bad time. If something happens, then they just pray to God. But in good times they forget.

s: Why do you think that is?

m: Maybe because of how they were raised. Maybe because of parents they have problems in their family. Maybe because of the war. They were in the war. They saw that war was for nothing. And they had enough from religion and stuff like that.

s: Are you concerned about how other Bosnian youth are responding?

m: Its not my business if they are going to the mosque or not. They don't think about school. Most of them they don't think about religions, about family, about their future, what they are going to do, how they are going to finish. They are just thinking about now, how to have an expensive car, how to get a job with money, but it doesn't make any sense now, if you have an expensive car, it doesn't make any sense.

s: What helped you to be different?

m: I think the life in Germany. And my family. Talking to me. About what's good and what's bad. How to do. What to do. How to behave. And my friends in Germany. My Turkish friends. I stayed with them. We never drank. I got a good attitude from them.

s: What is your opinion about how to relate to the experience of the war and politics?

m: The best thing is you don't think about that. Because it doesn't make any sense. The war didn't make any sense. The best thing for you and your future is not to think about it. It was very bad. You can never forget stuff like that. What happened there was very bad. You won't be able to ever forget it. But you have to try not to think about that. Not to talk about that. That's the best way.

s: Does that really work?

m: Yeah, it works, not to talk about it, like with some different people, with some other religion people you know, you will always get into fights. It wasn't making any sense. There's no end to talk about it.

s: How about in your family? Do you talk about it there?

m: Yes, sometimes we talk about it. But most of the time we don't talk about it. It just brings bad times.

s: Then what would you say is the way to respond?

M: Believe in your religion. War is not a good solution. There's no solution for that. Many people died. You got enemies over there. Never try to get friends with them. That's a bad thing. Because they always get you behind your back. Stuff like that.

S: What do you imagine you will teach your children?

M: I am going to teach them how the war was, what was it like, who was fighting. Teach them about the religion, to believe in God, stuff like that. To be very careful with your friends who are the enemy.

Maid is one of a number of Bosnian youth who have returned to religion—returned in the sense that these families always considered themselves Muslim, but since the war they have strengthened Islam's role in their lives. This takes various forms, including regularly attending the mosque, daily prayers, reading the Koran, not drinking, and believing in God. For Maid, deepening his connection with Islam happens to coincide (not contradict) with learning how to make his way in American society. Through his connection to God he finds purpose and strength that he cannot find elsewhere. Through partaking in the Muslim life, he stays away from the troubles that other Bosnians in America have fallen prey to, for example, through exposure to ghetto culture. Maid's Islamic faith is less about community or politics and more about prayer to God and about culture. His experience with religion is not one that provides him with mentorship or teaching, although it is conceivable that someday it may.

Maid suggests that the turn to religion is complicated for Bosnian youth and their families. There are many for whom the experience of the war moved them further away from religion. Many of these families were not strong believers before, and some were even less so after the war. Maid does not see it as his role to convert them. It is up to them, not him, to choose their path. Still, he recognizes what many youth do not. They are caught in the middle of a profound cultural struggle, and how they resolve it will be a big determinant of their paths in life.

Religion competes with contemporary American youth and mass culture for the attention of refugee youth. There are many youth who have not made the connection with other Islamic youth, like Maid did in Germany, but have made the connection with American youth who are not Muslim. Maid also suggests the important role families can play in shaping the teen refugee. The efforts of parents like his to assist teens in developing a sense of moral clarity and purpose are very helpful. But many families are not like this.

Adana: Learning How to Live

Adana is a 19-year-old senior at Lincoln Park High School. She is one of very few Bosnian students who managed to reach this school, which is one of the top Chicago public schools. She spent the war in Foca and Sarajevo and came to Chicago in the last year. Weine invited her to join him and a group of other Bosnians for a panel at Cranbrook Academy in Birmingham, Michigan. There she presented a strong yet sensitive voice that was tremendously impressive to the listeners. We spoke a couple of times before that event and talked about the situation of Bosnian youth in the diaspora and in Bosnia-Herzegovina. She offered to write a text in preparation for the event, and the following is what she wrote.

My voice is one of a child because that is the only one I can comprehend. It might seem odd but whenever I look back at the war period I feel simultaneous pain and joy. Yes, the grenades were flying all over outside the building in which we lived. But inside of it a union existed, made of the people from all over Bosnia, all ages and even religions. We all had two things in common: we were Bosnians and we needed to survive. And somehow we got through the evilness of war, with many losses that we all shared. As I am writing this some instances just pop up and I cannot [help] but go back.

In those times we had to survive without electricity, running water, or gas. We accepted not having those things as a quite common thing, and thought the couple hours when we would get connected to the power sources as privileges. And I remember the people that we might as well call heroes. Men were at the front lines while mothers struggled to keep everybody else alive with the hope of a better tomorrow. They are true heroes I will forever be indebted to.

After the war it seemed like everybody was trying to bring back things the way they were, but it was impossible. Why? Because nobody was able to erase from people's minds the memories of all the deaths and horrors. Surely, nobody would take the responsibility, and once again people were hampered by the few that had the control.

As far as most children my age, we just wanted everything to stop so we could get a taste of life. Now we learned about our identity, what it meant to be Bosnian, the fact never mentioned during Yugoslavia. As teenagers we dealt with many things ordinary teenagers never encounter. Politics and hatred between the nations of Bosnia permeated every aspect of our lives.

As far as the world goes, we were a new nation emerging, asking for our place and position in it. Most of the people my age felt the need to repair the mistakes of our predecessors. We do not want our children to be ignorant of their identity, culture, and tradition. All of us gave promises to ourselves that the war will not repeat and that we would try to destroy its roots. The only way this is possible is through learning, about us and others, ours and their country, and ours and everybody else's history.

Moving to America is another step in my learning of the world and gaining the new perspective. I cannot say that the idea of migrating ever made me happy. There are only two ways in which to look upon my coming here. First, I can say how fortunate I am. To assure myself I look back at my friends that stayed in Bosnia. What kind of future is there for them? The whole country is very divided, not only literally. Opinions are inconsistent, and the government does not seem to be agreeing on any proposition. A mere child can see that it is not a way to move forward. What is it that my friends have there, then?

The time has come for me to see how much I am capable of and finally I do have some control over my future. Everybody used to tell me how schools in America are very easy, a joke practically, and how children get to just paint coloring books through elementary school. When I started school here I saw completely another picture, the true one. Things seem to depend on how well you are doing in school because then people try to challenge you more. The fact that I can actually end up educated excites me in many ways. In my family education is very significant and I will always strive to make my family proud, since there is no other way to get a better recognition. That and I never again want to see my parents working for minimum wage and having to leave their whole life behind in order to provide my sister and me with a normal life.

And that is the other way in which to look upon my migrating here. We left everything behind, our roots, country, and the place in which we felt that we belonged. Whenever I think about it this, wrenching pain comes about. I neglect to tell that to people. They might blame me for feeling that way and they might think me dissatisfied with America, for which I have no right. I got the things here that I never dreamed of getting, and there is still more to get.

But what am I guilty of? I cannot find a better way for explaining this except asking them to try to envision themselves in my position. What if any of them had to leave America in the same way? Can they imagine the feeling? I bet they can attempt to. I refuse to be treated reprehensibly or looked at condescendingly. This feeling of torment is inescapable, not just for me but for everybody who has been through good and bad times with their mother country but had to desert it in the worst. I know a girl that lived her whole life in Chicago but then she went for several months to study abroad, in Rome, while she was in college. "Sometimes," she would say, "I would get up in the morning and make myself sandwiches, the way I used to do that while I was home. I missed it inconceivably." We use the word *nostalgia* to describe that feeling. But sometimes I feel I could pile up all the words in my vocabulary in order to try and explain my emotions. And nobody will understand it until they go through the same.

Sometimes I do feel like the speaker in one of the Margaret Atwood's poems, as if "I am the word in foreign language." I seem to be lacking conviction that I will ever belong here, although I feel accepted. We did an analysis of this poem in my English class recently, and it felt as if I was looking at this poem like in a mirror. Sadly, I felt very competent to conclude our analysis of this poem, so I did it.

What happened in Bosnia is just another display of us, people making the planet a bad place for living, although it is not such. What I had seen I would not wish for my worst enemy to see. Forever I retained the instinct to fight the unjust and wrong, giving my dismal contribution in making our lives be the way they should—worth living.

Adana views the experience of political violence from within a voice that is extraordinarily self-reflective. She sees what she experienced in the war and how she is now experiencing the war years. She sees what the experience was like for herself, as a child and a young woman, and what it was for the various other "we's" to which she belongs. She did not ask for any of these horrible things to happen; having lived through them, she feels obligated to learn from those experiences and use what she learns to help others. Hers is a voice that ethically transforms experiences of suffering and marginalization into opportunities for building knowledge, vision, and leadership.

One example is that she let herself learn something new about American schools. What she learned is that if you ask for more challenges, you will get them. This may be a typical attitude at her high-status high school, but it is far from typical among Bosnian teen refugees. Far too often, it seems as if Bosnian teens set their sights on doing the least that is expected of them and schools are not prepared to challenge them. What is also remarkable is that Adana has a long-term view of her education. It shows in the school she attends and in her ambitions for the future.

Adana learned that to be Bosnian means something because of the way Bosnians shared sacrifices and suffered together. She sees ethnocultural issues with a subtlety unusual for her years. It is important to know who you are, and it is also important to know who the others are. What kind of multicultural knowing is this? It is both knowing the self and knowing the other on the field of ethnonational politics. On the field of immigration, she feels the pain of exile. But she turns even that into a kind of moral knowing. She knows loss, separation, and nostalgia. She sees her experience in relation to the experience of others who are not Bosnian.

She learned that there is the obligation to work for a better tomorrow. She certainly feels that obligation toward Bosnians and more so as a part of a larger human family. She even feels bad for what the Bosnian people contributed to the history of human violence, and it serves to fuel her drive to make a difference in the world.

Teen Refugees in Resettlement and the Trauma Bundle: An Interpretation

This inquiry did not fully answer Mr. Berkson's questions regarding the impact of the traumas of political violence on teen refugees and the measures needed to assist them. It may have provided some sense of how and where to look for such answers. This is the kind of contribution one may reasonably expect from a narrative inquiry. Wolcott said of such narratives, "The effective story should be 'specific and circumstantial,' but its relevance in a broader context should be apparent. The story should make a point that transcends its modest origins. The case must be particular, but the implications broad" (1994, p. 98).

These narratives illustrate that teen refugees experienced not only genocide and war but multiple other difficult life experiences. They were displaced from Bosnia-Herzegovina and are immigrants beginning a life of exile in the new Bosnian diaspora. They left their villages, towns, or small cities for a major U.S. city to face a new set of challenges in an urban environment. Of course, they must meet these external challenges while transitioning to adulthood. Traumatic stress theory tends to prioritize the traumas of exposure to violence (in this case, war and genocide) and place less emphasis on other life experiences in the resettlement context. Even when trauma resulting from political violence is a predominant concern, these teen refugees' accounts reveal that other life experiences are also happening simultaneously or subsequently, and there is likely to be a large amount of interaction between them. Therefore, to address Berkson's questions requires rethinking refugee trauma in ways that acknowledge this complex interplay.

These teens' first-person accounts support a view of refugee trauma from political violence not as a narrowly conceived psychiatric disorder but in broader terms that may be called a *trauma bundle*. Sociologist Edward Tiryakian (1997) proposed the idea of a cultural bundle comprised of "race, ethnicity, religion, and nationalism" to understand why persons go for changes in individual and collective identities as part of nationalist movements. The trauma bundle proposed here recognizes that the traumas of teen refugees are not restricted to acts of political violence and may occur on multiple levels. Thus, traumas come directly from prior exposure to acts of political violence but also come from current experiences of life changes related to forced displacement, exile, immigration, and urbanization. Moreover, these traumas occur not only to the individual but also at broader levels, impacting historical, social, cultural, economic, political, and familial processes. Thus, to answer Berkson's questions from the perspective of a trauma bundle involves rethinking trauma as part of multilevel, multidimensional, and multiphasic processes, as described by Yael Danieli (1998). This is the type of framework that should be used to inform further research that investigates the consequences of trauma among teen refugees.

The trauma bundle may be considered alongside other constructs that professionals and scholars have devised to adapt the construct of trauma to describe situations of enormous social, cultural, political, economic, developmental, and psychological complexity. One strategy has been to generalize on trauma, as is represented in the phrase "secondary traumatization" (Stamm, 1999). For example, it is said that an asylum hearing can provoke secondary traumatization for a refugee. Another strategy is to add socially oriented qualifiers to the term *trauma*, such as "social trauma" (Das et al., 2001) or "collective trauma" (Erikson, 1995). Another strategy has been to abandon the word *trauma* altogether and go with another descriptive phrase, such as "social suffering" (Kleinman et al., 1997) or "positional suffering" (Bourdieu, 1993). In our opinion, by locating trauma within the social realm, all of these constructs have something valuable to offer. The reason the trauma bundle retains the word *trauma* is for the purpose of emphasizing the extreme disruptions across multiple dimensions of the lives that are reported by persons experiencing political violence, such as these teen refugees. But it needs the word *bundle* to expand beyond the focus of particular discrete traumatic events and instead emphasize the impact of trauma across a diffuse network of historical, social, cultural, economic, political, and familial processes. It is also important to recognize that the bundle is meant to incorporate not just trauma-induced disruptions but also resilient processes that protect against traumas negative impact at any of these levels.

The idea of a bundle also implies multiple factors may be involved, some more strongly and some less strongly. Although there may be some identifiable linear or even causal relationships, it is highly unlikely that the complexity of nuance of the interplay of multiple factors could be reduced in such a way. It is for this reason that reductionistic dichotomizing propositions must be rejected. This includes both the traumatologists' explanation that most wants to know who is traumatized and who is not? (as if trauma always trumps culture or history). The culturalists' position that most wants to know the cultural differences between, say, Americans and Bosnians (as if cultural differences must always exceed cultural interactions). No doubt, further research is needed to elucidate the complex interactions that are involved in the trauma bundle for a given individual, group, or population.

First-person accounts of living within "difficult spots" are valuable because persons who stand within these experiences can describe aspects of the changes, consequences, and contexts that experts may miss when looking through the lenses of known constructs. Adolescents, given their stage of cognitive development, may be especially open to exploring and communicating the phenomenological multiplicities, fragments, and contradictions that are part of the trauma bundle but are often difficult to represent. Their words may offer clues to strategies or interventions that may prove to be more helpful than existing services. Here we address several important points that these teen refugees made to respond to Berkson's question regarding how one might better help them.

Although these teens have been through difficult times, they have not lost hope for a better life for themselves, their families, their communities, or their countries. Traumas cause adverse changes, but they may also stimulate adaptive responses, especially in families, which can lead to positive outcomes. This underscores the importance of a family strength and resilience approach with teen refugees (Rolland, 1994; Walsh, 1998). Refugee families are able to find ways to adapt to even the most difficult trauma-related circumstances. In a prior ethnographic study of more than 100 Bosnian refugee families, we described the construct of families rebuilding lives, which specified the helpful strategies families have devised to cope with the adverse consequences of war and forced displacement (Weine et al., 2004). This study highlighted the need for professional clinicians or researchers to listen for signs of hope, resilience, and strength within these families that often become muted when emphasis is placed on what has been broken or lost. Detecting family protective factors and mechanisms is one step toward developing interventions that seek to enhance those inherent resources.

However, we cannot overlook the fact that several of the teens mentioned their desire that parents would do more to help them face adversities and challenges. They are aware that parents face enormous difficulties themselves, and this is part of the problem. There are many different ways parents could receive additional support and education that would enable them to be more helpful to their teenagers. In particular, community-based, family-oriented preventive interventions (such as CAFES) that we developed and evaluated show promise for helping teen refugees (Weine et al., 2006; Weine et al., 2008). Family interventions are able to impact family processes, such as family knowledge, attitudes, beliefs, communication, and accessing community resources, that may have a positive impact on teen refugees. If future research were to focus on family preventive interventions for teen refugees, it might yield some helpful answers to Berkson's queries, especially given that the family plays such an important role in facilitating children's development and education.

It is also important to think about how teachers and schools could be more helpful to these teen refugee students. The impression from these narratives and from listening to many other teen refugees is that many do not feel well understood by their teachers, counselors, or school administrators. Although there are exceptions, many teachers are not as committed or curious about teen refugees' experiences as Mr. Berkson is; he as a bilingual teacher who was very aware of the difficulties faced by refugees. But knowledge is not enough, and bilingual teachers also need adequate support, resources, or training to do their work. Sometimes they think of refugees as migrants like any other and do not consider that their status as any different. To make matters worse, many teen refugees' parents lack even the most basic level of involvement with teachers and the school. This is not surprising given that there are so many obstacles to parental involvement for teenage refugees (e.g., parents' work, unfamiliarity with educational system, language barriers). These teens' stories suggest that there is far more that psychosocial services could be doing both to help families understand school processes and to help educators better partner with refugee teens and parents. This calls for building new models of preventive services that link youth, parents, schools, and communities to promote parental involvement in education.

The accounts presented here also reveal the importance of rethinking the role of culture in relation to the trauma bundle in teen refugees. There is a need to go beyond the existing refugee mental health discourse on culture, which is limited in several important respects. First, it has typically been framed as a linear process of acculturation when most of these teens and refugee families are experiencing something closer to a far more multifaceted "transnationalism" (Baumann, 1999; Berry, Kim, Minde, & Mok, 1987). Second, the current discourse is often subsumed under a psychopathological rubric that restricts the focus to the issue of psychopathological symptoms expressed in different cultures (e.g., defining culture-bound syndromes). When we take time to listen to what teen refugees have to say, we realize that these conceptions of culture do not attend to important cultural processes that shape their lives. This includes such issues as religion, transitional families, diaspora communities, and the U.S.-led war on terrorism. In the contemporary globalizing world, marked by mass migration, global communication, and mass violence, there is a need for more complex models of the cultural processes impacting refugee youth. This includes a more sophisticated understanding of the processes that could inform designing, implementing, and evaluating interventions.

In conclusion, we are afraid that what Mr. Berkson says of teachers is also true for many (if not most) helping professionals working with teen refugees. In many respects we, too, do not know enough about how to help them. Although there are many teen refugees doing outstandingly well, it is too easy for many to get off-track, and it can be hard for them to find their way back. Perhaps it will help if we keep seeking their stories and being responsive to what they reveal of their needs, meanings, preferences, and strengths.

Acknowledgments   The research described in this text was supported by the National Institute of Mental Health (K01 MH02048-01). The authors thank Nadina Bambur, Maid Salcin, Alan Berkson, Amir Campara, Hasan Maksumic, and Ivan Pavkovic for their participation and support.

References

Bauman, Z. (1993). *Post-modern ethics.* Oxford: Blackwell.

Baumann, G. (1999). *The multicultural riddle: Rethinking national, ethnic, and religious identities.* London: Routledge.

Becker, D. (1995). The deficiency of the concept of posttraumatic stress disorder when dealing with victims of human rights violations. In R. J. Kleber, C. R. Figley, & P. R. Gersons (Eds.), *Beyond trauma: Cultural and societal dynamics* (pp. 99–110). New York: Plenum Press.

Berry, J. W., Kim, V., Minde, T., & Mok, D. (1987). Comparative studies of acculturative stress. *International Migration Review, 21*, 491–511.

Bourdieu, P. (1993). *The weight of the world: Social suffering in contemporary society.* Stanford, CA: Stanford University Press.

Bourdieu, P. (1998). *Practical reason: On the theory of action.* Stanford, CA: Stanford University Press.

Bracken, P. (2002). *Trauma: Culture, meaning, and philosophy.* London: Whurr.

Cohen, J., Bernet, W., Dunne, J. E., Adair, M., Arnold, V., & Benson, R. S. (1998). Practice parameters for the assessment and treatment of children and adolescents with posttraumatic stress disorder. *Journal of the American Academy of Child and Adolescent Psychiatry, 37*(suppl. 10), 4–26.

Danieli, Y. (Ed.). (1998). *International handbook of multigenerational legacies of trauma* (Plenum Series on Stress and Coping). New York: Plenum Press.

Das, V., Kleinman, A., Lock, M., Ramphele, M., & Reynolds, P. (Eds.). (2001). *Remaking a world: Violence, social suffering and recovery.* Berkeley: University of California Press.

Erikson, K. (1995). Notes on trauma and community. In C. Caruth (Ed.), *Trauma: Explorations in memory* (pp. 183–199). Baltimore, MD: Johns Hopkins University Press.

Hacking, I. (1998). *Mad travelers: Reflections on the reality of transient mental illness.* Charlottesville: University of Virginia Press.

Kleinman, A., Das, V., & Lock, M. (1997). *Social suffering.* Berkeley: University of California Press.

Marsella, A., Friedman, M. J., Gerrity, E. T., & Scurfield, R. M. (Eds.). (1996). *Ethnocultural aspects of posttraumatic stress disorder.* Washington, DC: American Psychological Association.

Rolland, J. S. (1994). *Families, illness, and disability: An integrative treatment model.* New York: Basic Books.

Stamm, B. H. (Ed.).(1999). *Secondary traumatic stress: Self-care issues for clinicians, researchers, and educators,* 2nd ed. Lutherville, MD: Sidran Press.

Tiryakian, E. (1997). The wild cards of modernity. *Daedalus, 126*(2), 147–182.

Walsh, F. (1998). *Strengthening family resilience.* New York: Guilford Press.

Weine, S. M. (1999). *When history is a nightmare: Lives and memories of ethnic cleansing in Bosnia-Herzegovina.* New Brunswick, NJ: Rutgers University Press.

Weine, S. M. (2006). *Testimony after catastrophe: Narrating the traumas of political violence.* Evanston, IL: Northwestern University Press.

Weine, S. M., Becker, D., McGlashan, T., Vojvoda, D., Hartman, S., & Robbins, J. (1995). Adolescent survivors of "ethnic cleansing": Notes on the first year in America. *Journal of the Academy of Child and Adolescent Psychiatry, 34*(9), 1153–1159.

Weine, S. M., Feetham, S., Kulauzovic, Y., Besic, S., Lezic, A., Mujagic, A., et al. (2008). A multiple-family group access intervention for refugee families with PTSD. *Journal of Marital and Family Therapy, 34*(2), 149–164.

Weine, S. M., Kulauzovic, Y., Besic, S., Lezic, A., Mujagic, A., Muzurovic, J., et al. (2006). A family beliefs framework for developing socially and culturally specific preventive interventions for refugee families and youth. *American Journal of Orthopsychiatry, 76*(1), 1–9.

Weine, S. M., Muzurovic, N., Kulauzovic, Y., Besic, S., Lezic, A., Mujagic, A., et al. (2004). Family consequences of political violence in refugee families. *Family Process, 43*, 147–160.

Weine, S. M., Ware, N., & Lezic, A. (2004). An ethnographic study of converting cultural capital in teen refugees and their families from Bosnia-Herzegovina. *Psychiatric Services, 55*, 923–927.

Wolcott, H. (1994). *Transforming qualitative data.* Thousand Oaks, CA: Sage.

Young, A. (1995). *The harmony of illusions: Inventing post-traumatic stress disorder.* Princeton, NJ: Princeton University Press.

Chapter 12

Making Sense and No Sense of War
Issues of Identity and Meaning in Adolescents' Experience with Political Conflict

Brian K. Barber

This chapter has been written in a style different from most of my previous material about youth and political violence. I chose such an approach to mirror my own gradual understanding—as elicited by my involvement in the project detailed here—of the explanatory systems of meaning sometimes available to war-involved youth and their potential impact on the well-being and identity formation of war-involved adolescents. Such a departure from my own prior assumptions and methods of inquiry on other topics (i.e., departing to grounding in a variety of disciplines, extensively engaging over the long-term with youth, alternating quantitative and qualitative methods, and, most significant, soliciting carefully and thoroughly the perspectives of youth themselves) lent itself to an unconventional written approach. Although these various components of inquiry evolved logically, they were not planned or foreseen but were inspired by progressive new awareness or discovery of information—or, more important, by the recognition of the need for more awareness or different information. Moreover, the new information was often unexpected and thus would not have been anticipated or properly appreciated through a priori hypothesizing (i.e., issues such as the surprising competent functioning of many youth exposed to and involved in sustained and severe conflict, the sophistication of youths' processing of conflict, or the essential importance to them of understanding the meaning of conflict).

In short, much of the understanding I have come to have in this area is attributable to the process that evolved in its discovery. Thus, although the substantive content presented here hopefully represents a useful contribution to the growing literature on adolescents and political violence, this chapter presents the additional opportunity of describing how those findings came to be made. Hopefully that narrative will also be useful in illustrating how important information on new and complex issues can be gleaned, that is, by the methodological strategies and their sequence that are dictated when carefully engaging the subjects to be studied and their culture.

Because the key topics discussed here (identity and meaning) are rich and central constructs for social science, much of the extensive, relevant literatures have been reviewed. However, to not distract from a more descriptive style (i.e., narratives both of the research process and of the youth interviewed), most of this material is included as notes for those wishing a fuller understanding of the diverse scholarship currently available on these issues.

The Data

Before proceeding, some fundamental detail on the interview data used primarily for this chapter is presented so that the reader can evaluate the substantive content accordingly. Participants in this portion of the project were several dozen youth from Bosnia and Palestine, most of whom had spent at least three of their teen years during political conflicts—1987 to 1993 for the Palestinians and 1992 to 1995 for the Bosnians. Groups, typically consisting of four to eight participants, were interviewed with sequential, tape-recorded translation by bilingual native translators who were mostly of similar age to the participants. In both cases the interviews were conducted approximately two to three years after their respective conflict had ended—1996 (and thereafter) for the Palestinian groups and 1998 for the Bosnian groups. The data therefore include these youths' retrospective accounts of their experiences in the conflict and their perceptions of its role in their current, postconflict lives (i.e., at the time of the interview). Mixed-gender group interviews were conducted with the Bosnian youth, who, although Muslim, were quite secular; therefore, it was culturally normative for males and females to meet together socially or officially. The Palestinian groups were all male because, as a highly orthodox Muslim population, mixed-gender interactions were not acceptable, nor was it appropriate for females to meet privately with a male, particularly a foreign interviewer. A few females did agree to be interviewed either individually or in pairs, in both cases with a translator well known to them. The Bosnian interviews were conducted in a meeting room at a landmark downtown Sarajevo hotel that was a notorious target of the Serbian siege. The Palestinian interviews took place typically in the parlors of various homes in the Nuseirat, Khan Yunis, and Maghazi refugee camps in the Gaza Strip. The interviews with females were conducted in the lobby of the YWCA in Gaza City.

The same semi-structured interview protocol was used for both groups, except for minor changes to accommodate differences in the two conflicts—for example, for the Palestinians, questions about the conflict referred explicitly to "the Intifada" (the 1987–1993 [first] uprising against the Israeli occupation), whereas for the Bosnians, questions referred to "the war" (the 1992–1995 war in Bosnia and Herzegovina). The introductory question for both groups was, "Please describe for me your first memory of [the Intifada; the war]." Subsequent questions included similarly open-ended queries about, for example, the nature of the conflict; their understanding of the purpose of the conflict; if, how, and why they participated in the conflict; any experiences they had with violence toward them or around them; and the effects they perceived the conflict to have had on them psychologically, socially, and civically.

Evolving Toward Appreciating Adolescent Experience in Political Conflict

These interview samples are part of the Adolescents in Political Violence Project (APVP),[1] a program of research that began in 1994 that also included extensive survey data from large samples of former adolescents in both regions. The APVP was not designed a priori as a comparative project. It began as a single, large, cross-sectional survey of Palestinian youth and their parents in the West Bank, East Jerusalem, and the Gaza Strip, but then evolved to incorporate an ethnographic/interview phase, primarily in Gaza (from which the data presented in this chapter emanate), and then a second survey administered to Gazan youth that was designed to incorporate culturally relevant insights gathered through the preceding two phases of the project (see Chapter 9 for a report of findings from this second survey).

The initial survey of Palestinian families in the occupied territories was conducted by a team of U.S. sociologists who invited me to join the group to add a focus on adolescent development. That survey was done competently, that is, the available literatures (in English) were reviewed in preparation for its content; the sampling frame included all ninth-grade (refugee) adolescents and both of their parents in the West Bank, East Jerusalem, and the Gaza Strip; response rates from all family members exceeded 90%, resulting in an overall sample of 7,000 families; and sophisticated statistical analyses have been conducted and findings have been published concerning a variety of issues included in the data set (e.g., Chapter 9; Barber, 1999a, 2001; Fronk, Huntington, & Chadwick, 1999; Huntington, Fronk, & Chadwick, 2001).

It became clear during the weeks spent in the territories conducting the survey, however, that no level of rigor in accomplishing academically sound surveys of this population would equip researchers like ourselves (all from a majority, Western culture of relative privilege and free of political violence) to understand the experience of adolescents and their families in that part of the world generally, let alone their experiences during that most unique and intense period of political conflict that was the First Intifada. This was a pivotal moment in professional development that instructed centrally on the recognition that the method of data collection must be suited to the level of prior understanding of both the issues and people under study to maximally and, more important, accurately produce new and useful understanding (see the closing comment to the chapter for explicit elaboration on the value of the process of the research).

For a culture so unfamiliar, it seemed that the only way to begin to understand it was to penetrate it as fully as possible. Accordingly, beginning in 1996 (extending to 2000), I arranged for a series of long residences (some 18 months in total) with families in or near refugee camps in the Gaza Strip (see Marks, 2001, and Hart, 2004, for similar methodologies in work among South African youth and Palestinian refugees in Jordan, respectively). By then it had become clear that Gaza was a critical corner of the occupied territories. This is so because it has always been the home of both the fledgling governments that Palestinians have occasionally tried or been permitted to form, as well as the home base of the major radical fundamentalist groups that have often been at odds with secular approaches to dealing with the occupation. In addition, Gaza's isolation from the rest of the territories has preserved very strong cultural ties, religious orthodoxy, and high levels of poverty, housing density, and unemployment. For all of these reasons, Gaza has typically had the highest rates of conflict with the occupying Israeli Defense Forces (IDF), especially during the First Intifada. It seemed to be the best place, therefore, to take the various pulses of Palestinian experience.

The goal of this effort was to experience as much of everyday refugee experience in Gaza as possible and specifically come to know youth experience, particularly as it related to the Intifada. Approaching such an understanding meant always residing in homes, studying the native language (Arabic), and participating in key cultural events, such as marriage ceremonies, wakes, the yearly fasting month of Ramadan, feast celebrations, and, most ubiquitous, endless hours of social chatting among and between families. Naturally, an outsider never knows the degree to which he or she has penetrated a culture, but one evidence of the success of this immersion was the eventual and regular welcome to be in the private sphere, that is, in the presence of the women of some families, in many cases even the private rooms (i.e., those behind the entry parlor) where guests are not permitted.

The time in Gaza also included hundreds of hours of association with youth in all of their contexts—home, school, play yards, and on alley corners. In addition to this informal involvement, which afforded much opportunity for observation, I conducted dozens of formal interviews with Palestinian youth, using a snowball sampling approach whereby youth or adults would refer me to other youth who they thought could give particular insight into the Intifada, and so on. No official effort was made to randomize the interview samples (that was attempted in the survey that followed), but every effort was made to include youth who represented the diversity that characterizes Gaza. Most critical, this diversity included varying political factions who during the Intifada had developed differing strategies of coping with the conflict and, importantly, different beliefs relative to how peace should and could be achieved. Thus, the interview samples contained members of the major political groups: Fatah (secular pro-Arafat, now Abbas), Popular Front for the Liberation of Palestine (PFLP, communist), and the two most prominent Islamic groups, Hamas and Islamic Jihad.

This contact with the Palestinian youth—particularly the formal interviews during which their Intifada experience was discussed in depth—was the impetus to add the comparative portion of the APVP (i.e., in Bosnia). Unexpectedly, youth accounts of the conflict—their overall perspectives, actions, and reactions—were so often noteworthy and surprising that it seemed important to do a check on other adolescents in similar conditions to understand how bound these Palestinian youths' experiences were to their particular culture and conflict. A thorough presentation of accounts of Gazan youth experience during the First Intifada are presented elsewhere (Barber, in press), but some brief elaboration will be provided for background to understand both the impetus for a comparative study and the basis against which to contrast the youth.

The challenge to understand this (to me) foreign population of youth was complicated by the need to appreciate a variety of dimensions of experience and, importantly, the complex of contexts that help shape those experiences. Thus, coming to understand how youth functioned in and after political violence (the prime research question driving the APVP) involved detailed study of the history, geography, and politics of the region, but it also required extensive observation of how individuals function daily as they live their lives amid the concomitant demands of poverty and isolation. Generally, I was ill prepared to understand people in these circumstances by both my lack of familiarity with conflict zones and by a naive trusting of the stereotypes that are constantly transmitted by broadcast media's sound byte coverage, especially of Gaza. In contrast to those images, I encountered none of the hostility, harshness, or vengefulness supposed to be characteristic of the "hornet's nest" that would be Gaza (see, e.g., Hass, 2000). Instead, there was a calm but eager warm welcome by all, particularly the youth, who above all yearned to be heard.

In a real sense, Gaza was primitive in many ways, including what felt like the Palestinians' own naive trusting. Indeed, the predominant response to my presence was an innocent incredulity that someone from the outside—from America no less—would deign come to Gaza. Repeatedly, this insecurity was voiced with such questions as "What do you think of us?" and "Will you come back?" In one notable discussion with a group of early college students in Deir-el-Bellah, a small town in the central part of the Strip, this question pair was posed verbatim six times within an hour, as if the students couldn't get enough of my positive answers to both questions. (Note: It is the case now, as it was then, that many foreigners come to Gaza, especially representatives from supportive governments and nongovernmental organizations. Most, however, reside in Gaza City, the urban, relatively modern center of the Strip. Camp residents had then and still have now relatively little long-term exposure to foreign residents.)

Another surprising aspect of Palestinian youth demeanor was the level of deference shown to authority. Clearly, the quite patriarchal culture of Gaza prescribes some of this deference, but it was surprising that such respect had so thoroughly survived the 6 years of often daily violence that was the Intifada, in which these youth had participated substantially both as perpetrators and recipients (see Chapter 9 for quantitative documentation of these experiences). Many have expressed anecdotal concern that might appear to contradict this point—that is, unruly, disrespectful behavior toward teachers, parents, and other adults both during and after the Intifada. Indeed, an original impetus for studying Palestinian families was accounts from some parents to one of the lead investigators of the initial phase of the APVP that they were losing control of their children, particularly their adolescents.

There is no doubt that relational patterns among adolescents and adults were different during the Intifada than they were before it, if only because of the heightened personal autonomy expressed by most adolescents as they participated in and often led the uprising. Had there been data collected on relational dynamics between parents and their adolescent children pre-Intifada, careful research post-Intifada might well have shown a lasting shift. Even if that were to be the case, however, it would only be a matter of degree. That is, whatever alterations in respect for authority that may have occurred as a result of adolescent involvement in the political conflict, it clearly was not of a magnitude that either consistently or comprehensively dissolved authority structures within the society. The apparently instinctive deference to adult status and authority was everywhere evident, whether in the form of the gentle manners that were expressed in individual conversations or in the broader, authority-driven relationship patterns with parents and teachers.

The complexity of the cultural immersion in Gaza included the paradoxical juxtaposition of this deference to "legitimate" authority with an unequivocal and unyielding defiance of perceived "illegitimate" authority, in this case, the Israeli occupation. This defiance was evident behaviorally during the Intifada through the adolescents' concrete political activism, and was still very apparent afterward through their unambiguous assessment that despite the "peace agreement," the occupation persisted on the ground in its unabated unjustness (Barber, 1999b). (To demonstrate the complexity further, it is important to note that on the political front, the balance and, indeed, targets of both defiance and deference have been even more substantially complicated since the First Intifada because of the perceived corruption of the "legitimate" authority of Palestinian political entities post-Oslo, the February 2006 electoral rejection of the Palestinian Authority in favor of a Hamas-led government, and most recently the Hamas military takeover of the Strip in June 2007.)

This opposing duality of fundamental ways of being among Palestinian youth presented a complexity of identity that is interesting precisely because of its inconsistency—an inconsistency, notably, of structure, not content. As such, it is not consistent with some classic renditions of identity formation (e.g., ego identity status; Marcia, 1994) which, although allowing for cultural variation in the content of identity, require that the structure or form of identity is invariant—for example, that identity must be coherent and consistent (and that it develops in the same sequence from diffusion to achievement) within an individual and across time. The contradicting components of Palestinian youth identity may, instead, illustrate the necessary revision (or correction, in part to be more consistent with Erikson's original thinking; Erikson, 1968) some recent writers on identity formation are suggesting, namely, that—particularly when considering identity formation in complex cultures where individual lives are unusually and fundamentally impacted by historical, political, ethnic, geographic (i.e., territorial) forces or moments—identity becomes organized into (non–internally consistent) configurations that represent responsiveness to the complexity of lived experience (see, for example, Schachter, 2004, 2005, for an elaborated discussion of these identity issues; see Straker, 1992, and Marks, 2001, for discussions of similar identity complexities among South African youth). Notably, the varying elements of the configuration (in the present example, defiance and deference) themselves are inconsistent over time, adjusting as they do to the frequently shifting, politically generated demands of their daily life (i.e., depending on the relative presence or intrusion of perceived illegitimate authority to be defied).

It seemed that the Palestinian youths' experiences illustrate another classic element of Erikson's (1968) notions of identity formation—in this case regarding the interrelationship between youth and the adults in their lives, particularly fathers and grandfathers. In contrast to many social or political conflicts in which youth (typically college students) protest as a cohort, the Intifada was a classic, popular movement in which all segments of the society were deeply committed and regularly engaged. The historical meaning given to the struggle (see following discussion) was passed on continually through stories of earlier stages of the Jewish/Arab conflict by youths' fathers and grandfathers, particularly in the refugee camps where the three generations are in close contact, perhaps facilitating both the personal and cultural continuity or persistence some scholars of identity have recently emphasized (e.g., Chandler, Lalonde,

Sokol, & Hallet, 2003). No doubt, also, the youths' commitment and engagement was absorbed in part by the older generation as a validation of their own identity as strugglers, perhaps illustrating a mutuality in which generations contribute to each other's development (Erikson, 1968; see also Youniss & Yates, 1997, for an illustration of the value to identity of cross-generational purpose).

The broader lesson from this immersion experience—again, profound only for those of us who have not experienced or witnessed human functioning in times of real hardship and conflict—was that life simply goes on, and most people do reasonably well given available resources (see Cairns & Darby, 1998, for similar observations in Northern Ireland). For their part, the seasoned adolescent fighters of the Intifada spent their young adulthood not in disarray and despair but in the day-to-day routine of fulfilling family duties, going to college, seeking employment or creatively scratching together some sort of income, playing soccer, watching TV, smoking cigarettes, napping, and otherwise filling the boredom of refugee camp life with typically quiet and calm conversation about the past and the future.

Engaging Political Violence

Apart from these rather fundamental insights into how a population of unusually conflict-weathered adolescents carry on, the youths' characterization of the Intifada itself was most surprising and at first a bit bewildering, frankly. The rather primitive lens that still characterized my orientation to youth experience with political conflict—shaped simply by recognizing the sheer amount and duration of violence the youth had engaged in and experienced—was primed for recitations of the violence itself, with perhaps some thrill and some fear but nevertheless intensely negative. As is evident in the overview presented in Chapter 2, such an expectation was natural given the predominant attempt among researchers to document the trauma, stress, and dysfunction of war populations. In part, the lens was poorly focused because of my own instinctual fear of violence and conflict; not because of past personal experience but, precisely to the contrary, because of a lack of experience in feeling and witnessing the levels of sophistication and complexity with which humans can process extreme circumstances like political violence.

The Palestinian narratives were indeed intense, yet it was (not always, but overwhelmingly so) an intensity of passion, not despair; of commitment, not chaos; of pride, not dismay; and of welfare, not wound. The violence, as severe, frequent, and enduring as it was, seemed to be incidental background to narrations of engagement that were loaded with emotion and purpose and noticeably absent of any concentration on stress, trauma, or negativity. They were so remarkably absent of the negative functioning I had expected that it felt necessary to provide a check on their validity. It made sense, then, to listen to another cohort of adolescents who had been involved in similar experiences before knowing how much to credit the Palestinian experience as generally instructive about adolescents or as uniquely enlightening about Gazan youth experience (see following discussion for illustrative excerpts from their interviews).

The Bosnian situation appeared to be a useful comparison at the time. The targeted population of Sarajevo (the main city placed under siege by Serbian or Serbian-backed forces) was largely Muslim. The youth had been confronted by several consecutive years of regular and severe political violence, and, not unlike for the Palestinians, the region had experienced substantial political instability over the preceding decades. The APVP was therefore expanded to include a replication of the Gaza interviews (and eventually, the survey as well; see Chapter 8 and McCouch, 2006, for a report of those survey findings).

The narratives from the Bosnian youth were striking and intense, but their tone and substance was as far from that of their Palestinian counterparts as one could imagine. There, finally, in the Bosnian narratives was the concentration on the stress and trauma of the violence that had been missing in the Palestinian interviews. The negativity overwhelmed the discussion. The fervor to express it in that moment was partly because the youth recognized that they had not yet had an opportunity to actually discuss their war experiences among themselves (even that many years after the end of the conflict). As the interviews went on, it was clear that the trauma was the essence of their experience, not just a venting prelude to something more positive. There was real terror in their memories and substantial dysfunction in their accounts of self.

Elna, for example, was terrified by the violence. She hadn't heard gunfire before. The sound of the first bullets was like "lightning," and then the grenades began falling. Emir, stunned by the sight of the gun he had never before seen in his father's hand, had a "terrible fear to die"—a fear so pronounced that it made his legs shake and brought him near tears as he was suddenly participating in defending his home, "even though we didn't know who was the enemy at that time or who we are fighting against." For Armin, the gunfire felt like "fury," paired with the panic he experienced when he thought the gunfire might have struck his brother. Still "a child," Muamer couldn't understand why, all of a sudden, he was restricted to the basement. He began to shake and "bit by bit" understand that war had confined him. For Faruk and others, the violence was so sudden and strange that it felt surreal, "but as time passed I saw that this movie will never end." These youth saw wounded people for the first time and began to fear for their own survival. For Ervin, "everything had been turned upside down." He began taking life more seriously, praying for survival.

Above all was a dense theme of personal loss in the Bosnian narratives. Candidates for loss surely included family (particularly fathers) who disappeared for various reasons, but for these youth it was their "friends" who inexplicably left them. "They all left," recalled Naida, referring to about half of her classmates who suddenly disappeared three or four days before school ended. "They went somewhere. We had no idea there was going to be a war." Some of them she has seen since the war, but "it is not the same. I was burned by the war. I lost my uncle, and there are no friends for me." Naida had another friend, a Croat. They were like sisters. One day the friend said she had to go to her relatives, and they joked that Naida would go with her. The friend somehow knew the war was coming, and afterward, "she doesn't want to contact me." Emin's Serbian friends were "simply disappearing," and he had not seen a single once since then. Armin turned down an invitation to go to Belgrade with one Serb friend. Why? "I thought it [the war] will end soon."

Apart from the dramatic distinction of tone and valence between the Bosnian and the Palestinian youth narratives, there was a stark disparity in the richness of the narratives. Both were emotional (i.e., passionate); whereas one set was sterile and empty of elaboration in its preoccupation with trauma (Bosnian), the other was packed with explanatory discourse in its declarations of sense and purpose. In short, the Bosnian youth were able to make no sense of the violence, but the Palestinian youth drew essential, intricate, and inspiring meaning from their conflict.

The comparative portion of the APVP therefore turned out to be critical in demonstrating how very differently youth experience political conflict. This disparity is generally instructive in cautioning against overgeneralizations of youth experience with war, and, more specifically, it gives insight into where we might focus to better understand the disparity in processing and adapting to political violence. In this case, it was clear that an ability to understand the conflict (i.e., interpret, make sense of it) was a significant parameter that distinguished the degree to which youth felt injured by the violence. Moreover, it was also clear that the meaning Palestinian youth attached to conflict (i.e., explanations sourced in history, politics, culture; see later discussion for an elaboration) was not the sum of inert facts but of information that was vibrant in empowering the youth as individuals and social actors.

Despite differing fundamentally in the demeanor, tone, and content of their expressions, the narratives of both groups share parallel, contingent themes: *competence/ growth* and *meaning*. The contingency of these themes—that is, feeding on and informing each other—was not explicitly articulated in the narratives, but the linkage can easily and logically be inferred. Palestinian youth did not convey in the interviews that they felt substantially enriched by their involvement in their struggle because the conflict made sense to them. Similarly, the Bosnian youth did not verbalize explicitly that their continued suffering was because of the nearly total absence of sensibility of the war. Interview questions were not designed to determine such associations among experiences but to solicit a report—a description—of their experiences and feelings (e.g., "your first memory," "did you participate," "why," "how did you feel," and so on). The pure frequency of mention of both growth (or its absence) and meaning (or its lack), however, makes the linkage dynamic and interpretable. This is all the more so given that the connection is also quite apparent in much recent social science writing (as will be referenced shortly).

Political Violence and Competence/Growth

The competent functioning of the Palestinian youth that was so evident in their narratives is quite consistent with one major trend in the research on youth and war (a literature that I was not at all aware of before conducting the APVP interviews). Indeed, increasing calls are being made to expand the focus of both research and interventions to concentrate on the ability of persons to function normally or positively in war environments (e.g., Almedom, 2004, 2005; Bolton, Neugebauer, & Ndogoni, 2002; Bolton & Trang, 2002; Boyden, 2003; Das, Kleinman, Lock, Ramphele, & Reynolds, 2001; Powell, Rosner, Butollo, Tedeschi, & Calhoon, 2003; Pupavac, 2002; Summerfield, 1999; see Straker, 1992, for a review of psychoanalytic theory of the benefits of violence). (Note: This impetus to focus on competent or positive functioning is consistent with much broader, social science literatures as well.[2]) Much of this emphasis has been in specific reaction against the prevailing focus on posttraumatic stress disorder and other related elements of negative psychological functioning in work on war populations (e.g., Chapter 1; Cairns & Darby, 1998; Summerfield, 1999) that was so evident in the specific review of studies on adolescents and political violence presented in Chapter 2. As noted there, the relative paucity of empirical evidence for competent functioning of youth in war zones is not due to the inability to detect such effects but rather to the lack of effort to test for them in the first place. Those relatively few studies that have tested for positive functioning have often found evidence for it (see Chapter 2 for an overview of those studies, and Chapters 5, 10, and 11 for new evidence. See also recent compatible findings from a thorough study by UNICEF of Ugandan soldier and nonsoldier youth: Annan, Blattman, & Horton, 2006; Annan, Blattman, Carlson, & Mazurana, 2008; Blattman & Annan, 2007). Furthermore, the review notes as well that up to 20% of studies that assess negative functioning do not find evidence of it.

With specific regard to Palestinian youth, the second set of survey data from the APVP provides support for the youth's growth narratives. In that sample of 900 Gazan youth (contemporaries of those who were interviewed), involvement in the Intifada was associated not only with their subjective assessment of personal growth and their willingness to participate again should another phase of the conflict ensue (Barber, 2008; Barber & Olsen, 2006), but also with various measures of their civic and social competence behaviors 5 years after the end of the Intifada (Chapter 9).

The absence of any clear evidence of personal growth as a result of their conflict experiences expressed by the Bosnian youth—indeed, their sustained emphasis on substantial personal and social difficulty—stands in direct contrast to the Palestinian youth experience. This is also supported in the survey data from the APVP, where, in the sample of 600 youth from Sarajevo (again, contemporaries of those who were interviewed), war experiences were directly related to numerous indicators of personal and social dysfunction (see Chapter 8 and, for a more elaborated treatment, McCouch, 2006). In essence, the Bosnian results (which themselves are widely supported in other research, e.g., Freedman & Abazovic, 2006; Jones, 2002, 2004; Jones & Kafetsios, 2005; Kerestes, 2006), as contrasted with the distinctly different findings from Palestinian youth, beg the very important and refining questions: "Which youth will be substantially disabled by experiences with violence?" "Which youth will function competently or experience growth in the face of political violence and which will not?"

The Meaning of Political Violence

One answer to these questions appears to be the extent to which the youth in the respective regions were or were not able to make sense of their experiences—that is, the degree to which the conflict had meaning for them. Both sets of interviews revealed the salience of the interpretability of the conflict. The Palestinian narratives were packed with multifaceted meaning that they ascribed to the conflict in which they participated, and the Bosnian narratives were demonstrably vacant of such meaning.

In this section, I advance the construct *identity-relevant meaning systems* to help capture the type of meaning that was revealed in these interviews. The construct of meaning has received much attention over the decades in attempting to describe human functioning in general (including adolescents specifically),[3] and of particular relevance here, numerous calls have been made by scholars of children and political violence for more attention to the meaning adolescents attach to the conflict they experience (e.g., Barber, Schluterman, Denney, & McCouch, 2005; Cairns, 1987; Cairns & Dawes, 1996; Garbarino & Kostelny, 1991; Jones, 2002, 2004; Punamäki, 1996; Straker, 1992; Straker, Mendelsohn, Moosa, & Tudin, 1996; Wessells, 2006). However, although elements of the traditional formulation of meaning have clear relevance to the work presented here, the type of meaning illustrated in these interview data is different enough in fundamental ways to warrant separate conceptualization. Essentially, classic renditions of the meaning (making) construct describe it to be a psychological (broadly human) attribute that is searched for and invoked on behalf of self and in response to trauma or pervasive challenge. Though it is most likely the case that both Palestinian and Bosnian adolescents engaged in this fundamentally human response to difficulty, the meaning that was so salient to their retrospectives on conflict was of a different type. That meaning, in contrast, was a collection of existing explanatory information sourced outside the self in the social ecology that was, or would have been, essentially useful before and/or during the conflict.[4]

Identity-Relevant Meaning Systems

Although there are types or forms of meaning that (once searched for and found) appear to be critical to human functioning in adapting to challenge or difficulty, there are other features of meaning that differ notably along the facets of classic meaning and have been well illustrated in the Palestinian and Bosnian narratives. This different type of meaning (or different facet of the overall meaning construct) is more static and less personally sourced or driven and, rather than provide a remedy for already experienced stress, gives explanation or clarification to significant events as they occur in one's contexts. This type of meaning is informational—made up of ideas, folk or historical knowledge, values, doctrines, and so on—and is possessed (or not) by an individual who uses it to process and make sense of surrounding events. This type of information comes packaged in sets or systems of meaning.[5]

Although there may well be an inescapable egocentric element to meaning, it is the information itself, collected as it is in a variety of systems of meaning (see following discussion), that has struck me as pivotal in understanding how youth have processed their experiences with political conflict in these two instances. More precisely, it appears to be the *availability* (and salience) of this informational meaning that appears critical—that is, meaning that need not be searched for but rather exists before or accompanies the event in question. Consistent with the Bosnian narratives introduced above, Lynne Jones's work in Bosnia (e.g., 2002, 2004; Jones & Kafetsios, 2005), for example, makes clear that the absence of meaning—particularly when it is searched after by youth—figures prominently in the difficulty youth can have in response to political conflict. Stated differently, the (in)comprehensibility of political conflict is quite likely a critical element of youth's negative response to it (Elbedour, Bensel, & Maruyama, 1993; Summerfield, 2000).

Because this type of meaning partly informs issues outside the self, it distinguishes itself from classic meaning in that it is not primarily used for self-serving purposes. Thus, the meaning that was so evident throughout the Palestinian narratives appeared to be utilized by them, not first (or, for most, at all) in service of their personal survival or well-being, but rather to interpret, explain, and inform the purpose, utility, legitimacy, and urgency of the conflict itself. In short, if humans are naturally motivated to make meaning of their lives, it follows that the effectiveness of that meaning making would be substantially enhanced by the presence of information that provides the meaning.

Clearly, meaning systems overlap, particularly regarding political conflict where often historical, political, ethnic, religious, and cultural systems combine to precipitate, define, and maintain the conflict. Heuristically, however, it is useful to isolate the systems to illustrate the complexity of information that youth can process as they confront conflict.

History as a Meaning System

In writing about civic engagement among U.S. youth, McClellan, Yates, and Youniss (1997) noted that youth seek to locate themselves historically by "adopting ideological traditions that older generations have sustained and still merit" (see Erikson, 1968). If this is true for Western adolescents, then it is surely so for youth in other parts of the world, for many of whom the history of their people is quite literally unfolding via the conflict of which they are part. The youth narratives analyzed for this chapter illustrate this well, and once again, the contrast between the Palestinian and Bosnian discourse is striking. When talking with Palestinian adolescents generally (and often much younger children as well), one is struck by the degree to which history infuses their worldview. This was particularly so among the cohort of adolescents studied in this project regarding the nature of the conflict in which they so thoroughly participated (see Tesfai, 2003, as cited in Almedom, 2004, for similar salience of history among Eritreans).

Universally, Palestinian youth attributed the conflict to the Israeli occupation, against which their people fought for the whole of the adolescents' lives but that also had longer historical roots in pre–State of Israel tensions between Arabs and Jews (i.e., since the turn of the twentieth century). Some accounts from the youth were general and ubiquitous—for example, the Intifada occurred because of "the suffering from the occupation," or "we have suffered from childhood"—whereas others included specific historical events that gave meaning to the conflict. Thus, for Mohammed, one day's demonstration at school was to mark "Black Sunday," a notable moment when many Palestinians were "martyred." The reach to historical causes of the conflict often invoked family. For Wajdi, it was that "my father and grandmother lost their country." Sami recalled querying his parents as a child as to why "we have no lands." For Saher, the essential meaning came when seeing his parents weep while watching a TV news report that featured Abu Amar (Yasser Arafat, the then-exiled leader of the Palestine Liberation Organzation, the PLO) and Abu Jihad (Khalil Al-Wazir, then second in command in the PLO and assassinated early in the Intifada). "That was the beginning of my love for Fatah [the main political party representing the PLO]."

Specific features of the history of this conflict, particularly imprisonments, figured prominently in the youths' system of historical meaning. Thus, Miasra's commitment to the struggle was "an extension of my father's spirit"; like so many fathers and youth,

Miasra's father had been imprisoned. Hammam was born just after his father was imprisoned many years before the Intifada erupted, and the whole of his formative years were defined by his visits with his mother to see his father in prison. Furthermore, and ironically, the prison experience not only represented part of the history of the conflict (as typically passed on via oral histories of parents and grandparents) but quite literally educated and expanded on that history. On his third prison-directed seizure, Abu Fida proclaimed to the arresting soldiers, "Take me to the Academy of the Palestinians," referring to the famed Ansar III prison in the Negev desert where there were rigorous, prisoner-organized schools that taught the history and politics of the struggle. At the same prison, Khalil "had a look at our history—not [just] our history, but all of the world's history with revolutions and occupations" (see Barber, in press, for an elaboration of the nondeterrent effect of imprisonment on Palestinian youth).

This saturated richness of the historical foundation and meaning that youth attached to the Palestinian conflict contrasted vividly with the Bosnian experience. This is seen most profoundly in the virtual absence of any historical explanation or guide to their war. Instead, the youth were both surprised and mystified by its onset. Ervin thought it odd that his parents, who normally would be working, were at home when he awoke on March 2, 1992. He was happy when they said he didn't have to go to school that day, but he "couldn't understand what was going on." The TV news of mass gatherings of people whose movement was impeded by soldiers was "like a movie . . . that couldn't happen in my town." He attended a protest meeting with his father that night, and everything "had a happy ending." Then "the same thing happened on April 6th," but this time the protests felt more serious and "the true war started—grenades and everything. Simply, everything turned upside down . . . I started to see things more serious and I was praying for survival basically." Edin watched the TV coverage of the shots from snipers at people huddled at a downtown hotel, but it was only when the first artillery shell hit that he knew that "something was going on."

Emir couldn't recall if it was the April 2 or 4, but he remembered that it was a "beautiful morning, like every holiday" when the war descended—barricades, killings, shooting—and when his town was totally cut off from others. "We didn't know where we could go." The shooting of an innocent girl while crossing the bridge "shocked" Muamar and filled him with bitterness. Elma remembered the March barricades, not going to school that day, and seeing soldiers around her building. "There was something very strange that was happening." Her parents were talking a lot with the neighbors, "they didn't know what was happening." Senka thought, "it's impossible for this to happen in the capital of western Herzogovina." It was Anis's birthday: "I was confused and didn't know what was happening."

Alen mused that had they been older, perhaps they would have known about the history of warfare in the Balkans. But as Alma indicated (as quoted in Chapter 11), they did not: "Serbs and Croats [unlike Bosnian Muslims] knew about history, not only from books, even the ones that were not educated knew a lot because they talked about it at homes, they were singing about great 'heroes,' they worked hard and are still doing the same at teaching new generations and refreshing memory of older generations. What we need the older generation to understand is that we were silent observers; we witnessed genocide, ethnic cleansing, human behavior at its worst." This historical vacuum was sensed similarly in Croatia, where "younger generations don't know anything about how this war came about, what were its causes. I believe we should talk about it more" (Freedman & Abrazovic, 2006, p. 65).

Politics as a Meaning System

When Emir saw a gun in his father's hand, he deduced that there was a need to defend oneself from an enemy, yet "we didn't know who the enemy was or who we are fighting against. Where are we to go?" Nedim "understood the war as an attack on Bosnia-Herzegovina as a state." Yet he only came to know this because he saw the "Serbian marks all over the tanks." Markings on the planes that were operating out of the airport led Almir to the same unwitting conclusion. "Where is the enemy?" Senka had not thought that the Serbian soldiers were enemies "until we realized that they were actually pointing their guns towards the people, towards the civilians, towards us." In retrospect, some vague signs were there. Almir noted that previously all youth had gone out together, and "a small separation started at the very beginning of the war . . . we would play ball and we would have two groups—Serbian groups and Muslim groups . . . and then the war started." Armin also had sensed a separation occurring—"they were not harassing me, but they really had something against me." He had noticed that the Serbs had been wearing religious symbols and clothes (T-shirts), but "I didn't know what this meant. Why are they wearing this? I thought it was pointless." Nonetheless, "we were not aware that they were preparing [for war]." Amar "figured out that this is politics now," when all of a sudden all the Serbs had left. "I don't know where they went. But I found out that they are fighting because I am a Muslim," an aspect of their political identity that Bosnian families apparently did not make central to their own self-definition (e.g., see Alma's interview, as quoted in Chapter 11).

In contrast to this vacuum of political knowledge in which Bosnian youth were forced to deduce from circumstantial evidence what was happening around them and who they and others were as people, Palestinian youth did not need to expend any effort in understanding the Intifada. Their conflict had a vibrant legacy, and its meaning, even for the youngest of them, was patently and unambiguously political. First, the history on which they were weaned by parents and grandparents was defined by political aspirations. To this was added the study of the history and philosophy of revolutions (as Khalil noted in his description of the prison education: "in Vietnam, Nicaragua, Russia, Algeria, Syria, and so on."). This was particularly the case for those youth who enlisted during the Intifada in the more ideologically driven factions, such as the PFLP. Regardless of faction, the prevailing assumption about the situation was punctuated by indictments against real political players, nations, and individual citizens alike. For Abu Sharif, for example, the Intifada taught him that his land "had been stolen" and that the occupation was assisted by "Great Britain and other countries for political reasons and persons." For Nader, it was "Clinton and his administration who follow the Israelis without even thinking what is right or wrong." For him, there was also plenty of political blame to be spread around: "Now we are not living the perfect life we dreamt of, this is our fault, I think—not the fault of the people, of the young people, of the children who threw stones—it was the fault of the leadership." For Abu Omar, politics was fused with human rights: "I am human and have human feelings inside myself, just as every people in the world: like Americans, like the British, like the French. They have their own land, they have their country, they have their flag, they have their rights. We are all humans, so, I have to have my rights, I have to have my country, I have to have my flag, just like all." (See Rafman, 2004, for a treatment of how politics, psychology, and morality merge in war, including the protective role of political meaning.)

Culture as a Meaning System

One additional source of meaning for Palestinian youth can be broadly conceived as the culture that prevailed during the conflict; that is, the beliefs and behaviors of the community as a whole. There were several features of Palestinian culture that were invoked by the youth as they described the essence of life during the conflict, all of which bound the society together in ways that imparted to the youth vital and motivating meaning.

Whereas a sense of isolation is apparent in much Palestinian self-discourse (i.e., a sense of identity-challenging marginalization; see Khalidi, 1997), for Gazans the isolation has a particularly tangible geographic component, given its literal separation from other concentrations of Palestinians, especially from those in the West Bank and East Jerusalem, not to mention more broadly from other Arab countries. Thus, for Abu Fida, one essence of the Intifada was "to break the loneliness of the Gaza Strip. It's a sealed area [and we wanted] to break it and get contact with the neighboring Arab countries." Critically, in his evaluation (which was very representative of the youth perspective overall), this meaning was shared by the whole culture: "It was for the good for all of the people; to save all the people. We were together."

This unity was evident in the breadth of participation across the society. Many youths expressed initial incredulity at the extent of participation—an amazement that quickly transformed to pride. For Miasra, for example, "the number of people that participated was strange . . . it involved all sectors of society." Khalil's first recollection of the Intifada was a demonstration that began in his camp on the first day of the uprising: "At that day, I saw what I had never seen before—about 40,000 people from Khan Yunis had gathered and started to drive, to walk . . . and at that moment, if you had stopped anyone of them and asked him, 'Where are you going?' he wouldn't be able to answer. We were just driven by emotions . . . we wanted to fight . . . to finish our suffering . . . to end the occupation itself." Ayman said that that participation was unlimited: "Even the children, you would see them throwing stones." For Naji, the cultural unity of purpose was self-evident: "Of course everybody participated in doing anything against the occupation . . . [it was] something for Palestine."

The unity the youth perceived was enriched by the inspiring mutual support. First, there were the traditional distributions to the poor at the annual Muslim feasts. Hussam recalled, "Some people before a feast distributed money, clothes, food, arranged some small parties for children, trips to factories in order to make some sense of fun and entertainment for those children whose fathers are in prison." Otherwise the displays of support were many and varied, including defending the arrested, warnings of approaching IDF patrols, lending a friend whatever money one had, holding secret classes when the schools were closed, and so on. Abu Fida's mother kept the clothes of the "wanted" youth (those who had been identified by the IDF and thus changed their garb before the next activity). "My mother was very happy . . . they respected her very much."

Youth were particularly impressed with the sacrifices during the most severe moments, like the long and frequent curfews placed on neighborhoods, camps, or towns. Again, Hussam: "During the curfews some people were going to a village near Nuseirat camp where vegetables are growing. They were bringing these vegetables and distributing them to people who are in black need for such things." Khaled remarked:

> I learned that my people are really great people because during the hard times, they could be just like one family. We used to have curfews for maybe ten or sometimes fifteen successive days. And you know what that means: no family, no house has the basic needs, the food actually, to live for fifteen days. And I remember that when my neighbors were cooking something, and we had no food, they were sharing the food with us . . . now when I recall these moments, I'm really proud to be a Palestinian.

Naturally, there were also tensions within the society. Political divisions surfaced particularly strongly during the latter half of the Intifada with the proliferation of competing religiopolitical factions. Ironically, the widespread unity also challenged cultural roles. This occurred particularly for women, whose participation was at once both welcome and awkward. Ibtisam, for example, recalled struggling with the gratification of participating in acceptable ways (e.g., making and distributing food) but with the sense that "our customs forbade us to share like the men." There was also ample generational tension, with parents often acutely ambivalent about their children's activism. Adel's father, prototypically, "was always nervous . . . waiting for us near the door . . . if we were late, asking people if they had seen us. He was always afraid that something might happen to us." Some youth were angry at parental intervention in their involvement, yet there was often also a negotiated appeasement that ultimately prioritized the unified struggle. "We would say," offered Khalil, "be relaxed, we just want to go out for five or ten minutes if it is okay with you. They said, 'Okay. You are our sons and our guards. It is our duty to you.'" Hussam's father didn't prevent his activism: "Just be aware, and maintain your study during the actions. So, in fact, after the actions, I always came back home and began to study."

Clearly, any group that is subject to assault—particularly one that so directly assails their essence as a people—bonds with some degree of unity. Thus, some of the Bosnian youths' commentary on their experiences implied a measure of cohesion. Notably, it was defensive in nature, stemming from a shared victimization. The Palestinian youth narratives clearly included the sense of collective violation, but salient also to their cohesion was the collective activity just described. Furthermore, full solidarity was compromised for the Bosnians precisely because of the absence of historical or political meaning, even by or from parents or other adults. Melika summed up the experience of most:

> I was a child, thirteen years old. I couldn't understand the situation the way it was. It was without any meaning. My parents didn't know and they didn't know what to tell me, why this was happening, what is going to become of us, are we going to be alive. They were frightened; they didn't know how to cope with the situation or how to explain

it to us—what to do, whether to leave or stay, where to go, if we are going to be alive or not. They told us they would protect us, but they didn't know what to do.

Supportive of this is the conclusion made by others who have listened to Balkan youth that the general sense of depression and malaise among them was fed in part by feeling abandoned by adults, who were unhelpful in assisting youth to know how to heal or think about the future (e.g., Freedman & Abazovic, 2006).

Religion as a Meaning System

Despite the fact that religion is possibly the most explored of all of these meaning systems (e.g. Silberman, 2005), very little of the narratives of either group of youth focused on it. Reasons for this absence probably vary. Bosnia is a relatively secularized Muslim region, and thus it is easy to understand why religious explanations for the conflict or response to it were not abundant. Gaza, in contrast, is considered quite an orthodox Muslim culture, and thus an explanation for a relative inattention to religion is not as forthcoming, except to note that because Islam's scope covers all realms of living (i.e., social, cultural, political) it is neither natural nor necessary to invoke religion independently. The fusion of religion with politics was quite evident, however, in the narratives of those who did speak explicitly about religion.

Without exception, these were members of the minority radical Islamic groups Hamas and Islamic Jihad. El-Zeldeen noted that Hamas depended completely on Islamic doctrine. Because it "doesn't confess the existence of Israel as an independent state in the Middle East," he explained, "we will work to end the occupation of the Holy Land of Palestine." His Intifada years were the happiest of his life, and were he to have it to do over, he would participate constantly, but, referring to the failed Oslo Agreement, he would not endorse "any thinking of making peace with the Jews." Several noted that there would be continuous conflict between Arabs and Jews, and Abu Ahmad indicated, referring to parents: "It is their duty, it's their religious duty, their national duty to encourage their kids, their babies, to defend their lands and to stop the occupation. And if they lose their kids or their children, that's their faith, it is for God's sake." Abdullah's self-description is telling as to the role of religion in his identity:

> I learned from the Intifada to be very courageous, and I didn't care if I was going to die today or tomorrow. In prison I learned something deeper—that everybody lacks something of his religion. When I began to learn about Islamic Jihad, I felt terrified . . . The word *jihad* means death and I was terrified at that moment to believe in such an ideology. I suffered from a self-conflict. I was divided in myself. I wanted to support them but also I was afraid. So I suffered so much of that inner conflict. Then I began to devote myself to *jihad*. First of all I began to recite the Quran. I began to read, to study, the rules how to recite the Quran. Then I began to change my behavior. I got rid of my habits, such as playing dominos and cards. I learned that as a Muslim, according to Islamic heritage, welfare should be distributed equally. For example, I am against America to have very rich people and very poor people. If they would follow the heritage of Islam, for example, they would divide all the wealth in a manner to be equal between the peoples.

As indicated, some Bosnian youth deduced that war was upon them by way of religious garb or by the splitting into religious groupings. Otherwise, to the degree that religion was conceived, it was vexing. Jasmin was resentful and in the end made his own analogy to the Palestinian conflict:

> The only thing that I regret about everything is the young people that died—really for nothing: for nationality, for religion. I don't understand how somebody could kill somebody because of their religion or nation. I don't know. I am filled with bitterness because of everything. I never believed that this can happen here in this state . . . we have Serbian, Croats, and Muslims, we have also other nations here: Hungarians, Czechs, Gypsies. What if they were all fighting for their rights? My friends were saying that this will not last for a long time. It was just religious problems. They will solve it somehow. But they didn't. I don't know what I am bitter at. I don't know. We have a lot of religious people here and I am not one of them. They believe it's the act of God. I don't believe that it is an act of God. I think it is human acts. Muslims are victims . . . we are the biggest victims as the Palestinians in Israel are . . . Palestinians are fighting against Israel for fifty years and they haven't achieved anything. At least we achieved something. At least we have our country. They don't even have a state. Israelis are of my opinion the same as Serbs were here. I am not a nationalistic man, but I am not defending Palestinians because of their nations but because of their beliefs that this is their country.

Identity-Relevance of Meaning

The identity-relevance of these systems of meaning lies in the substance they provide for identity. In contrast to much past work that has concentrated on the process of identity formation (i.e., attributing to adolescents the task of exploring available identities, selecting from among them, and committing to one of them), systems of meaning provide information that can be used to understand and define oneself within events or experiences with which one is confronted. Although these two elements of identity formation are likely not mutually exclusive (i.e., at some level of consciousness adolescents surely evaluate and commit to the identity or identities that are defined by the meaning systems provided them), they differ fundamentally in process and implications for the nature of adolescent experience. The more commonly discussed exploration/commitment scenario primarily describes an intrapsychic process over which the adolescent has directive control as well as responsibility for effective resolution. In contrast, meaning-driven identity is sourced in the (multidimensional) context and implies that adolescents not only act but become to some degree that which their contexts permit, facilitate, or encourage. Unlike in many stable, relatively prosperous, developed cultures where a menu of potential identities is available for adolescents' selection, in much of the world the prevailing contexts (e.g., cultural, social, political, ethnic) are both commanding and not highly diversified in defining available or acceptable identities.

Indeed, war environments might be particularly powerful in determining the level at which adolescent identity might be formed. Classic identity theories have always emphasized multiple identity types (e.g., personal, collective, social), but how these levels might be contingent or feasible and facilitated by prevailing context has not been clearly articulated. The data analyzed for this chapter suggest that—at least in war conditions—it may not be easy, desirable, or even possible to favor or separate domains of identity. In both cases, the threat or urgency of the conflict was so profound as to result (whether by active decision or by default response—see following discussion for an elaboration) in a concentration on group identity. Thus, regardless of however active or conscious the processes of individual identity may or may not be in adolescents of various cultures, political conflict can clearly intercede to derail or render it subordinate to the group. For Bosnians, their group membership (as Muslims) was forced on them as the cardinal currency of their (despised) identity. For Palestinians, allegiance to and cohesion with a clearly identified, historically fueled, sociopolitical legacy easily trumped concern with self.

Dynamic Identity versus Identity-by-Default

Finally, there is one identity-relevant element that was very apparent in the narratives and clearly amplified the dynamic nature of a meaning-sourced identity. This is the degree to which youth had opportunity to express—or live—the identity or identities imparted from their systems of meaning.

Dynamic Identity

The value of youth involvement in social issues and affairs has been emphasized in much and varying work, concluding that such active involvement can result variably in cultural consolidation, character development, efficacy, and so on.[6] In the Palestinian youth narratives, the elucidation of identity-relevant meaning was very often accompanied by recitations of acting that identity, and that pairing appeared to make for a dynamic, efficacious identity. Hussam noted, for example:

> Before the Intifada we were children. The only thing we thought about was football. Sometimes we studied, or watched TV, or did many things which were not so important. But during our actions or involvement in the Intifada, we began to think in another way. We began to have a role in our society. We changed the way people thought. We become leaders when we were children, so we began to think that we had a great role to perform. . . . By this we achieved self-satisfaction, self-assertion.

Mahmoud: "I struggled and I was active and I was in prison and I was injured two times. It might be abnormal in other countries, but for me, I am honored and I do not regret." Wajdi: "Our people had strong determination and courage because we hoped to achieve [our] rights. When I realized that my father and my grandmother lost their country, we hoped . . . to liberate our country. . . . We believed in many things, in principles, in moral principles." Khalil recalled, "My emotions took me. Where? I didn't know. I just wanted to fight and help end our suffering. We wanted this occupation to end. I can't describe, believe me, I just can't describe what a wonderful feeling it was to share with my people in the struggle against the occupation." Adel: "What I learned is that we as Palestinians have our voice. We can make people listen to us in the world. We can do many things as a result now, we can see what we have done. We lived as a big family, and we shared in many things. We made things easy for us, but it was difficult. There were hard circumstances around us and we learned how to ignore the fear that was surrounding us."

Identity by Default

For the Bosnian youth, not only were the potential meaning systems empty, there was also essentially no opportunity to engage in the conflict to discover or defend self through action. Critical components of identity had to be deduced by youth from circumstantial evidence—identities were formed by default, as it were.

AMAR: When you wake up and when you see one day that some people are gone. First you look around for neighbors. And you were thirteen years old. You go to see a friend and he is not there, nobody is there. They were always there. You have to, I don't know, to think about. You're so young . . . that sucks this first memory.

BRIAN: Where did these friends and neighbors go?

AMAR: I don't know where they went. But I found out that it is like this. That they are fighting because I am like a Muslim; I am Muslim and they were Serbs and they went away.

Adisa was equally as oblivious to her ethnic identity: "Before, I didn't know what being Muslim Serbian was, because we weren't religious people. I didn't know what word *Muslim* means until 1994, when they said to me, I have one friend and she said, maybe one month before the war, she said to me, 'I am Serb, we will kill the Muslims.' I didn't know what he was talking about." Ismir elaborated on how the defaulted identity has shaped him:

> Before the war, I didn't know the meaning of the word *Muslim, Croatian, Croat* . . . But now I know that Serbs attacked us and they tried to kill us, my people . . . so I am feeling a little bit different than maybe before the war. If someone told me that so-and-so was a Serb before the war, I would say, "Who is that? Who is that guy?" because I didn't know . . . but now I am feeling a little bit different when someone tells me about the Serbs and the Serbian people because I know they tried to kill and do those nasty things to us.

Senka captured the defenselessness, dislocation, and disconnection when describing her experience living in a settlement near the Sarajevo airport:

> In the morning around five o'clock, there was an intensive shooting around the buildings. There was about five people that were actually guarding the half of the street, this was like territorial defense, this is just one part of this building defense. And then we tried to defend from the aggressor. They couldn't defend the place and the soldiers went around the building and they were saying to the people that they should go away because the Chetniks are entering into the settlement. We were all sleeping in the apartment that we thought was more protected from the rest of the apartments that were facing the airport. So my mother entered and she woke us up and she said that we should go down to the basement. This was their plan that we should go to the basement in order to hide so that we can avoid Chetniks who had imprisoned my parents and put us in this tent concentration camp outside of Sarajevo. And I can say that this was very memorable for us, for one month I wasn't aware of what happened with my parents. I felt like an orphan because I couldn't hear anything or see anything when it comes to my parents so that with one word I felt miserable because I was twelve years old and then I felt that I didn't have any hands to protect me.

Alma (as quoted in Chapter 11) summed up the identity effect of the empty meaning: "My Serbian classmates, kids that I grew up with were carrying weapons. In one day they became complete strangers. In some ways I became a stranger to myself, too. My life and the lives of my family members were in danger because of our names and religion. I never knew those things mattered, which means that I did not know many things about my self too. That is what made me a stranger to my self."

Conclusion

This chapter concentrates on the interview data from a multistage project on adolescents and political violence. It is not common to have so much detailed and comparative information from young persons involved in war, and hopefully, the chapter thereby contributes meaningfully to understanding the very serious issues of both political conflict and youth functioning within it. Some commentary on this substantive contribution is offered immediately, followed by some brief comments on the evolution of the overall research project, the description of which was another intended contribution.

Most fundamentally, the data instruct on the complexity of youth functioning in extreme circumstances. That is, although on the surface it is easy and appropriate to evaluate war as a plaguing and destructive experience, it is nevertheless too simplistic to conclude that youth response to it is similarly straightforward or unambiguous (and that by extension, applied efforts to support youth in war zones can be uniform). On the contrary, the experiences of the two groups of youth studied in this project illustrate highly varying experiences with their respective political conflicts. Elsewhere (Barber, 2008), I have used other data from these youths' contemporaries to describe the literal differences in the structure, strategy, and types of political violence that characterized the political conflicts the two groups were exposed to (i.e., significantly more passive experience with death and destruction for the Bosnians and significantly more experience with proximal conflict, active involvement, and humiliating and harsh personal treatment for the Palestinian youth), but the interview data presented here reveal similarly demonstrable differences in the psychological processing of the conflicts by the two groups of youth.

Data from the youth indicate that they are anything but psychologically passive or ineffectual processors of complex and painful circumstances, and also that potentially determinative in the nature of their response is the explanatory information that is or is not available to them as they confront and manage the experiences of war. Thus, it was manifestly evident in the narratives of both groups that they understood that the events surrounding them were critical and urgent and that they wanted to place themselves constructively in those profound contexts. At the same time, it was obvious that their evaluation of that predominant context—and their decisions or ability to respond to it—fed or wanted to feed on what the conflict meant about their own lives as members of society.

I have suggested that this search for meaning appears different than the classically characterized quest for meaning as a self-focused, post-trauma coping process. Rather, the meaning that was so salient to these youth was embodied by contemporaneous information that would explain the fact, purpose, logic, and legitimacy of the conflict itself (and by extension, the relative value and ability to deal with its traumas). The presence or absence of this explication seemed critically relevant to how youth adapted to the wars that beset their regions. It seemed that precisely the lack of this explanatory information—in any of the variety of cultural, political, historical, or religious systems that it could have been packaged—was what frightened, embittered, and traumatized the Bosnian youth. In contrast, it appeared to be just this type (and depth and breadth) of meaning, clearly understood and endorsed by the Palestinian youth, that superseded their suffering.

Beyond simply endorsing the long-acknowledged but often too thinly studied role of context in individual functioning (i.e., as opposed or in addition to the intrapsychic explanations), the narratives of these youths have illustrated that the content of the context might be as critical as the context itself. Thus, for example, as illustrated throughout this volume, it does not seem sufficient to acknowledge or test for the effects of contextual experiences by chronicling amounts or degrees of exposure (in this case to political violence); rather, it is also necessary to understand to what degree and how youth attribute meaning to those contextual moments. This insight into the relative role of context in shaping individual development has seemed particularly relevant for the study of youth identity development. Thus, at one level, it is an endorsement of the importance of acknowledging the external (to self) components of identity (e.g., social, cultural, collective) that have always informed main theories of identity. Yet these data hint further that these external forces, at least in the case of war, can be commanding in shaping identity by literally defining, delimiting, or prioritizing identity options. The fact and intent of the war defined Bosnian youth for themselves—as part of a (hated) group. Palestinian youth needed no self-definition, but their war surely prioritized and provided opportunities to actualize their highly prized and marginalized group identity.

As useful as it is to know that youth response to political violence can be largely contingent on information-enriched cognitive processes, such as the identity-relevant meanings systems discussed here, it alerts us to at least two areas of further complexity. The first flows from the commanding role of context in shaping identity. If identities have been substantially shaped because of and in the context of war, then surely the postwar conditions will be also be critical—in either sustaining or frustrating that identity. This emphasizes the need for longer term assessments of the prevailing contexts in which youth continue to live both in determining the degree to which they generally offer key opportunities (e.g., economic, educational) but more specifically if and how they inform on a youth's war-won sense of self and identity. Thus, in determining the real effects of political conflict on Bosnian youth, it would be critical to assess if and how the postwar environment has enabled them to erase or at least counter the war-induced stigma of being part of a hated group. Given the protracted continuance of their conflict, assessments of longer term Palestinian youth well-being would need to determine if and how they have accommodated the failure of their efforts to facilitate a tangible national identity and freedom from perceived oppression (see West, 2004, and Summerfield, 1998, for the relevance of postconflict governmental failures to young men's and women's evaluations of the utility of their conflict efforts).

The second realm of complexity raised by the influence of identity-relevant meanings systems lies in the content of the meaning itself. War is, by definition, laden with ideology (political, ethnic, moral, etc.). The same conflicting values that often lead to and maintain war characterize divergences in judging the relative propriety of ideological positions. Thus, for some, violence of any kind is morally unacceptable; for others, violence, though undesirable, is justified if other attempts to rectify inequities have failed; for still others, violence is an elected and preferred strategy to accomplish ideological objectives. This means that there will probably always be debate and discomfort with crediting the identity-shaping power of ideology depending on the values used to appraise its morality and worthiness. The matter becomes more intense and intricate when considering children and youth, given the additional value held by many that these groups require special protection because of their presumed vulnerability and dependence (see discussion in Chapter 1).

If nothing else, however, what these groups of youth have offered us through the narratives of their conflict experiences is the substantially valuable awareness that they are highly capable of confronting and processing demanding sociopolitical and violent realities, and—whether one's goal is to reinforce or dissuade their further experiences—that crediting the meaning they attach to their experiences is critical in understanding who they have become as a function of their experiences.

Finally, some closing comments about the process of the research are in order. The reader will notice that the narrative of the evolving stages of the APVP that was presented in the first part of this chapter did not link to the variety of relevant material on methodologies of social-psychological inquiry. This was done intentionally to preserve the development of the research and the researcher. That is, I was not trained in cross-cultural psychology, cultural psychology, or anthropology, and to have grounded the research narrative in those disciplines' rich and relevant methodologies would mislead readers that they were elected a priori as the proper methods to pursue for the various stages of the project. They were not; rather, steps evolved as seemed naturally appropriate and requisite to deal with the new awareness that the progressive engagement with the youth dictated.

It happens, nevertheless, that that the APVP does illustrate well (albeit not purely so) some important, well-articulated principles of the study of individuals in different cultures. First, although useful in validating some patterns of interaction, the initial survey of Palestinian families that began the project (characteristic of an approach from cross-cultural psychology of transporting and testing concepts and measures from one culture to the next; e.g., Berry, Poortinga, Segall, & Dasen, 1992; Greenfield, 1997), was not adequate in revealing essential aspects of Palestinian youth experience or the culture of conflict. Second, the immersion phase and interview components of the APVP were consistent with approaches recommended by cultural psychology and anthropology that were essential in discovering what to ask and what to know (Greenfield, 1997; Schegloff, 1993, as interpreted by Greenfield, 1997). These approaches included the openness to understanding the youths' culture through ethnography, participant observation, and interview (e.g., see Greenfield, 1997, for a thorough review of empirical methods of studying cultures) and reducing interviewer bias by doing so for long periods of time and by interacting with everyday people (e.g., Miles & Huberman, 1994; Wassmann & Dasen, 1994). Finally, this engagement with the youth and their culture led to the ability to construct much more culturally informed and ecologically valid surveys (i.e., illustrating the synergistic inclusion of both quantitative and qualitative approaches; Greenfield, 1997; Jahoda & Krewer, 1997).

Above all, the lesson of this unplanned, evolving sequence of inquiry methods—and here this closing methodological commentary unites with the substantive summary—is the reality of culture and the requirement to engage it to understand it and its members. Though there are surely commonalities in human experience generally, and within wars and political conflicts specifically, it is clear that political conflicts have their own cultures and that youth embody and help create those cultures (in part by absorbing and acting the meaning that relevant systems do or do not provide them), the richness and intricacy of which cannot be adequately learned without respecting and listening to the youth who live them.

Acknowledgments   Sincere appreciation is expressed to Jim Youniss and Janis Whitlock for very helpful comments on this chapter.

Notes

1. Work on the APVP has been supported by funds from the U.S. Social Science Research Council, the Rockefeller Foundation Bellagio Italy Study Center, the Jerusalem Fund, the United States Institute of Peace, the BYU Jerusalem Center for Near Eastern Studies, the BYU Kennedy Center for International Studies, and the BYU College of Family, Home, and Social Sciences.

2. See, for example, the broader movement in anthropology, psychology, sociology, and, most recently, clinical psychology and trauma studies to focus on the positive features of human development (e.g., wellness, self-actualization, maturity, full functioning, and individuation) (e.g., Buhler, 1935; Hobfoll et al., 2007; Jung, 1933; Layne, Warren, Watson, & Shalev, 2007; Layne et al., 2008; Maslow, 1968; Rogers, 1961; Seligman, Steen, Park, & Peterson, 2005; Snyder & Lopez, 2002; see Ryff & Keyes, 1995, for a review), particularly in demanding environments, including, for example, social and (parental) mental health adversities against which children's "resilience" is tested (e.g., Masten, 2001; Masten & Coatsworth, 1998; Rutter, 1995, 1999); environmental stress and demands in the face of which individual's "hardiness" or "efficacy" is monitored (e.g., Antonovsky, 1979); workplace burnout against which employees' "fortitude" or "strength" is assessed (e.g., Strumpfer, 2003); "resilience" in the face of severe personal grief or stress (e.g., Bonanno, 2004; Folkman, 1997); and trauma, counter to which "post-traumatic growth" is assessed (e.g., Calhoun & Tedeschi, 2006; Tedeschi & Calhoun, 1995). See Almedom (2005) for a more detailed review of such work.

3. As Molden and Dweck (2006) have recently reviewed, philosophers, scientists, and lay people have historically tried to make sense of the world via a search for intrinsic meaning. Indeed, so fundamental is this search for meaning that many scholars have concluded that humans are "meaning-making creatures" (e.g., Raeff, 2006). This search to make sense out of experience, discover life's purpose, and find one's place in the world is viewed as an essential feature of human nature that is central to psychological well-being (Vignoles, Regalia, Manzi, Golledge, & Scabini, 2006). As these authors note, meaning is a critical element to a number of social and identity theories (Vignoles et al., 2006). Others note its centrality to existential theories (e.g., Antonovsky, 1979; Frankl, 1984; Ryff & Keyes, 1995; see Strumpfer,

2003, for a review). There is enough thinking on the topic, in fact, to devote entire volumes (e.g., Frankl, 1984; Polanyi & Prosch, 1975) and handbook chapters (e.g., Baumeister & Vohs, 2002; Mash & Barkley, 1996) to its explication and to assert that understanding it is a primary goal of psychological sciences (Molden & Dweck, 2006). As for youth, classic Western characterizations of adolescence (e.g., Erikson, 1968) clearly invoke meaning in young person's attempts to establish personal and social identities. This has been emphasized in the recent work on youth civic involvement and activism (e.g., Sherrod, 2005; Yates & Youniss, 1999; Youniss & Yates, 1997) and in the growing work on youth and conflict. Some sociologists have bemoaned the absence of attention to the role of ideas and beliefs in assessments of social movement participation in general (e.g., Sherkat & Blocker, 1997).

4. More specifically, there are three basic facets of the traditional conceptualization of meaning that, although undoubtedly applicable to human experience broadly (at some level and/or under certain circumstances), differ importantly from the meaning invoked in the interviews with these youth from conflict zones: (1) the locus of the meaning, that is, occurring within or outside of self; (2) its timing, that is, post-trauma versus pre- or during difficulty; and (3) the need to search for it, as opposed to it being present or readily available in individual or social consciousness of those enduring difficult circumstances.

As to the locus of the meaning, the classic rendition of meaning appears to be essentially *egocentric* to the extent that it is conceptualized as a personal, psychological trait, or "dispositional orientation" that serves the purpose of personal well-being, self-integrity, or survival (Antonovsky, 1987, p. xvi). As such, it is consistent broadly with conceptions of a fundamental, human "meaning motive" (Vignoles et al., 2006) or need that is thought to be basic to coping and identity enhancement (see Vignoles et al., 2006, for a review of relevant material and theories).

As to the timing of the meaning sought or produced, the classic work has focused on identifying the role of meaning in assisting individuals to adapt in response to events or circumstances. Indeed, most of the attention to meaning has been to evaluate its role in the adaptation to difficulty, which includes workplace burnout (e.g., Strumpfer, 2003), illness (e.g., Folkman, 1997), stress of various kinds (e.g., Antonovsky, 1987; Rutter, 1985, 1999), bereavement (e.g., Bonanno, 2004), and political crisis (e.g., Almedom, 2005), among other forms. This might be called "post-trauma, adaptive meaning making."

One of the more elaborated conceptual frames that illustrates these locus and timing features of classic meaning is that of Antonovsky (1987), who conceptualized "generalized resistance resources" (e.g., money, ego strength, cultural stability, social supports) as phenomena that are "effective in combating a wide variety of stressors" (by making sense of them) as part of a "global orientation [that] . . . expresses the extent to which one has a pervasive, enduring though dynamic, feeling of confidence that one's internal and external environments are predictable and that there is a high probability that things will work out as well as can reasonably be expected" (pp. xii–xiii). More specifically, Antonovsky's (1987) "sense of coherence" construct (a coping resource made up of components of "comprehensibility," "manageability," and "meaningfulness") (pp. 258–59) was conceptualized as a "stable, enduring, and generalized orientation to one's world that characterizes a person throughout adulthood" (pp. 182–85) that is crucial in making "order out of chaos" and coping with the "ubiquitous stressors of living" (pp. 163–64).

The third feature of traditional meaning—the search for it—flows from its post-trauma timing. Essentially, the bulk of the work echoes Frankl's (1984) classic endorsement of the survival value of meaning and the related and widely explored construct of coping with stress (e.g., Compas, Malcarne, & Banez, 1992; Lazarus & Folkman, 1984; Mash & Barkley, 1996). It is also consistent with the attention paid in political violence circles (e.g., Rafman,

2004; Waysman, Schwarzwald, & Solomon, 2001) to psychosocial transformations *after* crisis (Almedom, 2005).

5. In their historical overview of meaning, Molden and Dweck (2006) noted that from early on psychology has attempted to capture the idea that "people structure their environments using cognitive or affective systems of meaning" (p. 192). Compatible concepts have emerged in stress research, both in terms of coping with stress and the social support that might mitigate it. Thus, as examples, Lazarus and Folkman (1984) write of "beliefs" as "preexisting notions about reality which serves as a perceptual lens" (p. 63); Aspinwall and Taylor (1977) describe "proactive coping" as "the accumulation of resources and the acquisition of skills that are not designed to address any particular stressor but to prepare in general, given the recognition that stressors do occur" (p. 417); and Jacobson (1986) defines "cognitive support" as "information, knowledge, and/or advice that helps the individual to understand his or her world and to adjust to changes within it" (p. 252). Although all of these references still raise the egocentric, stress-response (or preparation for response to stress) features of meaning, they also indicate the relevance of existing collections of information that might be used in determining one's behavior.

   "Meaning system" is itself an explicitly identified construct that is characterized as containing "descriptive beliefs as well as motivational or prescriptive beliefs" that have "descriptive postulates" concerned with beliefs about self and the nature of the world and their interrelations. Meaning systems can be both individual (i.e., "idiosyncratic") and "collective" (Silberman, 2005, p. 645), whereby the system contains a shared reality that in some instances can be so vital as to actually define a group's essence (Bar-Tal, 2000).

6. Involvement is seen to lead to a sense of cultural consolidation (Erikson, 1968), connecting the actor to the broader polity and thereby exposing him or her to social conditions and concerns, political and moral structures, and others' perspectives, leading to character and identity development through facilitating potency (Flanagan & Syvertsen, 2005; McClellan et al., 1997; Yates & Youniss, 1999; Youniss & Yates, 1997). The resulting sense of efficacy is one of "four needs of meaning" that Baumeister and Vohs (2002, pp. 610–11) have identified (along with purpose, values, and self-worth). At the political level, McAdam (1989) has written of "effective agency" (p. 15) and political action accompanied by a sense of generational potency and being involved in historic moments, and several scholars have noted the value of youth making history through their involvement (e.g., Braungart, 1984; Levine, 1993; McAdam, 1989; Youniss & Yates, 1997).

   Daiute (2006) reviews work supporting concepts of psychosocial interdependence stemming from youth engagement and negotiation with states or multinational businesses in Africa and elsewhere. Whyte (1983) has written of the identity-consolidating role of enacting cultural/political traditions in the Northern Ireland conflict, as have several authors in describing the specific modes of youth political involvement in various other conflicts (e.g., Bornemann et al., 1994; also Chapters 5 and 10). Freedman (Freedman & Abazovic, 2006; Freedman & Ball, 2004) builds on Bakhtin's concept of "ideological becoming" in suggesting that effects on youth of political violence can be meaningfully understood to the degree that the involvement assimilates "authoritative discourse" (i.e., past, acknowledged cultural, political, religious, authority) and "internally persuasive discourse" (i.e., of peers and everyday citizens). The assimilation of these social and personal meanings contribute to the whole "ideological self." Youniss and Yates (1997) noted the same synergistic benefit of seeing individual agency coupled with that of previous generations, and thus, "By partaking in ideological positions that have historical legitimacy, youth can come to share in the collective meanings that ground identity in a truly social way" (p. 156). See also Janoff-Bulman and Frantz, 1997, as cited in Rafman, 2004, for dual levels of meaning.

References

Almedom, A. M. (2004). Factors that mitigate war-induced anxiety and mental distress. *Journal of Biosocial Science, 36,* 445–461.

Almedom, A. M. (2005). Resilience, hardiness, sense of coherence, and posttraumatic growth: All paths leading to the "light at the end of the tunnel"? *Journal of Loss and Trauma, 10,* 253–265.

Annan, J., Blattman, C., & Horton, R. (2006). The state of youth and youth protection in Northern Uganda: Findings from the Survey of War Affected youth (SWAY). A report for UNICEF Uganda. Available at www.sway-uganda.org.

Annan, J., Blattman, C., Carlson, K., & Mazurana, D. (2008). The state of female youth in Northern Uganda: findings from the Survey of War Affected Youth (SWAY). A report for UNICEF Uganda. Available at www.sway-uganda.org.

Antonovsky, A. (1987). *Unraveling the mystery of health: How people manage stress and stay well.* San Francisco: Jossey-Bass.

Aspinwall, L., & Taylor, S. (1997). A stitch in time: Self-regulation and proactive coping. *Psychological Bulletin, 121,* 417–436.

Barber, B. K. (1999a). Political violence, family relations, and Palestinian youth functioning. *Journal of Adolescent Research, 14,* 206–230.

Barber, B. K. (1999b). "Youth experience in the Palestinian Intifada: Intensity, complexity, paradox, and competence." In M. Yates and J. Youniss (Eds.), *Roots of Civic Identity: International perspectives on community service and activism in youth.* New York: Cambridge University Press.

Barber, B. K. (2001). Political violence, social integration, and youth functioning: Palestinian youth from the Intifada. *Journal of Community Psychology, 29,* 259–280.

Barber, B. K. (2008). Contrasting portraits of war: Youths' varied experiences with political violence in Bosnia and Palestine. *International Journal of Behavioral Development, 32*(4), 294–305.

Barber, B. K. (in press). *One heart, so many stones: The story of Palestinian Youth.* New York: Palgrave/Macmillan.

Barber, B. K., & Olsen, J. A. (2006). Adolescents' willingness to engage in political conflict: Lessons from the Gaza Strip. In J. Victoroff (Ed.), *Tangled roots: Social and psychological factors in the genesis of terrorism* (pp. 203–226). Amsterdam: IOS Press.

Barber, B. K., Schluterman, J. M., Denny, E. S., & McCouch, R. M. (2005). Adolescents and political violence. In M. Fitzduff & C. Stout (Eds.), *The psychology of resolving global conflicts: From war to peace. Volume 2: Group and social factors.* Westport, CT: Praeger.

Bar-Tal, D. (2000). *Shared beliefs in society: Social psychological analysis.* Thousand Oaks, CA: Sage.

Baumeister, R. F. (1991). *Escaping the self: Alcoholism, spirituality, masochism, and other flights from the burden of selfhood.* New York: Basic Books.

Baumeister, R. F., & Vohs, K. D. (2002). The pursuit of meaningfulness in life. In C. R. Snyder & S. J. Lopez (Eds.), *Handbook of positive psychology.* New York: Oxford University Press.

Berry, J. W., Poortinga, Y. H., Segall, M. H., & Dasen, P. R. (1992). *Cross-cultural psychology: Research and applications.* Cambridge: Cambridge University Press.

Blattman, C., & Annan, J. (2007). The consequences of child soldiering. HiCN Working Paper, 22.

Bolton, P., Neugebauer, R., & Ndogono, L. (2002). Prevalence of depression in rural Rwanda based on symptom and functional criteria. *Journal of Nervous and Mental Disorders, 190,* 631–637.

Bolton, P. & Trang, A. (2002). An alternative approach to cross-cultural function assessment. *Social Psychiatry and Psychiatric Epidemiology, 37,* 537–543.

Bonanno, G. A. (2004). Loss, trauma, and human resilience: Have we underestimated the human capacity to thrive after extremely aversive events? *American Psychologist, 59,* 20–28.

Bornemann, T., Ekbald, S., Marsella, A. J., et al. (1994). Trauma and violence among refugee children." In *Amidst peril and pain* (p. 248). Washington, DC: American Psychological Association.

Boyden, J. (2003). Children under fire: Challenging assumptions about children's resilience. *Children, Youth and Environments, 13*(1). Available from http://www.colorado.edu/jour nals/cye/13_1/index.htm.

Braungart, R. C. (1984). Historical generations and youth movements: A theoretical perspective. In L. Kriesberg (Series Ed.) & R. Ratcliff (Vol. Ed.), *Research in social movements, conflict and change* (vol. 6, pp. 95–141). Greenwich, CT: JAI Press.

Buhler, C. (1935). The curve of life as studied in biographies. *Journal of Applied Psychology, 19,* 405–409.

Cairns, E. (1987). *Caught in the crossfire: Children and the Northern Ireland conflict.* New York: Syracuse University Press.

Cairns, E., & Darby, J. (1998). The conflict in Northern Ireland: Causes, consequences, and controls. *American Psychologist, 53,* 754–760.

Cairns, E., & Dawes, A. (1996). Children: Ethnic and political violence—a commentary. *Child Development, 67,* 129–139.

Calhoun, L. G., & Tedeschi, R. G. (2006). *Handbook of posttraumatic growth: Research & practice.* Mahwah, NJ: Erlbaum.

Chandler, M. J., Lalonde, C. E., Sokol, B. W., & Hallett, D. (2003). Personal persistence, identity development, and suicide: A study of Native and non-Native North American adolescents. *Monographs of the Society for Research in Child Development, 68*(2), 1–130.

Compas, B., Malcarne, V. L., & Banez, G. R. (1992). Coping with psychosocial stress: A developmental perspective. In B. N. Carpenter (Ed.), *Personal coping: Theory, research, and application* (pp. 47–63). Westport, CT: Praeger/Greenwood.

Daiute, C. (2006). General introduction: The problem of society in youth conflict. In C. Daiute, Z. F. Beykont, C. Higson-Smith, & L. Nucci (Eds.), *International perspectives on youth conflict and development* (pp. 3–22). New York: Oxford University Press.

Das, V., Kleinman, A., Lock, M., Ramphele, M., and Reynolds, P. (Eds.) (2001). *Remaking a world: Violence, social suffering and recovery.* Berkeley and Los Angeles: University of California Press.

Elbedour, S., Bensel, R., & Maruyama, G. (1993). Children at risk: Psychological coping with war and conflict in the Middle East. *International Journal of Mental Health, 22*(3), 33–52.

Erikson, E. E. (1968). *Identity: Youth and crisis.* New York: Norton.

Folkman, S. (1997). Positive psychological states and coping with severe stress. *Social Science & Medicine, 45,* 1207–1221.

Flanagan, C., & Syvertsen, A. K. (2005). Youth as a social construct and social actor. In L. R. Sherrod, C. A. Flanagan, & R. Kassimir (Eds.), *Youth activism: An international encyclopedia. Volume 1.* Westport, CT: Greenwood Press.

Frankl, V. (1984). *Man's Search for Meaning* (3rd ed.). New York: Touchstone.

Freedman, S. W., & Abazovic, D. (2006). Growing up during the Balkan wars of the 1990s. In C. Daiute, Z. Beykont, C. Higson-Smith, & L. Nucci (Eds.), *International perspectives on youth conflict and development.* New York: Oxford University Press.

Freedman, S. W., & Ball, A. F. (2004). Ideological becoming Bakhtinian concepts to guide the study of language, literacy, and learning. In A. F. Ball & S. W. Freedman (Eds.), *Bakhtinian perspectives on language, literacy, and learning* (pp. 3–33). New York: Cambridge University Press.

Fronk, C., Huntington, R. L., & Chadwick, B. A. (1999). Expectations for traditional family roles: Palestinian adolescents in the West Bank and Gaza. *Sex Roles, 41,* 705–735.

Garbarino, J., & Kostelny, K. (1996). The effects of political violence on Palestinian children's behavior problems: A risk accumulation model. *Child Development, 67,* 33–45.

Greenfield, P. M. (1997). Culture as process: Empirical methods for cultural psychology. In J. Pandey, J. W. Berry, Y. H. Poortinga (Eds.), *Handbook of cross-cultural psychology, Vol. 1: Theory and method* (2nd ed., pp. 301–346). Needham Heights, MA: Allyn & Bacon.

Hart, J. (2004). Beyond struggle and aid: Children's identities in a Palestinian refugee camp in Jordan. In J. Boyden & J. de Berry (Eds.), *Children and youth on the front line: Ethnography, armed conflict and displacement* (pp. 167–188). Oxford: Berghan Books.

Hass, A. (1999). *Drinking the sea at Gaza: Days and nights in a land under siege.* New York: Owl Books.

Hobfoll, S. E., Hall, B. J., Canetti-Nisim, D., Galea, S., Johnson, R. J., & Palmieri, P. A. (2007). Refining our understanding of traumatic growth in the face of terrorism: Moving from meaning cognitions to doing what is meaningful. *Applied Psychology: An International Review, 56,* 345–366.

Huntington, R., Fronk, C., & Chadwick, B. A. (2001). Family roles of contemporary Palestinian women. *Journal of Comparative Family Studies, 32,* 1–19.

Jacobson, D. E. (1986). Types and timing of social support. *Journal of Health and Social Behavior, 27,* 250–264.

Jahoda, G., & Krewer, B. (1997). History of cross-cultural and cultural psychology. In J. W. Berry, Y. H. Poortinga, & J. Pandley (Eds.), *Handbook of cross-cultural psychology: Vol. 1. Theory and method* (2nd ed., pp. 1–42). Needham Heights, MA: Allyn & Bacon.

Janoff-Bulman, R., & Frantz, C. M. (1997). The impact of trauma on meaning: From meaningless world to meaningful life. In M. J. Power & C. R. Brewin (Eds.), *The transformation of meaning in psychological therapies: Integrating theory and practice* (pp. 91–106). Sussex, UK: Wiley.

Jones, L. (2002). Adolescent understandings of political violence and psychological well-being: A qualitative study from Bosnia Herzegovina. *Social Science & Medicine, 5,* 1351–1371.

Jones, L. (2004). *Then they started shooting.* Cambridge, MA: Harvard University Press.

Jones, L., & Kafetsios, K. (2005). Exposure to political violence and psychological well-being in Bosnian adolescents: A mixed method approach. *Clinical Child Psychology and Psychiatry, 10,* 157–176.

Jung, C. G. (1933). *Modern man in search of a soul* (W. S. Dell & C. F. Baynes, Trans.). New York: Hartcourt, Brace & World.

Kerestes, G. (2006). Children's aggressive and prosocial behavior in relation to war exposure: Testing the role of perceived parenting and child's gender. *International Journal of Behavioral Development, 30,* 227–239.

Khalidi, R. (1997). *Palestinian identity: The construction of modern national consciousness.* Chicago: University of Chicago Press.

Layne, C. M., Beck, C. J., Rimmasch, H., Southwick, J. S., Moreno, M. A., & Hobfoll, S. E. (2008). Promoting "resilient" posttraumatic adjustment in childhood and beyond: Unpacking life events, adjustment trajectories, resources, and interventions. In D. Brom, R. Pat-Horenczyk, & J. Ford (Eds.), *Treating traumatized children: Risk, resilience, and recovery.* New York: Routledge.

Layne, C. M., Warren, J., Watson, P., & Shalev, A. (2007). Risk, vulnerability, resistance, and resilience: Towards an integrative model of posttraumatic adaptation. In M. J. Friedman, T. M. Kean, & P. A. Resick (Eds.), *PTSD: Science & practice—a comprehensive handbook* (pp. 497–520). New York: Guilford Press.

Lazarus, R. S., & Folkman, S. (1984). *Stress appraisal and coping.* New York: Springer.

Levine, E. (1993). *Freedom's children.* New York: Putnam's.

Marcia, J. E. (1994). The empirical study of ego identity. In H. A. Bosma, T. L. G. Graafsma, H. D. Grotevant, & D. J. DeLeviata (Eds.), *Identity and development.* Newbury Park, CA: Sage.

Marks, M. (2001). *Young warriors: Youth politics, identity and violence in South Africa.* South Africa: Witwatersrand University Press.

Mash, E. J., & Barkley, R. A. (Eds.). (1996). *Child psychopathology.* New York: Guilford Press.

Maslow, A. H. (1968). *Toward a psychology of being* (2nd ed.). New York: Van Nostrand.

Masten, A. (2001). Ordinary magic: Resilience processes in development. *American Psychologist, 56*(3), 227–238.

Masten, A., & Coatsworth, J. D. (1998). The development of competence in favorable and unfavorable environments. Lessons from research on successful children. *American Psychologist, 53,* 205–220.

McAdam, D. (1989). The biographical consequences of activism. *American Sociological Review, 54,* 744–760.

McCouch, R. J. (2006). *Destruction and reconstruction in the aftermath of armed conflict: Assessing risk, resilience, and youth decision-making in post-war Bosnia.* PhD dissertation. Heller School for Social Policy and Management, Brandeis University.

McLellan, J., Yates, M., & Youniss, J. (1997). What we know about engendering civic identity. *American Behavioral Scientist, 40*(5): 619–630.

Miles, M., & Huberman, A. M. (1994). Drawing valid meaning from qualitative data: Toward a shared craft. *Educational Researcher, 13,* 20–30.

Molden, D. C., & Dweck, C. S. (2006). Finding "meaning" in psychology: A lay theories approach to self-regulation, social perception, and social development. *American Psychologist, 61,* 192–203.

Polanyi, M., & Prosch, H. (1975). *Meaning.* Chicago: University of Chicago Press.

Powell, S., Rosner, R., Butollo, W., Tedeschi, R. G., & Calhoun, L. G. (2003). Posttraumatic growth after war: A study with former refugees and displaced people in Sarajevo. *Journal of Clinical Psychology, 59,* 71–83.

Punamäki, R. (1996). Can ideological commitment protect children's psychosocial well-being in situations of political violence? *Child Development, 67,* 55–69.

Pupavac, V. (2002). Pathologizing populations and colonizing minds: International psychosocial programs in Kosovo. *Alternatives, 27,* 489–511.

Raeff, C. (2006). *Always separate, always connected: Independence and interdependence in cultural contexts of development.* Mahwah, NJ: Erlbaum.

Rafman, S. (2004). Where the political and the psychological meet: Moral disruption and children's understanding of war. *International Relations, 18,* 467–479.

Rogers, C. R. (1961). *On becoming a person.* Boston: Houghton Mifflin.

Rutter, M. (1985). Resilience in the face of adversity: protective factors and resistance to psychiatric disorder. *British Journal of Psychiatry, 147,* 598–611.

Rutter, M. (1999). Psychosocial adversity and child psychopathology. *British Journal of Psychiatry, 174,* 480–493.

Ryff, C. D., & Keyes, C.L.M. (1995). The structure of psychological well-being revisited. *Journal of Personality and Social Psychology, 69,* 719–727.

Schachter, E. P. (2004). Identity configurations: A new perspective on identity formation in contemporary society. *Journal of Personality, 72*(1), 167–200.

Schachter, E. P. (2005). Context and identity formation: A theoretical analysis and a case study. *Journal of Adolescent Research, 20*(3), 375–395.

Schegloff, E. (1993). Reflections on quantification in the study of conversation. *Research on Language and Social Interaction, 26,* 99–128.

Seligman, M. E. P., Steen, T. A., Park, N., & Peterson, C. (2005). Positive psychology progress: Empirical validation of interventions. *American Psychologist, 60,* 410–421.

Sherkat, D. F., & Blocker, T. J. (1997). Explaining the political and personal consequences of protest. *Social Forces, 75,* 1049–1070.

Sherrod, L. R. (2005). Youth activism and civic engagement. In L. R. Sherrod, C. A. Flanagan, & R. Kassimir (Eds.), *Youth activism: An international encyclopedia.* Westport, CT: Greenwood Press.

Silberman, I. (2005). Religion as a meaning system: Implications for the new millennium. *Journal of Social Issues, 61,* 641–663.

Snyder, C. R., & Lopez, S. J. (2002). *Handbook of positive psychology.* New York: Oxford University Press.

Straker, G. (1992). *Faces in the revolution—the psychological effects of violence on township youth in South Africa.* Athens: Ohio University Press.

Straker, G., Mendelsohn, M., Moosa, F., & Tudin, P. (1996). Violent political contexts and the emotional concerns of township youth. *Child Development, 67,* 46–54.

Strumpfer, D. J. W. (2003). Resilience and burnout: A stitch that could save nine. *South African Journal of Psychology, 33,* 69–79.

Summerfield, D. (1998). The social experience of war and some issues for the humanitarian field. In P. Bracken & C. Petty (Eds.), *Rethinking the trauma of war.* London: Free Association Books.

Summerfield, D. (1999). A critique of seven assumptions behind psychological trauma programmes in war-affected areas. *Social Science and Medicine, 48,* 1449–1462.

Summerfield, D. (2000). Conflict and health: War and mental health: A brief overview. *British Medical Journal, 321,* 232–235.

Tedeschi, R. G., & Calhoun, L. G. (1995). *Trauma and transformation: Growing in the aftermath of suffering.* Thousand Oaks, CA: Sage.

Tesfai, A. (2003). *Two weeks in the trenches.* Trenton, NJ: African World Press.

Vignoles, V. L., Regalia, C., Manzi, C., Golledge, J., & Scabini, E. (2006). Beyond self-esteem: Influence of multiple motives on identity construction. *Journal of Personality and Social Psychology, 90,* 308–333.

Wassmann, J., & Dasen, P. R. (1994). "Hot" and "cold": classification and sorting among Yupno of Papua New Guinea. *International Journal of Psychology, 29,* 19–38.

Waysman, M., Schwarzwald, J., & Solomon, Z. (2001). Hardiness: An examination of its relationship with positive and negative long term changes following trauma. *Journal of Traumatic Stress, 14,* 531–548.

West, H. G. (2004). Girls with guns: Narrating the experience of war of FRELIMO's "female detachment." In J. Boyden & J. de Berry (Eds.), *Children and youth on the front line: Ethnography, armed conflict and displacement* (pp. 105–129). Oxford: Berghan Books.

Wessells, M. (2006). *Child soldiers: From violence to protection.* Cambridge, MA: Harvard University Press.

Whyte, J. (1983). Everyday life for 11 and 12 year-olds in a troubled area of Belfast—do the troubles intrude? In J. Harbison (Ed.), *Children of the troubles.* Belfast: Stranmillis College.

Yates, M., & Youniss, J. (Eds.). (1999). *Roots of civic identity: International perspectives on community service and activism in youth.* New York: Cambridge University Press.

Youniss, J., & Yates, M. (1997). *Community service and social responsibility in youth.* Chicago: University of Chicago Press.

Part IV

CONCLUSION

Chapter 13

Moving Forward with Research on Adolescents and Political Violence

Brian K. Barber

The intent of this volume is to illustrate the complexity of the study of adolescents and political violence. In Chapter 1, I discussed many of the central issues of concern, virtually all of which had to do with either refining existing, basic findings or, more important, expanding the scope of inquiry to better capture the intricacy of youth experience with political conflict. The evaluation included coverage of both sides of the equation—that is, the assessment of both the experience with conflict and the breadth of indices of youth functioning thought to be impacted by their experiences with political violence. In the chapters of this book, authors addressed a realm of relevant issues, all of which were useful in illustrating the need for this expanded attention. The chapters included reviews of existing literature, scrutiny of predominant theoretical and measurement issues, and both quantitative and qualitative analyses of youth experience with political conflict in many regions of the world. Importantly, the book as a whole focused attention on the perspectives of youth themselves, a key element needed in the expansion of the current knowledge base. The purpose of this brief closing chapter—rather than repeat the elaborated summary of the volume's content and contribution found in the opening chapter—is to outline a set of specific recommendations that stem from the discussion and findings of this volume as a whole and that could be useful in guiding future research. The specific chapters that justify and support these recommendations are indicated in parentheses.

The following recommendations are not exhaustive, but they do cover many areas in need of further specification, elaboration, or extension. These recommendations for future research are organized according to the basic outline articulated in the opening chapters (Chapters 1 and 2), namely, (1) studying adolescence as a focal group more explicitly (i.e., both focusing research more precisely on adolescents, distinct from other age groups, and suggesting realms of development of most relevance to be studied); (2) refining the dominant trend in current studies of linking exposure to negative functioning (i.e., identifying key mediators and moderators of the effect of conflict exposure); and (3) expanding the scope of inquiry (i.e., broadening the assessment of experience with political violence and the consideration of the types of youth functioning that should be investigated). An additional recommendation is for work that better synthesizes research and policy interests.

Adolescents and Political Violence

Recommendation 1: Adjust Research Designs to Permit the Testing of Age-Related Differences in the Experience of Political Violence

As was evident in the overview of the empirical literature outlined in Chapter 2, relatively few studies have focused specifically on adolescent populations. Instead, most have blurred the age distinctions between children and adolescents and have not tested for age variations in effects of political conflict (beyond sometimes assessing differences in prevalence of exposure). The question of how to define adolescence, distinct from other age groupings, remains an open question and will likely remain so given the broad variations across the world in acknowledging, conceptualizing, and circumscribing adolescence. Thus, developmentally oriented researchers first have the task of clearly specifying their study-specific definition of adolescence and then designing studies that properly test for the issues they believe are relevant to that age group. Given that the construct of adolescence—however its age range might be bounded—is invariably developmental in that the focal group is thought (by the assignment of an age-related label to it) to differ from other age groups, designs should explicitly include testing to demonstrate the degree to which the phenomenon of political violence in all its parts—exposure, involvement, motivation, understanding, adaptation, and so on—is or is not experienced differently by this age group. Critically, such studies must consider the degree to which all of these parameters vary by culture (see Chapters 1, 4, 6, and 12).

Recommendation 2: Concentrate on the Sociocultural Aspects of Adolescence

In accomplishing Recommendation 1, it is important to respect the skepticism about the relevance of classic principles of adolescent development as they have been understood and pursued in Western research (e.g., Brown & Larson, 2002; Gielen, 2004; Larson, 2002). This concern is even more critical when considering youth functioning in extreme conditions, such as war, where a jumble of powerful political, economic, historical, ethnic, and other forces shape day-to-day life pre-, during, and postconflict. If researchers wish to maintain attention to the heavily intrapsychic and self-focused tradition of studying adolescents, then careful and more elaborate studies need to be conducted to document the relevance of that domain of experience given the current absence of such developmentally targeted research.

More useful both theoretically and for applied reasons would be a more heavily social-cultural approach to studying adolescents and political conflict, one that concentrates primarily, for example, on how conflict impacts youth's social bonds, cultural integrity, and readiness to assume the roles that their respective cultures prescribe for them (see

Chapters 4, 7, 8, 10, 11, and 12). Critical here are two components that will be elaborated in recommendations to follow: (1) the conflict's impact on the postviolence economic and political structures that determine the opportunities adolescents have to move on with their lives (recognizing that much of the quality of adolescents' later lives has very much to do with such broader forces; see Recommendation 9); and (2) the ways experience with political violence has shaped youths' identity (i.e., their sense of membership in as well as their willingness and capacity to contribute to the family, social, cultural, ethnic, and political spheres of their lives; see Recommendation 10).

Refining the Dominant Finding of Negative Psychological Correlates of Political Violence

The overview of empirical research presented in Chapter 2, along with numerous other reviews of the state of inquiry into children's experience with political violence, makes clear that the central focus of work to date remains the testing of the association between conflict exposure and impaired, predominantly psychological functioning. Recommendations relative to broadening the scope of that narrow question follow, but the basic question is important enough to warrant recommendations for specification.

Recommendation 3: Elaborate the Effort to Specify the Negative Effects of Political Violence on Youth

War is violent and destructive, often massively so. Naturally, therefore, continuing efforts are critical to document and understand how these experiences cripple its participants. Research continues to show, nevertheless, that many (indeed, most) youth are neither automatically nor substantially impaired psychologically or socially as a result of their experiences (see Chapters 1, 3, 5, 8, and 10). This is a challenging finding. At least two avenues should be pursued to address it. First, given that the absence of widespread debilitation may be in part artifactual—to the degree, for example, that research methodologies to date (due to their relative simplicity) have not been up to the task of identifying the real suffering that actually is present—increasingly sophisticated and elaborate efforts should be pursued that better identify the trauma experienced (in all its parts, e.g., incidence, type, severity). As discussed extensively in Chapter 1, such efforts need to be guided by the relative meaning that cultures ascribe to trauma, suffering, and well-being. Particularly relevant here also would be longer term assessments of functioning—not only to assess late emerging or lasting effects of conflict but also to gauge how postconflict conditions (including resumed conflict) dynamically impact later well-being (e.g., the degree to which the equity or nationalistic goals for which youth may have fought and sacrificed have or have not been realized). For discussions of the intersection of politics and psychology in work with children and war, see Chapter 12, and Rafman (2004).

Second, efforts should persist and be elaborated toward identifying which members of a war's population—that is, individuals or groups—will suffer substantially. Although traditional efforts to identify psychological coping styles of individuals is worthy of further pursuit, acknowledging and assessing both the breadth and power of prevailing economic, political, and cultural forces that accompany conflict will likely bear more fruit in understanding functioning during (see Recommendation 6 for an elaboration) and after conflict (see Recommendation 9 for an elaboration).

Recommendation 4: Conduct More Research that Explicitly Focuses on Females

It might be true that in most conflicts males are more directly involved than females are, but it is also true that females are, in varying degrees, affected by all conflicts, that they participate to significant degrees in some conflicts, and that in selected conflicts their victimization can be particularly severe (see de Berry, 2004, Swaine & Feeny, 2004, and Annan et al., 2008 for illustrations of this and of girls' competence in the face of this victimization). Thus, for both theoretical and applied reasons, much more careful work needs to be done to understand female youths' experience with political conflict. It is not a question of if females are affected by conflict but in which ways their experiences (e.g., exposure, processing, adaptation) might be unique. Cultural prescriptions for gender roles and status clearly impact definitions of and expectations for female (and male) functioning and well-being; thus, they must be considered carefully in assessing the effects of conflict on females as well as on efforts to program and write policy to enhance their adaptation and successful progression through life. It should be recognized that the relative (lack of) prominence of women in the public sphere of many traditional societies has little to do with the salience of their experiences to a culture's response to war. Thus, regardless of how much official or public role they might have in setting the agenda of a society, women have critical influence on the stability of society. Accordingly, understanding their experiences with political conflict is necessary—not just how it affects their own well-being (which is reason aplenty to call for more and better research) but also how it shapes the degree to which they might instill, encourage, and support conflict/peace-relevant values and ideologies in their siblings, spouses, and eventual children.

Expanding the Scope of Inquiry

This volume has been critical of the narrow focus of much of the research that has been conducted to date on youth and political violence (i.e., the continuing dominant trend of linking violence exposure with stress). As summarized in Chapter 1 and as the succeeding chapters have illustrated, youths' experience with conflict is intricately complex and can only be captured with more elaborated research designs. This complexity extends to virtually all aspects of the phenomenon but particularly to three basic components: the nature of the political conflict itself, youth exposure/involvement with violence, and the psychological/emotional/social processing of the conflict. Recommendations for each follow.

Recommendation 5: Acknowledge the Distinctiveness of Political Conflicts

Research intended to assess and evaluate a youth's conflict experience should extend past cataloging the number of stressful or traumatic experiences with war. In part, this requires recognition that political conflicts vary on a realm of features relevant to how and why the conflict is being fought, and these characteristics, in turn, have implications for how youth experience and are impacted by the conflict. Wars are waged with different tactics, strategies, and goals. This can include the type, frequency, and relative proximity of political violence. Thus, for example, the Bosnian war entailed very high levels of destruction (of both life and property) that was caused largely by distal bombardments and sniping. In contrast, youth during the Palestinian (First) Intifada experienced less destruction but much more proximal contact with violence in the form of personal and often humiliating mistreatment of self, family, and neighbors, as well as their own violent or quasi-violent activist behaviors (for an elaboration, see Barber, 2008). These "structural" aspects of war (i.e., type, proximity, and target of violence) likely have real implications for youth response because they can define the tenor of the conflict, as in, for example, the level of threat and fear (e.g., the sense of unpredictability and defenselessness that distal attacks can produce), the degree and type of passion experienced (e.g., the sense of intrusion and insult that proximal conflict can inspire), and the relative activeness (e.g., opportunities for resistance) or passiveness with which the violence will be met.

Relatedly, as Cairns and Darby (1998) and Gallagher (2004) have noted, disputes also differ on fundamental geographical and demographic parameters that speak directly to how an individual might experience political conflict and/or postconflict futures. Thus, in the case of the Troubles of Northern Ireland, for example, the feud has been among people inhabiting the same territory and for whom the conflict and its potential resolution have been seen in zero-sum terms (Gallagher, 2004), where an accession at any level is viewed as victory by one side and as defeat by the other side. This rigid polarization might well ascribe an intense consequentiality to discrete conflict events and thereby shape the day-to-day intensity of youth responses during the conflict, especially when the conflicting parties share the same territory (even the same neighborhood). The Israeli-Palestinian conflict, in contrast, centers instead on the degree of sharing territory (i.e., splitting, not cohabiting). The governing issues are equity of the split, self-determination, and parallel coexistence, and thus, discrete conflict events might be viewed as less momentarily consequential but rather with a longer term view as to how the trends in the conflict and the fruits it bears appear to be leading toward resolution of these postconflict goals.

Recommendation 6: Assess the Broader Sociopolitical Ecology of Conflict

Wars and political conflicts are typically expressions of social, economic, political, and/or religious tensions. Because violence is therefore symptomatic of these essential domains of conflict, they should be assessed when studying the effects of violence on youth. Specifically, research endeavoring to fully capture youth experience with political conflict should assess (among other factors) prevailing economic conditions (e.g., levels of poverty, neighborhood disorganization, destruction of infrastructure, degree of urbanization, access to health services), the social positioning of youth (e.g., gender, ethnicity, social class), cultural conditions (e.g., degrees of social support, intactness of cultural values, compatibility of traditional culture with imposed or developing cultures, levels of community violence), and political conditions (e.g., marginalization, representation, and status [displacement, refugee, exile]) (see Chapters 1, 4, 5, 6, 7, 8,

10, 11). Such an expansive assessment of the prevailing ecologies of conflict will not only permit a more realistic assessment of the true effects of violence but also help significantly in targeting interventions to ensure effectiveness. For further elaboration of this point, see Recommendation 9.

Recommendation 7: More Comprehensively Assess Youth Exposure and Involvement in Political Violence

Assessments of exposure to violence should continue to specify as completely as possible the nature of the violence experienced. Thus, frequency of exposure should be considered, but so should such issues as acuteness, chronicity, proximity, duration, severity, novelty/familiarity of violence, and so on (see Chapters 4, 6, 8, 9, and 10).

Particularly needed is an accounting of the degree of youth involvement in conflict, a realm that is itself complex. Regardless of whether youth involvement in political violence is coerced or voluntary, assessments of their participation are critical to understanding their overall functioning during conflict and after conflict has ceased (see Chapters 1, 5, 9, and 12). Beyond assessing frequency and type of involvement, useful insight into their overall functioning can be had from accessing the meanings they ascribe to the conflict (e.g., their understandings of the history, reasons, legitimacy, and goals of the conflict) and their role in it (see Chapter 12). For the particular relevance of these to identity development, see Recommendation 10.

Recommendation 8: Expand Assessment of Functioning Beyond the Psychological

Research into the effects of violence on negative psychological functioning will certainly continue and could benefit from more explicit specification of the types, severity, and persistence of stress and other difficulties. To be most fruitful, these efforts could benefit from consideration of indigenous conceptions of violence, suffering, adaptation, well-being, and so on (see Chapters 1, 3, 4, 5, 6, 7, 8, 10, 11, and 12). Critical, however, to an appreciation of youth functioning amid political conflict will be an expansion past individual psychological functioning to a more complete assessment of youth lives. Given prevailing values for collective integrity in many cultures that are in conflict, of particular importance in this regard would be evaluations of the impact of violence exposure and involvement on youths' social, cultural, institutional, civic, and political functioning. Research that includes such broader assessments would not just facilitate a better understanding of how well conflict-weathered youth are managing but also assist in signaling which specific aspects of youth experiences might benefit most from assistance. More generally, it would pave the way for investigating more precisely how youth reconcile harsh and violent experiences (e.g., to be debilitated by them, flex to them, become transformed by them, or balance them with positive experiences; see Chapter 1).

Recommendation 9: Assess the Postconflict Ecology

Following from Recommendation 6, the ecological complexities of conflict are as critical to understanding youth functioning postconflict as they are to both defining the nature of conflict and to youths' functioning during conflict. Thus, assessments of youth functioning postconflict, particularly over the long term, should monitor and assess the economic, social, cultural, and political realities youth face. Particularly important are the degree of lingering or reignited conflict, reconciliation and restoration of cultural unity, reestablishment of bonds with family, freedom from poverty, opportunity and equitable access to education and employment, family formation, and recognized participation and integration into community and cultural life. Assessments of the availability of these types of resources would aid greatly in identifying which youths are in need of particular assistance (see Chapters 1, 5, 8, and 10; also, Saraswathi & Larson, 2002).

It is important to note here that beyond improving the science, this expanded scope of investigation (as well as the related expansions elsewhere in these recommendations) would provide a natural and needed linkage between research and applied efforts—particularly those of clinical intervention, programming, and policy. Systematic, comprehensive assessments of youth experiences with conflict and the conditions they face postconflict will assist greatly in identifying those youth in particular and specific need for intervention as well as highlighting the sectors of their social ecology that are deserving of programming and policy initiatives (see Chapter 8).

Recommendation 10: Concentrate on Conflict's Impact on Identity Formation and Development

Many of the preceding recommendations alert one to the importance of studying how youths' identities are impacted through their conflict experiences. Far from being passive witnesses to or victims of political violence, adolescents in war zones actively engage cognitively and emotionally to make sense of their experiences and how the conditions of conflict define or determine their roles. Thus, much need and promise attends the study of identity development in the face of political conflict, particularly for developmentally oriented researchers. Effective study of identity in these complicated contexts requires broad considerations of multiple levels and configurations of identity (e.g., personal, social, cultural, ethnic, political) as well as issues of continuity and persistence that are likely highly contingent on the nature of the postconflict ecology (see Chapter 12).

Recommendation 11: Enhance Research Designs

Finally, all of the preceding recommendations imply the need for more elaborate research designs. As noted in Chapter 2, the current state of research into adolescents and political violence is still at a relatively basic level and could benefit from advances at all levels: theory, conceptualization, design, measurement, and analyses. In particular, given the relevance of multiple, conjoint forces that impact youths' experience with political violence, the scope of research designs needs to be elaborated to comprehend this complexity. For quantitative studies, measurement, adequate sampling, and sample size are critical, as is the use of multivariate statistical analyses. For qualitative studies, the careful formulation of research questions and probes are critical to access the various relevant components of youths' experiences with political conflict and violence, followed by thorough discussion and elaboration of the issues to mine their depth and breadth (see Chapters 2, 4, 7, 8, and 9). Regardless of the type of research, control group designs that compare adolescents from conflict zones with matched adolescents from nonconflict zones, as well as prospective studies that start before the conflict, would be very useful in specifying how adolescents deal with political conflict. Finally, periodic assessments of adolescents' functioning over the long term are key to the accurate assessment of conflict's impact on youth.

References

Barber, B. K. (2008). Contrasting portraits of war: Youths' varied experiences with political violence in Bosnia and Palestine. *International Journal of Behavioral Development, 32*(4), 294–305.

Boyden, J. (2003). Children under fire: Challenging assumptions about children's resilience. *Children, Youth and Environments, 13*(1). Available from *Children, Youth and Environments* Web page, http://www.colorado.edu/journals/cye/13_1/index.htm.

Brown, B. B., & Larson, R. W. (2002). The kaleidoscope of adolescence: Experiences of the world's youth at the beginning of the 21st century. In B. B. Brown, R. W. Larson, & T. S. Saraswathi (Eds.), *The world's youth: Adolescence in eight regions of the globe* (pp. 1–20). Cambridge: Cambridge University Press.

Cairns, E., & Darby, J. (1998). The conflict in Northern Ireland: Causes, consequences, and controls. *American Psychologist, 53,* 754–760.

de Berry, J. (2004). The sexual vulnerability of adolescent girls during civil war in Teso, Uganda. In J. Boyden & J. de Berry (Eds.), *Children and youth on the front line: Ethnography, armed conflict and displacement* (pp. 45–62). Oxford: Berghan Books.

Gallagher, T. (2004). After the war comes peace? An examination of the impact of the Northern Ireland conflict on young people. *Journal of Social Issues, 60,* 629–642.

Gielen, W. P. (2004). The cross-cultural study of human development: An opinionated historical introduction. In U. P. Gielen & J. Roopnarine (Eds.), *Childhood and adolescence: Cross-cultural perspectives and applications* (pp. 3–45). Westport, CT: Praeger.

Larson, R. (2002). Globalization, societal change, and new technologies: What they mean for the future of adolescence. In R. W. Larson, B. B. Brown, & J. T. Mortimer (Eds.), *Adolescents' preparation for the future, perils and promises: A report of the Study Group on Adolescence in the Twenty-First Century* (pp. 1–30). Ann Arbor, MI: Society for Research on Adolescence.

Rafman, S. (2004). Where the political and the psychological meet: Moral disruption and children's understanding of war. *International Relations, 18,* 467–479.

Saraswathi, T. S., & Larson, R. (2002). Adolescence in global perspective: An agenda for social policy. In B. B. Brown, R. Larson, & T. S. Saraswathi (Eds.), *The world's youth: Adolescence in eight regions of the globe* (pp. 344–362). New York: Cambridge University Press.

Swaine, A., & Feeny, T. (2004). A neglected perspective: Adolescent girls' experiences of the Kosovo conflict of 1999. In J. Boyden & J. de Berry (Eds.), *Children and youth on the front line: Ethnography, armed conflict and displacement* (pp. 63–84). Oxford: Berghan Books.

Index

Adolescence
  definition of, 316
  Western characterizations of, 6, 7, 9, 305
Adolescents, 73 (*see also* Youth)
  and cognitive and emotional processing of
    violence, 3–4, 10, 11
  and degree of exposure to conflict, 3,
    12, 25
  and degree of involvement in conflict, 25
  and development, 316
  in Israel, 12
  and moral complexity of understanding
    conflict, 15, 18, 25
  negative characterizations of, 4, 7
  in Palestine, 12, 71
  and sense of personal competence, 18
  and social aspects of experience, 17
Adolescent functioning and conflict, 3–6, 7,
    24 (*see also* Youth functioning; Youth
    competent functioning; Youth negative
    functioning)
  and adaptation, 25–26
  balance of, 21
  and competent functioning, 4, 7–8, 46,
    48–49,
  and employment,
  and family influence, 52
  and mediators/moderators, 49–51, 86,
    90–92, 95–99, 146–149, 151,
    170–171, 182, 315–316

and motivation for involvement, 3
and negative functioning, 45–46
and peer influence, 52
and political engagement as buffer, 51
and poverty, 24
research on, 35–56
and role of education, 24
and social isolation, 24
sociocultural approach to the study
  of, 316
and work, 24
Adolescents in Political Violence Project
  (APVP), 181, 283–285, 289, 303
Afghanistan, 105, 109, 115, 120
  and Northern Alliance, 105
  Soviet invasion of, 109
  and the Taliban, 105, 109, 120
  war in, 177
Africa (*see also* specific regions and
  countries)
  youth experience in, 24
Aggression
  and adaptive mechanisms, 64
  biological and social aspects of, 63–69
  inhibition of, 69
  and memory, 67
  and violence, 63
Aggressive Behavior (*see also* Youth negative
  functioning)
  of children, 64

323